Education Policy:
Globalization, Citizenship and Democracy

Education Policy:
Globalization, Citizenship and
Democracy

Mark Olssen, John Codd
and Anne-Marie O'Neill

SAGE Publications
London ● Thousand Oaks ● New Delhi

First published 2004

 SAGE Publications Ltd
1 Oliver's Yard
55 City Road
London EC1Y 1SP

SAGE Publications Inc
2455 Teller Road
Thousand Oaks, California 91320

SAGE Publications India Pvt Ltd
B-42 Panchsheel Enclave
Post Box 4109
New Delhi 110 017

British Library Cataloguing in Publication data

A catalogue record for this book is available from the British
Library

ISBN 0 7619 7469 5
ISBN 0 7619 7470 9

Library of Congress Control Number: 2003106638

Typeset by Dorwyn Ltd, Hampshire
Printed in Great Britain by Athenaeum Press, Gateshead

Contents

About the Authors

Mark Olssen is Reader and Director of Doctoral Programmes, in the Department of Educational Studies, University of Surrey. He is editor of *Mental Testing in New Zealand: Critical and Oppositional Perspectives* (University of Otago Press, Dunedin, 1988), author (with Elaine Papps) of *The Doctoring of Childbirth* (Dunmore Press, Palmerston North, 1997) and editor (with Kay Morris Matthews) of *Education Policy in New Zealand: The 1990s and Beyond* (Dunmore Press, Palmerston North, 1997). More recently he is author of *Michel Foucault: Materialism and Education* (Bergin and Garvey, New York, 1999). He has published articles in Britain in the *Journal of Education Policy*, the *British Journal of Educational Studies*, *Educational Psychology* and *Educational Philosophy and Theory* and the *British Journal of the Sociology of Education*. Released in 2003 from Peter Lang, New York, he is a co-editor with Michael Peters and Colin Lankshear of *Critical Theory: Founders in Praxis,* and from Rowman and Littlefield, New York, also with Michael Peters and Colin Lankshear, *Critical Theory and the Human Condition: Dreams of Difference.*

John Codd is Professor of Policy Studies in Education in the Department of Social and Policy Studies in Education at Massey University, New Zealand. He has co-edited five books of essays on education policy in New Zealand and published monographs on the philosophy of educational administration (1984) and organizational evaluation (1988). He is General Editor of *Delta: Policy and Practice in Education*, a former co-editor of the *New Zealand Journal of Educational Studies* and has contributed regularly to international journals, including the *Journal of Curriculum Studies, Discourse*, the *Journal of Education Policy* and *Educational Philosophy and Theory*. More recently, he is a joint author of *Education and Society in Aotearoa New Zealand: An Introduction to the Social and Policy Contexts of Schooling and Education* (Dunmore Press, Palmerston North, 2000).

Anne-Marie O'Neill is a Senior Lecturer in Education in the Department of Social and Policy Studies in Education at Massey University, New Zealand. She teaches graduate and undergraduate courses on curriculum sociology, educational/policy sociology and the sociology of gender and education, in which she has published widely in New Zealand. She is a Joint Editor of the refereed journal *Delta: Policy and Practice in Education*. In 1996 she published *Readings in Education Feminism* through Massey University, and is a joint author of *Education and Society in Aotearoa New Zealand: An Introduction to the Social and Policy Contexts of Schooling and Education* (2000). She is also the primary editor (with John Clark and Roger Openshaw) of two large volumes, *Reshaping Culture, Knowledge and Learning? Policy and Content in The New Zealand Curriculum Framework Vol 1* (2004) and *Critically Examining The New Zealand Curriculum Framework: Contexts, Issues and Assessment Vol 2* (2004) to be published by Dunmore Press.

Acknowledgements

Some paragraphs and sections of Chapters 7, 8, 9 and 10 by Mark Olssen on neoliberalism have been published previously in New Zealand by the New Zealand Association of Research in Education ('The neo-liberal appropriation of tertiary education policy', Monograph Number 8, 2002) and by *Access: Critical Perspectives on Cultural and Policy Studies in Education*. Some sections of Chapter 3, 6, 9, and 11 have been published by the *Journal of Education Policy* (vol. 11, no. 3, 1996; vol. 13, no. 1, 1998; vol. 15, no. 5, 2000, and vol. 18, no. 2, 2003). Some sections of Chapter 12 have appeared in *Globalization, Societies, Education* (vol. 2, no. 2, 2004). Some sections of Chapter 9 by John Codd on trust have been published in the *New Zealand Journal of Educational Studies*, vol. 34, no. 1, 1999 and sections of Chapter 4 on discourse in *Journal of Education Policy*, vol. 3, no. 3, 1988. The authors would like to thank these sources for permission to reproduce work in this book. The authors would also like to thank Christine Gardener, who typed many chapters between 1994 and 2000 in New Zealand, and Sue Starbuck at the University of Surrey who has tirelessly searched for lost or incomplete bibliographical reference data.

1
Reading Education Policy in the Global Era

- neoliberalism - eroded. the process of democracy

The thesis at the centre of this book is that education policy in the twenty-first century is the key to global security, sustainability and survival. The events of 11 September 2001 (9/11) have shown that the era of global interdependence and interconnectivity is also an era in which human survival is threatened not only by the actions of states with weapons of mass destruction (WMD) but also by the actions of transnational networks of individuals perpetrating acts of terrorism (AOT). Thus, the era of globalization brings urgency to the need for a new world order in which nation-states can develop policies that will contribute to and sustain forms of international governance. We argue in this book that education policies are central to such a global mission.

Globalization, we contend, is not a new phenomenon but it is becoming more complex and more pervasive with the advent of new technologies and the expansion of global markets. Contrary to what some would argue, nation-states, in our view, are not disappearing. However, internally they are changing in their spheres of control, while externally they are radically unequal in the extent of their international influence. Global governance, we argue, is necessary for global survival, but such governance cannot be established and maintained without the support of strong democratic nation-states. This has been clearly evidenced in the Iraq crisis of 2002–03, where the authority of the United Nations has been challenged both by Iraq, as an undemocratic 'rogue state' and also, paradoxically, by the USA and Britain, ostensibly democratic states that have been unwilling to concede to the majority view of the United Nations Security Council. Thus, the disparities of power amongst states can undermine processes of global governance and prevent the attainment of solutions to major crises. Because inter-state democracy at the global level is not viable, it is necessary to build durable democratic institutions within nation-states. The problem is, however, that the neoliberalism of recent times has seriously eroded the process of democracy within most ostensibly 'liberal democratic' states.

Our argument is that a deep and robust democracy at a national level requires a strong civil society based on norms of trust and active responsible citizenship and that education is central to such a goal. Thus, the strong education state is necessary to sustain democracy at the national level so that strong democratic nation-states can buttress forms of international governance and ensure that globalization becomes a force for global sustainability and survival.

Reading education policy

The book sets out a broad theoretical framework for a critical reading of state produced educational policy texts. To this end, it shows the inadequacy of earlier approaches to policy that have their origins in the hegemonic dominance of liberalism underlying traditional educational discourses. The development of the policy sciences, which sought to derive so called 'objective', value-free methods for the writing and reading of policy, represent an attempt to give technical and scientific sophistication to the policy process in order to buttress its intellectual legitimacy. Such approaches to policy-making and policy analysis, in our view, serve to legitimate forms of liberal and neoliberal state hegemony.

This study demonstrates the conceptual complexity of reading state-produced policy discourse. It argues that reading neoliberal educational policy is not just a matter of understanding its educational context or reading it as the 'pronouncements' of 'the policy-makers'. It requires an understanding of the dynamics of the various elements of the social structure and their intersections in the context of history. Policy documents are discursive embodiments of the balance of these dynamics as they underlie social relations at particular points in time. It is for this reason that the discursive formations they contain constitute a highly politicized form of public rhetoric; symbolic systems which await decoding. If official policy texts are political, cultural and economic as much as they are educational treatises, the meanings of the discourses embedded in these texts await decoding so as to reveal the real relations that this specifically cultural form of official discourse helps to construct, reconstruct and conceal. In the analysis of educational policy, this theoretical decoding has been done in different ways, depending upon the philosophical assumptions entailed within the theories used.

There was a time when educational policy *as policy* was taken for granted and policy-making was seen more as a democratic consensual process than a political one. Policy analysis, if it were even identified as such, was taken to be a somewhat sterile and invisible activity carried out by statisticians and officials in government departments. Clearly that is no longer the case. Today, educational policies are the focus of considerable controversy and overt public contestation. The analysis of such policies, moreover, is an activity undertaken both by officials within the system, who now call themselves policy analysts, and various commentators or critics outside the system who also presume that what they do is policy analysis. Educational policy-making has become highly politicized.

In the past 25 years, critical educational scholarship has endeavoured to place the formulation, meanings and real effects of educational policy within the wider theoretical context of critical theory. Indeed, 20 years ago, Prunty (1984: 3), in articulating the importance of what he called the 'critical-perspective', spoke of venturing 'onto an intellectual landscape with few paths and signposts ... a new social terrain'. The ways that critical theorists have traversed this landscape have varied according to their intellectual concerns and political commitments. For example, in a paper addressing the construction of inequality in state produced reports on education, Apple (1986: 174) argued that such texts were important ideological constructions, not only as indicators of shifts in rationales but as 'part of the cultural production of such altered public discourse and as such (they) need(ed) to be seen as constitutive elements of a particular hegemonic project'. Likewise, in a discussion on the development of a political sociology of educational policy-making, Torres (1989: 83) reiterated the need to situate such production within the context of a theory of politics. Thus, he argued for the application to policy of a critical theory of power, one which interrogated the role of bureaucratic organizations, interlinked to a theory of the state. thesis –

Recognizing the political nature of educational policy, this book argues for the need to reject the dominant liberal/idealist inclination of education studies and the technicist theories of the policy sciences. In essence, our argument is that education policy must be contextualized both nationally and globally as a transformative discourse that can have real social effects in response to contemporary crises of survival and sustainability, such as those that follow the events of 9/11. Primarily, this implies a rejection of their pervasive reliance on positivist epistemologies and positivist methodologies as well as many of the dominant insights in the liberal conception of the political system. In opposition to both classical liberal and neoliberal conceptions of policy, this study advocates a critical orientation to educational policy deriving theoretical and methodological insights from critical social theory, and more specifically from the work of the French post-structuralist, Michele Foucault. Central to such foci is a conception of policy as a politically, socially and historically contextualized practice or set of practices. Rather than aiming to present a detailed account of the whole field of educational policy, what we aim to do in this study is elucidate an approach to the critical 'reading' of educational policy. In other words, what we aim to present the reader with is a way of understanding, conceptualizing and analysing educational policy: what it is, why it is important and what it means. The meanings of policy texts, we will argue, do not reside unproblematically in the text itself as something to be 'discovered' or rendered 'visible', but in the relationship between the text and the social structure. The meaning and significance of policy at any particular historical juncture is something that must be rendered intelligible through a process of interrogation, by ascertaining the way that discursive contexts inherent within the social and historical process manifest themselves in and through textual production, formulation and articulation.

Although our analysis in this study is relevant to policy restructuring in Organization for Economic Co-operation and Development (OECD) countries such as the UK, the USA, Canada, Australia and New Zealand, our particular approach is dictated more by a concern with the supranational contexts of policy formulation and development than it is by particularized concerns with understanding policy development within specific national contexts. Notwithstanding certain tendencies within both recent postmodernist and 'older-styled' positivistic studies to emphasize the 'local' and the 'specific' as against the 'interrelatedness' of the 'political', 'economic', 'cultural' and 'social', our study seeks to illuminate how discursive practices and assumptions which operate supranationally come to effect specific national policy developments. Where we do focus on particular national contexts our examples seek to illuminate general processes at the level of nation-states and their interrelations. These include how discursive ideologies come to influence policy developments within a particular nation-state, and how the nation-state as a specific bounded region can no longer protect national community life from supranational influences, as the events of 9/11 have so dramatically shown. In this sense, the nation-state is 'too small' to be entirely effective and 'too large' to be entirely irrelevant. Yet a further issue concerns how the existence of dominant discursive contexts of policy development are, if not truly international, common to more than one country and how the patterns of this commonality must be understood historically, culturally, politically and economically.

Theories of globalization

Globalization theorists have emphasized the 'new' ways in which the individual nation-state is influenced by the international world order. Broadly these can be considered in relation to economic, cultural and political categories, each of which is interrelated. Moreover, the different forms of globalization have been shaped by technological progress. Thus the rapid development in the past 30 or so years of communication and transport technologies has reduced the possibility of individual nation-states maintaining separate economic policies. As a consequence of these new technologies, it is suggested that markets, governments and independent political groups within specific nation-states become 'more sensitively adjusted' to each other (Held, 1991: 145). As the patterns of interaction and communication typically cross-cut national boundaries, so the cultural identities traditionally defined within these boundaries are increasingly undercut (Wallerstein, 1974).

4

economic globalization—
transnational corporations, financials & share markets
Reading education policy in the global era

Economic globalization

Economic globalization is about processes that enable the free flow of goods, services, investments, labour and information across national borders in order to maximize capital accumulation. Thus, global capitalism involves the commodification of all kinds of human endeavour in order to produce surplus value and profit. The transnational corporation is the main vehicle through which this surplus value is appropriated and accumulated as profit. It also occurs through the medium of financial and share markets. Many transnational corporations have more power and are larger economic entities than a number of nation-states. In 1998, for example, there were 29 such corporations with larger economies than New Zealand (Rugman, 2001: 58). Moreover, as Kelsey (2002: 16) points out, 'the top 200 transnationals account for over one quarter of the world's economic activity, but employ less than one percent of its workforce'.

At an economic level, there is a major incongruence between the boundaries of the nation-state and the systematic interests of economic units within the international community. This relates centrally to the internationalization of production investment and exchange, and of financial transactions between international banks and investment houses which have little to do with, and which frequently are disjunctive with, the interests, goals and strategies of individual nation-states. Both multinational enterprises and financial institutions plan and execute their operations with a world economy in mind. As a consequence, the monetary and fiscal policies of individual nation-states are increasingly dominated by developments in international financial markets and by the decisions of the international financial and business community.

The well-known and controversial journalist, John Pilger (2002: 2) describes 'global economy' as a modern Orwellian term, such that:

> On the surface, it is instant financial trading, mobile phones, McDonald's, Starbucks, holidays booked on the net. Beneath this gloss, it is the globalization of poverty, a world where most human beings never make a phone call and live on less than two dollars a day, where 6,000 children die every day from diarrhoea because most have no access to clean water.

Predictably, economic globalization has strong opponents (Chomsky, 1999; Gray, 1998; Mander and Goldsmith, 1996) and equally strong advocates (Cable, 1999) as well as those who are cautiously sceptical (Soros, 2002; Stiglitz, 2002). Political parties that champion the so-called 'third way', such as New Labour in Britain and New Zealand's Labour-led government since 1999, consider economic globalization to be a reality that has to be accommodated with a mixture of enthusiasm and pragmatism.

Joseph Stiglitz, former chief economist of the World Bank and winner of the 2001 Nobel prize for economics, has recently argued (2002: 214) that although economic globalization has the potential to be a force for good, it has not worked for millions of people. He lays much of the blame for this squarely on the transnational economic institutions:

> Globalization has brought better health, as well as an active global civil society fighting for more democracy and greater social justice. The problem is not with globalization, but with how it has been managed. Part of the problem lies with the international economic institutions, with the IMF, World Bank, and WTO, which help set the rules of the game. They have done so in ways that, all too often, have served the interests of the more advanced industrialized countries – and particular interests within those countries – rather than those of the developing world.

Anthony Giddens, arguably the most influential theorist of third way politics, suggests that 'Economic globalization, by and large, has been a success. The problem is how to maximize its positive consequences while limiting its less fortunate effects' (Giddens, 2000: 124). In support of this claim, Giddens refers to improved global levels of employment and improved living conditions in some Asian countries. But Giddens (1999: 12) also acknowledges that globalization is 'a complex set of processes, not a single one'. Thus, globalization has cultural and political dimensions as well as economic dimensions (Burbules and Torres, 2000).

Cultural globalization

At a cultural level, globalization involves the expansion of Western (especially American and British) culture to all corners of the globe, promoting particular values that are supportive of consumerism and capital accumulation. Because culture is what makes life meaningful for people, global images and symbolic representations, such as those contained in marketing or advertising texts, popular music or films, can influence people's sense of identity and belonging, their values, beliefs and aspirations. While it is important not to conflate global culture and the communication technologies through which it is transmitted, there can be no doubt that such technologies have made possible the complex connectivity of cultural globalization (Tomlinson, 1999).

Cultural globalization is largely transmitted by the expansion of the transnational enterprises, such that, as the 1998 Nobel prize-winning economist, Amartya Sen (1999: 240), has commented:

> The contemporary world is dominated by the West, and even though the imperial authority of the erstwhile rulers of the world has declined, the dominance of the West remains as strong as ever – in some ways stronger than before, especially in cultural matters. The sun does not set on the empires of Coca-Cola or MTV.

This cultural hegemony that pushes the values of consumerism and standardization also invokes forces of resistance and movements for the assertion of

Neocolonization — invade with Coca-Cola, instead. of an army

local interests. Many indigenous groups, therefore, view globalization as a renewed form of colonization, threatening to destroy their cultures and exploit their peoples. Jane Kelsey (2002: 10) gives a biting account of these effects, as follows:

> Global capitalism reduces the natural and spiritual world to tradeable commodities and rationalizes its (and their) exploitation. This destroys the enduring relationships and balance between economic, social, cultural and spiritual life and denies their responsibility as the guardians of that lifeworld. Exclusion from, or exploitation on the periphery of, this global economy compounds the powerlessness, poverty and dispossession of previous eras.

As with economic globalization, cultural globalization is closely linked to the development of new information technologies. The Internet, for instance, has enabled the growth of mass communications that can reach to all corners of the planet. But this does not mean that all people have access to these forms of communication. The 'digital divide', both within nations and globally, has given rise to a new kind of structural inequality. While there is increased cultural interconnectedness across nations as a result of the mass media, and also as the result of greater movements of people in migration, tourism and the growth of global economic and political institutions, there is also a heightened awareness, if not understanding, of cultural differences. Hence, there is no tendency towards a single integrated global culture. On the contrary, cultural globalization has contradictory or oppositional effects, providing an impetus for the revival of local cultural identities. As Giddens (1999: 13) points out:

> Most people think of globalization as simply 'pulling away' power or influence from local communities and nations into the global arena. And indeed this is one of its consequences. Nations do lose some of the economic power they once had. Yet it also has an opposite effect. Globalization not only pulls upwards, but also pushes downwards, creating new pressures for local autonomy.

What is very clear, in both of these effects, is that globalization is about power; it is fundamentally a political phenomenon, in which dominant ideologies are vigorously contested and resisted (Rupert, 2000).

Political globalization

At a political level, policy is increasingly in response to international developments, and increasingly involves international agreements and collaboration, as can be seen in the rise to prominence and power of quasi-regional or supranational organizations such as the World Trade Organization (WTO), the North Atlantic Treaty Organization (NATO), European Community (EEC), World Bank (WB), or International Monetary Fund (IMF) or, with relation to

New Zealand and Australia, Closer Economic Relations (CER). The effect of 'private' or quasi-public organizations, such as 'think tanks', research groups and so on, can, with the development of rapid communication and information processing capabilities (the 'superhighway', for instance), also exert an influence which systematically and continuously cross-cuts the boundaries of individual nation-states. Moreover, the new information and communication technologies, especially the Internet, have provided a means for the mobilization of public opinion on a global scale that has never been seen before. This could be seen dramatically on 16 February 2003 when, for the first time in history, millions of protesters in more than 50 countries expressed united opposition to war against Iraq. This globalization of mass resistance substantially reduces the power of nation-states to control the availability of information and to manufacture consent.

Political globalization, in some accounts (Ohmae, 1996; Reich, 1991), is the most powerful form of globalization because it is a process whereby the autonomy of the nation-state is being radically reduced and its sovereignty eroded. In some ways it is a consequential effect of other forms of globalization. Thus, economic globalization means that governments are required to manage monetary, fiscal and other economic processes, over which they have little or no control because they are no longer contained within national borders (Held, 1995). Likewise, cultural globalization means that satellite communication systems can disseminate information, images and ideas with increasing degrees of freedom, opening up an enormous array of influences on socialization and weakening the notion of 'citizen' as a unified and unifying concept (Capella, 2000). Thus, within the context of political globalization, the nation-state surrenders some of its capacity to ensure citizenship rights or entitlements and to maintain non-economic policies having such aims as environmental protection or social justice.

The nation-state in the new global order

That the relevant focus of analysis is constituted by the communities of a bounded territory or state becomes deeply problematic as soon as the issue of global interconnectedness is considered. Tracing the patterns and effects of such interconnectedness between nation-states and the international world order is referred to as 'world systems analysis' (Herz, 1976; Kedgley and Wittkopf, 1989; Wallerstein, 1974) or as 'globalization theory' (Held, 1991; 1995; 1996; Held and McGrew, 2000; Held et al. 1999; MacEwan, 1999; McGrew, 1992), although more accurately it could be referred to as the 'process of western globalization' (Held, 1991; 1995). Amongst the major arguments by globalization theorists is the claim that there is a process of global transformation which eventually will render the nation-state of substantially reduced power, although not totally ineffectual. Thus theorists such as Castells (1996; 1997; 1999), Reich (1991) and Ohmae (1990; 1996) argue that new forces are witnessing the decline in influence of the nation-state. Ohmae (1990), for instance, argues for the development of what he calls the borderless state where national cultures are dissolved under the influence of global electronic communication, resulting in patterns of 'cultural hybridization'. Manuel Castells sees the rise of a 'powerless state' (1997: 121), where the 'instrumental capacity of the nation-state is decisively undermined by globalization of core economic activities, by globalization of media and electronic communication, and by globalization of crime' (ibid.: 244). In a similar way, the economist Robert Reich (1991) argues that with the growth of modern technologies, increases in the transfer of goods and services and information effectively undermines the autonomy and efficiency of the national economies. Reich sees the transnational corporations as being at the centre of this process, as they form the new 'global enterprise webs' which co-ordinate, transfer and exchange capital and information. Such forms, says Reich, are increasingly cosmopolitan, owing little allegiance to any particular national country, in relation to management operations, ownership, product manufacture and assemblage, as well as product sales and service. In Reich's extreme view, the process of global transformation will rearrange the politics and economics of the twenty-first century (ibid.: 1): 'There will be no more national products and technologies, no national corporations, no national industries. There will no longer be national economies at least as we have come to understand the term. All that will remain rooted within national borders are the people who comprise the nation.' Globalization – worldwide in scope

Adopting a more moderate position, David Held and his collaborators (Held, 1991; 1995; 1996; Held and McGrew, 2000; Held et al., 1999) hold that globalization implies at least two distinct phenomena. First, it suggests that political, economic and social activities are becoming worldwide in scope. Second, it suggests that there has been an intensification of levels of interaction and interconnectedness between states and societies, which make up the international world order. As Held (1991: 145) puts it:

– intensification & interconnectedness between states & society

> What is new about the modern global system is the chronic intensification of patterns of interconnectedness mediated by such phenomena as the modern communications industry and new information technology and the spread of globalization in and through new dimensions of interconnectedness: technological, organizational, administrative and legal, among others, each with their own logic and dynamic of change.

One important question that arises here is to what extent such global interconnections constitute a new phenomenon? It could be claimed that nation-states have always been 'interconnected' since the emergence of a world economy and the development of international trade over great distances have ancient origins. Whether we focus on the Mogul expansion throughout Asia, or the expansion of the Roman empire throughout the regions of the Mediterranean, we can detect the development of commercial trade relations across national boundaries in many pre-modern societies. In the modern era we can detect the expansion of trade through the growth of commerce since the end of the fifteenth century with the opening of international sea routes by Europeans, and again in the nineteenth century with the expansion of trade, international investment and banking finance activity, as a consequence of the Industrial Revolution. While in this sense 'globalization' is not a new phenomenon, the point being made by globalization theorists today is that the extent and nature of the interconnections have changed, affecting the sovereignty of nation-states and undermining their autonomy. Moreover, nation-states are now required in the post-9/11 era to respond to new threats to their security brought about by AOT and WMD. In this sense, late twentieth-century globalization has some distinctive characteristics, as Held (1991: 145) points out:

> It is one thing to claim elements of continuity in the formation and structure of modern states and societies, quite another to claim that there is nothing new about aspects of their form and dynamics. For there is a fundamental difference between the development of a trade route which has an impact on particular towns and/or rural centres and an international order involving the emergence of a global economic system which outreaches the control of any single state ... the expansion of vast networks of transnational relations and communications over which particular states have limited influence [and] the enormous growth in international organizations and regimes ... . While trade routes may link distant populations together in long loops of cause and effect, modern developments in the international order link and integrate peoples through multiple networks of transaction and co-ordination, reordering the very notion of distance itself.

Characteristically, the implications of the new global order for nation-states has been to create new patterns of both institutional and consumer conduct, new structures, opportunities and problems, as well as new incentives and disincentives. In the current period, globalization has involved a progressive deregulation by individual nation-states of the international movement of capital and goods. As well as pressures for free trade other related developments have involved:

- the emergence of new financial constraints by the state in response to international pressures and increased competition;
- the increasing importance of technological developments and knowledge production to national economies in order to compete in the international marketplace;
- the tightening of the relationship between states and business, and closer relationships between states and multinational business corporations;
- an increase in the state's interest in expenditure and conduct in the public

sphere, resulting in new regimes of control and accountability;
- the increasing trend to marketization and deregulation by states over social services including education at its various levels; and
- a new institutional norm of competition as a strategy to effect the efficient utilization of resources.

Nevertheless, while there are common trends, globalization has not produced the same responses in all countries. As Esping-Andersen (1996) has shown, welfare states have adapted to the global economy in different ways. He argues (ibid.: 10) that:

> Since the 1970s, we can identify three distinct welfare state responses to economic and social change. Scandinavia followed until recently a strategy of welfare state employment expansion. The Anglo-Saxon countries, in particular North America, New Zealand and Britain have favoured a strategy of deregulating wages and the labour market, combined with a certain degree of welfare state erosion. And the continental European nations, like Germany, France and Italy, have included labour supply reduction while basically maintaining existing social security standards. All three strategies were intimately related to the nature of welfare states.

Thus, it is important not to assume that globalization is a homogeneous or universalizing process. Its various dimensions – economic, political and cultural – will have different manifestations in different national contexts. In this study, our primary focus is on the Anglo-Saxon countries, particularly Britain, the USA, Australia and New Zealand.

Globalization, liberalism and neoliberalism

This book is about policy in education, more specifically how to contextualize it in the contemporary global era. It is not about 'globalization' or 'world systems' as such, except in terms of how an understanding of these contributes to an understanding of national and global contexts. What is important in this respect is that in order to understand the production of education policy within individual nation-states, we will argue that it is necessary to understand the origins and determining influences of that policy in relation to social, cultural, political and economic forces that transcend the context of its national production. This is so, for example, in relation to the impact of theoretical systems such as Keynesianism, but also in relation to the disciplinary knowledge systems of neoliberalism as well. In fact, the rise of various theories of macroeconomic management which have come to affect the development of education in all advanced capitalist societies is, as Tomlinson (1991: 103) has put it, 'one of the most striking features of the middle decades of the twentieth century'. In the post-war decades this was seen in terms of the effects of the 'Keynesian Revolution'. Although it manifested itself differently in different countries,[1] it became a dominant and effective theoretical force fundamentally affecting the structure and development of state-produced social and educational policy. Since the 1970s, a similar claim can be made with regard to significant modification of welfare policies and the resurgence of neoliberal or 'new right' policies. While in Reagan's America and Thatcher's Britain, and post-1980s Australia and New Zealand, all had quite distinct approaches to restructuring education and social policy, there is enough similarity of basic orientation and theoretical commitment to warrant an examination of the extra-national factors at play in the formulation and implementation of specifically national approaches. These extra-national factors constitute both material and discursive elements of policy formation.

Although the consequences of this highly interconnected global order mean that traditional domains of state activity, as well as the forms of economic, political and social policy, must be considered within a context that transcends national boundaries, we are not arguing a thesis of the 'powerless state'. While we accept that international developments in culture, politics and economics have become increasingly interconnected, we argue in this book that a particular nation-state, or block of nation-states, has the capacity to act with relative autonomy in political affairs, and indeed must assert its autonomy against globalization forces if nations are to thrive and prosper. In this sense, we are not uncritical of globalization theories. While it is undoubtedly true that new technologies change the nature and speed of world politics and economics, and that globalization forces affect national identities at a cultural and ideological level, we would argue that technological changes do not in themselves prevent national or regional autonomy at the political and educational level.

In this we concur with Hirst and Thompson (1996) who present a critical assessment of the globalization hypothesis in their book, *Globalization in Question*. While they recognize, as we do, increasing internationalization at the economic, political, educational and cultural levels, they argue that many of the claims of the globalization theorists are overstated. One claim they make is that internationalization has had greater effects in some countries and regions than others. Another argument is that the claims of the globalization theorists are often poorly conceptualized and fail to distinguish between the different forms and elements, (for example, investment, trade, political alliances, cultural and so on). Whether in relation to population movements, or trade or investment, internationalization has been sporadic and uneven in its advance. Although multinational corporations have an enormous stake in the world economy, in opposition to Reich's claim, the vast majority are not 'trans-national', but 'home-based', and in the main, their operations are closely controlled by their home country (Hirst and Thompson, 1996: 159).

Thus, for Hirst and Thompson, multinationals are still essentially located in national contexts. For the most part they still trade on the national nature of their services or products. Across a variety of dimensions, the 'home-orientated nature of MNC [multinational corporation] activity ... seems over-whelming. Thus MNCs still rely on their "home base" as the centre for eco-nomic activities, despite all the speculation about globalization' (Hirst and Thompson, 1996: 160). Thus, full (multilateral economic globalization is something of a myth) It has not been attained, and may not, in fact, be attain-able. Multinational corporations, which are, according to Rugman (2001:1), 'the engines of international business', are organized regionally rather than globally, and 'operate from the "triad" home bases of the United States, the European Union, or Japan, at the hub of business networks in which clusters of value-added activities are organized'. Rugman (2001:18) provides convinc-ing empirical evidence to show that: U.S. Europe, Japan,

> While there are some economic drivers of globalization there are extremely strong cultural and political barriers preventing the development of a single world market. Only in a few sectors, such as consumer electronics, is there a successful firm-level strategy of globalization, with homogeneous products being sold on price and quality. For most other manufacturing sectors, and all service sectors, regionaliza-tion is much more relevant than globalization.

Other economists, such as Hutton (1996), and Porter (1990) also argue for the importance of national context and 'local infrastructure' to business activity. While therefore, there are clearly important changes, and some strong 'globalizing trends', (the precise extent and nature of economic globalization is a contested phenomenon). At the political level, moreover, we claim that the state has potential autonomy notwithstanding important globalizing trends. For the forseeable future, more than ever before, it is important that the state plays a major role in two crucial respects: first, in co-ordinating and (providing social services,) as these are important to the continuity and stability of welfare in a global economic order; and, secondly, in funding providing and regulating education, which is not effectively protected, or provided for, by the institutions of global capitalism. (Education, we shall argue, becomes vital, economically, to the addition of value on goods and services, which enables nations to prosper, as well as for the basic growth and continuance of democracy.) In this sense, education becomes a central function of the state in the global order.) Our thesis concerns the rise of the education state, and the central functions that it fulfils in relation to the maintenance of democracy and welfare in the post-millennium era.

Central to our argument, then, is the claim that it is (imposed policies of neoliberal governmentality,) rather than globalization as such, that is the key force affecting (and undermining) nation-states today. Thus, while a great deal of recent educational policy can be explained in terms of the sociological concept of globalization, we argue in this book that it must be (theoretically represented in relation to the political philosophy of neoliberalism) No change

13

in the technology of communication or transport can radically affect the sovereignty, unity or power of the state, except perhaps in the shaping and mobilization of public opinion, as the anti-war protests of 2003 have shown. What is crucial, and yet largely ignored, has been the discursive politically developed context in terms of which international exchange has been directed. As a consequence of this, policy development within specific states is represented as explainable in terms of its relations to more fundamental political discourses, which have undergirded policy formation in western nation-states for some two centuries. Much of our attention is thus devoted to identifying the central relations between policy and specific forms of governmental reason. In fundamental terms the thesis developed in this book entails an examination of the role of the various forms of state reason as a basis from which policy has been formulated and enacted, and in terms of which it is capable of guiding the policy programmes of western nation-states.

In our view, liberalism, while incorporating many progressive elements in its classical, or original, formulation, especially as regards its democratic and constitutional safeguards, constitutes overall, an unsatisfactory basis from which nation-states can make or defend policy. Not only does it inadequately account for the dimensions of power and control, but it underemphasizes the effects of private property and social class as determinants of the political and social character of community life. In spite of the worthiness of its lofty ideals regarding rights, freedom and democracy, which we will seek to retain, we will argue that liberalism has an impoverished conceptualization of the individual, of human nature, of power, of the state, as well as of the international economic order, especially with reference to *free trade*. It also provides no consistent set of principles which could establish standards or priorities for the state in terms of its relations to individuals or groups or institutional sectors, such as the economy or education. Although it is in relation to liberal precepts and reason that state officials and politicians have sought to justify policy, liberal reason fails to provide the impetus for growth that it claims. Ultimately, also, it provides an untenable explanation of education, of the sources of educational success and failure, of the nature of individual agency and of the processes of national economic planning. Further, we will argue that through the mutations of its classical formulation, resulting as it has in neoliberal theories of the economy and management, those principles that were initially progressive in the classical doctrine, have themselves become corrupted. Rather than offering choice or freedom, neoliberalism, we maintain, becomes a new system of political and economic control. We contend, moreover, that Foucault's insights into the discursive manifestations of state-authored modes of power and control, together with the nuanced historicity of his exploration of how government becomes inscribed in the subject, provide a useful antidote to liberal views of globalization which see it simply in terms of expanding transnational

14

interdependence and interconnectivity. His account prepares the ground for a more deeply theoretical account of globalization.

The context for education policy

The substantive argument of this book, as explained in detail in the final chapters, is to argue for a new model of the welfare community as the basis for social policy in OECD countries. Our conception, seeks to formulate a democratic model which, while it would seek to preserve and protect the important principles of liberal constitutionalism, locates these within a communitarian context, where they are allied to a concept of social inclusion and trust. Only such a model, we argue, can support a conception of education as a public good. In its turn, education, for us, as once for Dewey (1916), is seen as pivotal to the construction of a democratic society, and for the model of citizenship that such a conception of society implies. This book, then, is essentially about the role of education in the construction and maintenance of democratic states, constituted within a new global order. Even more, today, we will argue, than in the welfare states of the past, the state must be an *education* state. This book, then, is about the rise of the education state.

As well as advancing a substantive argument in defence of a return to the welfare community, albeit in a new global context, this book also has an explicitly pedagogical purpose. As we have already stated, it aims to present students of educational policy studies, and social policy analysts generally, with a theoretical framework, and with the philosophical concepts and principles necessary for the critical analysis of educational policy. It is for this purpose that we cast the net widely: traversing topics in the sociology of education, theories of discourse and texts, policy analysis methodology, theories of the state, liberalism, neoliberalism, community, citizenship, democracy and conceptions of the welfare state – all of which are necessary for students in the field to achieve a deeper understanding of educational policy and policy-making by the state.

The structure of the study is as follows. This chapter has sought to set the scene by briefly examining some of the recent debates around theories of globalization and exploring connections between the education policies of nation-states and the current global context. This involves outlining the main forms of globalization and showing how all these forms have been shaped by neoliberalism. Chapter 2 provides an overview of Michel Foucault's theoretical position, explicating his concepts of power, knowledge, discourse and governmentality, and differentiating him from other post-structuralists. For Foucault, neoliberalism defines a form of state reason based on a revival of classical liberalism in political theory and neoclassical theory in economics. Our utilization of Foucault's theories and concepts as a framework for analysing policy is timely given the major interest in his work within the social sciences. Chapter 3 outlines a Foucauldian approach to critical policy analysis based upon his unique form of critique and his methods of archaeology and genealogy. Chapter 4 develops the approach further by elaborating a framework for the analysis of policy as discourse and as text based upon a materialist theory of language.

Chapters 5, 6, 7 and 8 all concern the themes of liberalism and the effects of liberal reason on models and conceptions of education. Chapter 5 outlines and critiques the political rationality of classical liberalism from John Locke in the seventeenth century to Adam Smith in the eighteenth century and through to Jeremy Bentham in the nineteenth century. Classical liberal axioms regarding the individual, freedom, the public and the private spheres, and the role of the state (laissez-faire) are outlined as constituting the necessary basis for an understanding emergence of neoliberalism in the twentieth century. Continuing the concern with the themes of liberal reason, Chapter 6 traces the rise of social democratic, or welfare state liberalism as it emerged in the nineteenth century with writers like Green and Hobhouse, and was finally realized in the economic formulations of John Maynard Keynes in the early twentieth century. Chapter 7 traces the ascendancy of neoliberalism. Twentieth-century neoliberalism centres around the increasing influence over state policy of the academic discourse of economics in writers such as Frederick A. Hayek, James Buchanan, Gary Becker, Milton Friedman, Oliver Williamson and Robert Nozick, and theories such as Austrian economics, Public Choice Theory, Human Capital Theory, monetarism, Transaction Cost Economics, Agency Theory, and the political philosophy of the minimal state and entitlement justice. These writers and their theories are central to any understanding of the resurgence of neoliberal restructuring of education and society that has occurred in the western world over the past 20 years. Chapter 8 continues with neoliberalism tracing the effects on institutional restructuring and educational management. Chapter 9 discusses the effects of neoliberalism on professionalism in education and higher education, as well as the effects of competition on the culture of trust.

In Chapter 10, neoliberal policies of choice are examined and in chapter 11 various educational policy issues are considered in the context of comparing liberal to communitarian forms of governmentality. Our endorsement of a communitarian position is based on the argument that communitarianism constitutes a more viable political philosophy than liberalism to understand the role of the state and education in relation to citizenship and democracy in a global order. Chapter 12 concludes by focusing on globalization and the importance of conceptions of citizenship and democracy for education. It theorizes a new conception of the political, moving beyond 'third-way' formulations, based on the relationship between democracy and education to advance a model of *the education state*.

Notes

1 Tomlinson (1991) maintains that, while Keynesianism strongly influenced Britain, Australia, New Zealand, America, Canada and most of Europe, in terms of macroeconomic policy it had very little influence on policies developed and implemented in France and Germany.

2

The Post-structuralism of Foucault

During the 1980s, educational policy sociology became much more directly concerned with the nature of policy discourse. This was due, in large part, to influences from the writings of the French post-structuralist, Michel Foucault. In this chapter, we attempt to unravel the key strands in Foucault's thought and to situate his work within the broad tradition of European critical social theory. We begin with his critique of Marxism which leads into his unique conceptions of knowledge and power. We then consider his views on the liberal state and the microprocesses of power that he sees as constituting forms of governmentality. We show how Foucault's thought engages with the central elements of liberal reason and, finally, we differentiate his form of post-structuralism from that of Derrida and the postmodernists. Thus we lay out the foundations for the Foucauldian approach that informs this study.

Foucault's critique of Marxism

Foucault's work was directed against the deep theoretical structure of Marxism at a level which rejected the functionalism of Althusserian Marxism. Essentially it criticized the holistic and deductivistic approach within which it located Marxism in general. His position not only rejected the primacy of the economy but also the approach which seeks to explain parts of culture as explicable and decodable parts of a whole totality or system. For Foucault, the explanatory quest is not to search for the organizing principle of a cultural formation – whether the 'economy' or the 'human subject' or the 'proletariat'. Rather, Foucault is interested in advancing a polymorphous conception of determination in order to reveal the 'play of dependencies' in the social and historical process. As he put it in 1968, he 'would like to substitute this whole play of dependencies for the uniform simple notion of assigning causality and by suspending the indefinitely extended privilege of the cause, in order to render apparent the polymorphous cluster of correlations' (Foucault, 1978a: 13).

There are three aspects to the play of dependencies. First, the *intradiscursive*, which concerns relations between objects, operations and concepts within the

18

discursive formation; secondly, the *interdiscursive*, which concerned relations between different discursive formations; and, thirdly, the *extradiscursive*, concerning the relations between a discourse and the whole play of economic, political and social practices. Rather than seeking to find the articulating principle of a cultural complex, Foucault was interested in discerning how cultural formations were made to appear 'rational' and 'unified', how particular discourses came to be formed and what rules lay behind the process of formation. In doing so he sought to produce accounts of how discursive formations like nineteenth-century psychopathology came to be formed, how it constituted its scientific legitimacy and shaped the thinking of a particular period. Thus in the case of nineteenth-century psychiatry and psychopathology Foucault shows how the term 'madness' came to be applied to certain types of behaviour, and how, in its very designation by what it was not, it helped establish our conceptions of 'the rational' and 'the sane'. What he resists, however, in all of these studies, is the temptation to explain the development of particular discursive formations as a result of any single cause or principle.

In opposing the Marxist conception of determination, Foucault explicitly opposes the conception of social structure present in Marxism and the determining effect of the economy on that structure. This reflected his Nietzschean heritage and his belief that Marxism was a mode of thought that had outlived its usefulness. Following Nietzsche, and the philosophy of difference, Foucault enunciates a theory of discursive formations and rejects Hegelian and Marxist conceptions of history. Although Foucault locates his work within a tradition beginning with Hegel, it is the rejection of the Hegelian dialectic with its implied beliefs in progress, enlightenment and optimism concerning the human ability to understand reality that characterizes Foucault's Nietzschean method. As a consequence of this, Foucault differs in fundamental respects from a theorist like Althusser. Whereas Althusser adopted the structuralist programme seeking to explain the whole by understanding the interrelations between its component parts, for Foucault the totality always eluded either analysis or understanding but, rather, was characterized by incompleteness, openness and chance ('alea') (Foucault, 1981: 69). Comparing Althusser and Foucault, Mark Poster (1984: 39–40) closes the balance sheet firmly in favour of Foucault:

> The theoretical choice offered by these two theorists is dramatic and urgent. In my view Foucault's position in the present context is more valuable as an interpretive strategy and ultimately, although this may strike a discordant note, more marxist. If by marxism one means not the specific theory of the mode of production, or the critique of political economy, and not even the supposed dialectical method, but instead a critical view of domination which as historical materialism takes all social practices as transitory and all intellectual formations as indissociably connected with power and social relations – then Foucault's position opens up critical theory more than Althusser's both to the changing social formation and to the social locations where contestation actually occurs.

Notwithstanding Poster's somewhat liberal use of 'marxism' as a concept, the passage highlights the important similarities and differences between the two systems of thought. While Marxism's focus upon labour and production was relevant to the rise of industrial capitalism in the nineteenth century, Poster identifies changes in the nature of the economy, an increase in the service and white-collar sectors, the increasing importance of information technology and communication together with the new possibilities this generates for a decentralization of political power that makes 'discourse/practices' the pertinent level of intelligibility for a critical social theory in the twentieth century (Poster, 1984).

In criticizing Marxism, Foucault also cautions 'circumspection' with regard to the use of the concept of ideology. Thus, in an interview conducted in 1977 (Foucault, 1980a: 118), he stated that:

> The notion of ideology appears to me to be difficult to make use of for three reasons. The first is that, like it or not, it always stands in virtual opposition to something else which is supposed to count as truth. Now I believe that the problem does not consist in drawing the line between that in a discourse which falls under the category of scientificity or truth, and that which comes under some other category, but in seeing historically how effects of truth are produced within discourses which in themselves are neither true nor false. The second drawback is that the concept of ideology refers I think, necessarily, to something of the order of a subject. Thirdly, ideology stands in a secondary position relative to something which functions as its infrastructure, as its material economic determinant, etc. For these reasons, I think that this is a notion that cannot be used without circumspection.

The third criticism Foucault lists expresses his rejection of the Marxist framework of base and superstructure and the problem of determination, already discussed, while the first and second express other issues central to his own approach. The first indicates Foucault's belief that marxism builds a conception of truth into its theoretical framework in advance. By representing a perspective as 'ideology', we not only imply that such a perspective is 'illusory' or 'false' or 'distorted', but we also imply that the perspective of the speaking subject is in fact true. This raises important questions about Foucault's own epistemology.

Foucault's epistemology: power–knowledge

Whether Foucault is arguing that truth is something that simply cannot be ever attained, the 'will to truth' simply being an expression, following Nietzsche, and the 'will of power', or whether he is suggesting, alternatively, that the issue of truth can be 'bracketed out', or, alternatively again, that he is simply not interested in the truth status of the discourses he examines, is not clear. While writers like Charles Taylor (1989) and Jürgen Habermas (1987a) charge Foucault with the 'crime' of epistemological relativism, there are some who seem less put out by such relativist implications (Dreyfuss and Rabinow, 1982). While within the context of his own framework of power/knowledge it does not seem that Foucault can avoid the charge of relativism, he certainly did not consider himself a relativist, and there is no shortage of truth claims, or 'claims to know', in his own analysis. In his writings on the physical and human sciences, in comparing organic chemistry to medicine and to various social sciences, Foucault's whole line of analysis is based upon the epistemological adequacy of their theoretical systems. He claims, for instance, that medicine has a much more 'solid scientific armature' than psychiatry (Foucault, 1980a: 109). In addition, the very focus of genealogy is to undertake grounded historical analyses. To the extent that there is an issue with relativism, it is not in the sense, then, of a *judgemental* relativism whereby it is claimed that all interpretations, or knowledge, are equally valid, or that there are no practical grounds for preferring one truth to another. Rather, it is in the sense of an *epistemic relativism* which claims that all beliefs or knowledge are socially constructed, so that knowledge is contingent, neither the truth values nor criteria of rationality exist outside of historical time.

While this is a potentially serious issue for Foucault,[1] it should be noted that Foucault did not deny that universal truths existed. To the extent they did so, however, they were always historically and discursively mediated. As he stated in his essay 'What is enlightenment?' (Foucault, 1984a: 47–8) he sees universalizing tendencies in the 'acquisition of capabilities and the struggle for freedom' which he says 'have constituted permanent elements'. Again, in the 'Preface to the History of Sexuality, Vol. 2', Foucault (1984c: 335) says that:

> Singular forms of experience may perfectly well harbor universal structures; they may well not be independent from the concrete determinations of social existence. However, neither these determinations nor these structures can allow for experiences … except through thought … this thought has an historicity which is proper to it. That it should have this historicity does not mean it is deprived of all universal form, but instead that the putting into play of these universal forms is itself historical.

Central to the analysis of Foucault's epistemology is the concept of *power–knowledge*. This concept suggests that knowledge and power are always inextricably related and that there are always sociological implications to the production of knowledge. However, it is not necessary to situate all knowledge (and all science) as a mere product or expression of power in order to isolate the interconnections between power and knowledge. As Dreyfuss and Rabinow (1982) maintain, Foucault focuses on discourses that claim to be advancing under the banner of legitimate science but which in fact have remained intimately connected to the microphysics of power. Because the different discourses interact with social structures in different ways, Foucault seeks to examine each specific discursive formation separately, to be able to evaluate its claims adequately to describe reality, as well as to assess the particular ways in which interactions with social structure and power take place. The problem with the concept of ideology then is not only that it predetermines discourses as overly coherent but that, by implication, it judges them as false.

The second issue Foucault raises in his statement on the concept of ideology relates to his view of the human subject. In what is a similar view to that of Althusser, Foucault attempts to advance a consistent social constructionist view of the constitution of the human subject. By social constructionism Foucault means that the subject is constituted discursively in history. It is by 'decentring' the subject in this way that he rejects essentialist views based on conceptions of 'human nature' or 'biology' or 'psychology'. Foucault's conception of subjectivity is central to his theoretical perspective. As he stated himself, his objective in the studies he conducted was to 'create a history of the different modes by which, in our culture, human beings are made subjects' (Foucault, 1982a: 208). Foucault recognizes three main ways by which subjects are so constructed: first, via the human sciences, which developed after the start of the nineteenth century; secondly, through the 'dividing practices' which objectify the subject, providing classifications for subject positions ('male', 'normal' and so on); thirdly, by human individuals themselves who have agency to turn themselves into subjects and, through resistance, change history. For Foucault, individuals identify with particular subject positions within discourses. It is with reference to this third view that Foucault has been criticized by writers like Giddens (1987: 98) for failing to explain how human agency is possible.

Discourse

Foucault replaces the concept of ideology with that of *discourse*. He represents discourse as one of a variety of practices whose most significant units are 'serious speech acts', both written and spoken. A discourse is defined in terms of statements (*énoncés*), of 'things said'. Statements are events of certain kinds, which are both tied to historical context and capable of repetition. Further, as Foucault (1972: 49) describes them, 'Discourses are composed of signs but what they do is more than use these signs to designate things. It is this move that renders them irreducible to the language and to speech. It is this "move" that we must reveal and describe'.

Discourses, then, as Stephen Ball (1990a: 2) summarizes them, 'embody meaning and social relationships, they constitute both subjectivity and power relations'. Although they comprise signs and consist of complex ways of conceptualizing objects of concern analogous to the idea of a 'frame of reference', discourses cannot simply be equated with language analysis of the sort undertaken by Austin and Searle. As Foucault (1972: 27) puts it:

> The question posed by language analysis of some discursive fact or other is always: according to what rules has a particular statement been made, and consequently according to what rules could other similar statements be made? The description of the events of discourse poses a quite different question: how is it that one particular statement appeared rather than another?

For Foucault, it is the relationship between the discursive and the extra-discursive that is central. This was especially the case in his writings after 1968 when Foucault became concerned with the analysis of institutional power and in the relations between macro and micro structures of power and between power and subjectivity. What differentiated discursivity from language and from textuality, as Michelle Barrett (1988: 126) explains it, is that discursivity is related to context. This is particularly important in the analysis of policy discourse where the context of implementation is to be differentiated from the context of policy formation. In Chapter 4, we argue that this is a key distinguishing feature of a Foucauldian approach to policy analysis, making possible a deeper understanding of how policy texts can have real effects on social structures and practices.

Foucault's concept of power was developed in opposition to the marxist idea of power and class dominance. In Foucault's analysis, power is exercised rather than possessed, and incorporated into practices rather than in agents or in interests. As the themes Foucault was interested in – psychiatric institutions, madness, medicine, sexuality, discipline and punishment, the care of the self – had only a limited significance in relation to economic considerations, the Marxist conception of power as resulting from economic oppression was of limited relevance. Power, as Foucault conceptualized it, was dispensed rather than centralized, worked from the bottom up rather than from the top down, and was positive and enabling as well as being negative and repressive, liberating as well as coercive. The fact that Foucault recognized no core or institutional basis to power accounts for a major absence of theorization in relation to the state.

Foucault and the state

Foucault's work challenges received ways of thinking about the state and about government, and in our view can be rendered complementary to the work of Gramsci on the basis that his concepts and theoretical ideas supplement, while not being inconsistent with, Gramsci's views.[2] Unlike much work within the Marxist tradition, however, Foucault does not see the state as all-encompassing, in the sense of subsuming the sphere of civil society altogether (as could be claimed of Althusser, for instance). With this caveat, however, the issues of the state, of political power, and of government are all considered important. In responding to earlier misunderstandings of his views, Foucault (1980a: 122) states:

> I don't want to say that the State isn't important; what I want to say is that relations of power, and hence the analysis that must be made of them, necessarily extend beyond the limits of the State ... the State is superstructural in relation to a whole series of power networks that invest the body, sexuality, the family, kinship, knowledge, technology and so forth.

To understand Foucault's conception of the state it is necessary to understand his views on power. Rather than being concerned with the contradictions of the state, or processes like legitimation, his interests are related to the more general issues of power within civil society, as well as presenting an historical analysis of how models of power have operated. In his earlier works, prior to the 1970s, Foucault was concerned with the microprocesses of power. In this conception, power is represented in terms of a multiplicity of force relations throughout the entire social formation. Foucault's central critique of traditional approaches to power is against the 'juridico-discursive' model of power which underpins not just Marxist theories but liberal theories of power as well. The three features of this model of power are (1) that power is possessed (for example, by the state, classes, individuals); (2) that power flows from a centralized source, from top to bottom; and (3) that power is primarily repressive in its exercise. In contrast, Foucault's alternative conception maintains: (4) that power is exercised rather than possessed; (5) that power is productive, as well as repressive; and (6) that power arises from the bottom up (Sawicki, 1991: 20–1).

In analysing the microprocesses of power, as he did in his earlier works, Foucault's attention focuses on the ways in which individuals are incorporated to the practical and efficient system of social regulation and control by which it constitutes its subjects as members. Such a process occurs, he says, through disciplinary practices of power as they operate in and through modern social institutions such as education. Such disciplinary practices constitute a technology of the political in terms of which individuals recognize themselves as members of the society and as social beings. Although power functions as an omnipresent dimension of human affairs, because power in society is a constantly changing relation, life is an open strategic game. Here Foucault takes Weber's point that power and freedom coexist. Power is not a substance, nor a mysterious property, but a certain type of relation between individuals, and the source of the constitution of their subjectivity. In *The History of Sexuality Vol. 1* (Foucault, 1978b) and in *Discipline and Punish* (Foucault, 1979), Foucault conceptualizes power as a *microphysics* by looking at the manner in which power acts on the bodies and behaviours of individuals.

Governmentality

Later, in the 1970s and beyond, Foucault became interested in power at *macro* levels of society, as it acted on populations through the exercise of governments, as *bio-power* developed in the early modern period. It was in this concern with *bio-power* and *governmentality* that Foucault is concerned to link micro and macro dimensions of analysis. By 'governmentality' Foucault refers to a form of activity aimed to guide and shape conduct, or as it is frequently represented: 'government is the conduct of conduct' (Gordon, 1991: 2). In his essay, 'Governmentality', Foucault (1991b) traces a genealogy where he notes that from the middle of the sixteenth century until the end of the eighteenth, political writings shifted from a predominant concern with 'advice to the Prince/Ruler' to a concern with the 'art of government ... of how to be ruled, how strictly, by whom, to what end, by what methods, etc.' (Foucault, 1991b: 87–8). It was a concern, he says, with the 'problematic of government in general' (ibid.: 88) and it articulated 'a kind of rationality' (ibid.: 89). Foucault traces the concern with government from its initial usage in relation to the management of the family, to its concern with territory, to its concern with the category of population, to its concern with civic society. In this manner, says Foucault (1991b: 92):

> The art of government ... is essentially concerned with answering the question of how to introduce economy – that is to say, the correct manner of managing individuals, goods and wealth within the family (which a good father is expected to do in relation to his wife, children and servants) and of making the family fortunes prosper – how to introduce this meticulous attention of the father towards his family into the management of the state.

In 'Governmentality', Foucault (1991b: 94) also fastens on to Guillaume de La Perrière's phrase that says that 'Government is the right disposition of things, arranged so as to lead to a convenient end'. This implies that there is a plurality of specific aims to be seen to by government; and that government is now not interested in imposing laws on men (as entailed in theories of sovereignty) but of *disposing of things*, that is, engaging in tactics and strategies rather than imposing laws. Whereas sovereignty rules through laws, Foucault sees a turning point in the eighteenth century, where government becomes more 'earthly', now ruling in accord with 'invisible' natural laws. In this sense government can be distinguished from sovereignty in that sovereignty has ends which are transcendental or truly legal – either God's laws, or those of an Absolute Sovereign.

For Foucault (1991b: 90), the art of government is also concerned with the issue of *security*, of stabilizing the fragile link between ruler and ruled, of rendering it legitimate, 'to identify dangers ... to develop the art of manipulating relations of force that will allow the Prince to ensure the protection of his principality'. The concept of *security* is, along with governmentality, a central concept for Foucault, and is concerned with the issue of how the state deals with unpredictable events, how it evaluates and calculates the costs and consequences, and how it manages populations within constraint, rather than through the imposition of rule. The issue of security became of increased concern in the eighteenth century. While sovereignty is concerned with the problem of rule through the imposition of *Law*, security is concerned with the *management of populations.*

In his later works and interviews, Foucault presents the outline of a genealogy of power, tracing the different historical modalities in the way models of power have functioned at different periods. In lectures given in 1978–9 and specifically in the Tanner lectures (see Foucault, 2001a), Foucault argues that a history of the forms of rationality by which power operates is more effective than an abstract conception or model of power. Power is rationalized in different periods in different ways, yet the basis of its rationalization is different from the rationality of economic processes, or of scientific discourses. What he is concerned to do is ascertain the form of rationality at stake. Although he says (Foucault, 2001a: 325) that 'for several centuries the state has been one of the most redoubtable forms of human government', it is important to examine the 'nascent state rationalities' in the course of their historical development if we are to understand the paradoxes of our present forms of government. Specifically he identifies four such rationalities: pastoral power, *raison d'état, Polizei,* and liberal (incorporating neoliberal) reason, spanning the period from ancient times until the present, all comprising specific arts of government or forms of governmentality.

Pastoral power

In ancient Greece, Foucault (2001a: 307) notes how Plato's *The Statesman* constitutes 'classical Antiquity's most systematic reflection on the theme of the pastorate'. Plato considers pastoral power as the individualized care by the rulers for each individual, like the care of the shepherd for his flock, involving leadership, duty, guidance, responsibility, and so on. But the pastoral model is rejected in *The Statesmen* as Plato argues that the model of individualized care exceeds the capability of a mortal Sovereign. What is significant about pastoral power for Foucault is that such a form of power revealed the complexity of the relation between the 'one and the many', between the individual and the totality, in the context of a population. This was the major theme of 'Omnes et Singulatim', and the significance of this for Foucault is that this theme continues to 'haunt' us today. Although Christianity altered the pastoral model of power, pastoral power did not triumph as a form of governmentality. Partly this was because pastoral power relations were difficult to reconcile with the predominantly rural and dispersed economic context of the Middle Ages; partly for educational and cultural reasons, relating to the skills and level of culture necessary for pastoral power to operate; and partly for reasons relating to socio-political structure, in that feudalism developed between individuals a tissue of personal bonds of an altogether different type from the pastorate. Notwithstanding all of this, the model of pastoral power did not disappear entirely in the medieval church. While it was not *instituted*, it was nevertheless a permanent thematic concern in the tissue of proximal cultural ties and bonds that defined life in that period.

Raison d'état and *Polizei*

What emerged in the sixteenth century in Europe were models of power that were altogether different, which represent the arts of government as an autonomous rationality. In this context Foucault points to two specific types of state rationality: *raison d'état* (reason of state), and the theory of *Polizei* (Police) which were crucial in the 150–200 years in which the modern state was being formed. *Raison d'état* emerged in the sixteenth and seventeeth centuries and formed a particular 'art of governing' not according to divine law, or natural law, or human laws, but which referred to 'a rationality specific to the art of governing states' (Foucault, 2001a: 314). It was concerned, at the most general level, with the principles that distinguished earthly states, that exhibited a 'system of rationality' (ibid.: 315) and constituted 'government in accordance with the state's strength'. Foucault (ibid.: 315) cites Botero who defines it as 'a perfect knowledge of the means through which states form, strengthen themselves, endure and grow'. In this, *raison d'état* is an 'art' or series of 'techniques' 'conforming to certain rules' (ibid.: 214). Understood as rational knowledge, it presupposed the constitution of a certain kind of knowledge, as government is only possible if the strength of the state is known, if the strength and capacities of the state's neighbours are known, and if they are known in a precise and detailed manner. While this tradition had much in common with other forms of governmentality, in that all are constituted by 'rationalities of government', it differed from the Christian and juridical traditions, in that *raison d'état* did not see the state as ruled by Divine Law, Natural Law, Human Laws or the laws of nature, but constituted a rationality internal to the state itself. Similarly, it differed from the Machiavellian tradition. Whereas Machiavelli was concerned with the relation between Prince and state, and how the power and control can be maintained by the Prince over the state, *raison d'état* is concerned with the very existence of the state itself.

The second form of state rationality, *Polizei*, emerged in Europe in the seventeenth and eighteenth centuries. For Foucault, as Gordon (2001: xxvii) notes, *Polizei* includes elements of pastoral power in that it defines its form of power as being 'of all and of each'; that is, reconciling each individual with the unity of the state. In this sense, *Polizei* is a form of governmental rationality which constitutes a detailed knowledge and regulation of the population. It does not refer to an institution functioning *within* the state, as it does today, but a governmental technology identical to the state itself. Foucault draws on

27

both French and German documents in support, but indicates that he is giving just a few examples of a huge literature which circulated in most European countries, and was especially influential in the seventeenth and eighteenth centuries, either as applied policies such as Cameralism or Mercantilism, or as subjects to be taught, such as *Polizeiwissenschaft* (the science of administration). The *Polizei* covers a whole new field in the seventeenth and eighteenth centuries 'in which centralized political and administrative power can intervene'. In this it constitutes a 'logic' of intervention which 'sees to everything' (Foucault, 2001a: 320), or as Foucault preferred, which 'sees to *living*' (ibid.: 321). The police state, says Foucault in *Discipline and Punish* (1977a: 140–1) was linked to a concern with the detail of security, and was part of:

> a history of Detail in the eighteenth century, presided over by Jean-Baptiste de la Salle, touching on Leibniz and Buffon, via Frederick II, covering pedagogy, medicine, military tactics and economics, should bring us at the end of the century to ... Napoleon, [who] ... wished to arrange around him a mechanism of power that would enable him to see the smallest event that occurred in the state he governed; he intended, by means of the rigorous discipline that he imposed, 'to embrace the whole of this vast machine without the slightest detail escaping his attention'.

In 'Omnes et Singulatim' Foucault (2001a: 322) cites Johannn Heinrich Gottlob von Justi's *Elements of Police*, which defines police as (1) enabling the state to increase its power and extend its strength in full, and (2) keep the citizens happy, and which defines the modern art of state rationality as being to 'develop those elements constitutive of individual lives in such a way that their development also fosters the strength of the state'. In his book von Justi also devotes attention to *Polizeiwissenschaft*, the theory, or science, by which methods of police were taught. Von Justi differentiates two functions of *Polizeiwissenschaft*, the first being *Polizei*, referring to the state's positive task of fostering citizens' lives and the state's strength; and, secondly, *Politik*, referring to the state's fighting against its internal and external enemies. Foucault also notes in 'Omnes et Singulatim' how the concept of *population* came to be used by the theorists of *Polizeiwissenschaft*, like von Justi, in the eighteenth century. A 'population' was understood as a group of live individuals, belonging to the same species, living side by side, that is, in a given area, and constituted the *object* of police concern. As a science of administration, *Polizeiwissenschaft* was both an art of government and method for analysing the population in a given area – 'a grid through which the state – that is, territory, resources, population, towns, and so on – can be observed' (Foucault, 2001a: 323).

Liberal reason

New liberal arts of government became important with the eclipse of the feudal order. The end of external wars, the growth of trade, the rise of capitalism, the impact of the Reformation in terms of the religious problematization of the individual, the dismantling of any notion of a private realm by the religious wars, as well as new demands for a discourse of individual direction, were all problematized by the transformation of social structure away from one based on hereditary status and community dependencies, obligations and ties, and the emergence of the new problem of 'population'.

For Foucault, the liberal art of government is not simply an ideology but a worked-out discourse containing theories and ideas that emerge in response to concrete problems within a determinate historical period. Within this framework, liberal partitions between the public and the private, or the governed and the government, constitute constructed spaces by which individuals can be secure in relation to their juridically assured rights. Liberalism, rather than being the discovery of freedom as a natural condition, is thus a *prescription for rule*.

As a prescription for rule, liberalism sought a political reconstruction of the spaces in terms of which market exchanges could take place and in terms of which a domain of individual freedom could be secure. As such a constructed space, liberalism, says Foucault, enabled the domain of 'society' to emerge in that it stood opposed to the *Polizeiwissenschaft* of the *ancien régime*. Hence the liberal art of government that one finds at the end of the sixteenth and beginning of the seventeenth centuries 'organizes itself around the theme of the reason of state' (Foucault, 1991b: 97). Liberalism emerges as a form of 'counter-'*raison d'état* with the seventeenth century jurists and philosophers 'who formalize or ritualize the theory of the contract. Contract theory enables the founding contract, the mutual pledge of ruler and subjects, to function as a sort of theoretical matrix for deriving the general principles of an art of government' (ibid.: 98).

Liberal reason constituted itself in relation to juridical, biological, economic and political doctrines that were to emerge from the seventeenth century and which anchored the scope of government in relation to the prevailing sciences of biology and evolution and in accord with the recognized scientific views concerning the individual. It is this formation of a 'savoir' proper to government, which is bound up with the knowledge of the processes related to population in its widest sense, and which incorporates also our contemporary idea of the 'economy', as pertaining not to the family but to the nation, that the problem of government came to be thought of outside the juridical framework of sovereignty. What enabled this were the new perspectives on population, and the discoveries through the new science of statistics, that populations contained their own laws and regularities. As Foucault (1991b: 99) says:

> Prior to the emergence of population, it was impossible to conceive the art of government except on the model of the family, in terms of economy conceived as the management of a family; from the moment when, on the contrary, population appears absolutely irreducible to the family, the latter becomes of secondary importance compared to population, as an element internal to population

Disciplinary power and 'bio-power'

At the same time as the liberal art of government found new spaces where the individual could practice freedom, Foucault (1977a) traces in *Discipline and Punish* the exercise of new *indirect* forms of power, executed through schemes and programmes which exacted greater disciplinary control. Here he describes the rise of the disciplinary society based on specific programmes of action, and executed through forms of legislation which were *indirect* rather than *direct*, to utilize a distinction employed by Jeremy Bentham.[3] Such schemes of action, says Foucault, were always constructed in response to some pressing social need. What was to emerge in the modern era, was the disciplinary society, which he sees as replacing the *Polizeistaat* of the cameralist and mercantilist eras. What defined the disciplines was a series of 'new techniques for assuring the ordering of human multiplicities' (Foucault, 1977a: 218). Such techniques were based in the new forms of power–knowledge characterized as the 'human sciences', which had arisen alongside the physical sciences in the Enlightenment. Foucault aims here to show how a new insidious form of 'positive' (but *indirect*) state power emerged at the same time as the liberal discourse on government, focusing its object upon society as a whole, and operating through the disciplines of expertise which became available on a widespread basis after the revolutions in statistics and *Political Arithmetic* permitted a new conceptual relation of the individual to the population. This was the emergence of *bio-power*, which for Foucault, as he discussed it in *The History of Sexuality Vol. I* (Foucault, 1978b), connoted a mixing of techniques arising from the Industrial Revolution with the growth of the human sciences. Bio-power signalled the emergence of 'population', as an economic and political problem, conjointly with the Industrial Revolution. With the growth of statistics and related disciplinary sciences, issues to do with poverty, fertility, diet and health could now be addressed in an altogether different way. What emerged was a new *positive* form of state administration, where control was exerted and achieved through *indirect* technical innovation, which coexisted with the arts of liberal governmentality. Thus two 'contradictory', 'discrepant' rationalities of power coexisted; two varied programmes and techniques, operated through variously *direct* or *indirect* state efforts. Hence, a carceral society, based on greater and greater individual control and surveillance, is the 'flip side' of a liberal regime characterized by individual rights, constitutional government and the rule of law.

The new forms of disciplinary bio-power were the eighteenth century's response to the new demands for increased controls. Foucault (1977a: 218) identifies a 'historical conjuncture' of forces:

> One aspect of this conjuncture was the large demographic thrust of the eighteenth century, an increase in the floating population (one of the primary objects of discipline is to fix; it is an anti-nomadic technique); a change of quantitative scale in the

groups to be supervised or manipulated (from the beginning of the seventeenth century to the eve of the French Revolution, the school population had been increasing rapidly ...). The other aspect of the conjuncture was the growth in the apparatus of production, which was becoming more and more extended and complex. The development of the disciplinary methods corresponded to these two processes, or rather, no doubt, to the new need to adjust their correlation. Neither the residual forms of feudal power nor the structures of the administrative monarchy, nor the local mechanisms of supervision ... could carry out this role.

Disciplinary power was organized as operating through a series of complex micro mechanisms, or techniques organized differently in different countries, and in different institutions, during the period of the Industrial Revolution. They were introduced in response to all manner of crises, such as control over epidemics of disease, fiscal control over markets, administrative control over crime, military control over deserters, the severity of which made the introduction and extension of controls 'essential'. The disciplines constituted the bases of a series of new schemes, developed by thinkers, philosophers, experts and writers, to deal with the problems associated with such changes in health and demography wrought by industrialization. There was a class bias to such disciplinary power in that it reassigned the way working life and social existence was organized, and coexisted with the liberal fictions which underpinned the privileges of the new bourgeoisie and of the leisured classes. In *Discipline and Punish*, Foucault considers many of the writers who introduced or devised the new schemes, such as Jeremy Bentham and Turquet de Mayerne, concerned as they were with the operations of power, that is, how to control inmates in prisons, how to contain dangerous diseases, how to ensure a docile and responsible workforce. Just as Bentham's *Panopticon* was designed to prevent autonomy, and render total compliance based on the principle of total surveillance, so disciplinary power in general, controls through classifying, differentiating, categorizing, excluding, individualizing, hierarchizing or identifying. Through the clever new design of a prison, the central features of *Polizeiwissenschaft* reappear. Because surveillance is now a total possibility, the prisoners begin slowly but surely to 'watch themselves', rendering their own conduct as compliant with the '*the power of the Norm*' (Foucault, 1977a: 184).

Normalization and *surveillance* constitute two of the main forms of disciplinary power. As Foucault (1977a: 184) states:

> Like surveillance, and with it, normalization becomes one of the great instruments of power at the end of the classical age. For the marks that once indicated status, privilege and affiliation were increasingly replaced – or at least supplemented – by a whole range of degrees of normality indicating membership of a homogeneous social body but also playing a part in classification, hierarchization and the distribution of rank. In a sense the power of normalization imposes homogeneity, but it individualizes by making it possible to measure gaps, to determine levels, to fix specialities and to render the differences useful by fitting them one to another.

31

A norm is a standard, by which it is possible to assess or measure or appraise without recourse to external standards. It is through the norm that the disciplines operate, through an assortment of techniques – examinations, exercises, practices, punishments, rewards – they both constitute and regulate individuals, while cloaking their explanations according to the liberal fictions of postulated metaphysical substances, such as those associated with the pre-social conception of the individual, with conceptions of genetic intelligence or with genetic disposition. Although the disciplines describe an array of normalizing regulatory techniques, and 'bend behaviour towards a terminal state' (Foucault, 1977a: 161) they do not enclose the human being within an 'iron cage of determinism', but show, rather, how new positive forms of state power infiltrate the social structure scientized under the guise of public administration techniques, aimed at the public good.

Foucault is not saying here that a society can operate without normative controls. Neither is he suggesting that all of the normative systems that have developed historically are inadequate because of that. Yet, he does think that systems developed in the past were often based on frames of reference that are today questionable, and there is a need for a critical reappraisal on the basis of present contingencies. In interviews such as 'The risks of security' (Foucault, 2001b: 381), or 'Confronting governments: human rights' (Foucault, 2001c: 474), Foucault makes the further point that the issues in terms of which populations should be differentiated or divided must be seen as *ethical* and *political*, rather than scientific or linked to foundational metaphysical premises. While he sees empirical research as vital, in order to bring the full facts of situations to people's (and government's) attention, he maintains that there is no 'univocal rule' (Foucault, 2001b: 378) or principle that can be brought to operate on the complexity of issues and problems confronting humanity in the twenty-first century. While he rejects the explanations of liberalism as 'cloaking myths', in terms of the juridical tradition of individual rights, conceptions of Divine Rights, or Natural Law, he is clearly striving towards a 'relational' conception of rights, embedded in a conception of community.

In the final analysis, to utilize a classificatory grid devised by Colin Gordon (2001: xxxiii), Foucault leaves us with 'three key formulations' in his theorizing about the state, government and power, which have implications for the twenty-first century. The first is 'security and autonomy' where Foucault speaks of the need for a 'new flourishing of governmental inventiveness to reshape the welfare state so that other demands (and achievements) in the area of individual social security are satisfied conjointly with new demands of personal autonomy'. The second relates to 'capacities and dominations', where Gordon notes Foucault's interests in maximizing the former while minimizing the latter. And the third relates to the issues surrounding 'relational rights' where he notes Foucault's concern, especially in advanced western cultures, with the 'impoverishment of the relational fabric'. Supplemented by our other discussions and observations in relation to liberal theory, it is these insights that will guide us later in this study. It is important, however, at this point, to distinguish Foucault's position from that of other post-structuralists, particularly the so-called 'textualists'.

Textualism

There is an important difference between Foucault's theory of discursive formations and the textualist position of the later post-structuralists (Lacan, Lyotard, Derrida). While Foucault operates in terms of the discourse/practice couplet, seeking to trace the relations between discourse and the extra-discursive, the textualists specifically reject the distinction between discursive and non-discursive practices. Whereas Foucault's theory of discursivity sees the meaning of discourse only in relation to context (Barrett, 1988: 126), the epistemological basis of textualism is self-referential; it privileges language over the world, is premised on a distinct anti-realism and, as a consequence, cannot give an account of the relationship between forms of discourse and social practice (Barrett, 1988: 126; Callinicos, 1989: 74–5; Said, 1983: 201). Foucault's materialist theory of discourse is elaborated and discussed more fully in Chapter 4. It is pertinent at this point, however, to differentiate his position from that of other post-structuralists, particularly Derrida.

While for Derrida each discourse produces its own truth, the actual meaning of this truth is held to be uncertain, an uncertainty which is based on Derrida's conceptions of textual dispersal and deferral of meaning where meanings are never made clear because the constituent terms can never be pinned down (Derrida, 1976; 1978; 1981; Lacan, 1977). Moving beyond Saussure and Levi Strauss, Derrida denies any systematicity to language at all. Rather, in his critique of 'The metaphysics of presence', he critiques the doctrine that reality is directly given to the subject. Language for Derrida is 'an infinite play of signifiers' where linguistic meaning 'consists in the play of signifiers proliferating into infinity', and any attempt to halve the endless play and invoke a concept of reference to the real world must, says Derrida, involve postulations of a 'transcendental signified' whereby the world is somehow assured to be present to consciousness without any discursive mediation. Hence the idea that our discourses of science or knowledge provide a veridical insight into the nature of the world or reality is just a myth: it is what Wilfred Sellars (1997: 33) has called 'the Myth of the Given'. In short then, for Derrideans, because we cannot secure the meaning of words in relation to their referent, we can never assume we are describing reality and the assumptions entailed in the 'metaphysics of presence' that the world is available to be understood through our discursive knowledge systems must remain assumptions. The 'Myth of the Given' is the myth that for Derrida propels empiricism, positivism, rationalism and historical materialism. Because it maintains that consciousness has direct access to reality with no requirement of discursive mediation, then 'discourse' cannot get in the way of apprehending reality. Derrida introduces the concept of *différance* to emphasize that it is impossible to escape from the 'metaphysics of presence'. 'Différance combines the meanings of two words – "to differ" and "to defer"'. It affirms a presence always deferred into the future or past but nevertheless constantly invoked' (Callinicos, 1989: 75).

Deconstruction for Derrida is the art of contesting the metaphysics of presence on its own terrain, a terrain from which there is no escape and to which no privileged discourse apparently has access. A major objective of deconstruction is to demonstrate that many of the binary oppositions that characterize traditional frames of reference, and forms of analysis (nature/culture, male/female, base/superstructure) are socially and historically constructed rather than natural or immutable (Anyon, 1991: 119; Hutcheon, 1989).

The influence of textualism, while in important senses referred to above and distinct from the post-structuralism of Foucault, has in education studies, feminism and other social science areas led to a proliferation of post-structuralist and postmodernist writings. While some educationists (Ball, 1990a; Kenway, 1990; Marshall, 1989; 1990) have been exclusively concerned with Foucault and the implications of Foucault for education, many others have not distinguished forms of post-structuralism/postmodernism but have drawn on the whole range of post-structuralist/postmodernist perspectives, 'overlaying' Foucault with the contributions of Derrida, Lacan and Lyotard. A major problem with this work is its lack of theoretical coherence in the reading of texts and its implicit denial that texts, including policy texts, can have real effects in the social world.

The postmodern turn

A related problem is the lack of any distinction between post-structuralism and postmodernism. Whereas post-structuralism represents a movement beyond the structuralism of those like Saussure, Claude Lévi-Strauss and Althusser, and is thus reasonably straightforward to understand, postmodernism remains more elusive and incorporates, as Anyon (1991) suggests, a number of definitions. Patti Lather speaks of it as 'a rage against humanism and the enlightenment legacy; a post-enlightenment frame of mind which has come to be coded with the term post-modern' (Lather, 1991). In this sense it represents a crisis of the human subject and a crisis in the prevailing modes of knowledge and representation. Yet, as Susan Bordo notes, there is something 'facile' and 'unspecific' about much of the theorizing that goes on about what 'postmodernism' is. According to Bordo, theorists in this tradition have a way of 'slip-slidin' away: through paradox, inversion, self subversion, facile and intricate textual dance, they often present themselves (maddeningly to one who wanted to enter into critical dialogue with them) as having it any way they want' (Bordo, 1990: 144).

In her own characterization of post-structuralism/postmodernism Anyon considers three major analytic heuristics which include an emphasis on the importance of the local, the validity of deconstruction and the centrality of discourse. We could add to these, following our analysis of Foucault and textualism, a rejection of totalizing conceptions of the social order, a rejection of 'foundationalism' and of 'meta-narratives', a rejection of binary oppositional forms of thinking and an affirmation of the radical contingency of all forms of knowledge.

Critiquing this tradition, Anyon identifies several contradictions all of which spring from the epistemological relativism of the textualists. While Anyon does not distinguish between Foucault and textualism, and while Foucault is not completely immune from all of the criticisms she makes, her criticisms are especially applicable to the later post-structuralisms of Lacan, Derrida and Lyotard. In directing her attention to several post-structuralist educationists (Aronowitz and Giroux, 1991; Cherryholmes, 1988; Ellesworth, 1989; Lather, 1991), Anyon (1991: 122) notes that, although these writers reject traditional forms of binary 'oppositional' logic, their own works are characterized by other binary dualisms. These include the 'postmodern/modern' and 'ad hoc theory/totalizing theory', 'local narrative/meta-narrative', 'non-scientific/scientific', 'many truths/one truth', 'deferral of meaning/fixed meaning' and so on.

Secondly, while these post-structuralists reject 'meta-narratives' and foundational thinking, they exhibit commitments to meta-narratives of their own. In this respect, Anyon (1991: 122) specifically criticizes Cherryholmes (1988) who claims to reject 'binary logic' and 'determinism' from all traditional educational theory. While Cherryholmes dismisses the enlightenment meta-narratives of universal truth, he exhibits, says Anyon (1991: 122), his own meta-narrative of indeterminacy: 'a metanarrative about the certainty of uncertainty'.

In a third criticism of these writers, Anyon points to their rejection of enlightenment values in relation to morals and politics while at the same time they claim that their theories contribute to emancipation and empowerment. In this respect, Anyon again identifies Cherryholmes, who claims a traditional commitment to enlightenment values such as 'dignity' while at the same time professing allegiance to the Derridean rejection of all moral systems.

Fourthly, those like Cherryholmes, Lather and Ellesworth who adopt Derridean positions radically neglect, in Anyon's view, the issues of class, race and gender. (This, we might add, is a consequence of Derrida's anti-realist epistemology.) This point is strongly made in relation to Elizabeth Ellesworth's book (1989), where she seeks to apply post-structuralist analysis to the classroom focusing on the 'local', rejecting the concepts of critical theory for being too 'abstract'. Anyon (1991: 125) comments thus:

> I want to raise a troublesome issue here ... when we read postmodern accounts of the local such as Ellesworth's account of classroom dynamics and institutional racism, we are reading accounts that have been fictionalized. By this I mean to point to the fact that analyses of the 'micro' always contain some understanding of the larger, the societal, the enveloping 'macro'. In the case of racism, for example, some knowledge of the ways in which racism is structured by the laws, conventions and histories of our society, some knowledge of the ways in which the economy, technologies, and sexism interact with racism – these are always present, even if implicitly in local power dynamics.

While Derridean textualism can, in new and novel ways, thus legitimate new forms of individualism, for Foucault the theory of discursive formation sought always to 'link' large-scale structures of power to the most mundane minutest bodily aspects of life. It was not against the possibility that 'connections' could be shown that Foucault reacted when he rejected the Hegelian theory of 'expressive totality' but against theoretical or philosophical frameworks of analysis that presupposed the nature of those connections as part of the theory, 'in advance', so to speak.

The return of the political

It is difficult for any theory caught in epistemological contradictions to contribute to a theory of the political. The real problem of textualism is the relationship to the real, and the fact that discourse is rendered as permanently discontinuous with practice or with the effects of practice. This is a serious limitation when it comes to the analysis of policy discourses.

Foucault's more materialist perspective offers several possibilities for politics and policy analysis. Much more than the textualists, Foucault emphasizes the political nature of discourse. A discourse implies a political apparatus and institutional technologies through which power is effected and subjectivity constituted. A theory of discourse can help an understanding of how people's identities are constituted and altered, of how social groups form and die out, of how cultural hegemony is secured and contested, and of the prospects for emancipatory social change.

Foucault's conception of social structure also speaks to a politics of pluralism whereby instead of privileging 'class' in relation to other salient divisions, the task of analysis is to focus upon the 'new social movements' centring around sex, gender, race, age, ethnicity or national identity. Education in all its forms is an appropriate focus for such analysis.

The concept of 'new social movements' utilized in post-structuralist theories also encapsulates a conception of the political, although only a limited one. Although, as Michelle Barrett says, the term 'new social movements' encodes its own historical 'marginality' in that they are only 'new' in the sense that they are not class, their 'emergence' has been particularly marked since the Second World War, and the concept stands to represent groups of diverse social and political kinds. Partly as a result of changes in the labour force, economics, communications, technology and ideology etc. post-1945, processes of bureaucratization and cultural massification have resulted in fundamental political and cultural changes, not the least of which have resulted in new demands for 'liberty' by traditionally marginalized and subordinated groups.

Many of the 'new social movements' can be theoretically grouped in terms of the categories of race, class and gender. Feminism is one such movement. In the 1960s, feminists began to question various images, representations, ideals, presumptions and practices that had been developed around women and the feminine. As Elizabeth Grosz (1989) says, initially feminists directed their attention to the structures of reproduction through which unequal gender regimes were continued and preserved. Later they were to direct their attention to 'patriarchal discourses': that is, political discourses that were openly hostile to and aggressive about women, or scientific discourses which embodied political conceptions of gender within the structures and institutions of society. Still later, theoretical divisions emerged as to what aims feminists should be employing. While initially they had sought equality with men in patriarchal structures, in the 1980s increasingly struggles became directed towards female autonomy – that is, women's right to political, social, economic and intellectual self-determination. As Grosz (1989: 193) maintains, 'this seems probably the most striking shift in feminist politics since its revival in the sixties'. Moreover (ibid.: 193):

> Autonomy implies the right to see oneself in whatever terms one chooses – which may imply an integration or alliance with other groups and individuals or may not. Equality, on the other hand, implies a measurement according to a given standard. Equality is the equivalence of two (or more) terms, one which takes the role of norm or model in unquestionable ways.

In the interests of 'autonomy' and 'self-determination', feminist scholars have eclectically borrowed from traditional (male) theoretical perspectives utilizing frameworks and methodologies tactically without necessarily retaining a general commitment to the framework. The basic unspoken assumptions of patriarchal theories are beginning to be analysed. The production of discourse is, for the first time, being examined. Conceptions of objectivity, science, the priority of class or the economy, and modes of thought not just on or about women but about any issue or object at all, including other theories, are being systematically retheorized.

The emergence of feminism and the central importance of gender is now a major emphasis in education and social sciences. The emphasis on race, sex, age and other 'non-class' movements has also contributed important new dimensions to analysis of the political in recent years. In these analyses, the insights of post-structuralist approaches have been significant, mainly however through reconceptualizing social structure and correcting some of the obstacles to analysis of Marxism.

Accepting some advantages to post-structuralist readings, there are also severe limitations to such approaches. The failure to distinguish between Foucault's post-structuralism and textualism has been one neglect. While Foucault's more materialist orientation offers a rich field of analytical and methodological possibilities for education and social science, the deficiencies of textualism, we believe, are irredeemable. And even though Foucault's analysis has possibilities, especially in relation to the conception of social structure as characterized by difference, the multidimensional conception of power within it also has limitations which need addressing. The central problem can perhaps best be expressed this way: if textualism has no conception of the political, Foucault offers us only one that is partial and incomplete. For Foucault, this relates to the sidelining of social structures such as the state, class and production, as well as an impoverished understanding of the institutional basis in which power resides and is mobilized. What is needed is a multidimensional understanding of the political. This is particularly important in the domain of policy-making and policy analysis, which traditionally have been dominated by technicist approaches based upon spurious assumptions of political neutrality.

Mainstream technicist understandings of how policy-making occurs in a democracy arose out of the dominant intellectual traditions of the social sciences, particularly those derived from the functionalist paradigm. Applied to education, such conceptions of the policy formation process, and its analysis, have buttressed the supremacy of orthodox liberal understandings of educational theory and practice for most of the twentieth century. Such understandings of policy are integral theoretical components not only in the maintenance of an intellectual, but also a much broader political and economic status quo. In the next two chapters, we reject these traditional technicist models of educational policy-making and policy analysis, and advocate a Foucauldian critical policy analysis approach.

Notes

1 For a discussion of the issue of epistemological relativism, see Olssen (1999) and Margolis (1993).
2 For the compatibility of Foucault and Gramsci, see Olssen (1999: ch. 7).
3 Bentham distinguishes 'direct' from 'indirect' legislation. Direct methods are those that 'forbid outright', whereas 'indirect' methods are those that have recourse to 'to oblique methods'. See Jeremy Bentham (1950: 175).

3
Critical Policy Analysis: A Foucauldian Approach

In this chapter, we consider the possibilities of adopting a Foucauldian approach to the analysis of education policy. We begin with an explication of Foucault's conception of critique as the basis for a deeper understanding of social institutions generally and educational institutions in particular. We then examine the distinguishing features of archaeology and genealogy as the two complementary forms of Foucauldian social analysis before discussing two recent attempts to apply Foucauldian methods to education policy analysis

Foucault's idea of critique

Critique, for Foucault, (aims at identifying and exposing the unrecognized forms of power in people's lives, to expose and move beyond the forms in which we are entrapped in relation to the diverse ways that we act and think.) In this sense, critique aims to free people from the historically transitory constraints of contemporary consciousness as realized in and through discursive practices. Such constraints impose limitations which have become so intimately a part of the way that people experience their lives that they no longer experience these systems as limitations but embrace them as the very structure of normal and natural human behaviour. Within these limits, seen as both the limits of reason and the limits of nature, freedom is subordinated to reason, which is subordinated to nature, and it is against such a reduction of reason to nature that Foucault struggles. His commitment is to a form of 'permanent criticism' which must be seen as linked to his broader programme of freedom of thought. It is the freedom to think differently from what we already know. Thought and life achieve realization through an attitude of 'permanent criticism' which does not have as its aim an objective of absolute emancipation, or absolute enlightenment, but rather aims at limited and partial operations on the world as well as acts of aesthetic self-creation framed within a critical ontology of ourselves and supported by an ethics and aesthetics of existence. As Foucault (1988a: 154) puts it:

A critique is not a matter of saying that things are not right as they are. It is a matter of pointing out on what kinds of assumptions, what kinds of familiar, unchallenged, unconsidered modes of thought, the practices that we accept rest. ... Criticism is a matter of flushing out that thought and trying to change it: to show that things are not as self-evident as we believed, to see that what is accepted as self-evident will no longer be accepted as such. Practising criticism is a matter of making facile gestures difficult.

The three central thinkers in terms of whom Foucault's notion of critique takes form are Kant, Nietzsche and Heidegger. While rejecting much of Kant, Foucault does take his idea that critique is a negative practice. In other words, that critique is concerned, not to postulate the conditions of an ideal society in contrast to an imperfect present, but solely to expose the contemporary limits to the necessary. Criticism is about escaping, not inaugurating, a new order. For Kant, the critical method of the Enlightenment was represented as an *Ausgang*, that is, an 'exit' or 'way out' of an existing impasse or state of affairs. Hence, for Kant, critical method must exit from our own state of immaturity, which makes us obey authority in a thoughtless and uncritical manner. For Foucault, the meaning and significance of a critical ethos is that it is a clarification of the present. It is a concern with, as he says (Foucault, 1988b: 121): 'what is happening right now, and what we are, we who are perhaps nothing more than what is happening at the moment'.

Where Foucault differs from Kant and Habermas is in asserting the contextual historical character of the categories that take root in, and develop in the social and historical customs and practices of a specific society. In this context, the role of the policy analyst is to understand the historical nature of the a priori through a detailed examination of the social and historical practices (customs, language, habits, discourses, institutions, disciplines) from which a particular style of institutional reasoning emerges and develops.

For Habermas, critical theory has both Hegelian and Kantian moments in that it attempts to realize an ideal historical state as well as to maintain universal claims for truth and moral reasoning. Foucault sees Habermas's reconstructive conception of critique as an idealist conception that traces the process of Enlightenment as the story of its movement toward its ideal realization or end state. This is the Hegelian theme which links Habermas's idea of critique to the realization of history's ultimate goal, and which sees history as the self-realization of humanity. Foucault also rejects assumptions concerning the systematic unity of knowledge and of the interests of the human race, which for Habermas, following Kant and Fichte, constitute the major divisions in the sciences of inquiry. This, in Foucault's view, is to ground one's form of critique on an analytic framework of anthropological interests that underpin both the Hegelian and Kantian moments. Hence, Foucault attempts to purge both the humanist as well as the idealist aims of critique as they occur in Habermas's project, replacing them, following Nietzsche, with a model of history as a continuous and never-ending process of changing practices.

For Foucault, the unresolved tension within the philosophical projects of Kant and Habermas is that they fail to appreciate the contingent and historically contextualized character of all truth-claims, that is, by advocating a notion of critique which claims to transcend specific historical conditions through the exercise of cognitive faculties (of understanding, reason and judgement) deduced a priori as timeless structures. The transcendental character of Kant's argument resides in positing a priori categories which are deduced to constitute the consciousness of the human subject, as that which organizes perception as a timeless and universal structure. In this sense, Foucault rejects Kant's claim to have established the universal grounds for the conditions of possibility of human knowledge. Hence, Kant's claims for transcendental reason are replaced for Foucault by a principle of permanent contingency. By extension, Foucault disputes Kant's claim to have established a secure foundation from which to differentiate types of knowledge claims, relating to science, practical reason or aesthetics. The objective is to switch from a conception of critique as being transcendentally grounded, to a conception of critique that conceives it as practical and as historically specific. Thus Foucault says (1984a: 45–6):

> Criticism is no longer going to be practised in the search for formal structures with universal value, but rather as an historical investigation into the events that have led us to constitute ourselves and to recognize ourselves as subjects of what we are doing, thinking, saying. In this sense the criticism is not transcendental, and its goal is not that of making metaphysics possible: it is genealogical in its design and archaeological in its method.

Foucault's project then is a critique of the modes of existing reason whereby he seeks to introduce what McCarthy (1994: 249) calls 'a sociohistorical turn' into the practice of philosophy. In order to explore 'the nature scope and limits of human reason' we have to understand (McCarthy, 1994: 243–4):

> the intrinsic impurity of what we call reason – its embeddedness in culture and society, its engagement with power and interest, the historical variability of its categories and criteria, the embodied, sensuous and practically engaged character of its bearers ... and this calls for models of sociohistorical enquiry that go beyond the traditional bounds of philosophical analysis. The critique of reason as a non-foundationalist enterprise is concerned with structures and rules that transcend the individual consciousness. But what is supraindividual in this way is no longer understood as transcendental; it is sociocultural in origin.

Thus Foucault adapts Kant to support his socio-historical conception through which individuals are constituted in relation to a world of already given practices of a determinate historical terrain. In order to do this he draws upon both Heidegger and Nietzsche. For Heidegger, *Being* constitutes the deceptively neutral and naturalized practices of our world. It constitutes the historical terrain onto which we are *Thrown*. Heidegger distinguishes between an unthinking mode of being, which is primary, and a reflective mode of being, which is derivative, but more relevant to critical thought, in Foucault's view. Central to such a conception is the idea that power, which functions invisibly, must be unmasked. Thus Foucault's notion of critique also parallels Heidegger in that he aims to 'denaturalize' the phenomenal world, and turn it into a matter for reflection.

The influence of Nietzsche

By drawing on Nietzsche's method of genealogy, institutions and practices are historically investigated in order to trace the forms of power and lines of opposition between and amongst them. For Nietzsche our habitual modes of action and thought have an historical origin and bear the marks of conflicting individual wills to power of people, groups and classes in history. In *On the Genealogy of Morals*, Nietzsche (1969) shows how our dominant moral codes emerged from the battle of classes and groups (for example, Romans and Jews) in the past. Genealogy seeks to trace the lines of the battles that have gone into making the world, as we know it in the present, natural. In this sense it contributes to problematizing our taken-for-granted beliefs and conceptions about the way the world is.

For Foucault, because the Enlightenment has not evacuated the problems and dangers of earlier periods in history, there is a connection to his notion of critique. His criticisms of Kant confirm his view that the basis of critique must be as a form of permanent interrogative thinking. As he puts it (Foucault, 1984a: 42): 'The thread that may connect us with the Enlightenment is not faithfulness to doctrinal elements, but rather the permanent reactivation of an attitude – that is, of a philosophical ethos that could be described as a permanent critique of our historical era.' In that the Enlightenment emphasizes 'permanent critique', it emphasizes a form of philosophical interrogation which 'simultaneously problematizes man's relation to the present, man's historical mode of being, and the constitution of the self as an autonomous subject' (Foucault, 1984a: 42). Critique, then, defines an 'ethos' which has both a negative and a positive heuristic. In terms of its negative heuristic, Foucault identifies the need to refuse what he calls 'the "blackmail" of the Enlightenment' (ibid.: 42). This refers to the pressure to be either 'for or against the Enlightenment', to 'accept the Enlightenment and remain with the tradition of its rationalism ... or [to] criticize the Enlightenment and then try to escape from its principles of rationality' (ibid.: 43). Rather (ibid.: 43):

> We must try to proceed with the analysis of ourselves as beings who are historically determined, to a certain extent by the Enlightenment. Such an analysis implies a series of historical inquiries that are as precise as possible; and these inquiries will

not be orientated retrospectively toward the 'essential kernel of rationality' that can be found in the Enlightenment and that would have to be preserved in any event; they will be orientated toward the 'contemporary limits of the necessary', that is, toward what is not or is no longer indispensable for the constitution of ourselves as autonomous subjects.

For Foucault, the Enlightenment comprises a set of events and complex historical processes located at a certain point in the development of European societies. This creates the necessity for a double conception of critique. On the one hand, it must proceed genealogically under the influence of Nietzsche through an examination of the historical a priori of all possible experience; on the other, it must seek to explore the possible limits to experience by exercising the transcendental freedom which Kant himself established as an essential foundation for critique. In this sense, the philosophical ethos of critique may be characterized as a limit-attitude, but in a different sense to that suggested by Kant. As he says (Foucault, 1984a: 46):

> Criticism indeed consists of analysing and reflecting upon limits. But if the Kantian question was that of knowing what limits knowledge must abstain from transgressing, it seems to me that the critical question today has to be turned back into a positive one: in what is given to us as universal, necessary or obligatory, what part is taken up by things which are actually singular, contingent, the product of arbitrary constraints? The point, in brief, is to transform critique conducted in the form of necessary limitations into a practical critique that takes the form of a possible transgression.

Rather than accepting pre-established limits to reason based on Kant's transcendental analysis, the theoretical task becomes one of testing the limits which establish to what extent we can move beyond them. Foucault defines transgression as 'an action which involves the limit ... the experience of transgression brings to light this relationship of finitude to being, this moment of the limit which anthropological thought, since Kant, could only designate from the distance and from the exterior through the language of dialectics' (Foucault, 1977b: 33, 49).

The objects of Foucauldian critique

What criticism refers to for Foucault, in a concrete and practical sense, is an autonomous, non-centralized kind of theoretical production, one whose validity is not dependent on the approval of the established regimes of thought. In this sense, criticism has a local character because the attempt to think in terms of totalizing strategies or models proves a hindrance to effective action. Criticism thus involves the role of the 'specific intellectual' and is linked to the insurrection of subjugated knowledges. By subjugated knowledges, Foucault is referring to the historical contents of knowledges that have been disqualified as inadequate to their task or insufficiently elaborated – naive knowledges that are defined as operating low down on the hierarchy of formal knowledge below an acceptable level of cognition or scientificity. But, Foucault does not mean by subjugated knowledge the unsuccessful paradigms of knowledge, but rather, as Habermas (1994a: 92) notes, he is thinking of:

> the experiences of groups subordinated to power that have never advanced to the status of official knowledge, that have never been sufficiently articulated. It is a question of the implicit knowledge of 'the people' who form the bedrock in a system of power, who are the first to experience a technology of power with their own bodies, whether as the ones suffering or as the officials manning the machinery of suffering – for example, the knowledge of those who undergo psychiatric treatment, of orderlies, of delinquents and wardens, of the inmates of concentration camps and the guards, of blacks and homosexuals, of woman and of witches, of vagabonds, of children and dreamers.

For Foucault it is through the re-emergence of these low-ranking subordinate groups and their knowledges that criticism performs its task. And, as Habermas (1994a: 93) has observed, there is a parallel here between Foucault's conception and writers like Lukács who attributed an immanent potential to the perspectives of the working class.

By 'buried', 'disqualified' or 'subjugated' knowledges Foucault is also referring to the 'local' or 'regional' character of knowledge, for genealogy can only do its work once the 'tyranny of globalizing discourses ... [is] eliminated' (Foucault, 1994a: 22). In this, Foucault strives repeatedly to distance the task of critique from its traditional pairing with the notion of revolution, or indeed with any ideal conception of an imagined society in the future. In this sense, historico-critical attitude must be an experimental one. This is to say, it must reject 'radical and global' forms of analysis, as 'we know from experience', he says (Foucault, 1984a: 46), 'that the claim to escape from the system of contemporary reality so as to produce the overall programs of another society, of another way of thinking, another culture, another vision of the world, has led to the return of the most dangerous traditions'. Thus, Foucault analyses 'specific transformations', which are 'always practical and local' (ibid.: 46).

On these grounds, Foucault's conception of critique does not appeal to standards in the past, in the future or in reason, yet it seeks to expose the unrecognized operation of power in social practices. This is why Foucault's conception of critique differs from the totalizing conceptions of Marxism, the Frankfurt School or the reconstructive conception of Habermas. His aim is not the realization of a rational society, but the more pragmatically orientated aim of revealing 'the contemporary limits of the necessary'. His critique, in that it is not Kantian, also does not share the faith in a future utopia of the sort advocated by Marxists or by the leading writers of the Frankfurt School, such as Adorno, Horkheimer or Habermas. As Rajchman (1985: 80) says, citing Geuss (1981), Foucault sees the model of an 'inverted Enlightenment' as definitive of the very idea of the model of critical theory that has been developed within Marxism, and most especially by the Frankfurt School. Such models presuppose, in Foucault's view, the revelation of some concealed emancipatory truth about our 'real' natures, just as much as they do about the real nature and limits to reason. It is the absence of some implicit or explicit ultimate measure or standard by which truth is assessed that explains why Foucault terms his own form of critical interrogation as 'practical'. In this sense, its most immediate and central concern is to sound a warning on the dangers of power.

Foucauldian methodology: archaeology and genealogy

Methodologically Foucault's works utilize two approaches: that of archaeology, concerned to describe the historical presuppositions of a given system of thought, and genealogy, concerned to trace the historical process of descent and emergence by which a given thought system or process comes into being and is subsequently transformed. While distinct, the two approaches can be seen as complementary forms of discourse analysis.

Archaeology = ANALYSING LANGUAGE

Foucault's method of archaeology constitutes a way of analysing the superstructural dimension of language statements constitutive of discourse. A discourse is defined in terms of statements (énoncés) of 'things said'. Statements are events of certain kinds, at once tied to an historical context and capable of repetition. Statements are not equivalent to propositions or sentences, or 'speech acts', neither are they phonemes, morphemes, or syntagms. Rather, as Foucault (1972: 114) states:

> In examining the statement what we have discovered is a function that has a bearing on groups of signs, which is identified neither with grammatical 'acceptability' nor with logical correctness, and which requires it to operate: a referential (which is not exactly a fact, a state of things, or even an object, but a principle of differentiation); a subject (not the speaking consciousness, nor the author of the formulation, but a position that may be filled in certain conditions by various individuals); an associated field (which is not the real context of the formulation, the situation in which it was articulated, but a domain of coexistence for other statements); a materiality (which is not only the substance or support of the articulation, but a status, rules of transcription, possibilities for use and re-use).

Foucault is interested in serious statements comprising subsets that have some autonomy, which contain truth claims and which belong to a single system of formation. A 'discursive formation' comprises the regularity that obtains between 'objects, types of statement, concepts, or thematic choices' (Foucault, 1972: 38, 107). It is 'the general enunciative system that governs a group of verbal performances' (ibid.: 117).

Archaeological analysis is centrally concerned to uncover the rules of formation of discourses, or discursive systems. In a technical sense, it proceeds at the level of statements (énoncés) searching for rules that explain the appearance of phenomena under study. It examines the forms of regularity, that is, the discursive conditions, which order the structure of a form of discourse and which determine how such orders come into being. It is not analysis of that which is claimed to be true in knowledge but an analysis of 'truth games'. Discourse is thus analysed in terms of the operation of rules that bring it into being. Archaeology attempts to account for the way discourses are ordered. As such, archaeology focuses attention on the link between perception and action and why at different periods specialists in knowledge perceive objects differently. The core of archaeology is thus an attempt to establish the discursive practices and rules of formation of discourses through asking 'how is it that one particular statement appeared rather than another?' (Foucault, 1972: 27).

In *The Order of Things*, for example, Foucault (1970) seeks to uncover the regularities which accounted for the emergence of the sciences of the nineteenth century by comparing forms of thought across different historical periods (Renaissance, Classical, and Modern). Archaeology here constitutes a method for examining the historicity of science by describing rules that undergird ways of looking at the world. These rules are regularities that determine the systems of possibility as to what is considered as true and false, and they determine what counts as grounds for assent or dissent, as well as what arguments and data are relevant and legitimate. These 'structures of thought' are termed epistemes. An 'episteme' refers to:

> the total set of relations that unite, at a given period, the discursive practices. ... The episteme is not a form of knowledge ... or type of rationality which, crossing the boundaries of the most varied sciences, manifests the sovereign unity of a subject, a spirit, or a period; it is the totality of relations that can be discovered for a given period, between the sciences when one analyses them at the level of discursive regularities. (Foucault, 1972: 191)

Robert Machado (1992: 14) characterizes an episteme as defined by two features. The first is its depth; an 'episteme' relates to the nature of 'deep' knowledge (*savoir*) and to the specific order or configuration that such knowledge assumes in a given period. This is to say that an episteme is governed by a principle prior to and independent of the ordering of discourse such as science, which is constituted of 'surface' knowledge (*connaissance*). The second is its general global nature. In any culture, at a particular point in time, there is only one episteme which defines the conditions of possibility of all

46

theoretical knowledge (see Foucault, 1970: 179). Archaeology is an historical analysis of this theoretical knowledge attempting to trace links between the different domains of 'life, work, and language', revealing relationships that are not readily apparent. In doing so it seeks to expose the 'historical a priori' of the episteme as it manifests itself in the body of discourses under study. In this sense, Foucault insists that epistemes are not transcendental in the Kantian sense, neither are they origins or foundations. Rather, they are practices to be encountered, that is, they are time-bound and factual.

In that archaeology's object of study is discourses, its methods are conceptual and it aims to search for explanations at a deeper level than those provided by science. Archaeology utilizes theoretical knowledge (*savoir*) in order to analyse forms of knowledge. It examines all forms of policy in their historical context, taking as its starting point the historical constitution of scientific concepts, detailing the types of progress which characterize them, the means by which truth is produced, as well as the criteria of rationality that they establish. However, while it yields rich insights, archaeology is limited by its inability to account for the historical emergence and transformation of discourses. Such accounts were to become the major focus of Foucault's work after 1968 when he shifted his methodological emphasis to genealogy.

Genealogy = POWER AND KNOWLEDGE

Genealogy offers a specific methodology for studying and writing history. As a method of interest to social and educational research, genealogy demonstrates the potential of discourse to impact and shape life at the physical level, based upon the interaction of power and knowledge in shaping historical conditions, which in turn makes particular structures realisable and particular conceptual frameworks possible. Although Foucault developed this approach during the 1970s, as a consequence of his turn to Nietzsche, it must be viewed as a supplement, not an alternative, to archaeology. As Arnold Davidson (1986: 227) puts it: 'genealogy does not so much displace archaeology as widen the kind of analysis to be pursued. It is a question, as Foucault put it in his last writings, of different axes whose "relative importance is not always the same for all forms of experience"'. Genealogical analysis aims to explain the existence and transformation of elements of theoretical knowledge (*savoir*) by situating them within power structures and by tracing their descent and emergence in the context of history. As such, it traces an essential, historically constituted tie between power and knowledge, and constitutes a causal explanation for change in discursive formations and epistemes. Because it is more historical it helps Foucault avoid succumbing to the temptations of structuralism. Yet, like archaeology, it avoids reference to a philosophical conception of the subject, radicalizing Nietzsche and Heidegger's opposition to the post-Cartesian and Kantian conceptions. Also, like archaeology, it is limited and justified as a method in terms of the fruitfulness of its specific applications.

Genealogy thus asserts the historical constitution of our most prized certainties about ourselves and the world in its attempts to de-naturalize explanations for the existence of phenomena. Policy discourses with their specific problems and solutions relative to a particular historical time are amenable to such an analysis. It analyses discourse in its relation to social structures and has an explicit focus on power and on bodies. It is interested in institutional analysis and technologies of power aiming to isolate the mechanisms by which power operates. Through its focus on power, also, it aims to document how culture attempts to normalize individuals through increasingly rationalized means, by constituting normality, turning them into meaningful subjects and docile objects. Power relations are thus pivotal. Genealogy thus shifts the model for historical understanding from Marxist science and ideology, or from hermeneutical texts and their interpretation, to a Nietzschean-inspired analysis of strategies and tactics in history.

As a Nietzschean strategy, Foucault (1977c: 142) is clear that genealogy opposes itself to the search for origins (*Ursprung*) or essences. To search for origins is to attempt to capture the exact essence of things which Foucault sees as reinstating Platonic essentialism. Rather than tracing origins, genealogy traces the process of descent and emergence. Descent (*Herkunft*) is defined by Foucault as pertaining to practices as series of events:

> To follow the complex course of descent is to maintain passing events in their proper dispersion; it is to identify the accidents, the minute deviations – or conversely, the complete reversals – the errors, the false appraisals, and the faulty calculations that gave birth to these things that continue to exist and have value for us. (Ibid.: 146)

In contrast to descent, emergence (*Entstehung*) traces 'the movement of arising' (ibid.:148). 'Emergence is thus the entry of forces; it is their eruption, the leap from wings to center stage, each in its youthful strength' (ibid.: 149–50). Unlike the continuities traced by those historians who search for origins, genealogy traces the jolts and surprises of history in terms of the effects of power, which Foucault, and those who have been inspired by him, like Edward Said (1978; 1983), have marked in terms of 'beginnings'. Foucault's genealogical histories thus challenge the presuppositions of past histories, the tendency towards totalizing abstraction, towards closure, to universalist assumptions regarding the human identity or the nature of existence. His approach also rejects the transcendental turn in philosophy and asserts the radical contingency of discourses in their historical context.

Further insights into Foucault's archaeological and genealogical methods are revealed from his lecture notes at the Collège de France, as published in the four volumes of *Dits et Écrits* (Foucault, 1994b). In these volumes,

Foucault reveals the importance of analytic method and the philosophy of language in relation to the analysis of discourse. In one essay, 'La philosophie analytique de la politique' (Foucault, 1994c), initially delivered in 1978 in Japan, Foucault spells out the superiority of analytical methods as used in Anglo-American philosophy compared to dialectical methodology. What characterizes analytic methods is a concern not with the 'deep structures' of language, or the 'being' of language but with the 'everyday use' made of language in different types of discourse. By extension, Foucault argues that philosophy can similarly analyse what occurs in 'everyday relations of power', and in all those other relations that 'traverse the social body'. Just as language can be seen to underlie thought, so there is a similar grammar underlying social relations and relations of power. Hence, Foucault argues for what he calls an 'analytico-political philosophy'. Similarly, rather than seeing language as revealing some eternal buried truth which 'deceives or reveals', the metaphorical method for understanding that Foucault utilizes is that of a game: 'Language, it is played'. It is, thus, a 'strategic' metaphor, as well as a linguistic metaphor, that Foucault utilizes to develop a critical approach to society freed from the historical determinism of Marxism: 'Relations of power, also, they are played; it is these games of power (*jeux de pouvoir*) that one must study in terms of tactics and strategy, in terms of order and of chance, in terms of stakes and objectives' (Foucault, 1994c: 541–2).

Foucault's departure from structuralism

Our characterization of Foucault is as a *post-structuralist* whose central methodological approach is historical. As Arnold Davidson (1997: 11) notes, Foucault borrows two central insights from structural linguistics: first, its 'anti-atomism', or the idea 'that we should not analyse single or individual elements in isolation but that one must look at systematic relations amongst elements'; second, its notion that 'the relations between elements are coherent and transformable, that is, that the elements form a structure'. Yet, although Foucault partially adopted a structuralist orientation, he departed from structuralism on several grounds.

First, Foucault rejected the notion, central to structuralism, that there is a system of *universal rules* or *laws* or *elementary structures* that underpinned history, and explained its surface appearances. This was clearly associated with structuralists such as Saussure, Barthes (at least in his early work) and Lévi-Strauss whose work demonstrated adherence to the notion that there was one original structure which was both universal and ahistorical. In this sense, the post-structuralist, as opposed to the structuralist approach, assumes that the regularities identified are not the same in all historical periods and in all cultures, but rather are specific to particular times and places. As a consequence of this, Foucault also rejected the structuralist and Marxist utilization of topographical or architectural metaphors such as depth/surface, or base/super-structure, in preference for an approach which focused at the level of the micro-practices of lived experience.

Secondly, Foucault always stood opposed to a marked tendency amongst structuralist writers to a *prioritizing* of the structure over the parts, or assuming the *pre-existence* of the whole over the parts, whereby the units could be explained once the *essence* of the structure is uncovered. This was again the case for structuralists like Saussure, Barthes, Lévi-Strauss and Althusser, as well as for the sociologist, Durkheim, and the philosopher, Hegel. For Althusser (1971), the economic mode of production 'explained', albeit 'ultimately' and 'in the last instance', the particular functions of the Repressive State Apparatuses as well as the Ideological State Apparatuses. Similarly, for Lévi-Strauss (1969: 100), human institutions were: 'Structures whose whole – in other words the regulating principle – can be given before the parts, that is, that complex union which makes up the institution, its terminology, consequences and implications, the customs through which it is expressed and the beliefs to which it gives rise.' Hence, although Foucault's conception of structural causality was arguably influenced by, and shows similarities to, certain features of a model of change adopted by structural linguistics, namely its holistic, non-atomist and non-linear conception of change, there is no representation of the structure or whole as *integrative* of the entire social formation, or as constraining the system of differences. This constitutes the essence of Foucault's *pluralism*, a principle on which he differed explicitly from writers like Althusser, but also from the whole structuralist tradition.

Thirdly, clearly apparent in Foucault's perceptions of the limits of structuralism was a failure to theorize adequately the *historicity* of structures. Amongst structuralists like Saussure, Barthes and Lévi-Strauss there was little sense of history, which is to say they privileged synchrony over diachrony in analysis. For Lévi-Strauss, indeed, the search for universal structures was a direct challenge to the established disciplinary concern with evolutionary historical development.

Foucault's dependence on structural linguistics is also central to understanding the nature of his analysis. Traditionally, the rationality of analytic reason, he says, has been concerned with causality. In structural linguistics, however, the concern is not with causality, but in revealing multiple relations that Foucault calls in his 1969 article 'Linguistique et sciences sociales' 'logical relations' (see Foucault, 1994d: 824). While it is possible to formalize one's treatment of the analysis of relations, it is, says Foucault (1994d.), the discovery of the 'presence of a logic that is not the logic of causal determinism that is currently at the heart of philosophical and theoretical debates'.

Foucault's reliance on the model of structural linguistics provides him with a method which avoids both methodological individualism and being trapped by a concern with causalism. Structural linguistics is concerned with 'the systematic sets of relations among elements' (Davidson, 1997: 8), and it functions for Foucault as a model to enable him to study social reality as a logical structure, or set of logical relations revealing relations that are not transparent to consciousness. The methods of structural linguistics also enable Foucault to analyse change. For just as linguistics undertakes synchronic analysis, seeking to trace the necessary conditions for an element within the structure of language to undergo change, a similar synchronic analysis applied to social life asks the question: in order for a change to occur what other changes must also take place in the overall texture of the social configuration (Foucault, 1994d: 827). Hence, Foucault seeks to identify logical relations where none had previously been thought to exist or where previously one had searched for causal relations. This form of analysis becomes for Foucault a method of analysing previously invisible determinations (see Davidson, 1997: 1–20).

The methodological strategies common to both archaeology and genealogy were also developed in response to Marxism, which is characterized by a specific narrow conception of causality (*un causalisme primaire*) and a dialectical logic that has very little in common with the logical relations that Foucault is interested in. Thus he maintains: 'what one is trying to recover in Marx is something that is neither the determinist ascription of causality, nor the logic of a Hegelian type but a logical analysis of reality' (Foucault, 1994d: 824–5).

Arnold Davidson (1997), in a review of *Dits et Écrits* to which our own analysis is indebted, points out that it is through such methodological strategies that Foucault proceeds to advance a non-reductive, holistic, analysis of social life. As he puts it (Davidson, 1997: 11):

> this kind of analysis is characterized, first, by anti-atomism, by the idea that we should not analyse single or individual elements in isolation but that one must look at the systematic relations among elements; second, it is characterized by the idea that the relations between elements are coherent and transformable, that is, that the elements form a structure.

Thus, in his dissertation on the knowledge of heredity as a system of thought, submitted as part of his application for his position at the Collège de France, Foucault seeks to describe the changes, transformations, and conditions of possibility that made genetics possible, that constituted it as a science based on a series of discourses concerning breeding, just as in *The Order of Things* (Foucault, 1970) he had done for natural history and biology. What factors led to the emergence of these fields as sciences? What elements changed to make such developments possible? What made them possible as systems of thought? Thus Foucault seeks to describe the relations among elements as structures which change as the component elements change, that is, he endeavours to establish the systematic sets of relations and transformations that enable different forms of knowledge to emerge.

In retrospect, we can see that even when Foucault's methodological focus privileged archaeology, it was within the context of historically constituted *epistemes* and the difference of his position from structuralism was already manifest in relation to several key dimensions. The dissociation became more apparent after Foucault's turn to genealogy and Nietzsche at the close of the 1960s, which led to an emphasis on history and power and a playing down of the importance of 'archaeology' and its concern with the purely formal (and more 'structuralist') analysis of discourse. With the turn towards genealogy, Foucault became more concerned with power and history, and the historical constitution of knowledge. In this process, however, there is no *integrative* principle and no *essence*. If the genealogist studies history 'he finds that there is "something altogether different" behind things: not a timeless and essential secret, but the secret that they have no essence or that their essence was fabricated in a piecemeal fashion from alien forms' (Foucault, 1977c: 142).

Foucault's materialism

Foucault's concentration on power signals an added and distinctive character to his post-structuralism in comparison with writers like Derrida, Lyotard and Baudrillard. In this, as has been maintained before (Olssen, 1995; 1996a; 1999; 2002b; 2003) Foucault's post-structuralism is a more materialist conception, rejecting the priority of the signifier and its overemphasis in relation to the signified, and the failure of other post-structuralists to contextualize both signifier and signified in the context of the pre-discursive. For Foucault, meaning is not produced through the free play of signifiers alone, but signification is effected by power. The material substance of the expression is the statement (*énoncé*) which serves as a mechanism constraining signification, which in turn is effected by social and historical context, and within such a context, by power. Culture for Foucault, as for his fellow Nietzscheans, Deleuze and Guattari, is not simply a system of signification but a system of material and discursive articulation. In this, genealogy puts an emphasis on *power* rather than knowledge, and *practices* rather than language. As Foucault (1980a: 114) says: 'one's point of reference should not be the great model of language (*langue*) and signs, but to that of war and battle'. For this he introduces the concept of 'apparatus': 'what I call an apparatus is a much more general case of the *episteme*; or rather ... the *episteme* is a specifically *discursive* apparatus, whereas the apparatus in its general form is both discursive and non-discursive, its elements being much more heterogeneous' (Foucault, 1980b: 197). Foucault's utilization of Nietzsche also differentiates him from Derrida's post-structuralism in relation to the focus on the body, as opposed to the signifier. The relationship between power and bodies operates as both power *over* bodies, and the power *of* bodies, the latter operating through Will and Desire, whereby Foucault discovers a force not determined by epistemic frameworks, and where the 'historical a priori' of discourse is underpinned by a more primary reality, which explains it. The post-structuralism of Foucault is thus not concerned with language, but with politics.

In *Discipline and Punish* (Foucault, 1977a), for example, Foucault observes how punishment cannot be derived solely from the force of the discourse, for torture, machines and dungeons are material, and have meaning because of the ideology of punishment. But we cannot derive the resultant forms solely from the discourse or the law, although they are clearly related. Rather, the social forms of discipline and punishment represent a synthetic and relatively autonomous compound of knowledge and technique and material objects. The developments of the prison, the clinic, the mental asylum are thus the outcomes of this multiple articulation. Foucault can be distinguished in this from other post-structuralist and postmodern writers, such as Baudrillard and Derrida, who as Gottdiener (1995: 73) says 'have ignored the interrogation of material forms' in the same way as western sociologists such as the symbolic interactionists have done. Unlike deconstruction, which confines itself to synchronic textual analysis, seeking to isolate the metaphysics in the text, Foucault is concerned to trace the historical constitution of our most prized certainties, to expose their contingent historical basis, and to track the inter-relations between power and knowledge within a particular historical period. In this schema, culture is not just a system of signification, but a system of material and discursive articulation in which meaning and the processes of signification are effected by power, that is, by material culture.

Foucault and critical policy analysis

If we ask, how does Foucault's historicist method work in practice, analysis is possible at several levels:

- at the level at which the discursive and the material are inextricably linked together (as apparatuses), as in the development of institutional forms such as the clinic, the mental asylum, the prison or the school;
- at the level where institutional-discursive apparatuses conflict, as for instance in the conflict over the control of birth between midwives and doctors; and
- at the level of the discursive as historically constituted material and ideological forces, rendered comprehensible via genealogy.

For us, Foucault's rich forays – archaeological, genealogical, ethical – suggest a multiplicity of models for a critical approach to reading education policy. Although this study presents a Foucauldian approach to the analysis of educational policy and the politics of education, there are some aspects of Foucault's work that are not accepted. Especially significant here is the fact that we depart from his apoliticism, localism and neutralism over ends and values, whereas some critics have detected these trends in his work (Trombadori,

1991). Although there is no Hegelian commitment to a pattern in history or a future utopian state of society, there is within Foucault's work, we argue, the basis for a broad commitment to a democratic and ethical vision of a new welfare community. Rather than employ him in a one-sided negative way that can be found in some readings of his work, we seek to utilize Foucault as an ally, sometimes going beyond the literal canon of his texts, but keeping within his general conception of critique in order to rearticulate and retheorize a new understanding of a social-democratic polity.

Foucault's methodological insights contribute to a critical policy analysis and are thus compatible with the contributions of writers like, Codd (1988; 1990a; 1990b; 1994), Dale (1986a; 1986b; 1989; 1999; 2000), Henry (1993), Scheurich (1994), Marshall (1995), Marshall (1997), Peters and Marshall (1990), Prunty (1984; 1985) Taylor (1997) or Gale (2001), as well as those who identify their tradition as 'policy sociology' such as Payne et al. (1981), McPherson and Raab (1988), Ball (1990b; 1993; 1994), Bowe et al. (1992) or McGuire and Ball (1994).

In his article 'Policy archaeology: a new policy studies methodology', James Scheurich (1994: 297) maintains that Foucault's work:

> completely reconceptualizes policy studies, and ... significantly expands its critical problematic ... Rather than acquiescing to the range of policy solutions debated by policy makers and policy analysts, it interrogates the social construction of that range. Rather than accepting policy studies as a 'neutral' social science, it questions the broader social functions of policy studies. And, finally, rather than concluding that social and education problems, policy solutions and policy studies are created by the conscious interplay of the free agents of history, policy archaeology proposes that the grid of social regularities constitutes what is seen as a problem, what is socially legitimized as a policy solution, and what policy studies itself is.

Although not claiming to have literally or correctly interpreted Foucault, and disavowing any wish to be captured by his theory, Scheurich acknowledges that Foucault is the inspiration for his excavations in policy archaeology. He divides his new policy studies methodology into four arenas of focus (Scheurich, 1994: 300).

The first ('Arena I') is labelled 'the education/social problem arena'. This concerns the study of the social construction of specific education and social problems. Scheurich indicates that (1994: 300):

> Instead of accepting a social problem as an empirical given ... policy archaeology ... questions or brackets this givenness ... Policy archaeology, refusing the acceptance of social problems as natural occurrences, examines closely and sceptically the emergence of the particular problem. By what process did a particular problem emerge, or, better, how did a particular problem come to be seen as a problem? What makes the emergence of a particular problem possible? Why do some problems come identified as social problems while other 'problems' do not achieve that

level of identification? By what process does a social problem gain the 'gaze' of the state, of the society and, thus, emerge from a kind of social invisibility into visibility? As Foucault (1972) said, 'how is it that one particular [discursive]] statement [that is, social problem in this case] appeared rather than another?' ...

The aim here is to investigate the 'historical a priori' of policy agendas and social problems, and to investigate 'the rules of formation [of social problems and policy choices, in this case] in order to define the conditions of their realization' (Scheurich, 1994: 301).

The second domain ('Arena II') Scheurich (1994: 300) labels as 'the social regularities arena: the identification of the network of social regularities across education and social problems'. In this arena, policy archaeology suggests that there exist 'networks of regularities' or 'grids', or a 'grammar' that is/are constitutive of a particular policy problem or issue, and which determines what will be counted as a problem or issue. In Scheurich's (1994: 301) view, however:

> This second arena of policy archaeology is a complex one. It is based on the assumption that social problems do not achieve their visibility or recognition or status as social problems in an idiosyncratic or random or 'natural' fashion, but that visibility is not primarily a function of the interactive intentions and actions of consciously involved social agents or groups. Nor is the range of policies that get considered to 'solve' a social problem primarily the function of the same intentions and actions. Instead, policy archaeology suggests that there is a grid of social regularities that constitutes what becomes socially visible as a social problem and what becomes socially visible as a range of credible policy solutions. Policy archaeology as a methodology proposes that it can identify this grid or network of social regularities.

Four additional points are made about these regularities. First, the regularities identified are not intentional, meaning that no particular group consciously created them, and no individual or group has conscious control over them. Secondly, such social regularities do not mechanically determine a particular policy solution, but according to Scheurich (1994: 302), citing Foucault (1972: 208) 'they constitute rather the set of conditions in accordance with which a practice is exercised [with which a social problem emerges]'. So although such regularities constitute social policy solutions and problems, it is not in a linear, mechanical deterministic sense, but in terms of a process that is 'incredibly complex with unaccountable macro- and micro-interactions occurring on an hourly basis' (Scheurich, 1994: 302). A third feature of Arena II is that such social regularities are historical, which is to say 'they change and disappear, and new ones emerge'. And a fourth feature involves a rejection of the structuralist metaphor of 'depth' or 'deep structure', and the post-structuralist assertion that 'all is surface' in the sense that all that occurs in life does so at the level of micro-practices.

The third domain of policy archaeology ('Arena III'), is termed 'the policy solution arena: the study of the social construction of the range of acceptable policy solutions' (Scheurich, 1994: 300). Scheurich maintains that 'just as the range of policy choices is shaped by the grid of social regularities, the range of acceptable policy solutions is similarly constituted'. Similarly, also, 'this shaping is not an intentional or conscious activity' (ibid.: 302). While for Scheurich, this arena functions as equivalent to arena II, as it simply parallels that arena, in our view it is not strictly necessary as a separate arena.

The fourth arena of policy archaeology asserts its epistemological function as an arm of the sociology of knowledge, by seeking also to examine policy studies as a series of historically constituted discourses that have emerged within a determinate historical order. Here Scheurich focuses on conventional and postpositivist policy studies seeking to trace their emergence as constituted by a specific set of social regularities. Within this four-pronged approach, Scheurich points out that such distinctions are purely conceptual, and that work on a particular problem-policy axis repeatedly passes through all four arenas. In the main body of his paper, he seeks to apply policy archaeology to an education problem, the school failure of urban children, and to a policy solution, the linkage of school, health and social services. In doing this, he identifies five 'regularities' – gender, class, race, governmentality, and professionalization – all of which interact in a pattern of 'grid-like intersections', and which together constitute the 'dominant liberal social order'. (Ibid.: 307)

While Scheurich's applications of Foucault to policy methodology are inventive and insightful, in our view it is unnecessary to reify a series of relatively useful insights into a typology of 'arenas', as though each is distinct and has an independent role to play at a methodological level. We would also dispute that it is worthwhile to analytically separate 'Arenas II' and 'III', and while it is important to emphasize the constitutive dimension of discursive regularities like class, gender, race and the like, it is important to preserve the insight that such 'constituted' frames are themselves historically woven material configurations, and express the particular patterns of determinate historical situations. Although we may not have enough evidence of Scheurich's ontological position, he has a tendency at times to overemphasize the autonomy of the constructionist dimension. In our view, ambiguities in the concept of 'social construction' make it advisable to avoid its use (opting for a phrase like 'historically constituted' instead).

Although Scheurich's insights are useful, what makes 'policy archaeology' less than satisfactory from a Foucauldian standpoint is the neglect of attention to Foucault's historical method of 'genealogy', which after 1968 came to play a role equally important to, and inseparable from, the methodological emphasis on archaeology.

A further approach to critical policy analysis which utilizes Foucault is contained in a recently published article by Trevor Gale (2001). Although, like

Scheurich, Gale claims to being 'influenced' by Foucault, but not always 'fully attentive to Foucault's renditions of archaeology and genealogy' (Gale, 2001: 384) he outlines 'three alternative and overlapping historical lenses with which to "read" and "write" policy research: specifically, policy historiography, policy archaeology, and policy genealogy' (ibid.: 384). *Gale*

Policy historiography relates to the 'substantive issues of policy at particular hegemonic moments' and seeks 'to trace the processes of educational change and to expose the possible relationships between the socio-educational present and the socio-educational past' (Kincheloe, 1991: 234, cited in Gale, 2001: 385). Gale lists five factors; the first three characterize 'policy historiography' and the last two 'critical policy historiography'. They are: (1) what were the public issues and private troubles within a particular policy domain during some previous period and how were they addressed? (2) what are they now?; (3) what is the nature of change from first to second?; (4) what are the complexities in these coherent accounts of policy?; and (5) what do these reveal about who is advantaged and who is disadvantaged by these arrangements? *Policy questions*

Not only do we dispute the piecemeal addititive way in which Gale seeks to differentiate 'policy historiography' from 'critical policy historiography', we would also maintain that this distinction trivializes the conception of what it means to be 'critical'. Before making further criticisms of Gale's approach, let us introduce his two other policy categories.

Gale defines 'policy archaeology' by drawing on the work of Scheurich, without simply reproducing his account. In Gale's (2001: 387) view policy archaeology 'tries to establish the rules of [policy] formation'. Citing Foucault (1972: 207), Gale distinguishes his own position from Scheurich's as follows:

> I suspect that I take [policy archaeology] to mean a little less than Scheurich – that is, I restrict policy archaeology to the analysis of constitutive rules and position 'the conditions of their realization' (Foucault, 1972: 207) as the interest of policy genealogy – and perhaps I mean a little more than Scheurich, including the licensing of policy makers and their relations as part of the process of policy formation. In this account critical policy archaeology asks: (1) why are some items on the policy agenda and not others? (2) why are some policy actors involved in the production of policy (and not others)? And (3) what are the conditions that regulate the patterns of interaction of those involved?

Finally, Gale identifies 'policy genealogy' as a third lens to analyse policy. Here he focuses on 'social actors engagement with policy' (Gale, 2001: 385), on the 'particulars of temporary policy settlements' (ibid.: 389) and on the 'modalities of power' (ibid.: 389). Thus, for Gale (2001: 389–90) 'genealogy'constitutes:

> an appropriate foil to policy archaeology's interest in policy settlement parameters. Indeed, it is genealogy that enables insight into policy 'realizations' that are defined by (archaeological) rules of their formation … . This should not be taken to mean the discovery of simple continuities between past and present, and parameters and

particulars, for 'genealogy seeks out discontinuities where others found continuous development … . Policy genealogy, then, is not convinced by analyses of policy production explained by 'bounded rationality' … or 'incrementalism' achieved through 'partisan mutual adjustment' … . Certainly, it asks (1) how policies change over time, but it also seeks to determine (2) how the rationality and consensus of policy production might be problematized and (3) how temporary alliances are formed and reformed around conflicting interests in the policy production process. Intentionally, 'what emerges out of this something one might call a genealogy, or rather a multiplicity of genealogical researches, a painstaking rediscovery of struggles together with the rude memory of their conflicts' …

The difficulty with Gale's typology of research methods, from a Foucauldian point of view, lies in his distinction between 'historiography' and 'genealogy' (which we would claim does not exist in Foucault's work, and should not exist in any research strategy). Quite simply, for Foucault, genealogy incorporates what Gale lists as being part of 'historiography'. Following Nietzsche, genealogy is at once 'historical' and consists of a tracing backwards from the present through the contested forces and struggles that constitute the lines of descent, and tracing forwards from the beginnings in terms of lines of emergence. Genealogy is an historical method and in Foucault's view, there is no other historical method. It is this method that for us lays the foundation for an approach to the analysis of education policy that not only recognizes the historical formation of policy but also its constitution as discourse. We develop this approach further in the next chapter.

4

Policy as Text and Policy as Discourse:
A Framework for Analysis

Having considered the broad parameters of a Foucauldian approach, in this chapter we focus more specifically on the discursive dimensions of policy, particularly in relation to policy texts. We argue for a materialist theory of language as the basis for an approach to critical discourse analysis.

While we acknowledge the valuable contributions of Scheurich, Gale and others to the growing body of Foucauldian policy analysis, we base our approach on a more comprehensive reading of Foucault that takes account of the emergent nature of his whole intellectual project, thus avoiding the limitations of locking into one period or facet of his work. By adopting Foucault, in this manner, our approach also overcomes objections from writers like Troyna (1994b: 71–2) that 'policy sociology' is inappropriate as a designation because it is 'no different from other social and political analyses of policy'. Utilizing Foucault in this way we see policy sociology as a form of critical policy analysis with no particular affinity or attachment to the discipline of sociology. Because Foucauldianism is not located within any existing discipline, it is more genuinely able to be *multi*disciplinary, thus also overcoming Troyna's objection to its ability to be multidisciplinary on the grounds of it being located within 'Sociology'. At the same time, we would claim to avoid what Henry sees as the problem of theoretical eclecticism, as advocated by Ball (1990b; 1993; 1994) as part of the 'toolbox' approach to policy, in that we claim that underpinning Foucault's approach is a coherent philosophical position (Olssen, 1999). In our view, our Foucauldian perspective enables us to incorporate a form of 'critical policy analysis' within a more grounded and theoretically worked-out 'critical social science approach' (see Ozga, 2000). The accent is not, however, on the disciplinary status or credentials of the enterprise as formulated, but on its distinctive critical edge. It is not a totalizing conception of critique, in the tradition of the Frankfurt School, or a reconstructive conception, in the tradition of Habermas, but rather a form of critique which aims at partial and local interrogations of the real, which confines itself to exposing the contemporary limits of the necessary, but nevertheless struggles against oppressive social structures. It is a form of critique

59 - 71

that, as Rehg and Bohman (2001) state in the title of their book, is associated with 'pluralism and the pragmatic turn' and 'the transformation of critical theory'. Above all, it is a form of critique that rejects linguistic idealism and emphasizes the material nature of language in the constitution and exercise of power.

Linguistic idealism in the interpretation of policy texts

A Foucauldian approach to critical policy analysis is based upon a theory of language that rejects the idealist assumptions underpinning traditional conceptions of the policy process. In the technocratic view, policy documents are interpreted as the expression of political purpose, that is as statements of the courses of action that policy-makers and administrators intend to follow. Within this view, the analysis of a policy document becomes a quest for the authorial intentions presumed to lie behind the text. The technocratic model assigns discrete functions to the policy researcher (who is a disinterested provider of information), the policy-maker (who produces the policy) and the policy recipient (who interprets or implements the policy). The document itself is regarded as a vehicle of communication between these agents within the process. Thus, policy statements or documents relate educational intentions, in the form of values and goals, to factual information resulting from research. These statements must then be interpreted by those who would either discuss or implement the policy. This can be represented diagrammatically as in Figure 4.1.

Because policy documents are construed as *expressions* of particular information, ideas and intentions, the task of analysis becomes one of establishing the *correct* interpretation of the text. When there is controversy surrounding the meaning of a document, it is assumed that some readers have misunderstood what was meant. One of the tasks of the policy analyst within this approach therefore, is to clear up such confusions and establish an authoritative interpretation. However, from a materialist standpoint we argue that such a task is founded upon mistaken idealist assumptions about both the nature of intentions and the nature of language itself. It is subsequently argued that these assumptions are widely held because they belong within a liberal humanist ideology which is largely successful in masking fundamental contradictions behind the rhetoric of many state policies.

The intentional fallacy

To assume that policy documents express intentions is to subscribe to a version of what in literary criticism has come to be known as the *intentional fallacy* (Wimsatt and Beardsley, 1954). In essence, this particular version of the fallacy holds that the meaning of a literary text corresponds to what the author

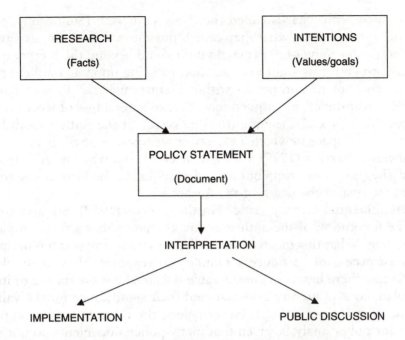

Figure 4.1 *Technical-empiricist model of the policy document*

intended, that is, the text is taken as being *evidence* of what the author intended to express. As Lyas (1973) points out, the fallacy can be shown to derive from an idealist confusion about the relevant sense of 'intention'. First, it is a mistake to think of intentions as private mental events (arguments which show this to be a mistake can be found in Wittgenstein's *Philosophical Investigations*, [1953]). Second, intentions are not the same as 'statements of intention' (people can be mistaken about their own intentions). Third, we must distinguish between an intention in the sense of a prior plan or design and an action that is done *intentionally*. In short, it is the adverbial sense of intention, rather than the nominal sense, that is relevant to the interpretation of texts. The crucial point, however, is that nothing can be said about an author's intentions apart from various features of the text itself and the context in which it is interpreted. As Fay (1975: 73–4) points out:

> Intentional explanations ... make sense of a person's actions by fitting them into a purposeful pattern which reveals how the act was warranted, given the actor, his social and physical situation and his beliefs and wants. An intention is no more 'behind' the action than the meaning of the word is 'behind' the letters of which it is composed, and it is no more an 'invisible mental cause' of an act than is a melody the invisible cause of the pattern of notes that we hear at a concert.

The place of intentional explanations in literary interpretation was first challenged by a group of literary critics in the 1940s and 1950s who have come to be associated with what is called the 'New Criticism' (Simonson, 1971). These critics insisted upon what they called 'the autonomy of the text' which implied that the meaning of a text could not extend beyond the literary object itself. Some structuralists went even further, insisting upon a complete negation of the concept of authorship within literary analysis. Roland Barthes (1977: 146) for instance, has argued that: 'A text is not a line of words releasing a single "theological" meaning (the "message" of the Author-God) but a multi-dimensional space in which a variety or writings, none of them original, blend and clash.' Barthes (1977: 148) goes even further when he adds that: 'A text's unity lies not in its origin but in its destination ... the birth of the reader must be at the cost of the death of the Author.'

Another influential literary critic, Northrop Frye (1957) has also totally rejected the invocation of the author as any guarantee that a text can have a single meaning. What this means, essentially, is that for any text a plurality of readers must necessarily produce a plurality of readings. Now, it should be recognized that there has been considerable debate about the nature of intentional explanations in literary criticism, and their significance for the validity of interpretation (Hirsch, 1967). Nevertheless, there are important implications here for policy analysis, given that many policy documents do not even have single identifiable authors and are inevitably addressed to a plurality of readers.

Linguistic idealism

Attempts to analyse policy documents by explicating the ideas within them and clarifying their intended meanings, presuppose a theory of language which may be called idealist because of the posited relationships between words, thoughts and the real world. These relationships were illustrated diagrammatically by Ogden and Richards (1923: 11) in what has come to be called 'the semiotic triangle' (see Figure 4.2).

Ogden and Richards argued that language bears an indirect relationship to the real world, one which is imputed because it is meditated by thought. The relationship between language and thought is direct and causal. Moreover, they (Ogden and Richards, 1923: 10–11) argued that:

> When we speak, the symbolism we employ is caused partly by the reference we are making and partly by social and psychological factors – the purpose for which we are making the reference, the proposed effect of our symbols on other persons and our own attitude. When we hear what is said, the symbols both cause us to perform an act of reference and to assume an attitude which will, according to circumstances, be more or less similar to the act and the attitude of the speaker.

Given these relationships, conceptual truth becomes a matter of the correctness of language in expressing what is thought and the adequacy of the lan-

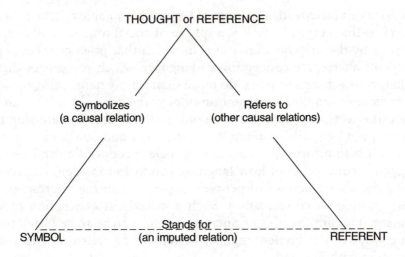

THOUGHT or REFERENCE

Symbolizes
(a causal relation)

Refers to
(other causal relations)

Stands for
(an imputed relation)

SYMBOL

REFERENT

Figure 4.2 *The semiotic triangle*

guage in producing a concurrency of thought in a suitable interpreter. Thus, within this theory of language, symbolic truth (coherence) is distinguished from referential truth (correspondence). Ogden and Richards (1923: 102) define symbolic (or conceptual) truth as follows:

> A true symbol = one which correctly records an adequate reference. It is usually a set of words in the form of a proposition or sentence. It correctly records an adequate reference when it will cause similar reference to occur in a suitable interpreter. It is false when it records an inadequate reference.

This means that a proposition can be empirically false and yet also be a correct expression of what the speaker thought. Conceptual clarity is not dependent on empirical truth and Ogden and Richards (1923: 102) make the point that: 'It is often of great importance to distinguish between false and incorrect propositions. An incorrect symbol is one which in a given universe of discourse causes in a suitable interpreter a reference different from that symbolized in the speaker.' This is the conception of language implicit in the work of policy analysts who seek to clarify the meaning of policy documents. The main point of their work is to make language transparent through correct use in order to produce commensurability of meaning amongst different readers of the text. Essentially, this kind of policy analysis takes language to be a transparent vehicle for the expression of experience. As Belsey (1980: 7) points out, it is a view of language in which: 'Our concepts and our knowledge are held to be the product of experience (*empiricism*), and this experience is preceded and interpreted by the mind, reason or thought, the property of a transcendent human nature whose essence is the attribute of each individual (*idealism*).'

What this empiricist-idealist view of language is unable to take into account, however, is that language itself is a sphere of social practice and is necessarily structured by the material conditions in which that practice takes place. This requires an alternative conception of language which recognizes that words, whether in speech-acts or texts, do more than simply name things or ideas that already exist. It requires a conception of how the use of language can produce real social effects, and how it can be political, not only by referring to political events, but by itself becoming the instrument and object of power. In particular, if it is to inform the analysis of policies produced by and for the state, it requires a conception of how language produces ideological effects by suppressing the contradictions of people's experience in the interests of preserving the existing social formation. Such a materialist conception of language has emerged within theories of discourse which can be traced back to the pioneering work of the French linguist, Ferdinand de Saussure, and reach their culmination with Foucault.

The socio-linguistics of Saussure

Saussure's work has had a major influence on the structuralist tradition which adheres to the view that language precedes experience at some levels, making the world intelligible by differentiating between concepts. While this is not the place for a detailed account of structuralist theories of language, it shall suffice to say that this tradition has totally rejected the idea that language symbolizes the reality of an individual's experience and *expresses* that reality in a discourse which enables other individuals to recognize it as true.

Saussure challenged the notion that words express pre-existent ideas and the assumption that language can be reduced to a naming process. He argued that language is not simply a static set of signs through which individual agents transmit messages to each other about an externally constituted world of 'things'. Rather, language is a set of social practices which makes it possible for people to construct a meaningful world of individuals and things. In his pioneering work, Saussure distinguished between *langue* (the normative rules or conventions of language) and *parole* (the actual utterances made by speakers in concrete situations).

In opposition to idealist theories of language, Saussure argued that the linguistic sign unites, not a thing and a name, but a concept and a sound image. This is not a causal relationship, but rather, as Saussure (1974: 66–7) pointed out:

> The two elements are intimately united, and each recalls the other. Whether we try to find the meaning of the Latin word 'arbor' or the word that Latin uses to designate the concept 'tree', it is clear that only the associations sanctioned by that language appear to us to conform to reality, and we disregard whatever other might be imagined.

Saussure argued that language is the product of social forces. It is *both* an arbitrary system of signs *and* a domain of socially constituted practices. Like any other social institution it will change over time but always within social and temporal limits. Such limits, or structures, both enable and at the same time check the amount of choice that is available to a community of language users.

Language is checked not only by the weight of the collectivity but also by time. These two are inseparable. At every moment solidarity with the past checks freedom of choice. We say *man* and *dog* because our predecessors said *man* and *dog*. This does not prevent the existence in the total phenomenon of a bond between the two antithetical forces – arbitrary convention by virtue of which choice is free and time which causes choice to be fixed. Because the sign is arbitrary, it follows no law other than that of tradition, and because it is based on tradition, it is arbitrary (Saussure, 1974: 74).

Theories of discourse

Saussure's work was to prepare the way for a materialist theory of language in which the term *discourse* has come to be used to embody both the formal system of signs *and* the social practices which govern their use. In this sense, *discourse* refers not only to the meaning of language but also to the real effects of language-use, to the materiality of language. A discourse is a domain of language-use and therefore a domain of lived experience. It can be ideological in the Althusserian sense because it can become an unconscious, taken-for-granted 'system of representations' (Althusser, 1969: 231–6). This form of ideology is *inscribed* in discourse rather than symbolized by it, in other words, is it not synonymous with a set of doctrines or a system of beliefs which individuals may choose to accept or reject. As Catherine Belsey (1980: 5) points out:

> A discourse involves certain shared assumptions which appear in the formulations that characterize it. The discourse of common sense is quite distinct, for instance, from the discourse of modern physics, and some of the formulations of the one may be expected to conflict with the formulations of the other. Ideology is *inscribed in* discourse in the sense that it is literally written or spoken *in it*; it is not a separate element which exists independently in some free-floating realm of 'ideas' and is subsequently embodied in words, but a way of thinking, speaking, experiencing.

Because people participate in a range of discourses (political, scientific, religious) there are manifold ways in which they can signify and represent the conditions of their lived experience. But this does not separate discourse from subjective experience. Rather, discourse itself is constitutive of subjective experience and is also a material force within the construction of subjectivity (Macdonell, 1986).

The point has been made earlier that theories of discourse are centrally concerned with the relationship between language and ideology. In this sense, ideology refers to the relations between systems of representation and power, as it is unevenly expressed in the social system. It refers not simply to 'false consciousness' as Marx held, but to meanings and representations that are partial, that is, are true, but which conceal other meanings or representations which are equally real. It includes all the ways in which meaning (signification) serves to sustain relations of domination (Thompson, 1984). While it is not necessary to think in terms of 'the ideology of the society' as 'the dominant ideology', but more accurate to speak of complexes of discourses and practices, it is still possible to accept that the languages, codes and discourses of the wider culture are ideologically weighted in favour of certain groups and interests.

To explain this further, it is necessary to invoke the notion of discursive power. Only within a materialist view of language is it possible to show how discourse can mediate the exercise of power, for it must go beyond the meaning of what is said to the act of saying it. As Bourdieu (1977b: 648) has stated: 'Language is not only an instrument of communication or even of knowledge, but also an instrument of power. One seeks not only to be understood but also to be believed, obeyed, respected, distinguished.'

To understand how language can be an instrument of power it is necessary to extend the concept of power itself. At one level, power can be readily understood as coercive force or restraint. What is much more difficult to comprehend is the idea of power being exercised through consent, through what Gramsci called 'ideological hegemony'. To recognize power in terms of sovereignty or exploitation is less problematic than to recognize the forms of power which penetrate consciousness itself. These latter forms of power are normatively exercised within structures of distorted communication and false constructions of social reality. As institutionalized forms of domination they constitute pervasive expressions of power without normally being recognized as such by those who are affected. These are the micro-technologies of power that have been studied with such acute concentration in the work of Foucault.

Foucault and the discourses of education

While rejecting the orthodox Marxist distinction between knowledge and ideology, Foucault has advanced the view that all knowledge is a product of power relations. Within this view, he has developed a non-economic analysis of power and power relations. Rather than being a possession or commodity, power is exercised through dispositions, techniques, examinations and discourses. Foucault (1994a: 31) argues that:

> In a society such as ours, but basically in any society, there are manifold relations of power which permeate, characterize and constitute the social body, and these relations of power cannot themselves be established, consolidated nor implemented

66

without the production, accumulation, circulation and functioning of a discourse. There can be no possible exercise of power without a certain economy of discourses of truth which operates through and on the basis of this association.

The power that is exercised through discourse is a form of power which permeates the deepest recesses of civil society and provides the material conditions in which individuals are produced both as subjects and as objects. It is this form of power which is exercised through the discourses of the law, of medicine, psychology and education. These discourses, however, are more than texts. They constitute material social practices, and as such they both mediate and constitute relations of power.

In most modern societies, the education system is controlled by the state, but it works to maintain relations of power throughout the society as a whole. For this reason, the official discourse of the state relating to educational policies (for example, core curriculum, transition education, systems of assessment or school management) are obvious instances in which discourse becomes the instrument and object of power. But discourses operate at a number of levels within educational institutions. Teachers, for example, have their own craft discourse relating to pedagogical practice. This discourse will impose limits upon what is possible in areas of classroom organization control and discipline, or the assessment of learning. More importantly, however, the whole schooling process is an apparatus for the distribution, appropriation and stratification of discourses. Foucault (1972: 46) writes about schooling in the following way:

> But we know very well that, in its distribution, in what it permits and what it prevents, it follows the lines laid down by social differences, conflicts and struggles. Every educational system is a political means of maintaining or modifying the appropriation of discourses, with the knowledge and power they bring with them.

In addition to these discourses embodied in school curricula, there are many theoretical discourses *about* educational phenomena which have been instrumental in the exercise of power and have had far-reaching effects upon the institution of schooling. The discourse of psychometrics, for instance, is an obvious case in point (Gould, 1981; Rose, 1979). During a period of 50 years, the language of mental measurement has penetrated the craft discourse of teachers and shaped their practices. A critical analysis of such discourse seeks to expose the connections between psychometric theories and administrative practices, revealing the effects of using this form of technical language to legitimate the exercise of power.

A framework for discourse analysis

In proposing a framework for the discursive analysis of educational policy texts, it is important to emphasize that we do not see discourse simply as 'text', nor just as 'langue and parole', but rather as the ensemble of phenomena in and through which social production of meaning takes place. Whereas Laclau and Mouffe (1985), in rearticulating a discourse-theoretical approach to Marxism, lapse into a form of idealism (Geras, 1987), for us discourse is a complex dimension itself anchored in extra-discursive conditions of a given political and economic order. While we do not deny the efficacy of this extra-discursive dimension, what we do maintain is that this extra-discursiveness is effective in and through the discursive, and against a background of multiple discourses which affect the conditions of its production and reception. In this sense, an analysis of social practice always necessitates at the same time an analysis of the discursive, as social practice is always mediated discursively. Likewise, in that policy discourses are 'texts', they are, at the same time, always more than texts; that is, they are always components of discourse and of social practices as well. Our position accords with that of Chouliaraki and Fairclough (1999: 6) who state that: 'It is important to recognize the social import of discourse without reducing social life to discourse – a reductionism characteristic of postmodern views of the social world that is a constant risk and temptation for discourse analysts.' While the material order of reality thus maintains, in our view, an autonomous ontological existence, in epistemological terms it is always mediated discursively. In this way, we would claim that our approach in this book avoids the pitfalls of both logocentrism and of textual reductionism; that is, we neither deny nor exclude the ontological status of extra-discursive realities, nor do we 'slip back' to simple textual readings.

Our adoption of Foucault's materialist conception of discourse has been influenced by the work of Norman Fairclough (Chouliaraki and Fairclough, 1999; Fairclough, 1989; 1992; 1995). While recognizing Foucault's immense contribution to theories of discourse analysis, Fairclough points to the neglect of textual analysis in his work, and suggests that this is a serious limitation. Foucault's work is concerned mainly with the social and political analysis of discursive practices as systems of rules, rather than with textual analysis of real instances of what is said or written, that is with the analysis of actual texts.

Fairclough attempts to integrate the social and political theories of discourse developed by Foucault and others with more linguistically orientated approaches to discourse analysis. Not only does this require a much sharper focus upon the particular uses of language within actual texts, but it also requires that attention is given to the relationship between those texts and the wider domains of discursive and social practices to which they belong. Thus, as Fairclough (1989: 26) argues:

> In seeing language as discourse and as social practice, one is committing oneself not just to analysing texts, nor just to analysing processes of production and interpretation, but to analysing the relationship between texts, processes, and their social conditions, both the immediate conditions of the situational context and the more remote conditions of institutional and social structures.

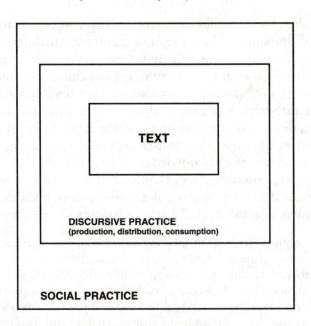

Figure 4.3 *Three-dimensional conception of discourse*
Source: Fairclough, 1992: 73

To this end, Fairclough (1992: 73) posits a three-dimensional conception of discourse, in which he seeks to integrate, or triangulate, three forms of analysis: analysis of *text*, analysis of *discursive practices* and analysis of *social practices* (see Figure 4.3).

Within Fairclough's framework, texts are specific instances of written or spoken language. They are one of the dimensions of a discursive event. Another dimension entails being an instance of social (political, ideological, and so on) practice. The analysis of discourse as text focuses upon linguistic processes, whereas the analysis of discourse 'as a piece of discursive practice' goes beyond the linguistic features of the text, and 'focuses upon processes of text production, distribution and consumption. All of these processes are social and require reference to the particular economic, political and institutional settings within which discourse is generated' (ibid.: 71).

Aims of discourse analysis

This framework is useful in analysing the discourses of educational policy. It provides, in particular, a basis for the recognition of different *discourse types* and explains why language is politically important in struggles over education policy. As Fairclough (1989: 90) points out, 'the struggle over language can manifest itself as a struggle between ideologically diverse *discourse types*'.

What is at stake in such struggles is which discourse type is to be dominant within the social domain of education, and therefore which practices are to be ideologically maintained or strengthened. One of the main purposes of critical discourse analysis is what Luke (1995: 19) has called 'the denaturalization of text' by showing how the representations within texts mask the sources of their status and authority. A critical analysis of text 'can model the possibility of alternative readings and interpretations, particularly those silenced by dominant social institutions that tend to privilege a particular analysis, reading position, or practice as official knowledge' (ibid.: 19).

In addition to exposing such representational functions of texts, a second purpose of critical discourse analysis is to reveal how texts define, position and control readers and listeners. Thus, according to Luke (ibid.: 19–20):

> Texts do not simply portray or misportray social relations of domination/subordination. With their relational functions, texts actually constitute inter-subjective relations of power, setting out a social relationship between text and reader, speaker and listener. Critical discourse analysis can make transparent asymmetries in those relations, revealing the textual techniques by which texts attempt to position, locate, define, and, in some instances, enable and regulate readers and addressees.

A third purpose of critical discourse analysis identified by Luke is to examine the effects that texts and discourses have 'in the world' through 'the construction of social subjectivities' or 'the construal and distribution of material and symbolic resources' (Luke, 1995: 20). In education policy, for example, the neoliberal discourses of accountability, efficiency and effectiveness (derived from neoclassical economics) have had real effects in shaping the ways in which educational resources are measured and allocated. In similar vein, Stephen Ball (1993: 15) comments that: 'We need to recognize and analyse the existence of "dominant" discourses – like neo-liberalism and management theory – within social policy.'

Such advice is particularly apposite within the current context of education policy in western welfare-capitalist states. Neoliberalism and management theory are both ideological currents that have infused and effected both educational and social policy in the 1980s and 1990s in Britain, Australia and New Zealand. While people are generally aware as to what the political consequences have been, the changes that have occurred go to a much deeper level than can be accounted for at the level of the school, or in relation to educational issues, on such topics as 'the restructuring of the administration' or 'the implementation of new policies for curriculum or assessment'. Such changes have taken place within the very discourses that shape our understanding of education as a field of social practice. Although they are manifested in particular linguistic forms and discursive practices, these changes also must be located in relation to the broader political and economic structures that provide their context. Not only do these structures shape discursive practices, but they also are shaped by discourse. Thus, it is a two-way relationship. In making this point, Chouliaraki and Fairclough (1999: 4) comment that: 'It is an important characteristic of the economic, social and cultural changes of late modernity that they exist as *discourses* as well as processes that are taking place outside discourse, and that the processes that are taking place outside discourse are substantively shaped by these discourses.'

Policy discourse and social structure

How we explain certain types of policy at certain junctures in history is deeply and intricately intertwined with the structuring realities of class, race and gender. Policy documents express and reflect these structuring realities, as well as perform certain functions of legitimation by establishing political consensus. Hence, just as certain policy documents of the 1970s in the western world expressed a liberal-humanist reaction to the technocratic discourses of the 1950s and 1960s, so in the 1980s we have seen the collapse of the Keynesian welfare state and the ascendancy of a form of neo-liberal monetarism manifesting itself in and through many of the policies of the state. The utility of a concept of 'discourse' is that it enables us to conceptualize and comprehend the relations between the individual policy text and the wider relations of the social structure and political system. If policy is a discourse of the state, it is by its very nature political and must be understood as part and parcel of the political structure of society and as a form of political action. By the same token, in that the state represents *unevenly* the influence of different groups and sectors of the society, state policy is inevitably ideological by its very nature and in its effects. Thus ideologies, not simply pertaining to politics or economics but related to curriculum, assessment, the nature of human abilities or human psychology or work, are expressed in and through its official educational policy documents. For example, in the post-war years, education systems came to be viewed increasingly in terms of the technological imperatives of the planned economy with the state representing itself, and being represented, as a sophisticated support system for school improvement. More recently, the ascendency of market-liberal discourses in the 1980s and 1990s has seen a major shift, as the policy discourses of education are replaced by the discourses of business and economics, providing a radically different model for the evaluation of educational performance and success. These redefinitions, shifts and transformations are, of course, reflected not only in the language of educational policy and politics, but also in the substantive and procedural policy preferences favoured by the state.

Policy here is taken to be any course of action (or inaction) relating to the selection of goals, the definition of values or the allocation of resources. Fundamentally, policy is about the exercise of political power and the language that is used to legitimate that process. Policy analysis is a form of enquiry which provides either the informational base upon which policy is constructed, or the critical examination of existing policies. The former has been called analysis *for* policy, whereas the latter has been called analysis *of* policy (Gordon et al., 1977: 27).

Analysis *for* policy can take two different forms: (1) *policy advocacy* which has the purpose of making specific policy recommendations; and (2) *information for policy* in which the researcher's task is to provide policy-makers with information and data to assist them in the revision or formulation of actual policies.

Analysis *of* policy can also take two different forms: (1) *analysis of policy determination and effects* which examines 'the inputs and transformational processes operating upon the construction of public policy' (Gordon et al., 1977: 28) and also the effects of such policies on various groups; and (2) *analysis of policy content*, which examines the values, assumptions and ideologies underpinning the policy process.

The central focus of this chapter is on the analysis or 'reading' of policy content, more specifically the analysis of the context of policy documents. We argue for a specific approach to the reading of educational policy. While we hold that policy documents can and should be regarded as texts which are capable of being decoded in different ways depending upon the social and historical contexts in which they are read, it is a specifically materialist Foucauldian analysis of the policy text that we argue for. By this we mean that in order to understand properly the significance of policy texts in the process of educational reform it is necessary to explain the material conditions within which such texts are produced and to examine critically the institutional practices which they are used to defend.

In that we can understand *the nature* of policy discourse through its language, at the level of *social practice* (politics, ideology) policy is more than just about the production of knowledge; it is a form of political action. In this respect, political action over education policy is operative and effective at both the level of the state, where policy is formulated, interpreted and, in the final analysis, either set aside, implemented or imposed, and at the micro-level of the school and local community where policies are discussed, debated, resisted, re-created or adopted. There are at each level corresponding empirical and theoretical implications which correspond to our conceptualization of policy as text, discourse and social practice. It is these implications that will be the focus of subsequent chapters.

5

Classical Liberalism

One of the key elements in the reading of educational policy is the philosophical context of both the policy discourse and the methods of reading it. The origins and the rise in the prominence of liberalism are of significance to the study of the nature of western capitalist societies. Liberal philosophies and ideologies have provided the basis upon which the political economy and the interlinked social and economic systems of these societies have been built. They have provided the guiding principles and ideological rationales for their organization and their social, political and economic reproduction. This is particularly so in relation to education. Liberalism has influenced the basic conception of what constitutes its meaning, and shaped the policies through which it has been provided. Historically, liberal assumptions within education have been understood as given, and unproblematic, and have remained, until the past decade, out of the sphere of rigorous critical enquiry.

This chapter and the next two chapters set out a general account of the discourses of liberalism as they emerged from the seventeenth to the twenty-first centuries. It is useful to trace the origins of the 'old' or classical liberalism which had its beginnings in the seventeenth century and was ascendant through until the last decades of the nineteenth century when it became challenged and then replaced by the 'new' liberal or 'social democratic' orthodoxy, which eventually provided the support for Keynesian-based welfarism. In this chapter we discuss the central tenets of classical liberalism which comprises both political and economic variants, and orbits a pivotal axis concerning particular conceptions of the individual, and the relations between the state and economy. After outlining the major features of classical liberalism, in the following chapters we will turn our attention to social democratic liberalism and Keynesian welfarism of the nineteenth century, and the revival of new forms of liberal discourse, which we will refer to as neoliberalism, based on the revival of neoclassical economics, which became a dominant form of state reason in the last three decades of the twentieth century.

73

Liberalism's common elements

In discussing the discourses of liberalism as forms of governmental rationality, our discussion will lead us to consider views on human nature as well as conceptions of political theory. This will lead into a discussion on the main characteristics of liberalism as a discursive art of government and as the basis of state-provided education in western nation-states. In Foucault's view, liberalism constitutes a specific form of governmental reason. As such, it is not simply to be represented as a 'philosophy', or 'explanation', but a complex system of political rationality comprising prescriptions as to how to rule, and how not to rule, of when to rule and when not to rule. The discourses of liberalism also set limits to the role of the state, provide for a democratized conception of sovereignty, and also for a series of more specific technologies of administration and rule, which they are able to do through the arm of law. Liberal prescriptions embody specific conceptions of the nature of human beings, the nature of the social world in which people act, the nature of democratic government, the role of the state, and the degree to which a central collectivity should intrude upon the lives of individual citizens. Its philosophical origins should not be understood as a static set of ahistorical rationales, however. Liberalism is a socially and historically variable set of discourses, the interpretation of which has been altered and reshaped, but certainly not disfigured out of recognition, to reflect its modernity.

Liberalism assumes that it is possible to govern differently from the science of Police (*Polizeiwissenschaft*) which constituted a model for administration in the German state during feudal times. The science of police had the aim of completely controlling social life and seeking to adjust the behaviour of individuals to the interests of the state. Through a complex series of political, economic, and epistemological changes, classical liberalism represented a new emergent form of governmentality that constituted a political-epistemological revolution. There were four central factors: first, the church's decline in unity and influence; secondly, the requirement of a new conception of political obligation in a more individualized and fragmented world; thirdly, the requirement of a technology of rule that was consistent with the new science of *political economy*, and more generally with the rise of capitalism, and fourthly, the emergence of the category of the population made possible by the science of statistics.

In Foucault's view, classical liberalism provided such a technology for rule. A genealogy of the modern state suggests two modalities of power, which can be distinguished in terms of the directions in relation to which power is exercised. Foucault was interested how, in the early modern period, 'individualist' principles replaced 'republican' ones, in a transition from: 'on the one hand, the state's exercise of power through the totalizing legal-political forms of its unity, and on the other, its exercise of an individualizing form of power through a "pastoral" government concerned with the concrete lives and conduct of individuals' (Foucault, 1988c: 67).

Totalizing forms of power are aimed at increasing the power of the state at the level of populations and characterize the *Polizeiwissenschaft* of the *ancien régime*. This reason of state is based on a unity of knowing and governing, as embodied in the conception of the state as a *leviathan*, where all that was happening in a society could be known and maintained by the state. *Individualizing* forms of power are applied to subjects of state power to which it recognizes a special responsibility. This conception questions the unity of knowing and governing, and maintains that the rationality of the state can not be calculative and regulative of the totality, but instead seeks to situate political reason within a matrix of unstable individual–state relations.

As a new reason of state, liberalism represented a new individualizing form of power that aimed to create subjects of certain kinds. Related to this, as Colin Gordon (1991: 15) has defined it, liberalism constitutes a critique of state reason, that is, a limit against the state's ability to act as it wants. Thus, it was in this sense, in the early modern period, that the discourses of liberalism arose constituting a critique of excessive government in the name of the rights and liberties of the individual. In addition, however, Foucault claimed that much of the liberal art of government involves a restructuring of institutions of the state in a manner consistent with the 'laws' of *political economy*. It was in this sense that the liberal formula of rule was inextricably tied to the security of the state, linked to a particular view of the nature of individuals, to a perspective of the relation between individuals and society, and to the needs of the economy. Its most important common elements will be introduced below.

The individual and human nature

Liberalism is individualist in relation to its embrace of a conception of human nature which asserts the moral and ontological primacy of the person as opposed to claims of social collectivity. In this, it rejected Aristolelian, medieval and religious accounts of subjectivity, which represented the self as a moral category with ends or purposes which each natural being was supposed to fulfil, for a conception of the self privileging the individual ontologically over the social historical environment. It justifies its ahistorical conception of the individual with reference to various theories of nature or, in the nineteenth and twentieth centuries, in relation to theories of genetics and biology. The liberal view of human nature sees human beings as driven from within by natural energy of innate desires and appetites. Each individual is driven in the pursuit of the gratification of these desires and appetites by the faculty of *reason*.

Within liberalism, such desires and appetites also account for the *agency* of the individual. From Hobbes through Locke, to Hume and Bentham, these writers constituted the given and unalterable mainstay of the liberal conception of human nature. In *Leviathan* Hobbes (1968) views human beings as part of nature, and subject to natural laws. Hobbes applied Galileo's law of inertia – 'When a Body is once in motion, it moveth (unless something else hinder it) eternally' (ibid.: 88). In Hobbes's view life is motion, and rest is death. To be in motion is to have desire, and desire knows no end but is constantly seeking new objects. As Hobbes (1968: 161) stated it, 'So that in the first place, I put for a generall inclination of all mankind, a perpetuall and restlesse desire of Power after power, that ceaseth onely in Death'. Reason *serves* desire, and in this sense, as for Hume, is the 'slave of the passions'. 'Desires', 'appetites' and 'aversions' thus constitute enduring characteristics of human nature, underpinning the liberal conception of the person as a self-interested egoist, as a person 'presumed to do all things in order to his own benefit' (Hobbes, 1968: 213).

Hobbes's pessimistic conception of human nature was never unreservedly accepted and was to be replaced by more optimistic, or qualified views by Locke, Bentham and the *political economists* within the classical tradition of political philosophy. Although Locke saw men as more social than did Hobbes, seeing men as having the potential to live together co-operatively in the state of nature,[1] primarily egotistical passions and appetites still undergirded his view of human nature, making man a creature dominated by both calculating self-interest as well as certain natural inclinations to peace and harmonious coexistence. The self-interested and ontologically separate and ahistorical conception of the self still dominated, as did the emphasis on the possessive aspect of the individual. This notion, which C.B. Macpherson (1962) sees as explicit in Locke,[2] traces the idea of self-possession to that of 'self-ownership', and to the broader theory of property, which became central to political and economic discourses of liberalism from the seventeenth century. Central to the liberal world-view was a conception of the person as owner of their own capacities, entailing a view that each individual is morally responsible to themselves, and not primarily to other people, groups or to the community as a whole.

In the eighteenth century, the conception of society as a natural order became intrinsic to the very idea of liberal reason of state. This involved the emergence of a space of society which operated according to its own laws, and which protected the autonomy and freedom of individuals. This social order, and especially the order of market exchanges, was self-regulating according to natural laws, and was sensitive to dysfunction with excessive state intervention. Liberalism, in Foucault's view, was thus not simply an absence of government but a 'reinscription' of the techniques by which a new form of civil society was to be managed. Such a conception presupposed a state–civil society relation, and more specifically a state–market relation. Liberty, in such a model, must be seen as a type of rule, or a way to rule. As Barry et al. (1996: 8) put it:

Liberalism is more like an *ethos* of government. Liberalism is understood not so much as a substantive doctrine or practice of government in itself, but as a restless and dissatisfied ethos of recurrent critique of State reason and politics. Hence, the advent of liberalism coincides with the discovery that political government could be its own undoing, that by governing over-much, rulers thwarted the very ends of government. Hence liberalism is not about governing less but about the continual injunction that politicians and rulers should govern cautiously, delicately, economically, modestly ...

As well as constituting a recurrent critique of the different forms of state rationality, liberalism defines the conditions and operational rules of liberal economy. It asserts a belief in progress through reason and science, as well as a commitment to the possibility of unilinear qualitative advancement or movement towards greater enlightenment. Consistent with the faith in neoclassical economics, in the international sphere liberals favoured 'free trade', involving the abolition of tariffs or subsidies, or any form of state-imposed protection or support, as well as the maintenance of floating exchange rates and 'open' economies. The belief in free trade involves the claim that international commerce, without government constraint or regulation, is the key to growth and stability.[3]

Liberalism also embodies principles about the workings of modern democracies. Although conceptions about the role of government vary, liberals generally have been committed to democratic political processes based upon constitutional government, the rule of law, popular sovereignty, government on the basis of consent, limitations on the size and role of government, as well as a variety of checks and balances designed to safeguard the freedom of the individual. Hence, during the seventeenth century groups such as the Levellers advocated limited manhood suffrage,[4] Locke theorized the legitimacy of government based on the consent of the governed,[5] Locke and Voltaire wrote on 'political tolerance'[6] and the need for political institutions which respect due legal process, and Montesquieu introduced the conception of the 'separation of powers'.[7]

Liberalism also can be characterized in terms of its internal discursive promises. Foremost here is a commitment to personal liberty, involving freedom of thought, of expression, of conscience, of emotion, of association, as well as rights to private property. Although a great deal of concern went into protecting the individual from the state, or from other interfering groups, the historical grounds for liberalism's claims have shifted. Up until the nineteenth century, the explanatory basis for liberal arguments was in terms of 'natural rights', established increasingly from the seventeenth century as the basis of reason (nature) rather than derived from divine purpose. During the nineteenth century, the rise of utilitarianism eclipsed natural rights, and consequentialist explanations which evaluated the effects of actions and policies in relation to their consequences in reference to a conception of the social good in terms of 'the greatest happiness for the greatest number' became prominent. The most well-known, certainly the most well cited, statement of the principle of liberty is that of John Stuart Mill (1859: 13):

> the sole end for which mankind are warranted, individually or collectively, in interfering with the liberty of action of any of their number is, self-protection. That the only purpose for which power can be rightfully exercised over any member of a civilized community, against his will, is to prevent harm to others. His own good, either physical or moral, is not a sufficient warrant.

In a Foucauldian sense, it is important not to analyse liberalism as an apology or cloaking ideology for ruling interests, nor on its own terms, but to examine, rather, the historical conditions within which the practices of freedom and guarantees of government have been possible. In this sense, as Graham Burchell (1996: 21) expresses Foucault's concern, early, or 'classical', liberalism emerged 'in relation to a problem of how a necessary market freedom can be reconciled with the unlimited exercise of political sovereignty', in direct opposition to, and as a criticism of, the early modern discourse of rule centring on the police state.

In as much as liberalism is a discourse of liberty, or a discourse of the economy, it was also, for Foucault, a discursive problematic concerned with security of the population as an end of government. As Mitchell Dean (1999a: 116) has pointed out, security was identified by Jeremy Bentham in *Theory of Legislation* (1950) as a subordinate end to the general utilitarian principle of 'the greatest happiness of the greatest number'. Liberalism provides techniques of government to enable it to regulate in the interests of security, that is, to control troublesome groups and to lead citizens to exercise responsible lives. From this perspective liberty becomes, as it was for Bentham, a 'branch of security' and an alternative conception to rule by police. But like police, it is concerned with the regulation of populations. This is what Foucault means when he says: 'liberty is a condition of security' (cited in Gordon, 1991: 19–20). That is, to govern effectively, whilst respecting the economy, it is also necessary to respect the interests of the individual. Liberal rationality, like *Polizei*, concerns the regulation and limits of the conduct of the governed but, while altering the techniques, retains the same concern with order and control.

In that it is concerned with security, liberalism constitutes a discourse of power that seeks to construct notions of law, seeks to maintain and strengthen the partitions of civil society revolving around 'private' and 'public' arenas, seeks to define the role and functioning of the market, and of market–state relations, as well as provide metaphysical constructs of our notions of progress, democracy and personal liberty. Liberalism has sought to establish laws and norms, as well as 'legal norms' of good conduct and good government. The law is central to a state's ability to intervene and to legitimate enforcement, as well as to conceptions of 'impartiality', 'corruption', 'democratisation' and 'participation' of the citizenry, as well as to the limitation of their involvement.

The historical development of liberal discourse

As a philosophical tradition, liberalism is not a homogeneous or unitary doctrine with definitively rigid objectives. Jaggar (1983: 28) argues that there are a number of forms, not all of which are internally consistent, but are unified by an underlying conception of human nature. Gray (1986: x–xi) reiterates that liberalism has no single unchanging essence but that there are certain distinctive features which characterize it as a discourse (for example, state–individual relations, the role of the market). He argues that (ibid.: x):

> The liberal tradition has sought validation or justification in very different philosophies. Liberal moral and political claims have been grounded in theories of the natural rights of man as often as they have been defended by appeal to a utilitarian theory of conduct, and they have sought support from both science and religion.

Notwithstanding different possible approaches to the study of liberalism, our own approach in this chapter is to distinguish the following forms: (1) political liberalism – emerging from the seventeenth century, (2) economic liberalism – emerging in the eighteenth century, and (3) social democratic liberalism – emerging in the nineteenth century.

Classical political liberalism had its roots in the religious political and economic reactions to the old order in the late sixteenth and early seventeenth centuries. In the late sixteenth century there was a breaking down of traditional forms of medieval communalism and a growing tide of individualism, both economic and religious. There was also a growing opposition to the authority of both church and state with increasing civil and political unrest in the early seventeenth century, culminating in the Puritan Revolution of the 1640s and the Glorious Revolution of 1688. These revolutions expressed the struggles of Englishmen against the overthrow of liberties bequeathed by their forebears. They appealed to ancient rights such as those expressed in the Magna Carta of 1215, and expressed them in new documents – the Petition of Rights of 1628 and the Bill of Rights of 1688. Thus we can trace the origins of liberalism as a political movement directly to the period of the English Revolution (1640–88). It was the result of a long accumulation of frustrations which the gentry and other men of property experienced as a result of the attempts by the Stuart monarchy to impose absolute rule in terms of both religious and state power. As a movement, however, it cannot be seen to represent a coherent class expression, but rather it constituted a diverse assortment of forces united in their opposition to Stuart absolutist rule.[8]

The major philosophical justification of classical political liberalism was provided by John Locke (1632–1704), although many of the central principles and beliefs of liberalism can be found expressed in the writings of Thomas Hobbes (1588–1679), in the political speeches of the Levellers, a group of seventeenth-century radical democrats, or in the views of political theorists such as Harrington. Locke was the most eloquent and coherent exponent of the liberal creed, and most consistently expressed the central liberal principles of civil rights, rights to property, a limited conception of state power and a broadly negative conception of freedom.

Together with the Kantian emphasis on the person as a moral being, Locke's conception constitutes the basis of the classical conception of liberalism which has enjoyed the 'upper hand' over the Rousseauian emphasis on the values of public life and on the notion that society might have a moral status over and above individuals. Lockean political theory was based on a theory of natural and non-legal rights, and Locke's central contribution was to frame a political conception of liberty to ensure liberty and market freedom within a conception of sovereignty based on contract. Although writers like Hobbes had earlier articulated a conception of human nature and distrust of state power which contributed many insights to liberal political philosophy, it was Locke who can be credited with enunciating liberalism as a coherent doctrine. This was articulated in his *Second Treatise of Government*, first published in 1690, and was concerned to safeguard the freedoms of the individual against the arbitrary power of the sovereign's rule. These freedoms included: government by the consent of the governed, the natural rights of citizens to private property which must be protected against infraction by any arbitrary acts of government, periodic popular elections to regulate the power of the ruling body through regular appraisal of the requirement to rule responsibly, and citizens' right of revolt against a despotic ruler who violates their natural rights (see Locke, 1960, II).

The classical liberals' distrust of state power was a central concern in Locke's writings, and Locke's answer to this concern was that laws rather than men should rule. In the state of nature, men were biased toward their own interests. What was needed, as the basis of sovereignty, was that there be an '*established*, settled, known *Law*' (Locke, 1960, II, para. 124). In the state of nature, men frequently would get carried away with passion and take the law into their own hands. What was needed, says Locke, was a '*known and indifferent judge*, with authority to determine all differences according to the established law' (Locke, 1960, II, para. 125). Also, the power of government to make laws should be limited to the public good of the society with respect to the enforcement of voluntary contracts and to the defence of the realm (Locke, 1960, II, para. 135). The government should only act according to the rule of law (Locke, 1960, II, para. 137), for should the government make arbitrary rules, the people would be worse off than they would be in the state of nature. The rule of law is important as the basis for state action and to regulate conflict between individuals with divergent interests.

As with Hobbes, there is a key sense in which Locke's individualist conception of the person is Cartesian. Although both Hobbes and Locke were hostile to Descarte's rationalism, their accounts of the individual are Cartesian in the sense that the individual's will is the source of his actions and that each individual has privileged access to its contents. In the Cartesian model, rights become subjectivist, and certainty resides in the inner recesses of intentionality. As developed by Hobbes and then Locke, man is represented as an autonomous chooser whose desire is shaped by self-interest. Thus, the individual is logically and temporally pre-social, and his wants and desires (undifferentiated by needs) 'belong unto himself' (Locke, 1979: 186–7).

Property rights in Hobbes and Locke

For Locke, property rights, like rights in general, are also natural, and the link between rights, property and democracy are a central concern. In the interaction of economic and political liberalism, McCloskey claims that liberalism derived from a commitment to the constitutional state rather than from any particular attachment to the free market. In its early development in the sixteenth and early seventeenth centuries, liberalism represented 'personal experience' and sought to champion liberty of the individual against the arbitrary power of the state. The privileged position it gave to capital and to the market as the desirable allocator of resources came later. In McCloskey's (1951: 2–3) words, it represented:

> a degeneration of the liberal democratic tradition ... . When he used the term 'liberty', the early democrat meant, first of all, freedom of experience – moral liberty – rather than freedom of business enterprise. His chief interest, in short, was in the right of the individual to realize his moral personality, and not the right to buy and sell and prosper economically.

Over the course of the seventeenth and eighteenth centuries, liberalism came increasingly to develop policies and attitudes which harmonized with the class interests of the expanding capitalist classes. England during this period was a transitional society between feudalism and capitalism, characterized by the emergence of modern notions of contract, a growing wage labour force and emerging national markets in a variety of commodities (Shapiro, 1986: 77).

Before Locke wrote, the writings of Hobbes can also be seen to legitimate this emerging capitalist order, both in terms of his conception of nature, and of rights. As Shapiro (ibid.: 77) has observed, for Hobbes individual property rights furnish the conceptual model for rights in general. These are essentially private and natural rights, which are the extension of the right to self-preservation. Such rights are not derived from natural law, but from Hobbes's psychology, in which man is driven by an insatiable power to accumulate.

Hobbes's conception of the state is also related closely to the defence of property rights. In Shapiro's (ibid.: 31, 77) words, 'Hobbes grounds property rights in positive law and thereby links the state to the preservation of private property ... . It creates and enforces a system of bilateral reciprocal contracts (and is thus by definition in opposition to large areas of medieval private law that still prevailed in Hobbes's England)'. As the state regulates private activity, including property rights, Hobbes effectively presents a negative libertarian view of society, where, as he puts it, 'The Greatest Liberty of Subjects dependeth on the Silence of the Law' (Hobbes, 1968: 271).

In his explication of seventeenth-century English political thought, C.B. Macpherson claims that Hobbes conforms to his thesis regarding 'possessive individualism'.[9] Although Hobbes's writing is, in certain senses, consistent with Macpherson's thesis, a number of important qualifications to Macpherson's argument are in order.[10] First, Hobbes was not solely, or even exclusively, concerned with the justification of specifically capitalist forms of appropriation.[11] Second, while his general model was consistent with the emerging market society, not all of Hobbes's philosophy was 'reducible to', or explainable in terms of, such an order.[12] In our view, Macpherson has over-extended his claims with regard to Hobbes. While his claims regarding the pre-social conception of human nature in respect to interest maximization are, we will claim, important, his attempt to link such a conception to a model of a possessive market order, and apply it to Hobbes and Locke, leads to insuperable difficulties. This is an issue which we shall take up below.

A more explicit and formal legitimation of capital and private property was to come later with Locke. According to McCloskey (1951: 5–6), the exalted position given to capital and private property in liberal discourse derived principally from two sources:

> The first from radical Christian democrats ... the second from the sober-sided English middle class bent on shaping a doctrine congenial to men of property ... . Locke fastened onto democracy the idea that the right of private property is fundamental; he set in train a materialization of democratic ideals that led ultimately to their perversion.

While the Levellers supported equal but limited rights to property in the seventeenth century as part of their campaign to extend the franchise, it was Locke who introduced into the liberal democratic cause an inalienable right to property. For Locke, rights to property were justified as natural rights, and one of the central functions of the state was to protect such property. In that Locke represents property rights, as well as rights in general, as natural and private, it is in the sense that they are justified by *natural* as opposed to *civil* law. This is to say, as Waldron (1988: 138) puts it, 'they are acquired as a result of actions and transactions that men undertake on their own initiative and not by virtue of the operation of any civil framework of positive rules vesting those rights in them'. In this sense, they are 'prior' to society. Every man, says Locke (1960, II, para. 190): 'is born with a double Right: *First, A Right of Freedom to his Person*, which no other Man has a Power over, but the free Disposal of it lies in himself. *Secondly, A Right*, before any other man, *to inherit*, with his Brethren, his Father's Goods'. As in the *Second Treatise*, in both the *Essays on the Law of Nature* (1958) and *A Letter Concerning Toleration* (1979) Locke justifies rights as 'pre-social' according to the laws of nature as decreed by Divine Will.[13] Rights are natural. What is natural is rational and also God's Will.[14]

In his justification of property rights, Locke's argument had several strands: (1) *initial common ownership*: that the earth and its fruits were originally given to mankind in common (Locke, 1960, II, para. 25); (2) *the right to appropriation*: whatever a man removes out of the natural state, he has mixed with his labour. By mixing one's labour with it, one makes it one's own property (Locke, 1960, II, para. 26); (3) *the spoilage limitation*: no person should take more than would not spoil (Locke, 1960, II, para. 31); (4) *the sufficiency limitation*: a person may appropriate as much as leaves 'enough, and as good' for others (Locke, 1960, II, para. 27).

These conditions applied both to possessions and to land. As Locke (1960, II, para. 32) put it: '*As much Land* as a Man Tills, Plants, Improves, Cultivates, and can use the Product of, so much is his *Property*. He by his Labour does, as it were, inclose it from the Common.' And as Ian Shapiro (1986: 90) points out, the right that each person has 'is in no way restricted to physical objects. We are proprietors of our own actions and have exclusive rights over the freedom and objects created as a result of those actions'. This is to say that each person has exclusive ownership of their own selves and capacities.

Although Macpherson's thesis is not problem-free when applied to Locke, it is in reference to the applicability and centrality of the possessive market model to Locke's writing that he makes his major contribution.[15] In his thesis, Macpherson documents the means by which Locke makes the transition from justifying a limited right to property to justifying an unlimited one (Macpherson, 1962: 197–221). This important development in Locke's thought hinges on the introduction of *money* as a form of exchange. To cite Locke (1960, II, para. 36):

> But be this as it will, which I lay no stress on; This I dare boldly affirm, That the same Rule of Propriety, (*viz.*) that every Man should have as much as he could make use of, would hold still in the World, without straitening any body; since there is Land enough in the World to suffice double the Inhabitants had not the *Invention of Money*, and the tacit Agreement of Men to put a value on it, introduced (by Consent) larger Possessions, and a Right to them …

According to Macpherson (1962: 211), it is through the introduction of money that the limitations on appropriation of property and wealth no longer hold and, as a consequence, 'Locke has justified a specifically capitalist appropriation of land and money'. Further: 'The spoilage limitation imposed by natural law has been rendered ineffective in respect of the accumulation of land and capital. … The sufficiency limitation … is less obvious to overcome by reference to the introduction of money by consent, yet there is no doubt that Locke took it to be overcome' (ibid.: 208, 211).[16]

Drawing on Locke's writings concerning entitlements to charity (see Locke, 1960, I, para. 42) Waldron (1988: 139) claims that special rights to private property are 'constrained by a deeper and, in the last resort, more powerful *general* right which each man has to the material necessities for his survival'.[17] This, we think, is an important qualification to Macpherson's view. All we would add is that such a concern that no man starve to death, as can initially be seen present in the 'sufficiency limitation', or in Locke's strictures concerning charity, hardly qualifies as a major egalitarian or social concern.[18] It is clear, however, from the voluminous writings from what we will refer to, following Macpherson (1970), as 'the Locke industry', that the real meaning of Locke's texts permit a wealth of interpretations and emphases. As our interest is not primarily in squabbles between scholars over the finer detail of what Locke really meant, but rather in the historical purposes that Locke has served in the functions of political legitimation, we will not be further delayed. Traditionally, in the conflict between liberty and equality, Lockean claims have served to justify the priority of the former at the expense of the latter. This was certainly the function Locke has served in the legitimation of American historical settlements. While strictures concerning charity can possibly be seen as having played a role, it has been only to the extent that it affords a minimal 'safety net', to cushion what in all other respects has been a justification to permit an *unlimited* accumulation of wealth. That the Lockean justification of property results in, and allows for, a massively unequal distribution of economic wealth introduces one of the central problems for classical liberalism.

Clearly the attempt to justify property in terms of natural right constituted liberalism as a doctrine, as Bowles and Gintis (1986: 174) point out: 'of dual etiology ... . On the one hand it constituted a reaction against the despotism of the modern state. On the other, it constituted an affirmation of the power of capital directly engendered by the state'.[19] What is common to this 'dual' doctrine relates specifically to the conception of individual rights as well as to a consistent view of human nature. Both Hobbes and Locke give a supreme value to individual rights and individual choice. Both begin from radically egalitarian premises. Both produce an argument which appears to treat all people equally every step of the way. And both arrive at a conception of the social world that is governed by market relations, in Shapiro's (1986: 73) words:

> as though such a view flows directly from men's natural equality ... . This is a device that would appear again and again in the subsequent history of liberalism: it turns on ascribing to presocial individuals a negative libertarian conception of freedom and gearing social institutions to the preservation of that freedom. This is how a system that can generate enormous inequalities gets its egalitarian gloss and can be justified via an appeal to egalitarian principles.

Liberalism as a dominant discourse

The period 1815–1920 saw the effective political realization of liberal policies throughout the western world as a consequence of the resolution of disputes and conflicts over the preceding centuries. Fuelled by popular pressures from below, as well as the advocacy of leading liberal thinkers – including Locke, Hume, Smith and Bentham in England and Scotland; Voltaire, Rousseau and Montesquieu in France; as well as Jefferson, Franklin and Paine in America – whose writing collectively served to heighten the contradictions between the theories of liberalism and existing political, social and economic practices, some of the privileges of the middle classes – those relating to personal and political rights – were gradually extended to the entire population. Once started, the tide was hard to stop. The advocacy of social democratic liberalism, while advanced in the nineteenth century by writers such as J.S. Mill, T.H. Green and L.T. Hobhouse, was to affect national policy-making only slowly, not becoming ascendant until after the third decade of the twentieth century.

The historical rise in the primacy of liberalism in political theory was integral to the emergence of capitalism and laissez-faire as an economic ideology and framework for state policy. Liberalism enabled the expression of the needs of the developing capitalist class so that the values of autonomy and self-fulfilment became intertwined with the right to privately appropriate property. Ironically, the development of capitalism enhanced the realization that the nature of the social relations it generated, meant that individuals (identifiable as collectivities) were affected by the actions of others in a whole diversity of ways. Contemporary theorists came to acknowledge that those in possession of wealth and power did exert an influence over the lives of those who did not have such resources. Thus the emergence of liberal political theory provided the philosophical rationale for the gradual enlargement of the public realm, through the extension of the responsibilities of the state, as it sought to protect the rights of its individual subjects (Rawls, 1971: 34). Concurrently, the economic, political and social re-emphasis on the primacy of the individual would provide the justification (through neoliberalism) in the twentieth century, for the withdrawal of those rights and the continued retraction of the state from civil society and people's lives.

Classical economic liberalism

The way the early economic liberals set limits to the state's capacity to rule was to represent society, and the arena of market exchanges, as natural arenas which could regulate themselves according to laws which were intrinsic to them. For these purposes, the doctrine of natural rights implied limitations to the sovereign's power, preventing government from acting without restrictions.

The ever-present possibility of a conflict between the self-interested drives and the necessary restraints of the contract led to representing *nature* not as something solely internal to individuals, but as a more encompassing ground-plan, and as providing a safeguard against the potentially destructive powers of egoism. In this context, the conception of a natural synergy between self-interested persons, and the peace, harmony and progress of society became widely circulated in the eighteenth century. Far from engendering endless conflict, as Hobbes maintained, this view asserted the belief, that individuals who pursued their own ends without regard to the interests or needs of others, produced as the unplanned and unintended result, the harmony and prosperity of the whole society

We shall refer to the theory in terms of which individual-society relations were structured as *invisible hand theory*. Essentially, this maintains the view that the uncoordinated self-interest of individuals correlates with the interests and harmony or good of the whole society. Although it was by no means a novel theory in the seventeenth and eighteenth centuries, it is most often associated with Adam Smith's writings on the harmonization of the private determinations of individual interests with the interests or good of society as a whole. Smith makes it clear that the workings of the hand have benefit only because it is invisible. There would be little good resulting from any attempt to direct the hand for the public good. Such a conception thus counters the heavily programmed conception as put forward by Hobbes in *Leviathan*, as well as the more indirect conceptions of state control as advanced by Quesnay in his economic 'Table', a device intended to allow the sovereign to monitor and direct the general order and health of the economy within the state. The notion of an 'invisible hand' thus constituted a counter to more 'interventionist' physiocratic conceptions of the role of the state. In addition to Smith, Montesquieu had developed a similar argument,[20] as did Vico in his *New Science*,[21] and Mandeville in *The Fable of the Bees*.[22] The idea had in fact been around for a long time. Some 40 years before Smith wrote, Pope, in his *Essay on Man*, had written:

> God and Nature link'd the gen'ral frame,
> And bade Self-love and Social be the same. (Epistle III, 317–18)

In relation to both the political and the economic spheres of society, the implication of invisible hand theory was a commitment to the maxim of laissez-faire. On the one hand this involved a commitment to free market economics, which entailed the view that given the nature of the individual as an interest-optimizer, a de-regulated competitive market system provides the best opportunities for people to utilize their skills and optimize their life goals. The market is represented as both a more efficient mechanism and a morally superior mechanism. Because it is a self-regulating order it regulates itself better than the government or any other outside force. In this, classical liberals show a distinct distrust of governmental power and seek to limit state power within a negative conception, limiting the state's role to the protection of individual rights. A commitment to laissez-faire also entailed a commitment to free trade.

There is an important sense in which interest establishes choice as central to human behaviour for economic liberals, and in this it stands in opposition to contract conceptions of right as found in the tradition of 'political liberalism'. Interests thus serve as the foundations of choice and in doing so make of the individual an isolated autonomous chooser, without the restraints of the contract. Thus *political economy* gives us a subjective theory of the individual which is more individualist than is posited in social contract theories of sovereignty. In this, Hume's and Smith's form of will is different from a juridical or contract conception. In the contract conception, individual interests are subordinated to a system of rights within contracts which transcends, and binds, individuals. Hence, as Foucault points out, the conception of interests as found in Hume and Bentham demolishes the contract theories of Locke and Blackstone. As Colin Gordon (1991: 21) summarizes Foucault's point:

> The postulate in social contract theory of an inaugural act of delegation and renunciation whereby the individual is constituted as a political and juridical subject is one which interest can never countenance as definitive: nothing can, in principle, exclude the possibility that interest will dictate the repudiation of such a contract. The subject of interest perpetually outflanks the scope of the act of self-imposed limitation which constitutes the subject of law.

This shift in rationalization, away from contract, towards 'invisible hand' conceptions was an eighteenth-century phenomenon. In the eighteenth century, science replaced philosophy as the principal means of uncovering the natural laws of society. It was able to do this because it no longer sought to criticize the political order from the viewpoint of abstract human nature, or in terms of divine purpose, but from the standpoint of economic social progress. There was a shift from the philosophical investigation of human nature to the scientific investigation of the laws that governed the economic progress of society. The development of the new sciences of *political economy* and *political arithmetic* facilitated at a political level a concern with the category of population. Different forms of property were considered, not solely according to natural rights, but increasingly also according to the contribution to progress. The change of focus signalled a growing concern with economic questions, and a new governmental concern with the regularities of populations. In this context, political philosophy gave way to political economy as the basis of a theory and science of society.

Classical economic liberalism, developed within the tradition of political economy, is best represented in the writings of Adam Smith, Adam Ferguson, James Steuart, John Millar, David Hume, Thomas Malthus, David Ricardo,

Jeremy Bentham, and James and John Stuart Mill. Many of their economic and social ideas were developed from the writings of the physiocrats whose theories came to dominate French views of society in the mid-eighteenth century. For the physiocrats, society is governed by natural laws. As Quesnay put it, these laws 'are immutable and indisputable and the best laws possible; thus they are the foundational rule for all positive laws' (cited in Meek, 1963: 53–4). Physiocratic doctrines were developed and applied directly to the contribution of large-scale agriculture, to the well-being of society as a whole, and in relation to the manner in which resources flowed between different social classes without the assistance of the state. Their models advocated a general regime of laissez-faire as the political basis of an expanded market. Society was no longer viewed as an expression of human nature but as a self-regulating and spontaneously ordering system; that is, a system regulated by its own laws rather than as a result of human design. If such laws were respected and not interfered with, the harmony of the entire society would prevail.

Many of the physiocrats' central ideas – notions such as the identification of the self-interests of farmers with the society as a whole, the necessity of laissez-faire as the basis of political stability, the necessity of the state to respect the natural laws of the economy if it was not to impede progress, and the view that the state should restrict its proper sphere of action to the protection of the realm and to the defence of individual liberty and property – were to be adapted by Adam Smith as the basis of his own economic and social theory. The theoretical limitation of physiocracy lay in its continued adherence to natural law doctrines and to its exclusive focus on agriculture as the basis of productive wealth. It was Smith who sought to overcome these limitations. It was Smith who recognized the productivity of manufacture by introducing the concept of 'capital' independent of land and labour, and modifying an emphasis on agriculture, fundamental to the physiocrats, to an emphasis on the division between capital and labour generally.

Adam Smith

In *An Inquiry into the Nature and Causes of the Wealth of Nations* (1976b) (hereafter, *The Wealth of Nations*), Smith maintained that the development of the market system was the best mechanism for the allocation of resources in a society. The voluntary exchange characteristic of the market mechanism brought economic gains to each party, and ultimately to the nation as a whole. Market exchanges are based on the price mechanism which is determined on demand and supply. The laws of demand and supply operate as indicators of under- and over-supply, as well as incentives for producers to produce high-quality, competitively priced goods for which there is an established demand. Markets thus provide fast and efficient methods of supplying information on consumer demand, and an effective way of making sure that producers and providers will respond.

As well as the emphasis on the market, Smith's major contribution was to describe how the pursuit of individual self-interest in the market automatically results in the overall collective benefit to society as a whole. The mechanism for this benefit was the 'invisible hand'. As Smith (1976b: 456) expresses it, in considering the choices of individuals, 'he intends only his own gain, as he is in this, as in many other cases, led by an invisible hand to promote an end which was no part of his intention'. In this, collective prosperity and the harmony of the whole society could be obtained through the workings of the market without state activity being necessary. As a consequence, the market will counteract the necessity for a strong state, and the 'interests' of the private citizen will counter the 'passions' of the sovereign (which was Smith's response to the Hobbesian problem of order). Thus, for Smith, the market and the state had their own distinct arenas, the result being a conception of the state which allowed for the freedom of the market. This meant a limited state. In fact, for Smith (1976b: 687–8), the sovereign had only three duties to attend to, although they were, he stressed, duties of great importance: first, there was the duty of 'protecting the society from the violence and invasion of other independent societies'; second, there was the duty of 'protecting, as far as possible, every member of the society from the injustice or oppression of other members of it'; and third, there was the duty of 'erecting and maintaining certain public works and certain public institutions, which it can never be for the interest of any individual, or small number of individuals, to erect and maintain; because the profit could never repay the expense to any individual, or small number of individuals, though it may frequently do much more to repay it to a great society'.

The extent of this third form of state intervention is central to the debate in contemporary economics over 'public goods'. One interpretation of Smith sees him as intending it conservatively. On this line, the theoretical aim of the state was to limit and minimize its role based upon postulates which included (1) universal egoism (the self-interested individual), (2) invisible hand theory which dictated that the interests of the individual were also the interests of society as a whole, and (3) the political maxim of laissez-faire, that government intervention in the economy and society should be confined within the bounds of the three functions as set.

During the later 1970s, Smith's work was reinterpreted by a new generation of scholars who criticized the 'liberal-capitalist' interpretation. The revisionist thesis emphasized the continuity between Smith's earlier and later works. Muller (1993: 2), for instance, maintains:

> Far from being an individualist, Smith believed that it is the influence of society that transforms people into moral beings. He thought that people often misjudge their own self-interest. He never used the term 'laissez-faire', and he believed that governmental expenses were bound to increase as civilisation advanced. He regarded the attempt to explain all human behaviour on the basis of self-interest as analytically misguided and morally pernicious.

That Smith's writing on human nature, the role of the market, and the role of the state was much more nuanced than many earlier writers have previously claimed, is a correction which is now thoroughly documented.[23] Whether it should lead us to accepting all of the claims of the revisionist thesis is another matter. It is true, for instance, in *The Theory of Moral Sentiments*, that he notes the importance of a range of qualities of human nature, which supplement 'self-interest'. Although we can accept the revisionist thesis that Smith recognized a wide range of qualities, such as sympathy, benevolence and the capacity for kindness, nevertheless the acquisitive drives were recognized by him as persistent: 'a desire which though generally calm and dispassionate, comes with us from the womb, and never leaves us till we go into the grave' (Smith, 1976b: 341).[24] In *The Wealth of Nations* (1976b: 341), Smith saw men as actuated by the 'desire of bettering [their] condition' and as motivated by 'an augmentation of fortune [as] the means by which the greater part of men propose and wish to better their condition'.

Self-interest

In Albert Hirschman's (1977: 48) view, the importance of self-interest was not simply that it was persistent, but it also came to constitute 'a dominant motive of human behaviour' in Smith's writing in particular, and in the second half of the eighteenth century in general. As he notes:

> [In *The Wealth of Nations*] there seems to be no place ... for the richer concept of human nature in which men are driven by, and often torn between, diverse passions of which 'avarice' was only one. Smith was of course fully aware of these other passions and had indeed devoted an important treatise to them. But it is precisely in *The Theory of Moral Sentiments* that he paves the way for collapsing these other passions into the drive for the 'augmentation of fortune'. Interestingly enough, he does so in the guise of doing the opposite; for he goes out of his way to stress the non-economic and nonconsumptionist motives that are behind the struggle for economic advance. (Ibid.)

That *political economy* could be established on laws of human behaviour became a dominant belief in the eighteenth century. Hume (1898), as well as Smith, believed in the possibility of a science of human nature, because it would then have a sure foundation in experience. Although humans are made up of diverse passions, what Hume (1898, vol. 1: 176) calls 'the interested affections', or 'avarice', or 'the desire for gain' constitute 'a universal passion which operates at all times, in all places and upon all persons'. Further, as Hume (1978: 492) states in the *Treatise*:

> 'Tis certain that no affection of the human mind has both a sufficient force, and a proper direction to counter-balance the love of gain, and render men fit members of society, by making them abstain from the possessions of others. Benevolence to

strangers is too weak for this purpose; and as to the other passions, they rather inflame this avidity, when we observe that the larger our possessions are, the more ability we have of gratifying all our appetites. There is no passion that is capable of controlling the interested affection, but the very affection itself, by an alteration of its direction.

The notion of 'interests' also underwent changes in the eighteenth century, and both Smith's and Hume's work reflected and expressed such changes. As Hirschman stated (1977: 42), '"Interest" became a new paradigm', and became accentuated as 'the key to the understanding of human behaviour' (ibid.: 43). Thus, drawing on Helvetius, it was argued that 'as the physical world is ruled by the laws of movement so is the moral universe ruled by laws of interest' (cited in Hirschman, ibid.: 43). According to Hirschman an important change took place in the attitude towards the passions from the seventeenth to the eighteenth centuries. Rather than being viewed as wholly vicious or destructive, they were 'rehabilitated as a potentially creative force' (ibid.: 47). Previously, interests had been counterbalanced by the other passions. Now, not only were interests the dominant passion, but they became a positive force. 'Interest', for Sir James Steuart 'will not lie to him or deceive him'; further, 'were a people to become quite disinterested: there would be no possibility of governing them' (cited in Hirschman, ibid.: 50).

This new line of thought was an eighteenth-century reaction against Hobbes and was especially characteristic of the 'sentimental school' of English and Scottish moral philosophers, from Shaftesbury to Hutcheson, including Smith and Hume. In the course of the eighteenth century, says Hirschman, interest in moneymaking and commerce became 'innocent' (ibid.: 56). While Hobbes had represented the emotion of 'insatiability' as a dangerous passion 'this very insatiability now became a virtue' which was seen to imply 'constancy' and 'harmlessness' (ibid.: 56). In this context, 'interest-motivated behaviour and money-making were considered superior to ordinary passion-orientated behaviour' (ibid.: 58).

In stressing the economic benefits of private interest-motivated behaviour, eighteenth-century philosophers superseded a concern that had hitherto been important, which emphasized the political dangers of such behaviour. Whereas seventeenth century writers like Hobbes had shown the political consequences of self-interest, the major impact of a book like Smith's *The Wealth of Nations* was to provide a powerful economic justification for the pursuit of self-interest. Hirschman (ibid.: 40) points out that *The Wealth of Nations* also effected a 'narrowing of the meaning of the term "interests"', substantially simplifying and 'blunting the edge of Mandeville's shocking paradox by substituting for "passion" and "vice" such bland terms as "advantage" and "interest"' (ibid.: 19). Whether Smith intended it or not (and Hirschman thinks he did)[25] the influence of his writing significantly promoted a much narrower concept of 'interest' both within nineteenth-century liberalism and as a construct in economic theory.

A different conception of human nature and of laissez-faire is present in Adam Ferguson[26] and John Millar[27] who see interests as only one factor amongst many. For Ferguson and Millar, society is allegiant or conflictual, varying from time to time and place to place. They do not posit an abstract, universal principle validated by an ahistorical human nature which is imposed on history, but rather a principle of historical contingency. People vary by nature in talent and strength, and interests can be variously 'self-interested', or 'other-regarding', or 'in-between', according to contingent historical circumstances. The task of liberal government becomes that of securing the conditions for rule, allowing for, and containing, the self-interested opportunism of the subjects that constitute the population.

Notwithstanding adaptations and variations of Smith's thesis by Ferguson and Millar, Smith's writing on the theory of the market economy has had a profound influence on the development of liberal economics and, refined and elaborated by economists such as David Ricardo, is incorporated into modern economic theory as the *perfect competition model*. According to this model, the free operation of the market economy results in an optimal allocation of societal resources. Such a model can be criticized for ignoring the existence and operations of monopolistic practices as well as for a whole range of other imperfections. There is controversy as to how efficiently the price mechanism operates to ensure 'market clearing', as large corporations can control the supply of goods and services, artificially distorting prices. The distorting effects of monopolies, as of practices such as advertising, within western capitalist economies makes the assumptions of Smith's 'invisible hand', which is based on the assumptions of small businesses with roughly equally weighted power, deeply problematic. The free market also fails to ensure any degree of equality of outcomes in the distribution of resources, which is to say, markets are inherently and cumulatively inegalitarian. And because goods and services are produced on the criterion of one's ability to pay, rather than need, the wants of the rich may well take precedence over the more urgent needs of the poor.

Within *political economy*, in the early nineteenth century, departures or deviations from the assumptions of laissez-faire were of course numerous, making the linkages between the economy and governmentality much more complex at the level of practices than the eighteenth-century theory might have suggested. In David Ricardo's revisions of English political economy, building in the more pessimistic insights of Malthus on population, the invisible hand plays a less obvious role, and the quest to understand man's incessant struggle for survival, regarding the cultivation of land and the productivity of labour is, as Dean (1999a: 115) puts it, 'ultimately enframed within the protocols of sovereignty'.

The contradictions of liberalism

It has been a common error of many radical analyses to reject liberalism *in toto*. As Bowles and Gintis (1986: 63) maintain in their book *Democracy and Capitalism*, there are many elements of liberalism – the conception of rights and choices, the doctrine of popular sovereignty, the advocacy of constitutional democracy – that have not simply been progressive but have exerted, at times, a distinct radical effect. In countries such as America, over the last century in fact, there has been more radical activity in the name of 'democracy' than there has been in the name of 'socialism'. Arguably, this is also true in countries such as Britain, Australia and New Zealand, in spite of the fact that these countries have supported more solid labourist traditions.

Yet for all its progressiveness, liberalism constitutes, overall, a contradictory set of principles which masks, or simply does not consider, the various sources of domination within western states. While social democratic forms of liberalism help ameliorate these contradictions, they do not overcome them. One major contradiction pertains to the tension between those rights conferred under the banner of democracy which grant universal suffrage and moral and religious equality, and those rights conferred in relation to property which underpin the legitimacy of capitalism and which are premised on the basis of inequality. While the principle of 'liberty' permits access to property on an unequal basis, the principle of democracy ensures popular sovereignty to all. Bowles and Gintis (ibid.: ch. 1) describe this conflict using the concepts of 'person-rights' and 'property-rights' and claim that the tension between these two sets of rights has been felt from the birth of the liberal movement and can be used, as an heuristic device, to conceptualize the dynamics of change within the liberal-capitalist state. Both sets of rights are 'expansionary', and one of the central conflicts of the political system is over whose set of rights should prevail.

In Bowles and Gintis's (ibid.: 63) view, the basic liberal argument is asymmetric, for while liberal-democratic theory supports the application of both liberal and democratic principles to the state, it only permits the application of liberty to the economy. Thus they maintain that liberal democracy supplies no coherent justification for this asymmetric treatment of the state and the capitalist economy. As a consequence, 'liberalism has suffered a congenital moral indeterminacy: the equality of all before the law is also the privilege of the wealthy to exploit the dispossessed'.

The contradiction between *liberty* and the *principle of equality* has been a constantly expressed theme, from the seventeenth to the eighteenth centuries, and it receives its most coherent expression in the formulations of the doctrines on the rights of man, and in Kant's philosophy, at the end of the eighteenth century. Yet in one strand of liberalism there is a consistent conception of human nature as egotistical and self-interested, which would seem to lend itself to a moral imperative to treat others as *means*, as is evident in Hobbes,

Locke, Bentham, Hume and even J.S. Mill. On the other hand, however, stalwarts of the liberal tradition such as Kant exhort 'every man is to be respected as an absolute end in himself', and not 'as a mere means to some external purpose'. This leads to an unresolvable contradiction.

At a political level, the contradictions of liberalism have been managed through various 'accommodations' which have sought to reconcile civic equality with economic inequality. Bowles and Gintis (1986) distinguish four such accommodations. The first was Lockean, which prevailed in the nineteenth century, whereby voting rights were limited to those who owned property. Two further accommodations are discerned with special relevance to the American environment – the Jeffersonian, and the Madisonian which were both concerned to disperse power (and property) more widely amongst the citizenry. A fourth accommodation was Keynesian, based on the practices of welfare economics whereby concessions were extracted from capital as a means of redistributing wealth. Each of these accommodations constituted an attempt to manage the contradictions between property rights and democracy. The neoliberal revival since the 1970s can be seen as the latest accommodation aimed to offset the difficulties of Keynesianism in an attempt to deploy 'the logic of the market' against labour's rising power and reverse labour's encroachments on capital without direct state intervention. Such an accommodation is likely, say Bowles and Gintis, to intensify 'the collision of rights' and highlight the conflictual nature of the liberal economy.

Human nature and the possessive individualism thesis

The possessive quality of privatized individualism is derived from belief in the personal capacity of people for possession of their own being and capabilities. Such a capacity emanates from the human propensity for rationality. This ontological precept came to provide liberalism with a philosophical basis from which to replace inherited privilege as the qualifier for citizenship. Macpherson (1962: 3) claims that this precept emerged in the seventeenth century in the writings of Hobbes, the Levellers, Harrington and Locke, and through the humanitarian writings of the French Enlightenment philosophers.

Individuals were conceptualized neither as 'moral wholes' nor as part of a larger social whole, but as 'moral agents', the private owners of their own 'essence' and accordingly their own social and economic fortune. This relation of ownership thus became paramount to an individual's freedom and the realization of innate potential. It became the core of the understanding of the nature of the individual. According to Belsey (1980: 67), 'the ideology of liberal humanism assumes a world of non-contradictory (and therefore fundamentally unalterable) individuals whose unfettered consciousness is the origin of meaning, knowledge and action'.

The main features of the conception of the individual emerged out of the rise of the male property-owning classes in the seventeenth and eighteenth centuries. The emergence of such a conception cannot be separated from the influence of the growth and development of industrialization and technology as well as the expansion of capitalism and the overall framework of the generalization of market relations of exchange. According to Macpherson, the foundation for this model of society emerged first in the philosophies of Hobbes and Locke. English political thought from the seventeenth to the nineteenth century, he says, was characterized by 'possessive individualism'. Its 'possessive' quality is found in the condition of the individual as the 'proprietor of his own person or capacities, owing nothing to society for them'. Thus, for thinkers 'from Hobbes through Locke, Hume, Burke and Bentham' (Macpherson, 1973: 198) the individual 'pre-figures' society and society will be happy and secure to the extent that individuals are happy and secure. Not only does the individual own his or her own capacities but, more crucially, each is morally and legally responsible for him or herself. The liberal conception of the individual also implied a model of society, however. Freedom from dependence upon others means freedom from relations with others, except those relations entered into voluntarily out of self-interest. Human society is simply a series of market relations between self-interested subjects. Thus, for John Locke, society is a 'joint-stock company' of which individuals are shareholders.

Notwithstanding his contribution to political philosophy, Macpherson's thesis on liberalism cannot be uncritically defended. Although we have already indicated the critical literature arising from his treatment of Hobbes and Locke, our own dissatisfaction stems from a number of concerns relating to his broader theoretical position. As a number of critics have identified,[28] there is within Macpherson's thesis both a form of Marxism and residual attachments to liberalism that we find problematic. Macpherson's Marxism is problematic in that implicit within his project is an assumption that some liberal-developmental conception associated with Mill and Marx could be realized by abolishing the market. There is a general assumption that market models or practices in themselves are problematic, an implicit perfectionism associated with notions of social harmony, an overly thick conception of the good, which assumes too much common agreement, and a tendency to emphasize the substantive over the procedural aspects of democracy.[29] To put this in a different way, Macpherson fails to appreciate the extent to which we live in a pluralistic world of ethical diversity. The implicit models of democracy he advocates are too utopian. His Marxist affinities place too much emphasis on economic class relations, on social harmony, on monist substantive and non-procedural notions of democracy, as well as a tendency to represent the world in terms of binary dualisms of possessive market capitalism versus socialism. His overall theoretical framework lacks applicability to

95

global capitalism, and the emerging issues to do with gender, race, class and the imperatives of ethical pluralism.

In terms of his residual attachments to liberalism, Macpherson's own preferred model of individual development draws its inspiration from J.S. Mill's conception of the individual as an 'exerter and developer of his capacities' (Townshend, 2000: 143–4). Objections to Mill's conception of the individual have been presented elsewhere (Olssen, 2000). In brief, Mill's individual, while he marks an advance over the classical conception, is not entirely freed from that conception. In *On Liberty* (Mill, 1859), the entire argument hinges upon a distinction between 'self-regarding' and 'other regarding' actions, which presupposes, and is much closer to it than at first appears, to the classical conception of the person. While the self may not now, in Mill's view, be 'self-interested', it is still an 'autonomous chooser', and insulated from society through an integral structural distinction separating the public from the private. As Hobhouse objected, the real difficulty is that such a distinction depends upon a prior conception of exclusively private or asocial interests. In Hobhouse's view, there were no such interests, as all were 'other regarding', and hence it could not serve as a criterion for determining the legitimacy of state interference in social and economic life.[30] As Hobhouse puts it, in *Liberalism* (1911: 120), 'there is no side to a man's life which is unimportant to society'. There are no actions which do not affect others, and furthermore, all individual actions are a matter of 'common concern' to others. Not only is individual welfare a matter of common concern, but all economic interaction among individuals has implications for third parties. For Hobhouse, the common good includes the good of every member of the community. By adding Marx to Mill, as Macpherson does, in our view, he creates the worst of all possible worlds.[31]

In order to address Macpherson's more specific arguments concerning classical liberalism and possessive individualism, it is necessary to outline the central axioms of his argument. Macpherson's thesis essentially involves the following claims: (1) that out of the struggles of the seventeenth century a new 'possessive' model of the individual as an indefinite appropriator arose; (2) that this new possessive model involved an almost total break with classical and medieval conceptions of the nature of the person, society and freedom; and (3) that seventeenth- and eighteenth-century writers, including Hobbes, the Levellers, Harrington, Locke, Hume, Burke and Bentham, were all committed to such a model of possessive individualism. As such, Macpherson's model is at once a conception of human nature, a conception of society and a conception of political society.

According to Macpherson, there are several assumptions or axioms that characterize the human individual. These include: (1) 'what makes a man human is freedom from dependence on the wills of others', (2) 'freedom from dependence on others means freedom from any relations with others except those relations which the individual enters voluntarily with a view to his own interest', (3) 'the individual is essentially the proprietor of his own person and capacities, for which he owes nothing to society', (4) 'although the individual cannot alienate the whole of his property in his own person, he may alienate his capacity to labour'; (5) 'since freedom from the wills of others is what makes a man human, each individual's freedom can rightfully be limited only by such obligations and rules as are necessary to secure the same freedom for others', (Macpherson, 1962: 263–4). In *Democratic Theory*, Macpherson (1973: 25–31) further qualifies the possessive individualist model of man as an 'infinitely desirous consumer of utilities' by three further claims: (1) that man is essentially a consumer; (2) that the desire for consumption is infinite; and (3) that infinite desire is both rationally and morally permissible.

As a thesis about market society, possessive individualism entails the further claim that human society consists of a series of market relations. In *The Political Theory of Possessive Individualism*, Macpherson (1962: 53–4) codifies the model of possessive market society as comprising eight postulates. These include: (1) 'there is no authoritative allocation of work'; (2) 'there is no authoritative provision of rewards for work'; (3) 'there is authoritative definition and enforcement of contracts'; (4) 'all individuals seek rationally to maximize their utilities'; (5) 'each individual's capacity to labour is his own property and is alienable'; (6) 'land and resources are owned by individuals and are alienable'; (7) 'some individuals want a higher level of utilities or power than they have'; (8) 'some individuals have more energy, skill or possessions, than others'.

Macpherson (1962: 61) claims such a model 'does correspond in essentials to modern competitive market societies', and that 'each of its postulates is required to produce that correspondence'. It is these claims, as well as the general attempt to devise a model of a market society, which is then applied across various thinkers spanning several centuries, which leads to a claim that he has overextended his thesis. It is such claims, as well as the formalism of the model, and his attempt to apply it universally, that has also led many others to criticize his thesis, as noted already in relation to Hobbes and Locke above. If it had been represented as general and schematic, and intended to trace emphases contained in these thinkers' views, a great deal of the criticisms directed at him might have been more effectively rebutted.

Hume and possessive individualism

David Miller (1980: 261) has defended Hume against Macpherson, claiming that 'Hume occupies only a minor place in the rogues' gallery of ... the political theory of possessive individualism'. On the issue of the applicability of Macpherson's model of market society to Hume's writing, Miller makes a strong and justifiable case. As with the criticisms of his treatment of Hobbes and Locke, if Macpherson is suggesting that we can project his model of possessive market society as an accurate description of the models of society from Hobbes to Bentham, then there is need for substantial correction and qualification. As Miller (1980: 277–8) puts it:

> Macpherson's model ... may serve as a guide to the ideology which became dominant in mid-nineteenth century Britain ... . When projected back into earlier centuries it seriously distorts the social attitudes prevailing in societies which were not predominantly market societies, even though market relationships were present and gradually increasing in significance ... . For that reason Macpherson's back-projection is not uniformly distorting. It reveals part of the truth about such figures as the Levellers and Locke, whose thought primarily reflected the attitudes of the 'middling rank', to use Hume's term – the small farmers, merchants and tradesmen; it fails to reveal the whole truth even here, because it ignores the extent to which this group remained embedded in an organic community and retained attitudes reflecting that fact. But when the template is held up against thinkers whose primary affiliations were with the landed aristocracy, such as Hobbes and Hume, the distortion becomes almost total.

Although Miller is on strong ground in criticizing the applicability of Macpherson's possessive market model, we would claim, *as a matter of emphasis*, that his thesis is by no means a 'total distortion' in relation to Hume and Hobbes, and is particularly relevant, even if not consistently correct, in relation to Locke and the Levellers.

On the issue of the individual, Miller's case is more problematic, however. Miller claims that while Hume certainly recognized the 'force of desire', there is no conclusive proof that he saw consumption as the 'ultimate desire', nor did he approve of it morally, or see it as 'infinite', in that 'the desire for commodities might be directed rather to preserving an existing standard of life than to expanding consumption indefinitely' and 'that commodities themselves might be desired as means to other ends' (Miller, 1980: 263). Miller (1980: 264) further claims that Hume posited a man who was not primarily self-interested, but where the positive passions balanced the selfish ones, and he cites Hume (1978: 487) from the *Treatise* that it is 'rare to meet with one in whom all the kind affections taken together, do not over-balance all the selfish'. To push his case yet further, Miller (1980: 264) claims that for Hume man is essentially social, in the sense that 'Hume clearly believes that the desire for society is intrinsic and omnipresent'.

If, as Miller claims, Hume doesn't fit Macpherson's 'mark I model of man as an infinite consumer' then that would be a noteworthy matter. It is unlikely, too, that all of the liberal writers Macpherson identifies from Hobbes to Bentham will fit his model in precisely the same way, or to the same extent. We can further agree that Hume certainly is not an individualist in precisely the way Hobbes is, or in the way that Locke, Burke, Smith or Bentham are. It may be, too, that Hume does not conform to all the separate additional criteria concerning Macpherson's model of the individual. For instance, he may not be, as Miller claims, an 'infinite' consumer, or, he may pursue consumer goods, as Miller also claims, for 'other ends'. Having said this, we cannot let Miller off from what is in our view a one-sided and misleading account. The evidence he presents on nearly every claim is less than decisive, and the reader is invited to share Miller's doubt, after citing one or two 'hard-to-reconcile' quotations from Hume, that Macpherson's model fits him very well. It is true, of course, that Hume frequently sees the interests balanced by the passions, but it is not true that Hume does not share, to all essential purposes, the classical liberal model of the self-interested individual. That he sees man as under the persistent sway of natural impulses, and consistently motivated by self-interested behaviour, is something we have already had cause to document.

This claim can be further supported, however, by drawing attention to several specific weaknesses in Miller's account. First, Miller (1980: 264) compromises his own case when he concedes that Hume's emphasis on the fact that the kind affections balance the selfish ones is strongly qualified, by the fact that 'sociability for Hume does not mean an abstract regard for men as such, but an affection for those we are connected to by the network of social relationships'. Yet, if we look slightly more widely in Hume's writings, we can find statements which not only further qualify this point, but which do so in a way that casts serious doubt on Hume's belief in man's fundamental sociability. As Hume (1978: 534) says in the *Treatise*, for instance: 'Nothing is more certain than that men are in great measure governed by interest, and that, even when they extend their concern beyond themselves, it is not to any great distance; nor is it usual for them, in common life, to look further than their nearest friends and acquaintance.'

While we can agree with Miller (1980: 265) that for Hume man has 'a powerful impetus to associate with others' and that 'the desire for society is intrinsic and omnipresent', this is in fact no different than for Locke,[32] and it does not alter the basic ontological condition of Hume's view of the individual as governed by strong self-interested passions that he brings with him from nature. As with the other classical liberals, Hume's question essentially is how is society possible on this basis of human nature. In addition, as Miller also concedes, Hume does regard rights to property as absolute,[33] although we can acknowledge, as Miller (ibid.: 267) points out, that he sees property as a conventional, rather than a natural institution,[34] and we can agree with Miller (ibid.: 269) that 'Hume does not see property rights as eliminating a man's natural obligations to those around him'. Taking all this into account, as Miller (ibid.: 269) concedes, Hume's model of man is still more akin to the possessive individualist model, than to a feudal conception of property. The real question, then, becomes, if Hume doesn't fit the 'mark I model', how much *less significant* is the 'mark II model'? (Miller, 1980: 266). Our view is that the metaphysical basis of Hume's conception of man still conforms in essential respects to the classical liberal conception. While man, for Hume, is clearly not a 'natural consumer or appropriator', he is still a 'naturally self-interested' subject. While his subject clearly had greater potential for sociability than Hobbes's man, and greater scope for collective determination over the rules of property than Locke's man, his writing was still able to provide rich fodder to be adapted and modified within traditions such as *political economy*. Hence, whatever scope there is for debating Hume's precise intentions, or degree of moderateness, his conception does not depart in the sense we are concerned with here from the classical liberal conception of the individual.[35]

The main point on which Miller's criticism is sound concerns the reductive economistic metaphor governing Macpherson's account of the individual.[36] The main problem with Macpherson's model of the individual in our view is in tying the individual's 'self-interest' so closely to 'property' or 'consumption', thus neglecting the more general, but more accurate, sense in which the individual is not an 'infinite consumer or appropriator', but an 'infinitely self-interested maximizer'. While property and possessions are clearly objects of this self-interest amongst some of the writers in this tradition, such things as status, position, reputation and security may also function as objects of desire, not adequately captured by Macpherson's narrow economistic formulation. To represent the individual of classical liberalism as a 'self-interested maximizer' rather than purely as an 'infinite appropriator of property', as well as modifying Macpherson's model of possessive market society, is in our view the major correction needed to Macpherson's account of liberal political philosophy, in order to correctly understand the importance of the liberal tradition to the contemporary era. By such a correction, many of the criticisms against Macpherson (the issues over appropriation or self-interest, including, for instance, Miller's point that Hume saw men as desiring things for 'other ends') effectively lose their force.

Liberalism, individualism and education

Notwithstanding the weaknesses identified in Macpherson's account, a critical analysis of his work has led to a more correct understanding of the commonalities in the classical liberal mind-set, spanning three centuries. What we have left is a conception of the classical liberal individual as a *self-interested maximizer*. This conception, which assumes that individuals are pre-social and that humans are basically solitary, with needs and interests which are separate or opposed to others, is the starting point of liberal theory and philosophy. Metaphysically this conception is central to all liberal analyses. It enables the limited acknowledgement of the presence and the influence that social groups can have on an individual's exercise of reason (for example, the development of speech). However, the reduction to the individual, always ensures the ontological and metaphysical separation of rationality from structural influences.

This is a tradition that has permeated philosophical, social science and educational scholarship and rendered the collective and structural effects of educational policies subordinate to an understanding of the individual's 'experience' of them. Within liberal educational discourse, an individual's ability to learn is seen as something determined by their inborn capacity, and their educational achievement is determined largely by individual effort, something for which they alone are responsible. In a model that discounts the influences of class, race or gender, schools are considered fair if they provide 'equal opportunity'. As Kenneth Strike (1989: 5) claims, 'liberals will tend to see schools as places wherein justice can be taught and implemented. Students can learn to treat one another fairly and democratically. They can learn to settle their differences by appealing to impartial and neutral standards whereby their differences can be rationally adjudicated'.

The intentions and choices of rational agents thus become the subject of the explicit political and economic theories of liberalism. Personal interests and desires are understood to be fulfilled through a 'privatized' motivation to secure a share of available resources. Historically, liberal discourses in education have always worked to suppress the role of various social processes, such as the development of language, the importance of the strategic resources that families provide children with, the salience of the hidden curriculum or the impact of the sexual division of labour upon the construction of subjectivity. Liberals have not primarily been concerned with the conditions for human growth and flourishing, or with the way individuals are formed. Liberals see individuals as 'self-creations' constituted by their free and rational choices. Such discourses have worked to suppress the reality of the social in the presentation of the individual as a free, unified and autonomous being. Social positioning is understood to be achieved quite independently of the influence of other people and structural barriers.

Modern individualism expresses its possessive quality, most obviously in the contemporary belief that humans are the pivotal architects of their own destinies (for example, the 'self-made man', meritocratic beliefs). In having proprietorship over oneself, individuals are thought free to alienate their own property and their capacity to labour. They are free from dependence on the will of others and are capable of voluntarily entering into contractual arrangements. Most centrally, this self-interested individual is still possessive and capable of infinitely appropriating; though, as we have reformulated this, it is no longer exclusively so. Irrespective of historical location or material circumstances, individuals are perceived as tending naturally towards egoism, or the maximization of their own individual powers or utilities. This maximization may at times be constrained by a scarcity of resources, by certain structural impediments, such as access to goods or services, or by certain moral considerations. All humans are understood to possess a common essence, or core, that is thought to fuel personal motivation and the expression of

101

aptitudes and abilities.

What can be designated as a 'static' or 'changeless' conception of human nature does accommodate the possibility of limited psychological differences between humans resulting from widely differing social circumstances. In addition to this, liberalism invokes an essentially ahistorical conceptualization of the individual. Historical location, class membership, ethnic belonging, gender identity – the basic divisions which organize the social world – are not perceived to be of any philosophical importance to the construction of individual subjectivity and rationality. Liberalism, however, realizes that humans are not born autonomous moral agents. In a somewhat limited fashion, it acknowledges they become like this. A liberal theory of education is concerned with how this happens. Yet, as Amy Gutmann (1987: 55–6) notes, education seems to present special difficulties for liberal theories. Because liberals in theory are neutral concerning a wide range of ways of life, the issue of 'which type of education' they opt for seems to necessitate or exert pressure in favour of accepting a notion of education being a matter of private preference. Any attempt to define the criteria for a 'good' education for all is likely to infringe the wishes and interests of the individuals concerned.[37] Yet to make education exclusively private opens up the possibilities of massive inequalities in resources and wealth as well as with respect to teaching, curricula and credentials.

A further problem with regard to the liberal conception of education relates to the historical tendency of liberals to take individual interests as given and not be concerned about the formative development of individuals as a matter of public policy. Of course the liberal model of the individual recognizes that preferences and capacities are affected by the environment. The formation of subjects and the education of children, however, have traditionally been concerns of the private sphere. The processes by which children become adults are the concern only of their parents as rational choosers. This is the crux of the distinction between 'choosers' and 'learners' that is sometimes made in liberal discourses. The idea of the rational chooser is epitomised in Mill's famous quotation on liberty above. The principle of liberty does not apply to children, however. As Mill (1859: 13–14) put it:

> It is perhaps hardly necessary to say that ... [W]e are not speaking of children or of young persons below the age which the law may fix as that of manhood or womanhood ... . For the same reason, we must leave out of consideration those backward states of society in which the race itself may be considered as in its nonage... . Despotism is a legitimate mode of government in dealing with barbarians, provided the end be their improvement ...

Mill's quote highlights what may today be seen as the *bête noire* of classical liberalism as a distinct social and political philosophy with consequences for the organization of education. Not only was it a philosophy of freedom but also of control and order. The status of rational autonomy applied in liberal discourse to the educated, white, male heads of households. The rest were 'learners' or 'dependants'. These included children, prisoners, the uncivilized, the insane and usually women as well. While the contemporary notion of the liberal individual is popularly understood to be a non-gendered form, classical liberal philosophers were decidedly androcentric and ethnocentric in their equation of humanity with rationality. They were referring to white, property-owning men. Such views, which were based on conceptions of a biologically determined female psyche and nature, remained influential through to the early to mid-twentieth century. In *The Subjection of Women*, Mill (1975) argued that the relations between husbands and wives formed an unjustifiable exception to basic liberal principles. He directed his argument against the legally sanctioned powers of husbands who were able to treat their wives as slaves. Mill, however, falls back on the same argument he criticizes when he assumes that even after social reform (including educational and legal changes), most women would still choose marital dependence. These assumptions contributed to the essential split between the public and private realms underlying both the 'old' and 'new' versions of liberalism. Middleton (1990) also points out that this split and these androcentric conceptions still permeate neoclassical liberalism and are most evident in the association between childbirth and irrationality. Of this patriarchal liberalism, Middleton (1990: 69) maintains that 'together with savages (non-Europeans), the indigent (unpropertied classes), and the insane, women were perceived as irrational creatures of passion, who could therefore justifiably be denied the rights of citizenship (such as the rights to own property or to vote)'.

Thus the early assumptions about human nature were premised upon the belief that even though liberal discourses implied universal categories, only some humans were seen as possessing the capacity to be choosing, rational, possessive agents. This rationality was an inherently 'mental' phenomenon that all had an equal potentiality for. Such a view is constituted on the underlying metaphysical assumption which places individuals as ontologically prior to society, and as not fundamentally shaped by social or cultural influences. This is an assumption that was to be heavily qualified within the philosophical and political traditions of social democratic liberalism. It is to a discussion of these that we turn in the next chapter.

Notes

1 Locke distinguishes the State of Nature from the State of War, and sees a condition of peace and co-operation as possible in the former. See Locke (1960, II: ss. 3, 19).

2 Locke states, for example: 'Man (by being Master of himself, and *Proprietor of his own Person*, and the actions or *Labour* of it) had still in

himself *the great Foundation of Property*'. See Locke (1960, II: ss. 5, 44).

3 David Ricardo originally advanced the theory of comparative advantage to bolster the intellectual rationale for free trade in the early nineteenth century. The theory claimed that if each country specializes in the production of those goods where it has a 'comparative advantage', then no country will be advantaged or disadvantaged overall compared to another.

4 Macpherson (1962: ch. 3) makes the point that the Levellers advocated for a much more limited conception of 'manhood suffrage' than had been often represented by historians. His point is supported by the historian Christopher Hill (1963).

5 See, Locke's (1979) *On Civil Government*, first published in 1690.

6 See, Locke's (1979) *Letter Concerning Toleration*, first published in 1689; see Voltaire's (2000) *Treatise on Tolerance*, first published in 1673.

7 See, Montesquieu (1900), *The Spirit of Laws*, first published in 1748.

8 Within the Parliamentary forces during the English Civil War (1640–49), there were a variety of political and social groups. These included the substantial men of property represented by Cromwell and Ireton; the small men of the city who opposed the big men of commerce, represented by Lilburn, the Levellers, with their radical programme of popular democracy for the poor sections of the community and even groups of landless labourers,

9 See C.B. Macpherson (1962), especially chapter 2. Hobbes conforms to his thesis, says Macpherson, because the value Hobbes places on property is defined as 'no more than it is esteemed by others', and this is essentially a market criterion (Macpherson, 1962: 152).

10 His treatment of Hobbes has been reviewed by Thomas (1965), Berlin (1964), Carmichael (1983), Letwin, (1972), Minogue (1963), Raphael (1977), Ryan (1988), Shapiro (1986), Sommerville (1992), Tuck (1989) Tully (1993), Viner (1963),Wood (1980) amongst others. Keith Thomas argued that Hobbes could not have championed capitalist interests. He argued that Hobbes's affinities were with the aristocratic and feudal rather than bourgeois, although he does concede that there are bourgeois elements represented in Hobbes's writing. He also concedes that in many respects Hobbes's state is the bulwark of property (Thomas, 1965: 222). He also admits that Hobbes expected laissez-faire to operate, but claims that overall Hobbes's interests are broader than purely market interests are. For example, Hobbes was concerned with aristocratic values, with values such as the nature of human reputation, which are not market indices. Also see Townshend (2000) for a summary of the debate.

11 Political and religious themes are also central to Hobbes's project.

12 Thomas (1965: 223, 225–7) points out that Hobbes legitimates various forms of behaviour which are contradictory to a market order, such as theft when hungry.

13 Kant later effected a parallel argument representing the subject and the basis

of morality as pre-social and ahistorical through transcendental arguments.

14 Waldron (1988: 141) points out the important point that Locke's account of ownership has a theological dimension. This does not concern us here. Our purpose is not to debate the correct interpretation of Locke, but concerns the political uses to which Locke has historically been put to legitimate existing political settlements.

15 While writers like Miller (1980), Shapiro (1986) and Townshend (2000) maintain that Macpherson's thesis has greater validity when applied to Locke than to Hobbes, they also maintain that there are still problems in applying an abstract model of market society to Locke's work. If Macpherson's thesis is that Locke's own views were a reflection of early seventeenth-century capitalist development, we think there are serious problems with it. To the extent that Macpherson is identifying Locke's theories as legitimating a certain model of future economic development, we think it very strong. Also see Andrew (1988), Ashcraft (1987), Berlin (1964), Dunn (1968; 1969), Hundert (1977), Laslett (1964), Ryan (1965), Tully (1980; 1988; 1993) and Wood (1984). One problem raised by several writers on Macpherson's interpretation of Locke is in interpreting whether Locke's strictures against 'covetousness' or 'greed', for instance, moderate his attitude to property. Macpherson claims that in relation to 'covetousness', Locke only saw it as a problem after the appropriation of 'large and unequal properties', and that in speaking of such, Locke is referring not to the accumulators of property but to those who would trespass upon the possessions of the industrious and rational, that is, those who are engaged in the pursuit of unlimited appropriation and accumulation. In his recent re-analysis of this debate, Jules Townshend (2000: 83, 87, 129, 155, 160) considers that Macpherson was unfairly treated by many of his critics, and makes the point that many of the criticisms are minor, tangential to the main argument, or unbalanced. Also, Christopher Hill (1963: 88) points out, that Macpherson has thrown 'new light on the two-facedness of Locke's theory' and significantly contributed to our understanding of the common frame of reference linking Hobbes, Harrington, the Levellers and Locke in relation to their common interest in the 'security of property'.

16 See Macpherson (1962: 208–11). A more succinct statement is provided in Macpherson (1980: xvi–xvii) where he says that money 'rendered inoperative the spoilage limitation, for one could now convert any amount of perishable goods into money, which did not spoil. The introduction of money also transcended the limitation about leaving enough and as good for others. The argument here was not quite as clear. In the first three editions of the *Treatise* Locke simply left it that the introduction of money would lead naturally to extensive commerce, which would make it profitable for individuals to appropriate more land than they could use the produce of, so that all land would be appropriated, leaving none for

others, and that this was justified because all had consented to the use of money. In later editions he added a new argument (in para. 37): land which is privately appropriated is ten times as productive as land left in common, so even when the land is all appropriated there is more produce for everybody. There is not enough and as good *land* left for others, but there is enough and as good (indeed more and better) *produce* for them. The original requirement had been that private appropriation should leave enough to meet everyone's equal right to subsistence, and that requirement was still satisfied after all the land had been taken up'. Macpherson (1980: xvii) continues: 'The third limit, that one could appropriate only as much as one had mixed one's labour with, was also transcended, or had quite a different meaning after the introduction of money. For when there was no land left, those without any would have to sell their labour, for wages, to those that had land. When B, C, and D sell their labour to A, their labour becomes A's property; it is then *his* labour which is mixed with what was in common: " ... the turfs my servant has cut ... become my property ... the labour was mine, removing them out of that common state they were in, hath fixed my property in them" (para. 28). Thus there was no limit to the amount one could appropriate by mixing one's labour with what had been given to mankind in common. Locke has thus in effect removed all the initial natural law limits on individual appropriation, and has established a natural right to unlimited amounts of private property'.

17 Waldron is drawing on H.A.L. Hart's distinction between 'special' and 'general' rights. See Hart (1955).

18 Our view here is that while we think Macpherson neglects the importance of Locke's strictures concerning charity, Waldron exaggerates the sense in which Locke was concerned with equality by suggesting that 'it could be argued that its effect is to extend the realm of legitimate state action and to provide a justifying ground for redistributive activism in the economic sphere' (Waldron, 1988: 139).

19 Representing liberalism as a 'dual etiology' helps to overcome some of the problems in the dispute engendered by Macpherson and his critics over which of these two 'poles' of the doctrine constitute the correct basis for interpreting seventeenth century liberalism. Thus, for example, Thomas's (1965) claims that Macpherson neglects aristocratic, religious and political themes in Hobbes can be accommodated if one is not concerned to render all aspects of Hobbes's theory compatible with a market model. There is a certain 'tired' repetition to the debate of the 1960s and 1970s as it is realized that both Macpherson and his critics sought to render liberalism 'coherent' by arguing whether liberals of the seventeenth century were defending liberty and democracy, or religious, or aristocratic, or Thomist, or feudal values, or seeking to promote the right to an unlimited appropriation of property. In our view the issue is not either/or but both/and.

They are not mutually exclusive positions, but rather are contradictory elements of a single doctrine. See also Ashcraft (1987: 265) where he argues, similarly, that Locke's thought manifests the contradiction or tension which is central to liberalism, 'as a social theory between its universalistic claims to moral and religious equality ... and its instrumentalist treatment of human beings as part of a process of capital accumulation'.

20 According to Montesquieu, when people strive after their own honour 'it turns out that everyone contributes to the general welfare while thinking that he works for his own interests' (cited in Albert O. Hirschman, 1977: 10).

21 See *The New Science*, paras 132–3 especially (Vico, 1968).

22 See Nathan Rosenberg (1963).

23 The 'revised' Adam Smith of the last two decades of scholarship is a much more reflective scholar who 'was fully aware of contemporary habits of mind and political practices he believed stood in the way of realizing liberal economic doctrines' (Teichgraeber, 1986: 87). As Teichgraeber (1986: 87 fn. 4) points out, much of the support for such a reading of Smith did already exist and had not been entirely overlooked. One person Teichgraeber does not mention is Albert Hirschman, who in his 1977 study, speaks of the 'Adam Smith problem' as the incompatibility between *The Theory of Moral Sentiments* and *The Wealth of Nations*. In his own reconciliation, Hirschman argues that while in *The Theory of Moral Sentiments*, Smith specifies that there are powerful non-economic drives, they all 'feed into the economic ones and do nothing but reinforce them' (1977: 109). As Hirschman puts it: 'In the former work, so it appears, Smith dealt with a wide spectrum of human feelings and passions, but he also convinced himself that, insofar as "the great mob of mankind" is concerned, the principal human drives end up motivating man to improve his material well-being. And logically enough, he then proceeded in *The Wealth of Nations* to investigate in detail the conditions under which this objective, on which human action tends to converge so remarkably, can be achieved' (ibid.: 109). Hirschman (ibid.: 108) also cites Smith from *The Theory of Moral Sentiments* for support: 'it is chiefly from [the] regard to the sentiments of mankind that we pursue riches and avoid poverty'. Notwithstanding Hirschman's account of Smith in *The Passions and the Interests*, a new generation of Smith scholars criticized the narrow 'liberal-capitalist' conception of Smith. See, for instance, Forbes (1976), Winch, (1978), Haakonssen, (1981), Hont and Ignatieff (1983), Robertson (1983), Dickey (1986), Teichgraeber (1986), Werhane (1991) and Muller, (1993). For earlier perspectives which asserted a 'revised' thesis on Smith, see Viner (1958) and Lindgren (1973). It was the studies of Forbes, and of Winch, that set the revisionist thesis in motion. For an unrepentant traditional interpretation of Smith, that upholds the liberal-capitalist conception, and is unconvinced by the revisionist accounts, see Himmelfarb (1984). Our own position here is to accept the revisionist thesis

that there was an emphasis by Smith on a broad spectrum of passions and human emotions, but we also accept Hirschman's view that interest became a dominant and persistent passion in the mid to late eighteenth century, which reinforced a concept of self-interest. Ultimately, however, that different interpretations of Smith are possible does not particularly concern us, or at least is not central to our own thesis, for as we maintain, liberalism is characterized by its contradictory nature. This means that irrespective of Smith's own views, or of eighteenth-century *political economy* in general, the possibility of exploiting an exclusive emphasis on interest, which we will claim occurred under neoliberalism in the twentieth century, manifests itself as a *latent* possibility within the discourse of classical liberalism.

24 See Hirschman, (1977: 63–6). The conception of self-interested behaviour as 'calm and dispassionate' was one accepted by the sentimental school, including Shaftesbury, Hutcheson, Hume and Smith. Shaftesbury had theorized the importance of affections such as benevolence and generosity, as well as the less admirable affections which were aimed at private advantages. Hutcheson simplified Shaftesbury's scheme, distinguishing between the benevolent and selfish passions on the one hand, and the calm and violent passions on the other. Hence Hutcheson talks of the 'calm desire of wealth', and Hirschman (1977: 65) comments that 'calm is the English equivalent of *doux* . ... A calm desire is thus defined as one that acts with calculation and rationality, and is therefore exactly equivalent to what in the seventeenth century was understood by interest'. Hume further adapted the distinction, to ensure that calm desires could win out against violent ones, by saying: 'We must ... distinguish betwixt a calm and a weak passion; betwixt a violent and a strong one' (Hume, from the *Treatise*, cited in Hirschman, 1977: 66).

25 See Hirschman (1977: 100–13).

26 Adam Ferguson (1996), *An Essay on the History of Civil Society* (originally published in Edinburgh in 1767).

27 John Millar (1990), *Observations Concerning the Distinctions of Ranks* (originally published in London in 1771). Also see, Lehmann's (1960) *John Millar of Glasgow*.

28 See Keane (1993), Connelly (1993) and Mansbridge (1993).

29 For a survey of criticisms of Macpherson see Townshend (2000).

30 Similar points were made by Ritchie, Bosanquet, Stephen and, later, by MacIver, Barker, and Anschutz, amongst others, all who maintained that because almost all actions could be classified as 'other-regarding', Mill's use of the principle as grounding a rule to determine the limits of state intervention fails (see Rees, 1966: 91–2 for a full summary).

31 For an analysis of Macpherson's utilization of Mill, see Wood (1978; 1981).

32 Locke also saw man as sociable and able to develop in society in this sense. As he says at the start of Book III of the *Essay*, 'God, having designed man

for a sociable creature, made him not only with an inclination and under a necessity to have fellowship with those of his own kind, but furnished him also with language, which was to the great instrument and common tie of society'.

33 Both in the sense, as Miller summarizes, that they are complete and in the sense that rights are not accompanied by corresponding legal obligations. See Hume (1978: 482); see Miller, (1980: 269).

34 Hume states that 'in the state of nature ... there was no such thing as property, and consequently could be no such thing as justice or injustice' (1978: 501). This is because for Hume property is a 'rule for the stability of possession' (ibid.: 492). Hence possession is negotiated as part of the contract, for such a rule is necessary if society is stable. Hume further says, 'Our property is nothing but those goods, whose constant possession is established by the laws of society, that is, by the laws of justice'. Thus, 'property has its origins in the artifice and contrivance of men' (ibid.: 491).

35 We acknowledge, of course, that Hume's man is not 'rational' in the Cartesian sense, and that there is an important sense in which Hume is an 'anti-rationalist', and this constitutes an important difference to liberals like Locke or Kant. Our point here is couched in terms of the debate between Miller and Macpherson over the metaphysical role of self-interest as central to the subject. While things other than reason drive self-interest, it is its central importance that makes Hume continuous with the liberal tradition, and a major influence on *political economy*, and on twentieth-century thinkers like Hayek. While Miller seeks to counter the importance of self-interest in Hume's theory of human nature, over-emphasising the importance of of the 'sociable' aspects, as part of his strategy against Macpherson, it is not supported by Hume's writings, in our view. Further endorsement of man's limited benevolence appears on pp. 466–467 of the *Treatise* where Hume (1978) states his view that 'each person loves himself better than any other single person', and while he acknowledges a mixture of passions, this does not result in a homogenized sociability but rather a conflicting array, which, as he puts it 'cannot but be dangerous to the new-establish'd union [of society]' (ibid.: 467).

36 Miller's approach is simply to take Macpherson's conception at face value whilst presenting contrary textual evidence from Hume, without attempting to make the reasonably minor adjustments that would have shown the strong kernel of truth in Macpherson's account.

37 This applies more to utilitarian theories than rights theories but the issue constitutes a difficulty for both forms. See Gutmann (1987) for a consideration of the essential differences between different types of liberal argument. Also see Strike (1989, ch. 3). Strike points out that because education necessarily involves the inculcation of values and beliefs, which for liberals is a private matter, state-provided schooling is problematic.

6

Social Democratic Liberalism

The virtual absence of theories of the state in educational policy is largely a reflection of the liberal ideology within which such analysis is generally undertaken. According to the liberal view, the state comprises a set of institutions produced by the consensual collective actions of individuals who enter a contract in order to protect their general interests and to make provisions for common social goods such as education, defence and the protection of property. With the rise of capitalism, this liberal view of the state became more deeply entrenched. Carnoy and Levin (1985: 28) summarize this trend as follows:

> With Bentham and Mill in the early nineteenth century, 'classical' theories of the state, which had been premised on a relatively homogeneous rural society of small-holders, shifted to a utilitarian view of democracy that incorporated the newly emerged capitalist class structure and provided an intellectual rationale for it. Utilitarians adopted Adam Smith's argument in *The Wealth of Nations* that, because of the guiding 'invisible hand' of the market-place, unfettered individual economic activity would maximize social welfare, that indeed there was no inconsistency between the unlimited pursuit of individual gain and social good, and that the State should thus limit itself only to the production of such public goods as defence, education, and the enforcement of laws.

Capitalism emerged as a mode of production in a specifically European cultural context. The gradual breakdown of the feudal system in the sixteenth and seventeenth centuries, involved the replacement of forms of medieval economic organization by those based on market exchange relationships between supposedly autonomous individuals. Governments representing the new bourgeois interests represented themselves as the legitimate custodians of popular allegiance and began to act internationally and domestically as the promoters of national economic development. The Industrial Revolution of the eighteenth and nineteenth centuries was seen primarily as the outcome of individual initiatives by the state.

The development of industrial capitalism was perceived by Marx to rest on a conflict of interests between capitalists and the vast majority of wage-workers. As the state for Marx was structurally aligned to the interests of

110

capitalists, the only resolution to the conflict lay in the violent overthrow of the system which would abolish the class structure and result in the collective social ownership and control of the means of production, distribution and exchange. What Marx failed adequately to see was the extent to which forms of social change were possible within capitalism and the extent to which the working class could secure concessions through both industrial (trade union) organization as well as through the extension of the franchise.

The development of an urbanized industrial economy made it clear that the state would have to assume a much larger role than it had in the past. According to Karl Polanyi, the growth of state intervention in the nineteenth century was neither deliberately planned nor politically motivated. Rather, it must be seen as a direct response to the pragmatic demands of the dysfunctions of the nineteenth-century market order. As he puts it (Polanyi, 1969: 16):

> The anti-liberal conspiracy is a pure invention. The great variety of forms in which the 'collectivist' countermovement appeared was not due to any preference for socialism or nationalism on the part of concerted interests, but exclusively to the broader range of vital social interests affected by the expanding market mechanism. This accounts for all but universal reactions of predominantly practical character called forth by the expansion of that mechanism. Intellectual fashions played no role whatever in this process ...

While state intervention was in this sense unplanned, in contrast, argues Polanyi (1969: 12), the road to the free market in the early nineteenth century was:

> opened and kept open by an enormous increase in continuous, centrally organized and controlled interventionism. To make Adam Smith's 'simple and natural liberty' compatible with the needs of a human society was a most complicated affair. Witness the complexity of the provisions in the innumerable enclosure laws; the amount of bureaucratic control involved in the administration of the New Poor Laws which for the first time since Queen Elizabeth's reign were effectively supervised by central authority; or the increase in governmental administration entailed in the meritorious task of municipal reform. And yet all these strongholds of governmental interference were erected with a view to the organizing of some simple freedom – such as that of land, labor, or municipal administration.

From the 1860s there was an expanding range of matters on which state action was taken, ranging from legislation relating to employment (child labour), to health and education. Polanyi argues, in fact, that the changes from liberal to collectivist solutions happened without any consciousness of deep-seated ideological and political changes on the part of those engaged in the process in countries as diverse as Prussia under Bismark, Victorian England, and France of the Third Republic. Each passed through a period of economic liberalism characterized by free trade and laissez-faire, followed by a period of anti-liberal intervention in regard to public health, factory conditions, child labour, municipal trading, social insurance, public utilities and so on.

111

Intervention in the market, especially as it related to employment, social services and education, was increasingly designed to influence the quality as well as the quantity of its provision, because in fact the free market proved to be 'a poor guide to the best means of satisfying the real wishes of consumers' (Shonfield, 1965: 227). In relation to education, the operations of the market proved to be particularly pernicious for, without a reasonably planned approach, one is driven to reliance upon considerations of economic costs and benefits as criteria for the setting of educational goals with the consequent danger that the determination of educational goals and objectives is taken out of the education realm altogether. This is in fact what happened under the technocratic models of educational policy-making that accompanied economic liberalism. The weaknesses of such economic principles were set out by Keynes in his original arguments against free-market policies which he made in an article entitled 'The end of laissez-faire' (Keynes, 1931a: 312):

> It is *not* true that individuals possess a prescriptive 'natural liberty' in their economic activities. There is *no* 'compact' conferring perpetual rights on those who Have or on those who Acquire. The world is *not* so governed from above that private and social interests always coincide. It is *not* so managed here below that in practice they coincide. It is not a correct deduction from the Principles of Economics that enlightened self-interest always operates in the public interest. Nor is it true that self-interest generally *is* enlightened; more often individuals acting separately to promote their own ends are too ignorant or too weak to attain even these. Experience does *not* show that individuals, when they make up a social unit, are always less clear-sighted than when they act separately.

This statement illustrates the early rejection of market principles by many moderate liberals earlier this century who wanted to reform capitalism rather than abolish it. The real issue, as Keynes saw clearly, was in seeking to ascertain 'what the state ought to take upon itself to direct by the public wisdom, and what it ought to leave with as little interference as possible to individual exertion' (Keynes, 1931a: 312–13).[1] His arguments against the minimal state were based on the discovery that there is no tendency towards efficient equilibrium in capitalist markets. Keynes was not the first to discover this of course. It had concerned economists in liberal and radical traditions, such as Marx, Hobson, Kalecki and others, before Keynes's idea achieved orthodoxy. Specifically, in this respect, was Keynes's theory of consumption functions and, in particular, his argument that the diminishing marginal propensity to consume creates a permanent tendency towards disequilibrium, or at least an inefficient equilibrium, as a result of the insufficient aggregate demand it generates.

For Keynes, and the social democratic or welfare state liberals in the early twentieth century, the failure of the labour market to regulate itself as adjudicated by the price mechanism, and the failures of the market to provide for externalities, that is, the consequences of its own operation, meant that action was required by the state. Keynes thus advocated a form of macroeconomic

112

fiscal policy whereby governments actively intervene in the economy to assist its regulation and assure the provision of public goods which the market did not provide or provided inadequately. For Keynes, as for many welfare state liberals and socialists, 'public goods' could not be reduced to 'private interests' of individuals, or seen simply as their aggregate expression. Public goods must be seen as those goods which have the characteristics of 'indivisibility' and 'nonexcludability' in that their use cannot be meaningfully divided between individuals (King, 1987: 81). To the minimal list of public goods which Adam Smith acknowledged, Keynes, influenced by the later nineteenth-century social democratic liberals, added issues related to the right to leisure, the right to work, the right to citizenship, as well as the right to a minimum, decent, standard of living.

Essentially, the expanded role of government translated to three distinct but overlapping functions:

- to supply public goods and services;
- to alleviate and regulate the failures of the market; and
- to arbitrate between competing social groups or classes.

Education was one focus of intervention. Henry Brougham's Select Committee (1820) reported that in 1818 only one in 17 of the total number of eligible children in England and Wales attended a school. Those children that did, attended either an exclusive private school or a small enterprise run mainly by voluntary societies. Although writers like James Tooley (1996) and E.G. West (1994) provide a romanticized account of life and education in this period in their attempts to argue for 'education without the state', few historians of education would agree with their account of social and educational conditions prior to Foresters Act of 1870. The physical conditions in which the working classes lived (especially in London and the bigger cities) presented a picture of the crudest and most unhealthy squalor, and education was not central to their life plans (see for instance, Maclure, 1970; McCann, 1977; Reeder, 1977; Rubenstein, 1969; Selleck, 1968; Sturt, 1970). Hence, as R.J.W. Selleck (1968: 5) reports for 1848, not only did the cholera epidemic in England claim between 200 and 400 deaths daily, but accounts of the general conditions under which the working classes lived and of the failure of social remediation through self-help and charity reinforced the belief by many, in spite of the Benthamite culture of Victorian England, that the state's involvement was an 'urgent social necessity' (Selleck, 1968:10). Education would reduce crime, spread 'useful information', provide the necessary skills and knowledge to prepare 'the lower orders' for the exercise of franchise which was gradually being extended to them, and help secure social order. All of these factors made it expedient, if not right and proper, that at least 'some' education should be provided to all the children of the nation.[2]

The state's involvement in education, as well as its growing role in the provision of welfare has a complex history. This related to the struggles of the

working classes against their exploitation, the requirements of industrial capitalism for a more efficient environment in which to operate, in particular the
need for a highly productive labour force, and the recognition by property
owners of the price that has to be paid for political security. The political
problems associated with social reform in Britain in the nineteenth century
became immensely complicated in the light of two factors: first, the emergence of the modern labour movement and, second, the extension of the franchise, which was significantly increased in 1884 when most of the miners and
agricultural labourers received the vote. Even then, many workers remained
outside the electorate, and the continuance of institutions such as plural
voting for property owners meant that the real gains to be expected from such
developments were to be slow in coming. In the long run, however, given the
working class's majority amongst the electorate, both Tories and Liberals were
forced to adapt themselves to the political demands of the new participants.

Many other factors contributed to the development of the welfare state: the
rise of trade unions, the formation of the British Labour Party, the growth of
socialist political and social thought, and the philosophical justifications for
the state's 'positive' role provided by intellectuals such as T.H. Green and L.T.
Hobhouse. Also important initially, however, were the activities of radical
political leaders like Bradlaugh, Dilke and Chamberlain who framed the
central assumptions upon which a welfare state of the twentieth century arose.
As Chamberlain asked in 1885 in his 'unauthorized programme' – an early
blueprint for the welfare state – 'What ransom will property pay for the security it enjoys?' (cited in Saville, 1977: 5). Although, as his biographer Garvin
explains, he was later to supplement 'insurance' for 'ransom', as the latter
went far beyond his real intentions. Chamberlain and his colleagues recognized that state intervention was developing and that labour was a progressive
force. In this sense the welfare state was seen as a concession granted by property. Chamberlain of course was not an opponent of private property. Rather,
he saw the role of the state as supplementing it where it was no longer adequate for social justice and national needs (Saville, 1977: 5).

Chamberlain advanced the cause of the welfare state from within the
framework of older political settlements. The emergence of 'new' socialist
groups such as the Fabians was also important and Fabian leaders such as the
Webbs provided detailed blueprints which influenced much legislation of the
twentieth century. Believing in the inevitability of gradualness, the Fabians
emphasized the ways in which collectivist practices and legislation had been
increasing steadily throughout the second half of the nineteenth century and
how the welfare state developed naturally and inevitably despite intensive
political opposition from the likes of Herbert Spencer and others who sought
to defend the Benthamite individualism of early Victorian England. As Sydney
Webb (cited in Saville, 1977: 6) wrote in 1889:

The 'practical man', oblivious or contemptuous of any theory of the Social Organism or general principles of social organisation has been forced by the necessities of time, into an ever deepening collectivist channel. Socialism, of course, he still rejects and despises. The individualist Town Counsellor will walk along the municipal pavement, lit by municipal gas and cleansed by municipal brooms and municipal water, and seeing by the municipal clock in the municipal market that he is too early to meet his children coming from the municipal school hard by the county lunatic asylum and municipal hospital, will use the national telegraph system to tell them not to walk through the municipal park but come by the municipal tramway, to meet him in the municipal reading room by the municipal art gallery, museum and library, where he intends to consult some of the national publications in order to prepare his next speech in the municipal town hall, in favour of the nationalization of canals and the increase of government control over the railway system. 'Socialism, sir', he will say, 'don't waste the time of a practical man by your fantastic absurdities. Self-help sir, individual self-help, that's what's made our city what it is.'

Webb's quote illustrates that the growth of municipal and state involvement in social and economic affairs in Britain had already proceeded a long way by the end of the nineteenth century. Some areas that Webb fails to mention in his statement include the important area of factory legislation, the beginnings of a housing policy, and the introduction of working men's compensation, the last of which constituted an especially important dimension of the welfare state, in the initial proposals put forward for it. In the twentieth century the main legislation for the British welfare state was put forward in three main periods of social reform. These included the period 1906–14, under the Liberal governments, which included legislation concerning education, the needs of children, employment conditions, pensions, health, unemployment and insurance. The second main period was between the First and Second World Wars, which saw the extension of social security and general modifications to policies in relation to maternity and child welfare (1918), housing and town planning (1919), unemployment insurance (1920) pensions for widows and orphans (1920) and extensions to state provided education (1926–7). The third main period, between 1945 and 1950, under the post-war British Labour government, was largely concerned with consolidation and minor modifications.

The emergence of the welfare state in Britain

The first decades of the nineteenth century marked the era of liberalism's triumph. As Stuart Hall (1986: 58) has observed:

From Waterloo until the outbreak of the First World War no other doctrine spoke with the same authority or exercised the same widespread influence. The great achievements of this period were all closely associated with liberal ideas. It served as the prophet of industrialism. It helped transform Great Britain into the workshop of the world. It was the exponent of free trade which created the world market. It espoused the gospel of progress.

At the start of the nineteenth century, issues such as the extension of the franchise and parliamentary reform preoccupied the foremost liberals of the period, Jeremy Bentham and John Stuart Mill. With Bentham, the liberal cornerstone of natural rights as the justification of liberal principles gave way to utilitarianism which was to serve as the new moral rationalization for liberalism. Although the principle of utility replaced natural rights as the calculus of moral evaluation, the central concepts of individual self-interest and laissez-faire remained at the basis of liberalism. It was within this adapted, and thoroughly modernist, frame of reference that Benthamite individualism came to dominate nineteenth-century political theory up until the 1880s.

In rejecting conceptions of natural rights, as Barker (1928: 205) tells us, Bentham paradoxically paved the way for increasing the interventionist role of the state in the second half of the nineteenth century. Bentham had advocated two principles which stood in a not altogether consistent relationship to one another. On the one hand, he had advocated the principle, which belongs chiefly to the economic field, of the right of each individual to pursue their own interest; on the other hand, he had urged, in the political sphere, the right and duty of the state to secure the greatest happiness of the greatest number. Time, says Barker, was to emphasize the second of these principles.

John Stuart Mill's writing also assisted in undermining the principle of laissez-faire, and helped prepare the way for new developments in English thought that occurred after 1880. It is Mill, more than any other writer of the nineteenth century, who serves as the bridge from laissez-faire to the idea of social readjustment by the state. In this sense, Mill is very much a transitional force between the individualism of which he remained ultimately a prophet, and the more collectivist solutions introduced at the end of the century. In his hands utilitarianism begins to be less individualistic, and assumes more and more of a social democratic quality. After the 1860s Mill became progressively uneasy with classical liberalism's inability to resolve the social chaos wrought by unregulated capitalism and the growth of collectivist politics. While he remained ultimately committed to the view that the new social and economic contradictions related to poverty, illiteracy and mass unemployment could be resolved within the framework of liberal capitalism, time and again he posed questions which tested the limits of liberalism's theoretical possibilities: how could the freedom of the individual be reconciled with extreme economic inequalities? Should the state play an active role in regard to the distribution of resources? Should the state intervene to remove obstacles which impede the free moral development of its citizens? In *The Principles of Political Economy*, (1965), he draws a distinction between the laws of production and the laws of distribution, and asks whether distribution is not a matter of artificial arrange-

116

ment which might not be regulated by the state (Barker, 1928: 205). In the same volume, Mill proposed taxation of the unearned increment of land, and makes other economic proposals which later were to be adopted by Fabian socialists as the basis of their economic programme. Further, in his *Autobiography* (1924), Mill reveals an ambivalence towards the liberal principle of self-interest when he explains that he looks forward to a time when 'the division of the produce of labour ... will be made by consent of an acknowledged principle of justice' (cited in Barker, 1928: 206). Much more than Bentham, Mill recognized the deeply contradictory nature of liberal democracy in an era of developing capitalism. Notwithstanding the searching nature of his questions and the sometimes radical appearance of his answers or suggestions, Mill remained fundamentally committed to liberal principles, however. He was generally opposed to state interventionism, although after the 1860s he increasingly broached the question as to whether it was not necessary in regard to some areas of social life. One example was his increasing enthusiasm for universal state-provided education as the basis of a liberal democracy on the grounds that neither liberty nor democracy could be practically realized except on the basis of informed choice.

While Mill acknowledged the deeply contradictory basis of liberal capitalism, in the final analysis he believed that the dislocations generated between democracy and inequality were remediable within the context of the market system. Ultimately his resolution to the problem of liberal democracy was, as Stuart Hall (1986: 61) observes, 'a series of compromises and postponements' within the liberal model itself.[3]

By the closing decades of the century, changes in the material economic, political and social context meant that liberalism could not survive without substantial rewriting. New ideals were needed for the new classes that had won the franchise. The central problems were related to the emergence of new class divisions consequent upon the rise of capitalism and a series of related social problems which unchecked capitalism generated.

From the 1880s, liberalism was restructured by a 'series of ad hoc "revisions" spanning five decades' (Hall, 1986: 64), frequently referred to as 'social democratic liberalism' or 'welfare state liberalism'. The major advocates of this new, more collectivist model included the neo-Kantian idealist philosopher, T.H. Green, the Oxford collectivist, L.T. Hobhouse, the 'liberal socialist', J.A. Hobson, the economist, Alfred Marshall and his student, John Maynard Keynes.

Essentially, social democratic liberalism supplemented 'negative' liberty with a 'new' form of 'positive' liberty (Berlin, 1969).[4] After the 1880s, these new liberals were to become progressively 'uneasy' with the extreme divisions in wealth and the widespread existence of poverty and, as a consequence, questioned whether 'freedom from' the coercion and interference of the state should not be matched with 'freedom to' food, shelter, education and a minimum level of security. In this, their analysis developed and extended that stated by John Stuart Mill.

Social democratic liberalism built upon the autonomy and self-fulfilment of the individual. In this it espoused what Macpherson (1977) has termed the developmental model of reason, based upon John Stuart Mill's conception of people as capable of infinitely developing their individual powers and capacities. It also encompassed a belief in each person's ultimate moral worth expressed politically in a broad commitment to egalitarianism. This, says Alison Jaggar (1983: 33), has been translated into the belief that 'all individuals have intrinsic and ultimate value ... their dignity must be reflected in political institutions that do not subordinate any individual to the will or judgement of another'.

This commitment is also linked to a theory of justice which affirms the worth of all and deals with all on the basis of impartial rules. A society's institutions must socialize people with a satisfactory regard for justice. Such a theory requires a certain view of how change occurs in a just society, and this centres around conceptions of rationality and democracy. The liberal conception of justice is rooted in the assumption that persons are autonomous and rational moral agents. In all societies humans must co-operate with each other to produce goods and services, while still having their own private interests, and while still being in competition with each other. There is a need for a theory of justice in order to determine how the social product will be distributed among those who produced it.

Precursors to the welfare state: Green and Hobhouse

In the 1880s the major 'new liberal' to build on the work of Mill was Thomas Hill Green at Oxford. If the great question which dominated political argument in mid-Victorian England concerned the scope and limit of state action, then Green contributed by theorizing the demise of laissez-faire through his reconceptualization of freedom. Green's reconceptualization was not the cause of the demise of laissez-faire, for state legislation in relation to education, employment, health and social issues had been steadily increasing throughout the century. Rather, what Green sought to do was to provide a philosophical defence for an extension of the state's role and to reconcile this with the freedom of individuals to pursue alternative options in life, a value which was central to the classical liberal mind-set. Thus, while classical liberals had defended a concept of 'negative' liberty where the state should do nothing but ensure that each individual is not interfered with or coerced by other human beings, Green added to this that it should also ensure the conditions for 'positive' liberty which related to the general development of personality or 'self-realization'. Green argued that government interference was sometimes necessary to ensure the true aims of liberty, in that its central role should be providing the conditions for all people to realize their positive powers or capacities and in ensuring that each person had an equal opportunity to do what is worthwhile. Unequal liberty through inequalities in the distribution of resources is also unfair, he reasoned, and thus equal opportunity is a desirable good. For Green then, liberty is not just a 'negative' quality which entails a state that leaves individuals to their own devices, but it must involve positively seeking to provide the conditions which enable people to actively realise their powers or capacities.

In Green's view, there was another basis for legitimate state action which the classical liberal had overlooked. While he agreed that the state should seek to protect individuals from *external* obstacles that impinge on their freedom, as was entailed in the negative concept of freedom, he pointed out that many hindrances to a person's freedom are *internal*. These internal hindrances are related to cognitive, emotional or some other developmental obstacle. He argued that it was the state's responsibility to seek to remedy the conditions which impede free action, for example, by seeking to remedy unsanitary housing, poor education and so on. In articulating this notion of positive liberty, Green's theoretical work constituted a decisive break with the past. While, in common with the idealists, he saw the ethical development of individuals as primarily an objective situation whereby a rational person conducts themselves in relation to the 'general will' of the society, for Green a subjective moment is introduced in that each individual freely chooses precisely how to fit themselves within this objective order. Freedom thus involves not merely a lack of restraint or coercion, but in addition a positive power or capacity.

Just as his conception of freedom differed from classical liberalism, so did his conception of society. Rather than represent it as a collection of self-sufficient individuals who contract to protect property on the basis of any natural right, or on the basis of any natural interests or capacities, rights are seen as social and must be maintained by the state. Hence, for Green, the state exists for maintaining the conditions of the good life which can only be lived in common. Hence, Green writes in 'The principles of political obligation' (1890: 353) that there are 'no rights antecedent to society, none that men brought with them into a society which they contracted to form'; and again (1890: 416), 'if the common interest requires it, no right can be alleged against it'. This introduces yet a further qualification to the liberal notion of freedom, for, rather than being the freedom simply to do as one likes, freedom now becomes *an ability to choose between alternative worthwhile courses of action defined in relation to the common good*. The role of the state must be to seek to increase real freedom not by encouraging the fulfillment of aimless individual gratifications, but by allowing a person to develop their powers in worthwhile ways. As he puts it in his famous tract 'Liberal legislation and the freedom of contract' (Green 1888: 371–2):

> When we speak of freedom ... we mean a positive power or capacity of doing or enjoying something worth doing or enjoying ... the mere removal of compulsion, the mere enabling a man to do what he likes, is in itself no contribution to true freedom ... the ideal of true freedom is the maximum of power for all members of human society alike to make the best of themselves.

For Green, and a growing number of followers, the idea that true freedom depends on conditions established by society stands in marked contrast to Spencer and the individualist tradition of classical liberalism. Rather than freedom being opposed to the extension of state activity and legislation, it in fact depends upon it for its maintenance. Thus the state was a prerequisite to liberty. One of Green's students, D.G. Ritchie (1895: 139–40), argued the case in relation to education, maintaining that universal publicly-provided education would extend the freedom of the citizens because it enabled them to develop their powers and capacities.

Another major voice in the 'new liberal' cause was Leonard Trelawny Hobhouse who became known for his interest in social reform in the 1890s. Hobhouse was indebted to both Green's 'social and ethical outlook' as well as to 'the requirements of liberty as set out by Mill' and to 'the Comtist conception of Humanity' (Collini, 1979: 149), which all added to 'the new demand for the extension of collective responsibility and the social control of industrial life' (ibid.: 149). He maintained an uncompromising hostility to Spencer's economic individualism and supplemented Green's original arguments, maintaining that 'self-reliance' and 'self-help' do not eradicate the need for state intervention, for the existence of law enlarges the realm of freedom.

Although influenced by Green's social and ethical outlook, Hobhouse was critical of the influence of Kant and Hegel in Green's work, claiming that it showed insufficient respect for the natural sciences, for knowledge based on experience, or for a general theory of evolution. In addition, Hobhouse was not prepared to reify mind as an ahistorical given in the traditional idealist sense but would treat it as 'an empirical fact within the world of time' and as something largely socially produced in the context of history (Collini, 1979: 157).[5] Hence, although his adherence to the themes of 'self-realization' and 'the common interest' showed traces of idealist influence, they were restated on a realist basis with a strong reference to the empirical sciences.[6]

While liberty was important, it is not a natural right of the person but a 'necessity of society' (Hobhouse, 1911: 123) and as such must be socially provided for. In addition it is only one of several values upon which society should be organized. Hence, 'freedom is only one side of social life. Mutual aid is not less important than mutual forbearance, the theory of collective action no less fundamental than the theory of personal freedom' (ibid.: 124). For Hobhouse, the ultimate end for the foundation of liberalism was his notion of the development of character. Liberalism, as he theorized it, should create as many choices for people as possible to enable the development of character, and the function of the state is 'to secure the conditions upon which mind and character may develop themselves' (ibid.: 158). To do this it is necessary to increase both negative and positive freedom. This entailed both trade union rights to organize as well as the extension of public education. Hobhouse and his friend J.A. Hobson also argued for major changes in existing social structures as being crucial for the securing of freedom. Thus Hobhouse (1911: 100) argues, similarly to Green, that in order to ensure freedom and equality it is necessary to extend the sphere of social control. Thus, he says, 'the "positive" conception of the State which we have now reached not only involves no conflict with the true principle of personal liberty but is necessary to its effective realization' (ibid.: 134).

In his account of the relationship between state action and the freedom of individuals, Hobhouse observes that many forms of collective action do not involve coercion but are in fact motivated by the desire for increased liberty. Hence, just as the public provision of hospitals or of education does not prevent people from employing their own doctors, or setting up their own schools, so the extension of state action in these areas is not necessarily an encroachment upon liberty. In this sense, Hobhouse (1911: 147) maintains that state control is distinct from individual choice:

> There is no true opposition between liberty as such and control as such, for every liberty rests on a corresponding act of control. The true opposition is between the control that cramps the personal life and the spiritual order, and the control that is aimed at securing the external and material conditions of their free and unimpeded development.

The state, for Hobhouse, has a duty to regulate in the interests of the general good – that is, in relation to education, crime, alcoholism and so on – and thus 'liberty and compulsion have complementary functions, and the self-governing State is at once the product and the condition of the self-governing individual' (ibid.: 153–4). Thus it is a question 'not of increasing or diminishing, but of reorganizing, restraints' (ibid.: 154). Hobhouse also favoured systems of progressive taxation, justified on the grounds that the individual, far from being the solitary independent being of classical liberalism, in reality owes more to the community than the early liberals recognized (ibid.: 149). What is frequently taken for granted by individuals is their debt to the community for their personal security and liberty of speech, as well as for the conditions of law and order and so on that permit free action in the pursuit of business and trade. There is a social element in production in that the individual cannot act in business by their unaided efforts. While the individual must provide energy and initiative, society provides conditions and opportunities (ibid.: 191). Hence an appropriately organized educational and economic infrastructure is necessary to maintain and stimulate personal effort (ibid.: 191). It is in this sense that 'the individual cannot stand alone, but that between him and the State there is a reciprocal obligation' (ibid.: 164).

Hobhouse thus supports a view of social democracy which must (1) be democratic, (2) represent the individual, (3) be founded on liberty, and (4) make for the development of personality. In this conception he (Hobhouse, 1911: 74–5) disputes the notion of the 'self-interested chooser' of classical liberalism as the basis of a market conception of the person, noting that: 'Men are neither so intelligent nor so selfish. They are swayed by emotion and by impulse, and both for good and for evil they will lend enthusiastic support to courses of public policy from which, as individuals, they have nothing to gain.' Through his conception of 'effective freedom' (ibid.: 139–40), Hobhouse advances an 'applied ethics' whereby he sees liberty as being commensurate with power and thus depending on equality.

Twentieth-century welfarism

After the First World War and the first Great Depression, the intervention of the democratic state into aspects of social, political and economic life came to be seen as necessary to mitigate the worst effects of a market economy. Like the 'negative' freedom from state intervention espoused by the classicists, 'positive' freedom (or intervention) became the philosophic justification for the dominant economic organization of the time. Most liberals accepted that the modern state with its managed (corporate) economy should also be charged with the task of guaranteeing a minimum standard of living and education for all. Accordingly, as Barry (1987: 2) states, it was no accident that the role of the state came to be:

> further extended into the interstices of economic and social life … . It was assumed that without the state people would be helpless victims of the 'blind' and unpredictable forces of the market. Furthermore, it seemed 'natural' that the state's welfare role should be extended into education and health. The rationale for this was not merely the relief of suffering by the creation of more equal opportunities. 'Social justice', where the term refers to the correction of a pure market determination of income so as to produce some desired social 'outcome', became perhaps the most predominant feature on the masthead of the new consensus.

Under the guiding rubric of 'consensus' the modern state at various junctures was still popularly expected to refrain from intrusion into the private lives of individuals, and from the imposition of moral values that might threaten personal autonomy. Contemporary liberalism emphasizes the preservation of civil liberties as well as the personal right to freedom from intervention.

The common view of politics which came to prevail under social democratic liberalism is that of its nature as a problem-solving method. Individuals, through interest group membership are thought to be able to utilize such processes. This has been accompanied by a view of the state in social democratic and moderately collectivist political thought, as benign. This conception is in turn linked to a theory of justice which sees that change occurs in a just society as a result of rational and democratic processes. These are thought to automatically respect the equal right of all to participate in deliberations about collective decisions and the equal right of all to have their interests fairly considered (Strike, 1989: 38–9). Rational deliberation about social choices requires criteria of choice which are impartial, universal and rationally accepted. This is necessary for effective social reproduction. The coercive features of the state and its role in the maintenance of structural inequalities have been downplayed by a theory and practice which assumes it to be the purveyor of welfare, and general beneficence (as opposed to the embodiment of legalized force or oppressive conditions). This social democratic view of the state has some affinities with the views of the conservative right, who believe in the preservation of a strong state to ensure maintenance of the social equilibrium. The right's conception of the breadth of state activity is, however, more limited and their use of coercive means more extensive. This portrayal is intimately connected to the ideological functions of the right's conceptions of democracy and the legitimation of the state within an entire social and political order.

In the twentieth century, John Maynard Keynes's economic theories served western nation states as the official policy discourse for the management of the economy. Keynes was the apostle of economic management in relation to unemployment, growth and equality. His central contribution to economic management was to reinterpret the role of government away from laissez-faire towards acceptance of a greater role for the state. In his essay 'The end of laissez-faire', written in 1926, he advances a consistent view of the role of the state. Drawing from Jeremy Bentham, he maintains that 'the chief task of economists at this hour is to distinguish afresh the *Agenda* of government from the *Non-Agenda*; and the companion task of politics is to devise a form of government within democracy which shall be capable of accomplishing the Agenda' (Keynes, 1931a: 313). Although acknowledging a debt to Bentham, he is careful to distance himself from Bentham's support for laissez-faire, maintaining his own commitment to the 'mixed economy', where the agenda and non-agenda would be determined, not in advance, but by the situation in hand. His only guidance consisted in the observation that: 'The important thing for government is not to do things which individuals are doing already, or to do them a little better or a little worse, but to do those things which at present are not being done at all' (Keynes, 1931a: 317).

Central to Keynes's approach was advocacy for *demand management*, exercised through forms of public planning as a means of regulating the economy by skilful management of fiscal and monetary policy. Intervention was to involve being prepared to run budget surpluses and deficits, as well as co-operation between government departments and with other governments and international agencies, such as the International Monetary Fund (IMF). Such ideas were to inform all of Keynes's economic prescriptions. Whether in response to unemployment or economic fluctuations, Keynes recommended a greater emphasis on fiscal than on monetary policy, and a greater role for economic management rather than market forces. His general attitude to public planning is made evident in 'The end of laissez-faire' (Keynes, 1931a: 317–18):

> Many of the greatest economic evils of our time are the fruits of risk, uncertainty, and ignorance. It is because particular individuals, fortunate in situation or in abilities, are unable to take advantage of uncertainty and ignorance, and also because for the reason big business is often a lottery, that great inequalities of wealth come about; and these same factors are also the cause of the Unemployment of Labour, or the disappointment of reasonable business expectations, and of the impairment of efficiency and production. Yet the cure lies outside the operation of individuals … . I believe that the cure for these things is partly to be sought in the deliberate control of the currency and of credit by a central institution, and partly in the collection and dissemination on a grand scale of data relating to the business situation, including the full publicity, by law if necessary, of all business facts which it is useful to know. These measures would involve society in exercising directive intelligence through some appropriate organ of action over many of the inner intricacies of private business, yet it would leave private initiative and enterprise unhindered.

Various forms of intervention were seen by him as indispensable to monetary management, especially controls on foreign and domestic investment, public works, the state direction over investment decisions and capital development. Such reflections as these, says Keynes (ibid.: 319) are 'directed towards possible improvements in the technique of modern capitalism by the agency of collective action'. Although acutely aware of the perversities of markets, he indicates his support for a free enterprise market economy, maintaining (ibid.: 319) that: 'There is nothing in these recommendations which is seriously incompatible with … the essential characteristics of capitalism … . For my part, I think capitalism, wisely managed, can probably be made more efficient for attaining economic ends than any alternative system yet in sight.' On this basis he rejects both liberal individualism and state socialist solutions, arguing (ibid.: 331) that the tasks for the future: 'Must be to decentralize and devolve wherever we can, and in particular to establish semi-autonomous corporations and organs of administration to which duties of government, new and old, will be entrusted without however impairing the democratic principle of the ultimate Sovereignity of parliament.' Keynes (ibid.: 313) then declares: 'That progress lies in the growth and the recognition of semi-autonomous bodies within the State – bodies whose criterion of action within their own field is solely the public good as they understand it, and from whose deliberations motives of private advantage are excluded.'

A further important strand of Keynes's thought was the need for international management. Although he supported individual governments maintaining sovereignty over the management of their affairs, he foresaw the management of each country's affairs as becoming increasingly difficult unless forms of international regulation and co-ordination were developed. His enthusiasm for such developments was articulated in the 1920s, and he was to be an influential voice at Bretton Woods, lobbying for the establishment of the IMF (Stiglitz, 2002: 11). In the late 1930s and 1940s his economic theories were to become influential in America, being spread by economists such as Alvin Hansen, Seymour Harris and Paul Samuelson. The appeal of Keynes to young American economists, says Robert Skidelsky (1978: 82), lay partly in his political radicalism. In 1938, an economic manifesto was produced by seven Harvard and Tufts economists proposing, 'a vigorous expansion of the public sector of the economy, sharp increases in the progression of the tax system, indefinite increases in the public debt, enlargement of old age benefits, assistance programmes for health and education, and massive commitments to housing and urban development' (Skidelsky, 1978: 83).

Whether the radical potential of Keynes's views and theories accurately reflect Keynes's own position on the political spectrum is a matter for some debate (Cranston, 1978). Although he fervently disassociated himself from all forms of state socialism, including Marxist socialism, and maintained a basic commitment to core liberal ideals,[7] as Maurice Cranston (1978: 101) observes, one of the main charges brought against Keynes was 'that he vitiated the theoretical purity of liberalism by introducing ... elements of socialism'. Cranston maintains that Keynes did introduce socialistic ideas to liberalism, seeing them as an extension of liberalism. Further, says Cranston, he was entitled to do so. Certainly, Keynes did apply the term 'socialism' to his own ideas from time to time. In 1924, he described himself as a champion of 'true socialism' (Cranston, 1978: 113). By this he clearly intended an ideal of 'liberal socialism', more in the spirit of Hobhouse, which he more accurately expressed in 1939, in a contribution to the *New Statesman*:

> The question is whether we are prepared to move out of the nineteenth century *laissez faire* into the era of liberal socialism, by which I mean a system where we can act as an organised community for common purposes and to promote social and economic justice, whilst respecting and protecting the individual – his freedom of choice, his faith, his mind and its expression, his enterprise and his property. (Cited in Cranston, 1978: 112)

The Keynesian welfare state consensus

There are several historical events which are significant to the international rise in the orthodoxy of the Keynesian economic doctrines and their socially ameliorative, state welfare policies. These are the Great Depression and the economic lessons learnt by governments through their participation in the two world wars.

For many, the collapse of the international financial system and the ensuing Depression cemented the horror of the realities of unemployment and destitution. This collapse followed the 1929 stock market crash. The contraction of credit led to a deflationary spiral which plunged the world into acute depression and led to a resurgence of protectionism and militarism which culminated in the Second World War. Moreover, the economic events of this time were not consistent with what the dominant neoliberal, anti-statist economic policies, which had dominated western economies, suggested should have happened.

Neoclassical, pre-Keynesian economics had underpinned liberal states for five decades after 1880. As a discipline it eventually narrowed its focus to that of scientific deductivism; primarily concerned with questions on the logic of choice for the 'self-interested, utility-maximizing and hence rational individual' (Gamble, 1986: 26). In the quest for generalizable hypotheses and universality, economics abandoned the prior analyses of capitalism, in particular historical and institutional contexts which had been so important to classical political economy. It focused on the relation between the price system and the co-ordination of a complex division of labour, and this had the effect of allowing capitalism to be presented as a rational and socially beneficial system (ibid.: 27). Within neoclassicism the reasoning underlying the relationship between value and price was entirely circular. Consequently, such theories fully legitimated the uneven distribution of surplus value, and the inequities which existed between capital and labour. The political and social nature of such inequities was never part of their problematic.

As the economic and social problems in capitalist democracies multiplied, the argument for laissez-faire and economic individualism became more difficult to sustain, and state interventionism came to be seen as the answer to the expansive problems which markets seemed unable to solve. The Beveridge Report, the Butler Education Act of 1944 and moves towards the establishment of a National Health Service established the conditions for the 'consensus of 1945' (Addison, 1975; Hill, 1993: 20). The Second World War had reinforced the lessons of the First; hence it was thought that the reconstruction of the international monetary system on a more secure basis so as to address the inter-war failure to free up credit and liberalize trade, would be central to post-war reconstruction. A strengthened accumulation process, it was thought, would facilitate the liberalization of world trade and secure the social and economic conditions to ensure the political incorporation of the working classes (Clarke, 1988: 150–3). Many western leaders assumed that the construction of a liberal world order based on the growth of extra-national credit would facilitate the pursuit of national expansionary policies. This incorporation lay at the basis of Keynesianism, although there was a sense, as the neo-Marxist O'Connor (1984: 201) maintained that 'the theoretical premises and goals which were structured into economic policy were stamped by class antagonisms'. Certainly from the perspective of the 1970s

126

and 1980s, the content of Keynesian economic policy can be seen to be shaped by, and embroiled in, the political class struggles between labour and capital, that manifested themselves in strikes and other forms of disruption throughout advanced western nations.

The publication in 1936 of Keynes's, *The General Theory of Employment, Interest and Money*, offered an alternative explanation for the economic realities of the depression, and a vision through which the above strategies could be achieved. Thus Keynes came to be seen as the architect of the reconstituted international monetary system. Keynesian economic policy-making sought to overcome the limits of classical liberal orthodoxy through the abandonment of its most cherished principles. The gold standard, which Keynes saw as inflationary due to the gold reserves held by the USA, was to be replaced by a managed system of international money and credit. Balanced budgets were to be replaced by discretionary fiscal policies. Its basic aim was to reconcile the sustained accumulation of domestic productive capital with the equivalent on a global scale. This would be done on the basis of a rising mass consumption and the expansion of international credit. Internally orchestrated demand-management policies were predicated on the assumption that they would assure full employment and economic growth within a mixed economic system. The excess revenues generated through the accumulation process and internal and external market dynamics would be redistributed by the state to meet the broader social and economic demands of the electorate. For neo-classicists a regime of free competition was understood to tend, in a normal state, toward a situation of full employment. Keynes argued strenuously that the system was not self-regulating, and that it exhibited a tendency towards subnormal activity (unemployment) while frequently remaining in a state of equilibrium. Hence the need for interventions through appropriate fiscal strategies or economic engineering. For Keynesians, the economic and social priority was full employment as opposed to the neoclassicists' economic priority of low inflation.

The 'historic compromise'

One of the main features of Keynesian social democracy was the 'accord' or 'historic compromise' which it sought to institute between capital and labour. Workers abandoned their calls for socialist reconstruction and their demands for structural change, and accepted government policies and the bargaining and welfare mechanisms the state set about to provide for them. Indeed it can be argued that most, if not all, twentieth-century bourgeois economic and social thought reflected this central compromise, entailing 'natural rights individualism and utilitarianism, property rights and human rights, liberalism and welfarism, capital and labour – a compromise which became increasingly embedded in economic policy' (O'Connor, 1984: 201).

127

Offe (1984: 194–5) maintains that this compromise shifted the central issue underlying class conflict from that of control of the mode of production, to the volume of its distribution and growth. It was based on the underlying belief that the interests of both workers and capital need to be secured in order to secure the interests of the entire system (the accumulative process and everyone involved in it). State welfarism thus diffused the revolutionary potential of the working classes. Personal needs were fulfilled collectively and were taken out of the realm of class and industrial conflict, 'leaving no room for fundamental issues and conflicts over the nature of political economy'. In theory, as Offe (ibid.: 194–5) claims, Keynesianism sought to promote 'active' economic policies which would: 'stimulate and regularize economic growth; the "tax dividend" resulting from that growth allows for the extension of welfare state programmes; and, at the same time, continued economic growth limits the extent to which welfare state provisions (such as unemployment benefits) are actually claimed.' The basis of these 'active' and 'stimulating policies' was the fundamental intent to expand productivity, production, and profits. O'Connor's (1973: 138) view is that this kind of social insurance was not primarily insurance for workers, but a definite kind of insurance for capitalists.

The enactment of policies underlaid by a Keynesian problematic resulted in the modification of the basic foundations of capitalism. The growth in state intervention ensured that internal governments became responsible for the general economic condition of their economies. The regulation of internal industries through monitoring agencies or most often through direct public ownership, occurred in most western democracies. This was achieved through the provision of various bureaucratic rules and legal regulations, guiding commercial transactions, as well as through the establishment of capital incentives for the production of certain goods and services, the provision of welfare services and the transfer, through the tax-system, of private income. In Britain, Australia and New Zealand, the state played an extremely active role through its Keynesian inspired, organized and ritualized intervention into civil society. It was this extensive intervention in the form of a strongly centralized educational bureaucracy, working closely with teacher organizations, which was attacked so vehemently in the neoliberal challenge to that settlement in the 1980s.

Thus, Keynesian economic principles not only underpinned economic policy, they also provided an inherently politicized 'vision' of the economy which came to embrace 'the ideological expression of institutionalized forms of class expectations of rising wages, increasing standards of public provision, and employment opportunities which could not simply be discarded at will'. (Clarke, 1988: 285). While this is undoubtedly true, Tomlinson (1988: 72–87) argues that the ideological ascendancy of Keynesianism and its collectivist policy implications was always much greater than their domination in practice. By this he means that redistributive imperatives should not overshadow the primacy of the basic market mechanisms and their facilitation of the privatized accumulation of surplus value. As Offe (1984: 195) states, the central rationale of liberal democracy has always been the reproduction of capitalism even though the welfare state can be shown to 'partially dispel the motives and reasons for social conflict while making the existence of wage labour more acceptable by eliminating part of the risk that results from the imposition of the commodity form onto labour'. Hence, the necessity to unpack and critically examine the ideological rationales which permeated Keynesian policies and the realities of their implementation. Although the pervasive view of the state throughout this century saw it as primarily benign, Keynesian policies contributed to this through the implementation of welfare measures and through their maintenance of the hegemony of liberal ideology. Thus they downplayed the state's coercive features and its embodiment as an institution of legalized force; and as the institutionalization of a multitude of power relations. In education, the belief in access and equality of opportunity for all constituted part of the democratic belief in the state's provision of education. It downplayed education's selective function and its role in social reproduction while legitimating the public welfare role of the state and its role in maintaining the balance of social relations.

The development of the welfare state in New Zealand

The final section of this chapter sets out a brief discussion of the main features of the historical emergence of the Keynesian social democratic welfare state in New Zealand. This is pertinent because the economic and social imperatives which underlaid this consensus-based liberal state were embodied in all its policy prescriptions, particularly in education, and have manifested themselves in policy documents produced at various junctures throughout its history. New Zealand, therefore, offers an exemplary case of Keynesian welfarism, both in its development following the economic depression of the 1930s and in its dramatic collapse with the advent of neoliberalism in the 1980s.

New Zealand, during the latter part of the nineteenth century and the first two decades of the twentieth, has been described as a 'classic example of the result of British nineteenth century laissez-faire economic policies and actions' (Sutch, 1966: 165). During the colonial period, most controlling economic interests were based in Britain. The New Zealand state, while supporting these interests, gradually assumed a minimal role in the provision of welfare and social security. Gradually there was an acceptance that the state had a 'positive' role in relation to social security. A conception of the welfare state derived from Britain, as well as a successful pattern of state intervention, forged at both a theoretical and practical level a viable role for the state aimed at civilizing rather than abolishing capitalism.

In response to the decade of depression that the country had been experiencing, the 1934 and 1935 conferences of the New Zealand Labour Party endorsed the strengthening of its economic policies and the 'fostering of economic interests' became part of its election manifesto. Upon its election in 1935, and spurred on by the Keynesian thesis, (particularly the British example of its implementation) the Labour Party, which was an alliance of small farmers, public servants, manufacturers and the working classes, sought to improve and strengthen the economy. It did this by 'building into it a consistently strong demand for goods and services; guaranteed prices for farmers; full rates of pay for all; higher pensions and new benefits; housing as essentially a state activity; and expanding public works' (Sutch, 1966: 177).

Consistent with the direction of growing state involvement in the social and economic life of the nation, a more complete model of the welfare state was erected by the first Labour government from 1936. The legislation introduced between 1936 and 1939 provided guarantees of employment and income, expansions of social security and increased access to social services and support systems, including education, health, housing and social work (Trlin, 1977: vi). These policies were based upon the philosophy that people should be able to help themselves in conditions of human dignity. In this sense, the foundations of the welfare state in New Zealand were the same as they were in Britain, as laid down by Beveridge and Keynes.

Thus, New Zealand's first Labour government, following its election in 1935, embarked upon a massive programme of social reconstruction. The right to waged work was recognized and relief jobs were abolished. Cuts in wages and salaries were restored and old age pensions were increased. The numbers of state servants were increased and many were employed in large-scale public works projects. Educational training programmes were restarted as were large-scale interventions into banking activities. Housing also became a public utility through the provision of state homes. The 1938 Social Security Act laid the foundations of a universal health care system. Manufacturing received considerable support, particularly in import substituting areas. A guaranteed price system for farmers was cemented into place to protect against the fluctuating British market. The Reserve Bank was removed from private shareholding so that one of its main functions became the implementation of government fiscal policy. There was a general political and economic commitment to industrialization, together with the goal of full employment, which it was claimed made possible the dignified self-help of every member of the community (Rosenberg, 1977: 53).

Central to New Zealand's unique version of social democratic liberalism, has been a strong political allegiance to egalitarianism. This has been pivotal to the growth and development of the nation. Historically, egalitarianism in New Zealand has come to signify, not equality of position or outcome, but access or opportunity for all, regardless of individual or social impediment. This popular belief, embodied in Keynesian policies, has masked the structural inequalities and contradictions within society which the school is strongly implicated in reproducing. Egalitarianism has subsumed notions of the 'possessive individual' and of personal responsibility for social success or failure, ensuring that membership of broader social groupings has been ignored in liberal analyses of the nature of New Zealand society. Thus, as James and Saville-Smith (1989: 10) have argued, egalitarianism has fostered:

> a view of society in which all are equally eligible to compete for society's rewards, irrespective of their birth or social position. The availability of this opportunity means that it is up to individuals to achieve. Such an understanding of equality is quite compatible with visible inequalities. It reinforces the idea that those inequalities are due to an individual's character or activities not to the organisation of social life.

Accordingly, the social and political milieu in which educational provision has emerged in New Zealand, as in Britain, has been framed against the backdrop of the 'myth' of equality of educational opportunity, an integral part of the ideology of egalitarianism. This myth, based on a belief in 'access' for all, was a product of nineteenth century liberal thinking, and is underpinned by the theory of meritocracy; the belief that intelligence quotient (IQ) plus effort, equals merit (Young, 1961). Essentially, it has ensured that the school has come to be perceived as one of the major avenues through which equality of opportunity within an egalitarian society can be achieved. This perception comprises one of the major ideological planks of Keynesian welfarism.

During a period of post-war economic prosperity, the egalitarian myth was relatively easily sustained within New Zealand. This meant the continual expansion of state resources directed into an ever-expanding system in order to maintain equal access to it. By the early 1970s, however, signs of economic strain were beginning to show. In order to sustain its expanding programme of Keynesian intervention and regulation, the New Zealand government began to incur considerable overseas debt. Continuing policies of deficit borrowing, combined with a long tradition of industrial protectionism, saw the beginnings of an emerging fiscal crisis that would reach its zenith in the mid-1980s.

However, even during the post-war period of relative prosperity, there were signs of the economic problems that lay ahead. In 1957–58, for example, the returns on wool, dairy produce and meat prices all fell simultaneously so that the total purchasing power of New Zealand exports fell by one-fifth. This meant that the deficit for this period was 54 million pounds (Sutch, 1966: 423). Wilkes (1989: 130–2) argues that this drop in revenues is the point at which the beginning of the fiscal crisis can be discerned. Terms of trade fell significantly again in 1966 which was of major significance, because growth in the international economy, at that point, was based on the exchange of manufactured goods. New Zealand was unable to participate and its income declined accordingly. Roper (1997: 3–4) claims that the turning point for the New Zealand economy coincided with the world recession that followed the oil shocks of the early 1970s. Thus, 1974 'separates an epoch of unprecedented growth and prosperity from an epoch of stagnation, declining real incomes, and rising unemployment' (ibid.: 3). Because of its size, its failure to diversify into other production areas, and the large numbers of its labour force tied up in a productive sector that no longer retained its previous global advantages, the New Zealand economy in the 1970s fell into serious economic decline. By the early 1980s, overseas borrowing had reached unsustainable levels and a two-year freeze on wages and prices became the final failed intervention by government in the economy. Keynesian solutions appeared to be no longer working.

Most analyses of the circumstances surrounding the collapse of the New Zealand welfare state in the 1980s emphasize the declining terms of trade and the precarious location of New Zealand in the global economy, as major contributing factors in the emerging fiscal crisis (Easton, 1980; Jesson, 1989a; Wilkes, 1989). There were, however, different explanations put forward by government policy analysts and advisers. In particular, the monetarists in the Treasury argued that increasing government intervention was to blame; whereas the Keynesians would argue that the comparative economic decline was due to structural problems combined with a relatively high population growth rate, observing that while New Zealand's economic growth rate was low in historical terms, it compared favourably with that of other countries (Roper, 1997: 9). In an earlier analysis, Roper (1991: 46) argued that the economic crisis of the 1980s was multifaceted and multidimensional, involving both internal and external factors. In his view (ibid.: 48) moreover:

> While external factors have been a major determinant of the economic crisis, internal factors have also been significant and so a sophisticated explanation must investigate both the specific configuration of New Zealand's integration into the world economy ('external factors') and the long term tendencies and recurrent crises of New Zealand's capitalist development ('internal factors').

Thus, it is the particular interplay of various internal and external factors inherent in the combination of Keynesianism and state welfarism, which have constituted a nexus of social, political and economic determinants of the New Zealand fiscal crisis of the 1980s. This crisis was significant not only for its economic and political ramifications, but also because it laid the ideological foundation for a massive change in the nature of the mode of accumulation and the nature of the entire social formation. In 1984, a newly elected Labour government commenced a systematic dismantling of the New Zealand welfare state under the ideological banner of neoliberalism. This radical transition from Keynesian welfarism to neoliberalism would bring the differences between these two forms of liberalism into stark contrast. In the next chapter we examine these differences and explore the theoretical bases and policy implications of neoliberalism.

Notes

1   Keynes is quoting from Burke.
2   What is called the 'over-education' controversy is an indication that while some education for the working classes was deemed necessary to secure peace, too much education was held to be dangerous. As Lyon Playfair, one of the leading advocates of the technical education movement noted in 1870: 'There is still ... a lurking though unexpressed fear that the lower orders may be too highly educated, and there is a sentiment, the offspring of that fear, that the state has done its duty when it imparts the rudiments of knowledge' (cited in Selleck, 1968: 15).
3   See also on the topic, Antony Flew (1975), 'J.S. Mill: socialist or libertarian'. It is frequently claimed that Mill's writing became more 'socialistic' under the influence of Harriet Taylor, and especially after the 1860s. While there is a sense in which he certainly became more progressively orientated in relation to social-democratic and socialist concerns during his later life, his commitments were never without qualifications of the sort that we have noted.
4   The distinction between 'negative' and 'positive' liberty was introduced by Isaiah Berlin (1969) in his famous article 'Two concepts of liberty'. It concerns the distinction, on the one hand, between the absence of external constraint, or absence of coercion (negative liberty) and, on the other hand, refers to a form of 'self-mastery' only effective through active state intervention. It concerns the ability to make decisions, to realize opportunities, to exercise agency (positive liberty). As Berlin (1969: 121–2) says, negative liberty 'is involved in the answer to the question "What is the area within which the subject ... is or should be left to do or to be what he is able to do or be, without interference by other persons?"' Positive liberty is 'involved in the answer to the question "What or who is the source of control or interference that can determine someone to do, or be, this rather than that?"'
5   Much of Hobhouse's thinking on the self is evident in his writings on biological social theory, excellently summarized by Collini (1979: ch. 6).
6   Various others, including Samuel Alexander (1859–1938) had sought 'ways to transpose some of the philosophy of Bradley and Bosanquet onto a realist basis', which as Collini (1979: 165) notes is a 'passable description of Hobhouse's philosophical aspirations of the time'.
7   See 'Am I a liberal?', in Keynes (1931b).

7

The Ascendancy of Neoliberalism

Neoliberalism constitutes a revival and continuation of earlier liberal perspectives that developed from the seventeenth century and continued right up into and through the nineteenth century. Marginalized by the ethical qualifications of the 'new' welfare state liberals of the late nineteenth century, and by the economics of Keynesian demand management in the twentieth century, the earliest writings of the neoliberals of the twentieth century showed all the hallmarks of a displaced embattled minority fighting a rearguard action for political survival.

The main purpose of this chapter is to elaborate the central elements of neoliberalism through an articulation of the principal intellectual and philosophical foundations. After having completed this, we shall provide an overview of the central effects of neoliberalism on social and educational developments in western nation-states, paying particular attention to changes in relation to culture, the self, knowledge, teaching and learning, and research.

The 'new right'

The concept of the 'new right' is closely related to neoliberalism and for the purposes of this analysis will be treated as essentially equivalent. To the extent that there is a difference, the concept of 'new right' tends to adhere more to the groups or interests, while that of neoliberalism has tended to be used to refer to the discursive philosophical, economic and political doctrines so supported. With reference to any discussion of the concept of 'new right', there are several issues that should be clarified at the outset, however. The meaning of this term is contentious both among its proponents and its critics. Many writers (Apple, 1982a; 1982b; 1996; 2000; 2001; Ball, 1990b; 1994; Kenway, 1990; King, 1987) have used it to refer to an alliance of interests comprising market liberals and political conservatives. While this is accurate in terms of describing the coalition of forces that have supported neoliberal policies within western nation-states, it is important to note that the precise alliance of interests differed in different countries. Thus in Britain, like

America, there were distinct groupings of market liberals, as well as 'old' and 'new' conservatives (Ball, 1990b) that lent general support to 'new right' policies, while in New Zealand there was more cohesive support around neoliberalism as a purely economic and administrative set of concerns.

Of the discursive monopoly the 'new right' has attained in Australia, Kenway (1990: 169) argues that it has drawn upon various ideological formations, modes of analysis and theoretical frameworks in order to cement its hegemony. These constitute an uneasy blend of conservatism, liberalism (leading into libertarianism) and right-wing economics. The former expresses itself in a concern for the preservation of authority, traditional values and institutions and the expectation that the state will protect these. Liberalism manifests itself in a belief in the sanctity of the market and the more recent opposition to any mechanisms thought to interfere with the 'freedom, prosperity and progress' supposedly guaranteed by it. Right-wing economics has advanced technical explanations which have incorporated these viewpoints into state policy, de-legitimating Keynesian welfarism and sponsoring the conditions for a crisis in education policy.

As for past usages of the concept 'new right', there are some differences amongst writers. Early writers, such as King (1987) and Barry (1987) argue, in a way similar to the position that we adopt, that it primarily constitutes a form of economic and political liberalism. In this sense, the 'newness' of the 'new right' entails a comparative reference to policies and practices which bear a resemblance to the principles and precepts of 'old' economic and political liberalism and, hence, constitutes a revival of it. Gary McCulloch (1991: 74) criticizes use of the concept on the grounds that to represent it as a coherent ideology disguises its internal contradictions. 'If the "new right" is seen as monolithic, homogeneous, and stable' he argues, 'it becomes unnecessary to access such aspects of change and development, internal conflicts, or competing social and ideological constituencies. For McCulloch (ibid.: 74), use of the concept constrains analysis of a complex area. In his view, '(t)he view of the "new right" as an abstraction, as a reified set of ideas, effectively cuts it off from historical analysis, it arises fully formed'.

While it is important to guard against the danger of attributing too much cohesion or unity to a particular group, it is not necessary, we would argue, to treat the 'new right' as a monolithic entity. Within western nations, the concept represents a broad alliance of liberal and conservative interests. While it is important not to exaggerate the cohesiveness of such alliances, the concept nevertheless serves as a useful proxy indicator to characterize those groups that support an expanded market and reduced public provision. Such a view is consistent with the conception put forward by Levitas (1986: dustcover): 'The New Right, however, is not a monolithic entity. The term may be applied to a wide range of ideologies and groups which support free market, anti-welfarist, or socially authoritative policies.'

Thompson (1990: 1) cautions against exaggerating the degree of cohesiveness as well. For him the 'new right' is a more expansive concept, describing:

> a particular set of discursive propositions and policy recommendations, and the political movement that articulates these. However, it is far from being a homogeneous discursive or political entity. Indeed, there are probably as many new rights as there are new right authors, and it can become difficult to pin down the exact limits to what is legitimate to include under the umbrella term of the 'new right'.

Thompson maintains that on the spectrum of conventional left–right political categories, the term indicates a position further to the right than most other forms of conservativism, but essentially this, like his general definition cited above, is an oversimplification. Most of the basic ideas underlying 'new right' doctrines are not new; it is their contemporary interpretation which is. If the 'new right' comprises a cluster of political groupings within western nation states, the basic principles – a belief in competitive individualism, an ideological representation of a 'reduced' role for the state and a maximization of the market – emanate from classical political and economic liberalism.

'New right' liberalism is a restatement of the basic tenets of such a position, in a version that has come to be known as 'economic rationalism' (Marginson, 1992; 1993; 1997) or 'neoliberalism' (Burchell, 1991; 1996; Foucault, 1992; Olssen, 1996b; 1998; 2000; 2002a; Olssen and Morris-Matthews, 1997; Peters and Marshall, 1990; Rose, 1993; 1996). Notwithstanding the important differences that we have discerned above, for most purposes the terms 'new right', 'economic rationalism' and 'neoliberalism', are interchangeable and, unless it is theoretically necessary to do so, we will not attempt to impose distinctions between them in this study. Our preference, however, is for the term 'neoliberalism' in that it focuses attention more on the discursive (philosophical, political and economic) doctrines than on the groups and factions that have tended to support them.

Defining neoliberalism

Notwithstanding a clear similarity between neo- and classical liberal discourse, the two cannot be seen as identical. Whereas classical liberalism represents a negative conception of state power, in that the individual was taken as an object to be freed from the interventions of the state, neoliberalism has come to represent a positive conception of the state's role in creating the appropriate market by providing the conditions, laws and institutions necessary for its operation. In classical liberalism the individual is characterized as having an autonomous human nature and can practise freedom. In neoliberalism the state seeks to create an individual that is an enterprising and competitive entrepreneur. In the classical model the theoretical aim of the state was to limit and minimize its role based upon postulates which included (1) universal egoism (the self-interested individual), (2) invisible hand theory which dictated that the interests of the individual were also the interests of society as a whole, and (3) the political maxim of laissez-faire. In the shift from classical liberalism to neoliberalism, then, there is a further element added, for such a shift involves a change in subject position from *homo economicus*, who naturally behaves out of self-interest, and is relatively detached from the state, to *manipulatable man* (an obviously gendered construct, see O'Neill, 1996), who is created by the state and who is continually encouraged to be 'perpetually responsive'. It is not that the conception of the self-interested subject is replaced or done away with by the new ideals of neoliberalism, but that in an age of universal welfare, the perceived possibilities of slothful indolence create necessities for new forms of vigilance, surveillance, performance appraisal and control generally. In this new model, the state has taken it upon itself to keep us all up to the mark. The state will see to it that each one of us makes a continuous 'enterprise of ourselves' (Gordon, 1991: 44) in what seems to be a process of 'govern(ing) without governing' (Rose, 1993: 298).

There are, as indicated above, important differences among the various advocates of neoliberalism. There are distinctions between consequentialist and rights-based neoliberalism (Barry, 1983) as well as many variations in relation to theories of the market and the state. Later in this chapter, we shall distinguish a 'libertarian' subgroup within neoliberalism as well. The common basis shared by neoliberals is more important than the differences between them, however. Some of the most widely known neoliberals are Frederich Hayek, Milton Friedman, Robert Nozick, James Buchanan, Gary Becker and Oliver Williamson. All share the basic commitment to individual liberty, and lobby for a 'reduced' state. All can be said to embrace one central defining feature that is based on 'a qualitative shift in both policy and ideology against government intervention, which was condemned as collectivist, socialist and economically misguided' (Levitas, 1986: 3).

Coupled with this shift, is a second political and economic tenet; the celebration of, and assumed superiority of, market mechanisms to ensure economic prosperity, the maximization of individual freedom and its provision of a base for all social interactions. Market forces should be allowed to operate as widely as possible within a social order that is understood to be capable of almost total self-regulation. There is thought to be no need for state intervention other than to minimize market distortions or offset certain dysfunctions. Indeed, within education, such intervention has been blamed by the 'new right' for a multitude of inadequacies.

Thus a model of life supposedly played out against the backdrop of the market is all-pervasive in neoliberalism. Every social transaction is conceptualized as entrepreneurial, to be carried out purely for personal gain. The market introduces competition as the structuring mechanism through which resources and status are allocated efficiently and fairly. The 'invisible hand' of

137

the market is thought to be the most efficient way of sorting out which competing individuals get what. Even though it is assumed to be an autonomous, apolitical and gender-neutral mechanism, it is not independent of the values and customs of those who participate in it. The centrality of the market is one of the central and distinctive features of the neoliberalism's theoretical and programmatic propositions.

Within the neoliberal model, then, the state seeks to assure the conditions for 'perpetual human responsiveness' and 'flexibility' that are advanced most forcefully in twentieth-century theories such as 'Monetarism', 'Human Capital Theory', 'Public Choice Theory', 'Agency Theory', 'Transaction Cost Economics' and the revival of various forms of 'managerialism'. These theories are variants of neoclassical liberal thought and share many of its major presuppositions:

- that subjects are economically self-interested;
- that competitiveness is a mechanism for quality and efficiency;
- that governments should rule from a distance through devolved management;
- that there should be a reduction of state services through privatization via user charges, contracting out, vouchers, and so on;
- that individuals are rational optimizers and are the best judges of their own interests and needs;
- that a 'flexible', that is, deregulated labour market provides the same opportunities for people to utilize their skills and therefore optimize their life goals;
- that free trade and open economies are required prerequisites for economic growth; and
- that tariffs, subsidies and controls on foreign investments or markets should be abolished.

In neoliberalism, although its advocates subscribe in principle to a 'reduced' state, it is a reduction of 'bureaucracy' but not 'control'. For neoliberals, then, the role of the state is now seen as that of the 'mediator' and 'instigator' of the successful operation of the market. In this, its role is to neither promote social justice nor develop public monopolies. In this model ethics becomes a matter for the private individual, it is no longer a concern of the state. Thus, the assertion of this new morality not only entails a revised conception of the individual, but a revised conception of the nature and process of democracy, of the role of the state, and by implication, of the policy-making process and its outcomes. State support for egalitarian policy initiatives is thought to be an attack on 'enterprise and endeavour', 'self-reliance', 'responsible self-management' and 'personal sacrifice' (Keat, 1991; Peters, 1992).

138

The doctrine of monetarism

The historical conjuncture of forces that permitted the political insertion of neoliberal policies came in the 1960s and 1970s as a response to inflation which allowed monetarist theories to challenge Keynesian demand management. Foremost amongst those arguing the case for monetarism was Milton Friedman who was strongly committed both personally and politically to economic and political liberalism. Initially, at a few centres like Chicago, the London School of Economics, and Manchester, Friedman and a growing group of supporting academics became increasingly predominant in their advocacy of monetarist accounts based on 'the quantity theory of money'.[1] This sought to argue that one could only solve problems in relation to stabilizing the economy, not through demand management in relation to such things as wage and price controls (for example, full employment, stable prices, rising living standards), but through the self-stabilizing properties integral to the market system. The 'quantity theory of money' suggested that the level of prices be directly related to the quantity of money in circulation. It sought to establish direct causal connections between total quantity of money, the general level of all prices, and the total amount of production. Although an old idea, its revived significance lay in relation to the renewed priority in controlling inflation in western economies. As Gamble (1986: 35) says:

> The break with a Keynesian framework and the polarization between Keynesians and monetarists was dictated by the political need to reassert the principle of sound money, to restrict government intervention and to give less importance to other economic objectives. What monetarists wanted was for inflation to be recognized as the major problem whatever its rate. There was no question of governments assessing whether inflation or unemployment was the greater evil which required policy action. Sound money had to become the government's main priority again; without sound money no other objective – such as full employment or faster growth – could be achieved.

The central idea is related to the importance of 'sound money' as the fundamental concern of state policy. If governments delivered sound money then the economy would be stabilized in relation to all other areas, and Friedman's theory about the 'natural rate of unemployment' followed as a consequence of this, as did arguments for monetarist techniques for controlling the money supply, like 'floating exchange rates',[2] setting monetary targets, fixing the definition of money and adopting medium-term financial strategies. In this sense, monetarism constituted a crusade against Keynesianism and a series of techniques, premised on a theory that inflation is always everywhere a monetary phenomenon (see Friedman, 1970: 24).

Although, originally, monetarism was a term used in technical debate on the supply and role of money in an economy that was based on the 'quantity theory of money', progressively throughout the 1960s and 1970s it evolved into a broader doctrine or set of economic analyses and prescriptions (Gamble, 1986: 25). The matter of sound money remained the central core, however, for Friedman argued that the excessive growth in monetary levels causes inflation, and that changes in the quantity of money are the only way to effect changes in nominal income. He therefore advocated state intervention to ensure a fixed level of monetary supply. Monetarism thus represents a synthesis of both the ideas of classical political economy and conventional twentieth-century economic analysis. This is a synthesis between the principles which should govern public policy, the nature of the society these policies seek to bring about, and the supposedly value-free generalizations of scientific economics. This rejuvenation has automatically meant a strong policy focus with practical strategies to change agendas in not only economic but also social policy when it has been adopted. Thus it encompasses a series of discourses not only of the workings of the economy, but also its relationship to the state.

In terms of its philosophical commitments, monetarism represents a resurgence of the classical economic model involving a renewed commitment to laissez-faire. The doctrine of laissez-faire economics positions the market as the central and guiding mechanism through which all commercial and interpersonal transactions should be conducted. Based on Adam Smith's notion of the 'invisible hand', as outlined in *The Wealth of Nations*, this is understood to result in collective societal prosperity. Transactions that occur are seen to be multiple and uncoordinated, unhampered by the effects of central direction. Such transactions are based on price mechanisms which are seen to contribute to the social order (because they provide a value derived from demand and supply). The market ensures a rapid response to changes in the allocation of resources and, in turn, the production of goods is responsive to market demands. This view maintained that the outcome of the market order is the mechanism which provides the most effective, impersonal allocation of scarce resources. Such an allocation is thought to be implicitly fair, because it makes no assumptions about the priority of objectives. There is no ordering of needs; thus it (along with minimal state activity) is the most successful way of organizing society and fostering its development. The technological and intellectual advances necessary for this to happen will be generated (like income distribution) through the market mechanism.

The pattern of market distribution is of no consequence in monetarist economics, for it is the order and function of the market which are primary. Monetarists concede that actual distribution may be a lottery, dependent on skill and effort to only a limited degree, but mainly on chance. Material and genetic inheritances are constitutive parts of that 'chance'. Thus individuals should make their own decisions about their own resources and their effective use of the market. Inequalities will naturally result, but these are thought to be the mark of a progressive society. This logic and its mechanism are defended on the grounds of economic efficiency and because of perceived

140

inadequacies in the Keynesian model. Public action and central planning produce bad results, inefficiency and infringement of optimal growth in the economic system, as well as individual freedoms.

The fundamental tenet behind laissez-faire, for monetarists, is that the economy is self-stabilizing at full-employment.[3] It has a tendency to equilibrium similar to the classical model, which to all intents and purposes it represents a continuation of. This is a situation where 'agents optimize' and 'markets clear'.[4] The economy is self-stabilizing at full employment due to the 'natural rate of unemployment'. Markets stabilize because supply and demand are balanced by the price mechanism. The role of the government in this process should be neutral, as government's attempts to influence the economy can only be detrimental, except in the short run.[5] Equilibrium is achieved when the supply of labour is equal to the supply of demand, when actual real rates of inflation match expected rates of inflation, and when full employment prevails.

The rise in the popularity of monetarism around the world in the 1970s was presented not as a modification to Keynesianism but as a complete overthrow of previous principles and policy. The changing world economy in the 1970s, and the internal preoccupation of governments with rising inflation rates, paved the way for its elevation from one component in a technical debate to an international policy to which all states committed to opening up the world economy felt obliged to subscribe. As world trade liberalized, monetarist controls were lifted so the importance of money in the co-ordination of unplanned market economies increased. By 1971 the Bretton Woods system had broken down and within the next decade all major currencies had floating exchange rates.[6] Keynesianism was criticized for failing to deal with inflation, and more, for making inflation worse through demand management policies. Essentially, argued the monetarists, it was not possible to achieve a desired unemployment rate while maintaining a stable inflation rate through government direction. Thus Keynesian attempts to 'fine-tune' the economy became the object of scorn.[7]

For monetarists, belief in the 'quantity theory of money' was based on faith in the premise that the level of prices is directly related to the amount of money in circulation. An increase in the money stock, or the speed at which transactions take place, leads to a rise in prices if the output of goods and services remains constant. This is one of the oldest and most commonsensical ideas in economics. Placing 'sound money' (which pre-war neoclassicism associated with the gold standard) at the pivotal nexus of policy-making, meant that unemployment levels and rates of growth became dependent on market conditions. Because government interventions to manage these features were seen as inflationary, monetarists argued that the money supply should not be adjusted in a short-term way in an attempt to offset fluctuations that might occur in the economy, as this would only destabilize it. Keynesians argued that money supply did not matter. Rather, what counted was the 'real economy',

141

the real output of goods and services and actual levels of investment and productivity. Employment thus attains an importance over inflation, whereas for monetarists, employment is juxtaposed against rising inflation. In policy terms, Keynesianism involved government 'fine-tuning' of the economy based on forecasting demand and growth in order to bring them into line. For monetarists, time-lags in the system, the difficulty of gaining accurate knowledge, or ascertaining accurately the required magnitude of the desired adjustment or of understanding the effects of interventions, make any government action to steer the economy bound to fail.[8]

Also of crucial importance in the monetarist doctrine is the 'natural rate of unemployment'. This is the level that obtains at the point where the economy is at equilibrium, and equates with a situation of 'full employment'. Breakdowns in the market system, which usually occur through government interventions, are thought to be the cause of such impediments as unemployment. Interventions are seen to stunt the ability of the market to make quick responses to changing market conditions. Labour market rigidities such as the power of trade unions, wage setting mechanisms and negotiated conditions of work, are also seen to contribute to unemployment.[9] The solutions, for monetarists, are to adopt 'supply-side' measures to increase the flexibility of labour, and thereby reduce the natural rate of unemployment. These include policies such as those adopted consistently by the Thatcher government in Britain, such as lowering taxes, reducing public expenditure, especially benefits and supplementary forms of assistance, and making unemployment more unpleasant, so as to increase incentives to find a job.

Austrian and Chicago economics

In broad terms, the Chicago school of free-market economics is associated with the work of Milton Friedman and his followers while the Austrian school, which began with Carl Menger (1880–1921), was continued on in America by Ludwig von Mises (1881–1973) and Fredrich A. Hayek (1899–1992).[10] The schools differ more in relation to specific details than general ideological outlook. Both advance consequentialist as opposed to rights theories of individual behaviour. Both also maintain an exclusive commitment to individualism – both methodological and political. Methodological individualism is the doctrine that collective phenomena can, for the purposes of explanation, be reduced to statements about individual activities and events. Entities such as 'classes', 'states' or 'societies' were seen as entirely fictitious in that they do not act, think, save, consume or invest and are thus merely abstract pseudo-entities. Only individuals do these things and hence, it was claimed, only individuals are real. Thus, economics must be based first and foremost on the analysis of people's subjective choices.

In terms of political individualism, adherents of both schools represent society as the aggregated composition of isolated individuals. Writers of both schools express their antipathy to socialism and the welfare state with much political and theoretical commitment. Both schools also support economic liberty as preferable to political direction, for the latter disrupts those mechanisms which would lead to the harmonization of individual actions. Both argue that liberty comes best with ignorance and unpredictability in the growth of knowledge. For both, knowledge is subjective and local in character, and hence only the market can co-ordinate such knowledge to produce an efficient and unintended outcome. Both schools also are subjectivist and non-cognitivist in their attitudes towards the foundation of ethics. They believe that moral statements do not convey information about the world but merely express the personal preferences of the speaker. The law of causality in economics is thought to be underpinned by certain regularities in the social world that observation reveals and scientific method substantiates. Economic science then, as Friedman (1953: 4) expresses it, is concerned to 'provide a system of generalizations that can be used to make correct predictions about the consequences of any change in circumstances'.

The major differences between the two schools relate to method. The adherents of the Chicago school are more positivistic in their approach to economics, arguing that causality in economic and social affairs can be substantiated through recourse to science. In claiming the status of a science for their theories, the Chicago economists sought to refute Keynesian claims by demanding the substantiation of interventionist policies through proof of their scientific validity. Chicago 'pragmatism' and the claim that competitive markets can exploit the natural motive of self-interest, and co-ordinate the disparate parts of a complex society, rest primarily on their empirical grounds. Barry (1986: 50) argues that this empiricism assumes a covert conception of the human as a passive responder to the social structure; an agent who reacts to stimuli rather than one who initiates and creates.

For the Austrian school, the underlying methodology was the opposite of the Chicago school. Instead of starting from observation, the Austrians started from 'introspection', and instead of seeing people in behaviourist terms as automata that can be predicted to respond to external stimuli, influenced by Kant, they see the human mind as the originating source of social phenomena. It is through deductive reasoning that the Austrians maintain that various forms of state interventionism in the economy must fail.

Frederich Hayek, as the leading intellectual of the Austrian school, is a writer of enormous importance and influence to the 'new right'. His major books, including *The Road to Serfdom* (1944), *The Constitution of Liberty* (1960) and the three volumes of *Law, Legislation and Liberty* (1973; 1976; 1979) represent the most complete and coherent statement of the liberal principles of individualism, of a limited, constitutionally specified role for the state, and of a faith in the market. Hayek's intellectual project was to develop the economic theory of liberalism as well as to de-legitimate the post-war theory of interventionism and oppose the extension of welfare rights throughout society. In spite of his consistent support for neoliberal principles, unlike libertarians like Ayn Rand and Murray Rothbard, he allows some role for the state to offset extreme hardships and suffering. In this sense, while recognizing certain public goods and a state-maintained legal framework, he does not think that state activity should be substantial. Rather, he maintains that a 'spontaneous order' emerges, through a process of *catallaxy*, from the unplanned interaction of consumers and producers in the marketplace.

If Friedman's approach to controlling inflation was confined to economic factors, the addition of Hayek's perspective, which shared the fundamental commitment to liberal axioms, was to extend the account of controlling inflation to include political factors as well. Hayek not only helped the monetarist attack on Keynesianism but he considered such things as the role of trade unions and of bureaucracy as more important factors in inflation. Rather than being simply a matter of incorrect economic policy, then, inflation was seen as spurred on by excessive government interference. In this way, Hayek was to shift attention to the nature of the public sector and the nature of the political order as it interfered with the market order and infringed its proper functioning.

Although Hayek must in many senses be considered a classical liberal, especially as regards his rigorous adherence to a negative conception of the state's role, his writings from the 1930s onwards contribute to neoliberalism. This is so, not only because he shares many of the themes of neoliberalism, but also because he deeply influenced later forms of the doctrine as manifested in Chicago economics, Public Choice Theory, Human Capital Theory, Agency Theory, Transaction Cost Economics, as well as the various forms of managerialism that developed in the 1940s to 1960s and became ascendant in forms of state reason from the 1970s to the 1990s.

Hayek can be considered a part of, and having major debts to, the Austrian School of Economics founded by Menger and carried on by von Wieser (1851–1926) and von Mises. Amongst the major themes of his economic and social philosophy are his argument that 'local knowledge', as is found in markets, is always more valid and effective than the forms of codified textbook-type knowledge that it is possible to introduce through planning. For this reason, markets have distinct advantages over state regulation or planning. The laws of supply and demand operate, via the price mechanism, as indicators of under- and over-supply as well as incentives for producers to produce high-quality, competitively priced goods for which there is an established demand. In a multitude of ways, markets provide fast and efficient methods of supplying information on consumer demand, and a sure way of making sure that producers and providers will respond.

Consequently, Hayek maintains that the proper functioning of markets is incompatible with state planning of any sort, either full-scale socialism or the more limited conception of the welfare state. A full-scale rational socialism is impossible because it would have no markets to guide resource allocation. In addition, central planning of any form, he claims, is not practical because of the scale of centralized calculation any effective attempt at allocation would require. On this basis, Hayek (1944) contends that all forms of state action beyond the minimal functions of the defence of the realm and the protection of basic rights to life and property are dangerous threats to liberty which are likely to lead down the 'road to serfdom'.

His main arguments against central planning are based on two claims: (1) its inefficiency, and (2) the threat to freedom of the individual. It would be inefficient, in Hayek's view, because real knowledge is gained and true economic progress made as a consequence of locally generated knowledge derived from 'particular circumstances of time and place' and the state is not privy to such knowledge (ibid.: 521). The market then is the mechanism which best allocates resources in society. Planning ignores this localistic character of knowledge and interferes with the self-regulating mechanism of the market.

One of the major ways that Hayek departs from classical economic theory relates to his acceptance of the Austrian school's subjective theory of value, the theory that value is conferred on resources by the subjective preferences of agents. As John Gray (1984: 16) puts it, it was this 'profound insight which spelt the end of the tradition of classical economic theory', marking a departure from economic theorists such as Adam Smith, David Ricardo, J.S. Mill and Karl Marx, all of whom had analysed value in objective terms as deriving from the labour content of the asset or resource under consideration. Like von Mises, Hayek defends subjectivism in economic theory regarding value, but goes further, noting that the data of the social sciences are themselves subjective phenomena and that social objects like money or tools are constituted by human beliefs.[11]

Also derived from von Mises, Hayek's work was characterized by a strong anti-socialism, most vehemently expressed in his opposition to Marxism, which he held did not constitute a rational means of organizing an economy. For Hayek, economies are the outcome of spontaneous evolution which demonstrate the superiority of unregulated markets for creativity and progress. A spontaneous societal order such as a market order can utilize practical fragmented knowledge in a way in which a holistically planned order cannot. Hayek states his theory of spontaneous order first in relation to a comment on Bernard Mandeville, (1978: 253) when he says: 'For the first time [he] developed all the classical paradigmata of the spontaneous growth of orderly social structures: of law and morals, of language, the market and money, and also the growth of technological knowledge.'

A spontaneous order emerges as a natural process. It can be observed in population biology of animal species, in the formation of crystals, and even in galaxies (Hayek, 1952a: 180; 1967: 76; 1973: 39; 1976: 39–40). It is this idea that self-organizing and self-replicating structures emerge without design, and that knowledge about some parts of the structure permit the formation of correct understanding about the behaviour of the structure as a whole, that Hayek is most keen to emphasize. It underpins his rejection of Cartesian rationalism, his anti-historicism, his anti-foundationalism, his theory of the evolution of mind (Hayek, 1978: 250). In that the market is a spontaneous order, it displays a tendency to equilibrium, although an actual perfect equilibrium is never achieved but must be viewed as a constantly changing process of tending towards orderliness. This is not only with reference to economic life and the spontaneous emergence of markets, but also in social life in relation to the growth of language where we find the spontaneous formation of self-regulating structures, as well as in relation to the development of moral norms. Hence, as Gray points out, the emergence of spontaneous systems is 'somewhat akin to the generalizations of Darwinian evolution' (Gray, 1984: 31) in that Hayek maintains that 'selective evolution is the source of all order' (ibid.: 32). Thus, in a market economy there is a real analogy to Darwinian natural selection in that the 'profit-loss system provides a mechanism for the elimination of unfit systems' (ibid.: 32) with the proviso that, in contradistinction to Herbert Spencer or W.G. Sumner, natural selection is not solely about individuals but is also about groups and populations. Such a thesis incorporates Hayek's arguments that social institutions arise as a result of human action but not human design (the 'invisible hand' thesis); that knowledge embodied in practices and skills that is practical, tacit and local, is primary in terms of its epistemological status; and that there is a natural selection of competitive traditions whereby rules and practices that confer success come to replace those unsuited to the human environment. Following closely in the footsteps of von Mises, Hayek argues that any attempt to supplant market relations by public planning cannot avoid calculational calamities and is therefore doomed to failure.

Human Capital Theory

Human Capital Theory (HCT) emerged, says Simon Marginson (1993: 35), from neoclassical economics in the second half of the nineteenth century. As a consequence of the marginalist revolution led by Jevons, Walras and Menger, the boundaries around economics were redrawn and narrowed. Economics, based upon mathematical methods, became the science of predicting universal economic behaviour in order to produce universal economic laws.

Human Capital Theory first emerged in modern form in the 1960s. Following the work of Theodore Schultz (1960a; 1960b; 1961; 1975), E.F. Denison (1962) and Gary Becker (1964; 1976), there was a renewed concern for investment in education. As Schultz (1960b: 571) put it:

> I propose to treat education as an investment in man and to treat its consequences as a form of capital. Since education becomes a part of the person receiving it, I shall refer to it as human capital … it is a form of capital if it renders a productive service of value to the economy.

For HCT, investment in education accounted for the fact of economic growth. As Marginson (1993: 35) notes, Schultz as well as earlier writers such as J.R. Walsh had noted that investment in education more than paid for itself. According to E.F. Denison (1962), as well, improved education was one of the major factors contributing to economic growth. Then, in 1964, a major publication by Gary Becker, *Human Capital: A Theoretical and Empirical Analysis with Special Reference to Education*, maintained that education was 'the most important single determinant' of economic growth (ibid.: 45). Like Friedman, Becker saw human capital as a tradable commodity capable of being organized according to the principles of market exchange. His own approach was to prepare mathematical models and formulae for calculating the private and social investment in human capital.

Like Hayek, Becker searches for the mechanism of functional adaptation in social systems which he sees as arising in a context of 'perfect competition'. Yet, while Hayek sees equilibrium as the product of the natural selection of competing practices, Becker's economic approach to human behaviour sees all human action as undertaken with ends or outcomes in view. Hence, the economic approach to human behaviour attributes a means-end calculational rationality to human agents, and it is under such a model, where rational human behaviour is seen as purposeful and goal-orientated, that individuals will invest in education. Becker's model is thus slightly different from Hayek's. For Hayek, man is a rule-following being and it is through an historical process of natural selection that maladaptive rules are filtered out. For Becker, the economic approach is purely and simply an 'economizing' and 'maximizing' strategy where humans are programmed to compete in order to maximize their opportunities. Hence, at the base of Becker's approach to human capital is a rational choice model which contains 'the combined assumptions of maximizing behaviour, market equilibrium and stable preferences' (Becker, 1976: 5). In this model, the economic approach explains institutions in terms of costs and benefits in maximizing the satisfactions of individual wants.

Although the human capital of a nation is the sum of skills, talents and knowledge embodied in its population, it is apparent that many influences increase the stock of human capital. These include job training, medical care, diet and formal education, amongst many others. The Human Capital perspective treats education and training as an investment and emphasizes the direct impact of skill creation on productivity. Thus, workforce and management skills are seen as essential determinants of national economic performance. Amongst the main propositions of HCT are:

- that education and training increase an individuals cognitive capacity;
- which in turn increases productivity; and
- an increase in productivity tends to increase an individual's earning;
- which becomes a measure of human capital.

A distinction within HCT is made between the private rates of return and the social rates of return. This stems from the distinction between education as a private good and education as a public good. As a private good, education is seen to be a tradable commodity in the market place for money and status, and hence is seen as used for the advancement of the individual where returns accrue to that individual. Education as a public good is seen in a number of ways, including the potential to develop the moral, ethical, social, cultural and political awareness of all citizens, as well as to assist in the effective operation of the democratic process.

The private rate of return is calculated by adding the benefits (earnings and consumption benefits) derived from education over a specified period of time. It is the private rate of return on human capital that provides individuals with the incentive to progress to further education (see Blaug, 1970: 22–32; Chia, 1989: 5–10). Individuals would invest in education to the extent that the increased private benefits were greater than the private costs. The HCT model suggests that rational individuals will invest in education as the benefits of higher earnings will more than offset the costs of that education. The model assumes that further education is geared for the labour market, that more education can be translated into higher productivity, and that the productivity results in higher earnings for the individual.

The social rate of return is meant to influence government decisions as to the level of investment that it will make in tertiary education. The normal method of calculation is to sum the net benefits to individuals and then subtract the government's costs of funding public education as well as the cost engendered by 'externalities'. The question as to what the externalities comprise, as well as how large they are, is a subject of considerable debate. While Keynesians tend to place a high emphasis on social externalities, Friedmanites do not see them as significant at all. Marginson (1993: 38–40) gives a more detailed account of the private and social rates of return from investment in human capital.

During the 1970s, a crisis of confidence in the human capital approach saw it eclipsed by 'screening theories' and other types of explanations as the fact of various recessions in Organization for Economic Co-operation and Development (OECD) economies made it apparent that there was no automatic relationship between education and economic growth, as the early Human Capital theorists such as Denison and Schultz had foretold. The rapid technological and structural change since the 1980s saw a renewed policy emphasis on investment in human capital adapted to a free-market form however. This neo-liberal version of HCT emphasized private rather than public investment in education and stressed that the benefits of investing in education accrued to the individual rather than to society.

The story of the neoliberal appropriation of HCT is provided by Marginson (1993). While HCT in the 1960s had been a general economic model about the importance of investment in education, the revived model of HCT of the mid-1980s, as demonstrated in various OECD publications, placed greatest importance on private individual investment in education. In its monograph, 'Structural adjustment and economic performance' (OECD, 1987), education was once again represented as an important source of flexibility and responsiveness in relation to technological and economic change. Again, the OECD was focusing attention on education, skills and knowledge as central to production. The difference from the 1960s was crucial, however. As Marginson (ibid.: 49) notes:

> The OECD did not recommend that its member governments adopt exactly the same policies as those of the 1960s. It called for a new reading of the relationship between private and social investment in education. The earlier period was dominated by the case for macro-level public investment, and private individual investment was downplayed … . The OECD now supported human capital econometrics for calculating the private rates of return on investment in education, but social rates of return were another matter. The earlier calculations of the social rates of return were no longer used 'as a criterion for public funding'. Screening theory was used to deconstruct the old form of argument for public investment in human capital. The OECD incorporated screening into its human capital framework, in a way that was compatible with the now dominant policies of smaller government and user payments for public services.

As Marginson also relays, while the neoclassical model of HCT was based on equilibrium and perfect competition, a revised model was influenced by studies of decision-making in agriculture which, while not discarding the neoclassical model, argued that in the actual world a pure exchange model of perfect information did not apply. Marginson (ibid.: 46) cites Nelson and Phelps (1966) who argue that farmers' capacity to implement and adopt new technologies depended on education, and, further, that the level of education determines the diffusion of new technologies. In addition, Marginson (1993: 46) cites a number of studies that argue that above-average levels of education are associated with enhanced efficiency (Fane, 1975: 452), or with innovation (Wozniak, 1984), ability to change, to incorporate technology or to deal with disequilibria (Schultz, 1975). Thus, as Marginson (1993: 46) explains, 'education is one of the determinants of competitive advantage'. The HCT coupled with the market liberal reforms would be seen throughout OECD countries as important to deal with change: 'To the free market school, investment in human capital could only be fully successful under the free market conditions assumed by the abstract human capital model: perfect competition and no government subsidies in the education market' (ibid.: 50).

Revitalized by the OECD in the mid-1980s, HCT represents human beings as the passive playthings of external forces who will 'deteriorate' (to use the OECD's term) if not kept in good shape through rigorous training programmes. In this model, investment in individuals' education will solve all the structural problems of the economy. Thus, central to the OECD's vision of HCT is a notion of 'perpetual training'. Such a notion, in fact, becomes:

> the new rationale for education and training systems in advanced countries pro-
> viding the link between education, in the broadest sense, and the economic system.
> It motivates both policy and practice, and, in terms of the prevailing human capital
> theory presently revitalized by the OECD, perpetual training becomes the basis for
> a vocational reorientation of the education system to meet the needs of the 'new'
> economy. (Fitzsimmons and Peters, 1994: 1)

Fitzsimmons and Peters argue that perpetual training will be available through the promotion of a 'training culture' which has developed in OECD countries like England, Australia and New Zealand. Such a change, they claim (ibid.: 2): 'is expected to bring improvements to industry in the form of a "highly skilled and adaptable work force" that will match the competitiveness needed in the international market place'. Skill, in this model, is the basis of all value, and, consistent with the notion of 'perpetual training', Human Capital theorists advocate infinite re-skilling as the basis of modern education and as the solution to economic problems. Consistent with these concerns, reports such as those produced by the OECD (1993: 83) point to: 'weaknesses in the skills of the current workforce ... that ... must be of concern given the shortages which may arise ... when the economic recovery gains momentum'. For HCT, the sum purpose of human existence is reduced to the skill level or performance capacity of its population. Ultimately the criterion of value is the self-interested individual. The assumption from neoclassical economics that individuals are rational utility maximizers resides at the basis of HCT and it is this assumption that lies behind the ascendancy of neoliberalism. At the core of all policies informed by neoliberal doctrines is the reduction of human beings to *homo economicus*. It is a conception of human nature premised upon the 'naturalness' of self-interested pursuits for economic gain and of individuals with the foresight and knowledge to enable this to happen.

While the core assumptions of neoliberalism, together with the doctrines of monetarism and HCT have their origins in neoclassical economics, many of the specific neoliberal policy prescriptions for institutional restructuring have been based upon more recent versions of neoliberal theory. These theories are described and critiqued in the next chapter.

Notes

1   The 'quantity theory of money' is based on the equation MV + PQ, where M is the quantity of money (or 'the money supply'), V the average velocity at which money circulates, Q the quantity of output produced by the economy, in real terms, in the course of a year, and P the price of this output (Stewart, 1986: 159).

2   Although this was the general position, some monetarists recommended a return to the gold standard. See W. Rees-Mogg (1974).

3   What this means within the discipline of economics is contentious. See Stewart (1986: ch. 8).

4   Markets 'clear' in the sense that all variables (such as the price of labour) adjust in such a way to equate supply and demand.

5   The 'Rational Expectations' variant of monetarism, rejects even short-run capability of government interference to effect real variables. The 'Rational Expectations' form is often referred to as the 'New Classical Economics'.

6   Exchange controls were abolished in 1974 in America, and 1979 in Britain.

7   Clearly Keynesian theory was perceived as unable to come to terms with inflation and its consequences. There was a difficulty of forecasting the inflation rate correctly. As Stewart (1986: 177) states, 'By concentrating on economic behaviour in "real terms" or at "constant prices"', Keynesianism failed to build into their models the consequences of expectations that there would be a *change* in the inflation rate. Monetarist models grasped the nettle of inflationary expectations, and accordingly provided a more illuminating account of an important part of the story.

8   Forecasting demand proved difficult, especially exports and private investment. As time went on, techniques of forecasting improved, although as Stewart (1986: 172) notes 'in due course confidence became overconfidence', and some Keynesian economists thought you could manage the economy on a month by month basis. Clearly Keynesianism needed some modification, but as Stewart (1986: 178) notes, this should not have necessitated the rejection of the entire theoretical system and its replacement by a theory which is based on the fallacious classical belief in a self-stabilizing economy. This assumption constitutes a 'fatal flaw' in monetarism and comprises an 'unreal assumption about how an economy works'.

9   A neo-Keynesian view would be that there is no reason to see the economy as self-stabilizing at full-employment, and that if there is no self-stabilization to the economy, then the very concept of a 'natural rate of unemployment' ceases to have meaning. The neo-Keynesian view is that the economy can settle at any of a wide range of unemployment rates depending on level of demand. Some Keynesians accepted that there was a link

between unemployment rate and inflation rate, and that there was an optimal level of unemployment when inflation would be stable. This gave rise to the 'non-accelerating inflation rate of unemployment' (NAIRU). This decreed that if unemployment falls below this rate, then inflation will rise and vice versa. But as there are no self-regulating forces, the government must do this through influencing demand. (See Stewart, 1986: 182.) Most neo-Keynesians see inflation as being caused by a multitude of factors, of which the rate of unemployment is only one. As well as demand-side measures, they would also support supply-side measures such as income policies, and training and re-training of the labour force. In speaking of the 'neo-Keynesian way ahead', Stewart (1986: 192) states, 'The government needs to engage in discretionary intervention in the economy if ... fluctuations in demand are to be minimized, and if, in particular, effective demand is not to get stuck at too low a level, leading to a high rate of unemployment which may persist for many years'. He advocates a 'middle way' which avoids 'equally the pitfalls of looking at the economy only in real terms and the dangers of looking at it only in money terms' (ibid.: 194).

10 Major statements of the Austrian school of economics can be found in von Mises (1949; 1951; 1958) and in Hayek (1935;1944; 1949; 1960; 1967; 1976; 1978; 1979). Major statements of the Chicago school can be found in Friedman (1962) and Friedman and Friedman (1980).

11 Hayek's earliest statement is in *The Counter-Revolution of Science: Studies in the Abuse of Reason* (1952b) where he defends a qualitative discontinuity between methods of natural and social sciences. There were also Kantian influences on Hayek's subjectivism in that, following Kant, he rejected the idea that knowledge could be constructed from a basis of raw sensory data, seeing order that we find in the world as a product of the creative activity of the human mind but suspecting that there are inherent limitations to the possibility of full explicit knowledge, and, in particular, an impossibility of ever fully explaining a mind as complex as our own (see Hayek, 1978: 45, n. 14). In addition, relatedly, Hayek denies the ontological independence of mind, as in Descartes's conception, denies the possibility of complete intellectual self-understanding, and denies any foundationalism, seeing all criticism of social life as immanent criticism, and social order itself as spontaneous creation rather than as a rational construction.

8
Neoliberal Theories of Institutional Restructuring

Although Hayek and Friedman are important influences on the rise of neoliberalism, because they advocate a minimal state, their own positions are technically classical liberal. Neoliberalism 'proper' arises with those theories that advocate an extension of market rules and principles to public and private sector organizational restructuring. This chapter seeks to outline some of the major institutional theories that have guided the contemporary restructurings of educational institutions. Having done this we will review the influence of libertarian political philosophy and conclude by outlining Foucault's account of neoliberalism.

Public Choice Theory

Inasmuch as the economy was a central object of neoliberal analysis and restructuring from the 1970s, the analysis and redesign of public sector institutions was also to receive attention. Unlike markets, the public sector, in the neoliberal view, lacked a comparable mechanism of economic efficiency to guide the utilization or allocation of resources. In addition, neoliberals claimed that the self-interested opportunism of bureaucrats and government officials would create conflicting loyalties and interests which would interfere with the implementation of policies in the genuine pursuit of the public interest. The school of Public Choice Theory (PCT) advocated the application of economic theories to public sector institutions in the interest of making public organizations subject to the similar costs and benefits as operate in the private sector. In this, PCT represents an application of economic models and theories to politics on the assumption that economic behaviour (*homo economicus*) describes the true state of human nature and thus is applicable to all aspects of life.

The central figure in the 'economics of politics' is James Buchanan who since 1969 was Professor of Economics and Director of the Center for Study of Public Choice at the Virginia Polytechnic Institute, Blacksburg, Virginia. A member of the Mont Pelerin Society and of the Institute of Economic Affairs advisory council, Buchanan describes PCT as 'the application and extension of economic theory to the realm of political or governmental choices' (1978: 3). Amongst his central books are included *Fiscal Theory and Political Economy* (1960), *Cost and Choice* (1969), *The Limits of Liberty* (1975) and, with Gordon Tullock, *The Calculus of Consent* (1962), which gave a lead to a group of economists at the Virginia Polytechnic Institute in America in the 1960s and 1970s. Buchanan claims to have come to PCT out of intellectual frustration with orthodox Pre-World War II Public Finance Theory, as enunciated by the likes of A.C. Pigou, Hugh Dalton in the UK and Harold Groves and Henry Simons in the USA. Public finance and economics could not be independent of a theory of politics, said Buchanan (1978). In this he claimed to be influenced by the nineteenth-century Swedish economist, Knut Wicksell, and by the political theories on voting behaviour of Duncan Black (especially his work on committees) and Kenneth Arrow (on social welfare). Impressed by Arrow's argument that a consistent social welfare function for a society could not be derived from individual preferences, Buchanan came to accept his view that any coherent social welfare approach must inevitably entail the imposition of will of some members or groups over others. In analysing how public goods were supposed to emerge from individual self-interested behaviour, Buchanan's achievement was to abolish any notion of the public interest as the derivation of the aggregate self-interest of individuals.

The analysis of public institutions by Buchanan constitutes a crucially important aspect of neoliberalism. In common with the work of Hayek and Friedman, Buchanan shares the major conclusions of monetarism, supporting restraints on the money supply and the public sector. In addition, he argues against Keynesian demand management, opposes growth in the role of government, supports privatization and commercialization of the public sector, opposes income redistribution, opposes full employment and opposes all 'collectivist' strategies in political decision-making.

Central to PCT are several interrelated arguments and ideas concerning the relationship between economics and politics. At the most general level, is the application of neoclassical analysis to non-market situations (Riesman, 1990: 136). In this view, politics was redescribed as an economic market. As Buchanan and Tullock (1962: 250) explain: 'One of the great advantages of an essentially economic approach to collective action lies in the implicit recognition that political exchange, at all levels, is basically equivalent to economic exchange'. With Hayek and Friedman, Buchanan characterizes economics as a process of *'catallaxy'*; that is, of the voluntary exchange of goods and services between competing individuals. Lying behind such an analysis is a strong normative commitment to free-market individualism which for Buchanan provides a common rationality linking the economic and political worlds. Political action is thus represented as being governed by the same interests and motivation that govern the market. Unlike Friedman, who maintains that monetarism was the consequence of a value-free scientific approach to economics (Friedman, 1953: 3–43, 1967: 86), Buchanan is self-consciously explicit about the political nature of his libertarian project as well as about the value-laden nature of scientific enquiry, maintaining a thoroughgoing commitment to a conception of the market order as a normative ideal (Barry, 1983: 101–5; Marginson, 1992: 45–57).

The libertarian quality of Buchanan's work is reflected also in his deeply individualist approach to public affairs. As far as political prospects were concerned, only those that resulted from the subjective choices of individuals were acceptable. Collective entities such as a 'society' or 'the public' were held not to exist because they were reducible to individual experiences. This 'methodological individualism' was fundamental to Buchanan's approach. As he acknowledged in *The Calculus of Consent*, 'the whole calculus has meaning only if methodological individualism is accepted' (Buchanan and Tullock, 1962: 265). This is an individualism that is both a method of analysis as well as a norm of organizing society as Marginson (1992: 47) notes. While in this respect, Hayek and Friedman also maintained an individualist approach, Buchanan is explicit in tracing his individualism to Hobbes (Buchanan, 1975: 147) and in declaring the political significance of individualism as the undergirding foundation for the overall theory (Buchanan, 1975: 146–8; Buchanan and Tullock, 1962: 265–70). Public Choice Theory is ruled by the imperative of a strict methodological individualism in which 'all theorizing, all analysis, is resolved finally into considerations faced by the individual person as decision-maker' (Buchanan, 1975: ix).

It is on this basis that PCT attacks as 'myth' the idea that government or public service is able to serve the public good. Influenced by William Niskanen's work on 'bureaucratic growth', Anthony Downs's pioneering work on political parties, Mancur Olson's work on 'interest groups' and Gordon Tullock's writing on 'rent-seeking' behaviour, it asserts the view that the notion of the public good is a fiction which cloaks the opportunistic behaviour of bureaucrats and politicians as they seek to expand their bureaus, increase their expenditures, and maximize their own personal advantages. In *The Limits of Liberty* (1975), Buchanan maintains that a coincidence of interests between the bureaucrats' private interests and their conception of the public interest ensues, such that 'within the constraints that he faces the bureaucrat tends to maximize his own utility' (Buchanan, 1975: 161). If preferences are inherently subjective then they cannot be known and transferred into a collective value judgement, such as a public good, for such a notion neglects the rights of consumers whose interests the public service and politicians are meant to serve, but do not.

As a further part of the argument against collective politics, or any notion of a public good, PCT suggests redesigning public institutions to make them reflect more accurately the preferences of individuals. This involves counteracting the possible forms of 'capture' which serve to deflect the interests of public officials from the public's real needs. To do this, PCT advocates a variety of quasi-market strategies, such as contracting out services to the private sector, increasing competition between units within the public sector, placing all potentially conflicting responsibilities into separate institutions, separating the commercial and non-commercial functions of the state, separating the advisory, regulatory and delivery functions into different agencies, as well as introducing an assortment of accountability and monitoring techniques and strategies aimed to overcome all possible sources of corruption and bias, particularly those arising from the pursuit of self-interest.

As a consequence of the individualist orientation, Buchanan's PCT maintains a strong commitment to the freedom and responsibility of individuals, and argues against the role and expansion of government in relation to social and welfare services. All dimensions of behaviour associated with personal morality or associated with the private sphere were 'off limits' as far as the social policies of state action were concerned. In the absence of state intervention, people will exchange in order to improve their well-being. As an individual's preferences are inherently subjective, they cannot, says Buchanan, be transformed into judgements of a collective sort. For this reason he is particularly hostile to the welfare state, as he maintains that it is impossible to derive the welfare functions of a state from the alleged preferences of individual economic agents. All individuals in PCT are rational maximizers of their own self-interest (Buchanan and Tullock, 1962: 309–10).

Extending these arguments, Buchanan maintains that market failure is rarely the basis for increasing or extending government action. The failure of markets to generate clean air, for instance, or to redistribute wealth in such a way as to sustain the entire community, does not justify any increased role for government. As Barry (1983: 104) explains:

> Collective action to solve public good problems is distrusted by the Virginia School because their individualism and subjectivism implies that we cannot say that such action represents genuine social improvement. It is claimed, therefore, that the assumption that market failure necessitates collective correction is false and has led, under the 'externalities' rubric, to numerous interventions which have violated individual preferences.

The 'externalities rubric' referred to by Barry pertains to the logic by which those problems or issues, which for PCT should be the problem of individuals, become defined as issues for governments. What is required is that they become 're-internalized', that is, taken back into and dealt with in the sphere of economic exchange between self-interested, legally accountable, self-maximizing individuals (ibid.: 105).

The rule regarding the government provision of public goods is that collective provision is acceptable only if it accords with the unanimity principle (Buchanan, 1975: 38–41). This principle underpins Buchanan's theory of political ethics. For Buchanan, 'the unanimity rule' replaces 'the majority rule' which prevents coalitions and group formations from controlling the political process. Developed as a political analogue of the Pareto-optimality principle of free-market economics, it specifies that no change is acceptable unless everyone agrees. As Barry (1983: 104) says, '(t)his obviously puts the status quo in a privileged position because it is always superior to any change which harms at least one person'.

It is not simply a conservative position which protects existing states of affairs, but it allows propertied groups to veto redistribution. Since most western democracies were welfare states at the time Buchanan was advocating his position, a rigid application of the unanimity rule would prevent the emergence of a libertarian society of course. While Buchanan is thus willing to relax the strict application of the rule, he is insistent that we must keep some distance from 'majority rule'. As Barry (ibid.: 104) explains:

> Thus, in *The Limits of Liberty* (1975) he produces an interesting abstract model, Hobbesian in method, of how self-interested maximizers would create a set of property rights and agree to a 'constitutional contract' which would authorize a 'Protective State' to enforce those rights and contracts, and a 'Productive State' to produce public goods. While the contract itself is unanimous, the Productive State itself could operate with a decision procedure of less than unanimity.

For Buchanan, property distribution emerges 'naturally' as people fight over scarce resources. The state is the outcome of an 'agreement' or 'contract' by people as a necessary evil to avoid anarchy. The formula is essentially Hobbesian. The task is to stop the state expanding beyond the basic protectionist role so that it does not infringe the preferences of individuals. Buchanan's distinctions between the protectionist role of the state and the productivist role of the state is fundamental here. The protectionist state has a definite legitimate function with respect to the defence of property and personal rights and contracts, yet even it is in danger of expansionary tendencies in relation to such things as legislating new laws. The productivist state, however, suffers much more from tendencies to expand its role and scope relating to the difficulties it has in limiting itself to the production of contractually agreed public goods and with the tendency to interfere excessively in the private economy (Buchanan, 1975: 160).

The underlying justification for property distribution is not, for Buchanan, based on Lockean natural law grounds but rather on contractarian foundations, ultimately justified out of fear, in a Hobbesian sense. The only appropriate role of the state is to defend individuals from coercion from other individuals, from groups and from the state itself. Beyond this the state has no role, and PCT writers spend considerable effort in emphasizing the dangers inherent in the growth of the public sector in order to maximize 'negative freedom' and expand the sphere of the individual. The 'calculus of consent' thus focuses on the costs of public intervention for the individual. Yet the dangers of bureaucratic and government expansionism are always imminent. For Buchanan, politicians themselves tend to be people who support the expansion of the collective activity of the state, as there is more to be gained politically through spending programmes than through tax cuts. In addition, expansionary pressures are created due to the continual need to appease pressure groups, including 'majorities' (Buchanan, 1975; Buchanan and Tullock, 1962).

Parallels between PCT as articulated by Buchanan and the approaches of Hayek and Friedman have been frequently made in several studies (Barry, 1983; Bosanquet, 1983; Heald, 1983; Marginson, 1992). Buchanan came himself to endorse the monetarist position and, in general terms, he, along with Hayek and Friedman, can be seen as constituting important 'organic intellectuals' for the revival of neoclassical liberalism. Marginson (1992) maintains, in a comparison of the three thinkers, that in each case their theories were driven by political commitments to the free market and in this sense it was a case of 'theory driven by politics' (ibid.: 6).

For Hayek, there was a strong political commitment from the start. In his 1948 lecture 'Individualism: true and false', for instance, he said, 'it is with the system which forms the alternative to socialism that I shall be concerned' (Hayek, 1949: 3). Inasmuch as his theoretical work was an important source of inspiration for neoliberalism, his political commitment was also important for the eventual discreditation and eclipse of Keynesianism as the hegemonic policy of western nation-states. Hayek was also politically active. Foremost amongst his contributions in this respect was the establishment of the Mont Pelerin Society of which he was a moving force. Established in 1947 at Mont Pelerin in Switzerland in order to debate the future of liberalism as part of the general concern for the preservation and extension of a free society, it was to become, in the words of the English newspaper, *Sunday Times*, 'the most influential but little known think tank of the second half of the twentieth century' (Lindsay, 1997: 1). As originally intended by Hayek, it has functioned as an 'international association of scholars' dedicated to 'regenerating the ideas of classical liberalism in order to refute socialism' (Lindsay, 1997: 2). In this, Hayek was explicit in articulating the function of intellectuals in creating the ideological conditions for change: 'The propertied class, now almost exclusively a business group, lacks intellectual leadership and even a coherent and defensible philosophy of life' (Hayek, 1960: 128).

Although a more traditional intellectual than Hayek or Friedman, Buchanan was just as politically committed. But unlike Friedman, who maintains a formal allegiance to positivist neutrality, Buchanan is explicit about his political ideals and the role they play in his work. For Buchanan, the free market is a normative ideal, and PCT is explicitly identified as advocating a specific political conception of society. As he declares in *The Calculus of Consent*, 'the only purpose of science is its ultimate assistance in the development of normative propositions' (Buchanan and Tullock, 1962: 308). Reinforcing this idea in his Nobel Prize speech, as Riesman (1990: 1) notes, he criticizes his fellow economists on the grounds that the motivation was not normative and that their work was not motivated by political commitments.

The one crucial respect in which PCT differs from classical liberalism, and from Hayek, relates to the positive gearing of the state's role as the constructor of the market order and guardian of individual wants and interests. Buchanan had little faith in the 'spontaneous' ordering of the market or in the efficacy of the social evolutionary process. For him, evolution may produce social chaos and dysfunctional patterns as readily as it may social harmony and equilibrium. As Buchanan (1975: 194n) says, in referring to Hayek's *Law, Legislation and Liberty*:

> My basic criticism of F. A. Hayek's profound interpretation of modern history and his diagnosis for improvement is directed at his apparent belief or faith that social evolution will, in fact, ensure the survival of efficient institutional forms. Hayek is so distrustful of man's explicit attempts of reforming institutions that he accepts uncritically the evolutionary alternative.

Rejecting all talk of automaticity and evolution, Buchanan expresses a much greater faith in conscious action to legitimate the 'long over-due task of institutional over-haul' (Riesman, 1990: 74) that many commentators recognize. It is on these grounds that he seeks to protect constitutional rules by the 'unanimity principle', as such rules will constrain the leadership as well as the citizenry. It is also on these grounds that he makes the distinction between the 'protective state' and the 'productive state'. While the former is concerned with the basic constitutional framework of rights enforced by law and with national defence, the latter is both 'policeman' and 'participant' (ibid.: 81). These two levels of state relate to, as Buchanan (1975: x) says, two stages of social interaction: one which involves the selection of rules and one which involves action within these rules as selected. While the distinction between 'protective' and 'productive' is the distinction between law and politics (Buchanan and Tullock, 1962: 69), importantly, in terms of the political theory of neoliberalism, it is also a distinction between 'negative' and 'positive' freedom, and of the 'negative' and 'positive' roles of the state in relation to this. Importantly in this context, Buchanan's state has a positive arm. Hence, while the stringent constitutional safeguards on the protective state make any change in the status quo or redistribution of property almost impossible, the positive arm of the productive state effectively extracts compliance from individuals in order to engineer a market order. In doing so it cuts across the traditional guarantees of classical liberalism regarding the spaces it sought to protect – a domain of personal freedom, the rights of privacy involving freedom from scrutiny and surveillance, as well as professional autonomy and discretion in one's work. Public Choice Theory effectively undermines and reorganizes the protected domains of its classical liberal forebears.

What is interesting in relation to neoliberalism is that only Hayek is at all consistent to this principle in developing a negative conception of state power.[1] Hayek's conception of 'spontaneous evolution' dictated his distrust of any form of direct or deliberate state action. He is in this sense, the true advocate of an unqualified laissez-faire. Those that came after Hayek, including Buchanan, Becker, Williamson and the *Ordoliberalen*, all represented the state as *positively constructing the market*. It is in this sense that, from the perspective of classical liberalism, *neoliberalism is a positive form of state power*, for it is in the constructive role of the state in engineering markets that it violates the normative criterion most central to the classical liberal mind-set.

Agency Theory

Central to this supply-side process of 'governing without governing' are a number of internal theories of organization through which efficiency and effectiveness are rendered operative in public sector institutions. Agency Theory (AT) has been widely used in the economic and social restructuring programmes in OECD countries, including the UK, the USA, Australia and New Zealand.[2] As a theoretical orientation, it represents work relations hierarchically as a series of contracts between one party referred to as the principal and another referred to as the agent. The theory is concerned with problems of compliance and control in the division of labour among work relationships. Although initially developed in relation to business firms, it became adapted and extended to public sector work relationships as a means of exacting the accountability and performance of employees where market incentives and sanctions did not operate. Agency Theory theorizes work relations hierarchically in terms of chains of authority and command which can be used to characterize authority relations at all levels of the management hierarchy. Hence, a single person will be principal to those further down the chain of command and agent to those further up. Central to its focus is how one gets an agent to act in accordance with the interests of the principal. Rather than specifying a broad job specification based on a conception of professional autonomy and responsibility, it specifies chains of principal–agent relationships as a series of contracts as a means of rendering the management function clear and accountable. Agency Theory theorizes hierarchical work relationships as contracts where a principal becomes a commissioning party who specifies or delegates work to an agent to perform in return for some specified sanction or reward. As such, it is concerned with how to extract compliance from a voluntary exchange relationship based on dependency. Hence, it speaks to the relationship between employer and employee in all types of work contexts – schools, government agencies, universities and businesses.

Like other neoliberal theories, AT assumes that individuals are rational utility maximizers and, because of this, the interests of principals and agents will inevitably diverge. In any management context, the problems encountered by the principal amount to a range of uncertainties and difficulties in obtaining information. In many senses, both principals and agents have access to information that the other party does not. In addition, agents will have an incentive to exploit their situation to their own advantage. They may, for instance, withhold information that would be to their disadvantage in the process of recruitment. In addition, in similar vein, there are many instances where the behaviour of agents is difficult for principals to observe. In order to minimize risks in the employment situation, AT specifies a range of monitoring, information eliciting and performance appraisal techniques which include the following:

- determining the best form of contract;
- determining the best way of motivating agents;
- determining the best way of spurring performance (via rewards and sanctions); and
- finding the best way of monitoring and specifying contracts to guard against excesses and dangers produced by opportunism on the part of the agent, due to 'shirking' deception, cheating or collusion.

Agency Theory, as well as the other neoliberal theories, is relevant to understanding the unprecedented disaggregation of the public sector that has occurred in OECD countries since the late 1970s. It has been central to the dramatic scale of the restructuring that has occurred in these countries. It has underpinned funder/provider and policy/delivery splits (the 'decoupling' strategies) both within the public sector bureaucracy as well as between the bureaucracy and the state, and resulted in policies of deregulation, corporatization and privatization. In addition, Althaus (1997: 137) notes that 'New Zealand and the United Kingdom have engaged in a unique application of agency theory which places them at the forefront of its application to the public sector'. Such a model, it was claimed, increased accountability and efficiency, rendering government departments analogous to private companies. As such, AT was, says Althaus (1997: 141) a:

> means of conceptualizing and rationalizing human behaviour and organizational forms ... [i]t is a scrutiny of the interaction between a distinct relationship between two parties – the principal and agent – within a context assuming individual self-interest maximization, bounded rationality, risk-aversion, goal conflict among members and the treatment of information as a commodity which can be purchased.

What were not noted by the political reformers, however, were the negative consequences of such disaggregative models. Research in Britain (Greer, 1992: 223; Hede, 1991: 38; and Trosa, 1994) and in New Zealand (Ewart and Boston, 1993) notes that when policy advice is separated from operations, the emergence of destructive subcultures can result, which can in turn lead to the duplication of advice and services as well as increased distrust, tensions,

161

rivalry and disruption instead of the theorized would-be benefits of greater contestability.

Transaction Cost Economics

Agency costs are effectively the subject of Transaction Cost Economics (TCE), which is another form of economic theory linked closely to Agency Theory, Public Choice Theory and Property Rights Theory.[3] Principally espoused in the work of Oliver Williamson (1975; 1983; 1985; 1991; 1992; 1994), it seeks to analyse and account for the efficiency costs of transacting business and the effect these have on organizational form. In this respect, as Charles Perrow (1986a: 18) puts it, TCE is 'relentlessly and explicitly an efficiency argument'. In this sense, TCE is used to evaluate the efficiency of alternative governance structures or sets of institutional arrangements for various kinds of transactions, especially those generated by the market. Like other neoliberal theories, it assumes a social-ontological context of 'uncertainty', 'bounded rationality', 'limited' and 'asymmetrical' information, and of the 'opportunism' of the 'self-interested' subject. Using theory-specific concepts such as 'small numbers bargaining' and 'asset specificity', TCE endeavours to show why various sorts of organizational forms (involving mergers or takeovers or various forms of organizational integration) may be preferred to a pure market form. In accounting for the increasing size of business organizations over the century, Williamson (1983: 125) argues 'that efficiency is the main and only systematic factor responsible for the organizational changes that have occurred'. In essence, then, TCE is about the most efficient method of organization given a particular market context.

It has a number of central theory-specific concepts. These are 'uncertainty', 'small numbers bargaining', 'bounded rationality', 'opportunism' and 'asset specificity'. While opportunism expresses the 'self-interested' nature of individual actions, bounded rationality attests to the absence of perfect information, or to the asymmetrical nature of information between two or more parties in any exchange relation. It is due to the absence of perfect information that the market equilibrium becomes unstable, introducing 'uncertainty', which in turn allows agents to act 'opportunistically'. For instance, where it is possible, a party to a contract may exhibit dishonest or unreliable behaviour in order to secure a market advantage. However, the ability to do so will depend upon the nature of the context, the degree of uncertainty in the environment and the extent to which information between the parties is 'asymmetrical'.

Williamson introduces several other concepts which attest to the bilateral nature of exchange and the distortions that are introduced and which need to be overcome when real-life interactions fail to match the precise model of the classical market. 'Small numbers bargaining' gives the parties to an initial contract an advantage over parties not so included in the contract, and tends to constitute a conservative pressure for firms not to change or not to be responsive to actual market signals. In this sense, the convenience of preserving an existing arrangement, or of continuing to hire existing staff, may override the fact that more competitive tenders exist, or that 'better' or less disruptive staff could be employed. The concept of 'asset specificity' is related, for long-term parties to a contract tend to have specific assets which become a form of bargaining power and, again, militate against change in line with the expectations generated by the classical model of the market order.

In the context of these potentially disruptive influences, TCE proposes that forms of administrative and governance structures can be instituted which counteract these adverse effects and which render transaction costs efficient relative to a specific form of market competition. Hence, while opportunism and bounded rationality produce different kinds of costs, these must in turn be offset by the types of governance structures in place. Agency Theory becomes relevant here in specifying a formalized structure of contracts between principals and agents to counter the possible distortions or costs associated with opportunism and bounded rationality. Forms of monitoring and performance appraisal also operate in this regard. In his later works, Williamson (1991; 1992; 1994) focuses attention on public sector governance issues and specifically on the problem of selecting governance structures which are most efficient, that is, which minimize the costs of the different organizational transactions involved.

Underpinning both Transaction Cost Economics as well as Agency Theory is Property Rights Theory (PRT), which is the fundamental grounding theory for the conception of self-interested human behaviour assumed in neoliberal theories. As such, the incentives structure of agents and principals in AT is assumed using PRT, which is essentially a theory of 'ownership' of property as it inheres in the individual. Central to PRT is the entitlement to scarce commodities and a conception of the system of exchange rules in terms of which such commodities may be transferred. As McKean (1974: 175) states, property rights are essentially 'one's effective rights to do things and effective claims to reward (positive or negative) as a result of one's action'. Such a theory assists in conceptualizing the structuring of incentives in relation to the management of institutions.

Transaction Cost Economics, with AT, PRT and PCT, are collectively represented as part and parcel of the New Institutional Economics (NIE) or of New Public Management (NPM) (Hood, 1991). The common language of such an approach stresses concepts such as 'outputs', 'outcomes', 'accountability', 'ownership', 'specification', 'contracts', 'purchase agreements' and so on. Central to such an approach is an emphasis on contract which ostensibly replaces central regulation by a new system of public administration which introduces such concepts as clarification of purpose, role clarification, task specification, quality assurance, reliable reporting procedures and the freedom to manage. According to Alex Matheson (1997), contractualism includes relations (1) where parties have some autonomy to their role, (2) where there are distinctions between roles and therefore where a clarification of roles is obtainable, (3) where the specific role components are specifiable and where as a consequence individuals can be held accountable, (4) where responsibility flows downwards, rather than upwards, that is, responsibility can be identified as fixed in terms of a specific role, (5) where the assignment of work is by agreement, (6) where there is an objective basis for judging performance, (7) where transparency is a feature of the agreement process, and (8) where there are explicit consequences (sanctions or rewards) for fulfilment or non-fulfilment.

The consequence of such a contractualism is to view all work relations as principal–agent hierarchies, thereby redefining the appropriate process in terms of outputs, and where services are viewed in terms of cost and quality. Such a system gives rise to new patterns of employment (fixed-term contracts) and new forms of accountability whereby relationships are more directly clarified and services more clearly described. Such an approach, says Alex Matheson, has low transaction costs, few legal fees and few direct compliance costs.

According to Graham Scott (1997), former Secretary to the New Zealand Treasury, the New Institutional Economics, especially AT, constituted a strategy that 'appeared promising' in terms of its commitments to (1) strategic management, (2) divestment of non-core activities (3) re-engineering to create customer focus, (4) de-layering/de-coupling, (5) total quality management, (6) use of modern information technology for management information systems, (7) improved accountability systems, and (8) establishing appropriate cultural values, teamwork and leadership. Not only was the NIE important for the selection and modification of governance structures, but it enabled a much tighter and clearer specification of roles, as well as greatly increased accountability. Such theories acted as influential forces on the people who were in key advisory positions in the OECD countries. The key concerns of the NIE were a concern with transaction costs, concepts and principles for analysing them through enhanced specification of tasks and goals, increased transparency, clear allocation of responsibilities and duties, the imposition of a heightened incentive structure, and a greater ability to monitor the contracts linked to a greatly increased accountability system. Central to the structural reforms in OECD countries, but especially England, New Zealand and Australia, were the following practices and principles derived from NIE:

- an emphasis on management rather than policy, in particular a new stress on management skills in preference to technical or professional skills;
- a shift from the use of input controls and bureaucratic procedures and rules to a reliance on quantifiable output measures and performance targets;
- the devolution of management control coupled with the development of new reporting, monitoring and accountability mechanisms;

- the disaggregation of large bureaucratic structures into quasi-autonomous agencies, in particular the separation of commercial from non-commercial functions, of policy advice from policy implementation, of ownership and purchase responsibilities, of policy from operations, of funding, purchasing and provision of services, and reallocation of functions for focus, synergy and information;
- a preference for private ownership, contracting out and competition between service providers for greater efficiency;
- the imitation of certain private sector management practices involving the use of short-term labour contracts, the development of quality control and audit procedures, involving the development of corporate plans, performance agreements and mission statements, new management information systems and a greater concern for corporate image; and
- a general preference for monetary incentives rather than non-monetary incentives, and a stress on cost-cutting and efficiency.

Libertarian political philosophy

In addition to neoliberal economic theories, the political philosophies of writers like Robert Nozick (1974) and John Hospers (1971) effectively serve to buttress 'new right' theories based on new theories of natural rights and of natural law. Both Nozick and Hospers can be classified as 'libertarian', along with writers such as Ayn Rand (1961; 1964) and Murray Rothbard (1978). The concept 'libertarian' is used here to refer to a particular political discourse which places a stress on the liberty and rights of individuals irrespective of or without relevance to the interests of society as a whole. Libertarianism entails the liberty of each person to live according to their own choices, provided that they do not attempt to coerce others and prevent them from living according to their choices. Libertarians hold this to be an inalienable right of people; thus libertarianism represents a strong commitment to the concept of individual rights. Although libertarians share a common concern with individual rights within a tradition of political philosophy, the specific extent of their anti-statism varies (for instance Rothbard and Rand have a stronger commitment to privatizing state functions than does Nozick) in the same way that neoliberals' perspectives on the state vary. To the extent that there is a difference between 'libertarians' and 'neoliberals', the former is a political discourse of rights, the latter is more an economic discourse of the allocative efficiency and progress of markets. While Hayek, like Adam Smith, sought to reconcile individual self-interest with social harmony (via catallaxy), libertarians, as the term is conventionally used, are more concerned with the 'interests' or 'entitlements' of individuals irrespective of the effects of such self-interest on the society as a whole.

In *Anarchy, State and Utopia* (1974), Robert Nozick's commitments are to reinstate a theory of individual property-based rights and a radically reduced state. Believing that the state should not diminish the liberty of individuals in any way, he argues for what he calls a minimal 'nightwatchman' state. In a project that can be seen as an attempt to reinstate the rational core of Locke's political philosophy, Nozick follows the natural rights, individualist tradition. In this tradition, Nozick sees the state as existing purely to safeguard the personal and property rights of individuals. Against the anarchists such as Ayn Rand or Murray Rothbard, Nozick argues that a minimal state is justified. Against the supporters of the welfare state, he argues that a minimal state is its only legitimate form. Hence the state only has the narrow functions of protection against force, theft, fraud and the enforcement of contracts. In essence, therefore, it is simply a 'Dominant Protection Association'. That is, it is a minimal state and has only two functions: (1) a monopoly on the use of force and the protection of all in its territory, and (2) the enforcement of voluntary contracts.

As a corollary to his theory of the state, Nozick reinstates a classical theory of 'self-ownership' where each person is the rightful owner of their self and body, and where each individual is surrounded by a protected sphere of rights. This idea of 'self-ownership' stands at the heart of classical liberalism and was developed in the writings of Locke, Kant and Mill. For Nozick, individual rights fill the whole political landscape, and the rights to life, liberty and property fall within the individual's 'protected sphere'. Consistent with the Lockean tradition, his conception of rights is exclusively negative, which is to say rights are restricted to 'non-intervention' rights – one person may not interfere with what rightfully belongs to another. There are no welfare rights or rights of recipience, for example, to food, medicine or decent social conditions. For Nozick, as for all libertarians, property rights are absolutely basic. In this Nozick follows Locke. Since in the pre-social world no one owns anything, everyone has an equal right to everything. What makes something mine is if I expend labour upon appropriating it; that is, taking it out of common ownership and into my own possession.

It is by taking account of how things actually came about, rather than by seeking to impose patterns or arrangements according to some predetermined principle of justice, that lies at the heart of Nozick's 'historical' conception of justice. Nozick's theory concerning the individual leads him to argue for an 'entitlement' theory of justice where considerations of how things came to be in history form the basis of entitlement, and entitlement rather than 'need' or 'merit' is the basis of the right to property. Nozick opposes all 'end-state' or 'distributive' principles (such as equality). Rather, he says (Nozick, 1974: 151), 'whatever arises from a just situation by just steps is itself just'. In this conception, there is no distributive justice though he does recognize that there can be redistributions for past violations of rights due to dishonesty or fraud. On issues such as taxation or health, however, Nozick makes no concessions: all taxation is unjust for it appropriates the legitimate property of the individual. Similarly, on issues to do with health, Nozick argues for self-reliance and self-help. For Nozick, it is 'user pays', the user being the isolated atomistic individual of classical liberalism.

Other libertarians adopt broadly similar conceptions, placing a fundamental emphasis on property rights. For John Hospers (1971), for instance, there are three sets of rights. The first concerns the right to life: each person has a right to be protected against the use of force by others. The second concerns the right to liberty: there should be no suppression of freedom of speech, of the press, or of assembly. In addition there should be no censorship of ideas, books, films and so on by the government. The third concerns the right to property: like all libertarians, Hospers supports the total protection of property rights of individuals against confiscation, robbery, trespass and so on.

Foucault's analysis of neoliberalism

In his lectures at the Collège de France in 1978 and 1979 Foucault focuses his attention on classical liberals such as Adam Smith, David Hume and Adam Ferguson, and two variants of post-Second World War neoliberals: the *Ordoliberalen* in Germany and the Human Capital theorists in the USA. (Burchell, 1991; 1996; Foucault, 1982b; 1984b; 1991b; 1992; 1993; 1997a; 1997b; 2001a; 2001b; Lemke, 2001).[4]

The *Ordoliberalen* comprised a group of jurists and economists in the years 1928–30 who published in the yearbook, *Ordo*. Amongst their numbers were included William Röpke, Walter Eucken, Franz Böhm, Alexander Rüstow, Alfred Müller-Armack and others. Preaching the slogan that 'inequality is equal for all' they devised a social market economy influencing the shaping of West German economic policy as it developed after the war. Foucault refers to these *Ordoliberalen* as the 'Freiberg school' who had some affinities (of time and place) with the Frankfurt school but were of a very different political persuasion. While they held that Nazism was a consequence of the absence of liberalism, they did not see liberalism as a doctrine based upon the natural freedom of the individual that will develop by itself of its own volition. In fact, for the 'Freiberg school' the market economy was not an autonomous, or naturally self-regulating entity at all. As a consequence, their conception of the market and of the role of competition, says Foucault, is radically anti-naturalistic. Rather than the market being a natural arena which the state must refrain from interfering with, it is rather constituted and kept going by the state's political machine. Similarly, competition is not a natural fact which emerges spontaneously from human social intercourse, as a result of human nature, but must be engineered by the state.

As a consequence of this, the traditional distinction between a sphere of natural liberty and a sphere of government intervention no longer holds, for the market order and competition are engineered by the practices of government. Both the state and the market are on this conception artificial and both presuppose each other. In Foucault's view such a conception means that the principle of laissez-faire, which can be traced back to a distinction between culture (the artificial state) and nature (the self-regulating market), no longer holds. For the *Ordoliberalen*, the history of capitalism is an institutional history. Capitalism is a particular contingent apparatus by which economic processes and institutional frameworks are articulated. Not only is there no 'logic of capital' in this model, but the *Ordoliberalen* held that the dysfunctions of capitalism could only be corrected by political-institutional interventions which they saw as contingent historical phenomena. What this means, says Foucault, is that the *Ordoliberalen* support the active creation of the social conditions for an effective competitive market order. Not only must government block and prevent anti-competitive practices, but it must fine-tune and actively promote competition in both the economy and in areas where the market mechanism is traditionally least prone to operate. One policy to this effect was to 'universalize the entrepreneurial form' (Lemke, 2001: 195) through the promotion of an enterprise culture, premised, as Foucault put it in a lecture given on 14 February 1979, on 'equal inequality for all' (Lemke, 2001: 195). The goal here was to increase competitive forms throughout society so that social and work relations in general assume the market form, that is, exhibit competition, obey laws of supply and demand. In the writings of Rüstow, this was called 'vital policy' (*Vitalpolitik*) which described policies geared to reconstructing the moral and cultural order to promote and reward entrepreneurial behaviour, opposing bureaucratic initiatives which stifle the market mechanism. To achieve such goals, the *Ordoliberalen* also advocated the redefining of law and of juridical institutions so that they could function to correct the market mechanism and discipline non-entrepreneurial behaviour within an institutional structure in accordance with, and supported by, the law. In this sense, the *Ordoliberalen* were not simply anti-naturalist, but constructivist.

In his analysis of neoliberalism, Foucault also directs his attention to the Chicago school of Human Capital theorists in America, focusing particularly on the works of Becker. These neoliberals also opposed state interventionism when it was bureaucratic and supported it when it fostered and protected economic liberty. For Human Capital theorists the concern was the uncontrolled growth of the bureaucratic apparatus as a threat to the freedom of the individual. Foucault sees the major distinction between the German and US neoliberals existing in the fact that in the USA neoliberalism was much less a political crusade than it was in Germany or France, for in the USA the critique was centrally directed against state interventionism and aimed to challenge the growth of the state apparatus. In his lecture of 28 March 1979, Foucault discusses Hayek and von Mises (whom he labels as the 'intermediaries of US neoliberalism'), Simons, Schultz, Stigler and Gary Becker, whom he says is the most radical exponent in the USA. The US neoliberals saw the *Ordoliberalen* as representing the political as being above and outside the market but constantly intervening to correct its bureaucratic dislocations. From their viewpoint, they wanted to extend the market across into the social arena and political arenas, thus collapsing the distinction between the economic, social and political in what constitutes a marketization of the state. No longer is the state independent of and outside the market, but itself now subject to market laws. In doing this, the US neoliberals extend economic criteria into spheres which are not economic and market exchange relations now govern all areas of voluntary exchange amongst individuals. In this model, the social and political spheres become redefined as economic domains. The government and the public sector will be 'economized' to reflect market principles and mechanisms. Thus the economic covers all of society and society is theorized as a form of the economic. The task of government is to construct and universalize competition to achieve efficiency and invent market systems. As Foucault states, for the US neoliberals, the market becomes 'a kind of permanent economic tribunal' ('une sorte de tribunal économique permanent') (Foucault, Lecture, 21 March 1979 – cited Lemke, 2001: 198).

As Foucault sees HCT, it is concerned with the problem of labour in economic theory. While classical political economy claimed that the production of goods depended upon real estate, capital and labour, neoliberals held that only real estate and capital are treated appropriately by the classical theory, and that labour needs greater illumination as an active, rather than as a passive, factor in production. In this sense neoliberals concurred with Marx that classical political economy had forgotten labour and thereby they misrepresent the process of production. In order to correct this deficiency, neoliberals theorize the role and importance of labour in terms of a model of human capital. In essence their theory starts with the human individual in terms of a classification of skills, knowledge and ability. Although, unlike other forms of capital, they cannot be separated from the individuals who own these resources, they nevertheless constitute resources which can be sold in a market. Becker distinguishes two central aspects to such human capital: (1) inborn, physical and genetic dispositions, and (2) education, nutrition, training and emotional health. In this model, each person is now an autonomous entrepreneur responsible ontologically for their own selves and their own progress and position. Individuals have full responsibility over their investment decisions and must aim to produce a surplus value. As Foucault puts it in his 14 March 1979 lecture, they are 'entrepreneurs of themselves'.

As Graham Burchell (1996: 23–4) puts this point, while for classical liberalism the basis of government conduct is in terms of 'natural, private-interest-motivated conduct of free, market exchanging individuals', for neoliberalism 'the rational principle for regulating and limiting governmental activity must be determined by reference to artificially arranged or contrived forms of free, entrepreneurial and competitive conduct of economic-rational individuals'. This means that for neoliberal perspectives, the end goals of freedom, choice, consumer sovereignty, competition and individual initiative, as well as those of compliance and obedience, must be constructions of the state acting now in its positive role through the development of the techniques of auditing, accounting and management. It is these techniques, as Barry, Osborne and Rose (1996: 14) put it: '[that] enable the marketplace for services to be established as "autonomous" from central control. Neoliberalism, in these terms, involves less a retreat from governmental "intervention" than a re-inscription of the techniques and forms of expertise required for the exercise of government.'

Notwithstanding this rather crucial difference between the two forms of liberalism, the common element expresses a distinctive concern. For both classical liberalism and neoliberalism, what defines this concern is a common orientation concerning 'the limits of government in relation to the market' (Burchell, 1996: 22). This was so, says Burchell, in relation to the early classical liberals, the Anglo-Scottish school, the *Ordoliberalen* of the Federal German Republic, the Chicago school of economic liberals, as well as other variants of neoliberalism in the twentieth century. Hence, as Burchell says (ibid.: 22–3), classical liberalism emerged 'in relation to a problem of how a necessary market freedom can be reconciled with the unlimited exercise of a political sovereignty'. The Anglo-Scottish school 'set limits to the State's capacity to know and act by situating it in relation to the reality of the market or of commercial exchanges, and more broadly of civil society, as quasi-natural domains with their own intrinsic dynamic and forms of self-regulation'. For modern forms of neoliberalism it is still a matter concerning the limits of government action in relation to the market. Hence:

> For the German school of *Ordoliberalen* that developed during and after the Second World War ... the problem is not one of how a space can be found within an existing State for a necessary market freedom, but of how to create a State on the basis of an economic freedom that will secure the State's legitimacy and self-limitation . .... . The Chicago school of economic liberalism ... also functions as a criticism of the consequences of too much government. What they have in common, putting it very crudely, is a question concerning the extent to which competitive, optimizing market relations and behaviour can serve as a principle not only for limiting governmental intervention, but also rationalizing government itself. Both are looking for a principle for rationalizing government by reference to an idea of the market. Where they differ from earlier forms of liberalism is that they do not regard the market as an existing quasi-natural reality situated in a kind of economic nature reserve space marked off, secured and supervised by the State. Rather, the market exists, and can only exist, under certain political, legal and institutional conditions that must be actively constructed by government. (Burchell, 1996: 22–3)

While there is thus an important difference between those forms of liberalism that existed from the seventeenth to the end of the nineteenth century and the forms of neoliberalism that emerged in the twentieth century, the special nature of the relationship between government and governed, and the priority of a market of free associations within this relationship, constitutes a central and continuous thread through the various different forms of liberalism. In this, as Burchell (1996: 23) points out, both early and later liberalism 'set out a schema of the relationship between government and the governed in which individuals are identified as, on the one hand, the object and target of governmental action and, on the other hand, as in some sense the necessary (voluntary) partner or accomplice of government'.

Neoliberalism as a mode of control

In addition to a common priority concerning the scope of the market, both classical liberalism and neoliberalism share common views concerning the nature of the individual, as rational self-interested subjects. In this perspective the individual is presented as a rational optimizer and the best judge of his or her own interests and needs. Being rational is to follow a systematic programme of action underpinned and structured according to rules. The rules are rendered coherent and permissible in relation to the 'interests' of the individual. Such a notion is located both within classical liberalism and classical political economy. It is epitomized in the writings of Thomas Hobbes, John Locke, Adam Smith, Adam Ferguson and David Hume amongst many others. Twentieth-century neoliberals endorse this view.

Neo- and classical liberals also endorse a strong commitment to free trade. Consistent with the faith in market economics, in the international sphere classical economic liberals favoured 'free trade', involving the abolition of tariffs or subsidies, or any form of state-imposed protection or support, as well as the maintenance of floating exchange rates and 'open' economies. These commitments are today central to the philosophies of neoliberalism, and constitute central planks in the economic policies of global agencies such as the World Bank and the International Monetary Fund.

With regard to the nature of the relations between individuals and society or the role of the state there are some major differences however. As we saw in Chapter 5 the theory by which individual–society relations are structured in classical economic liberalism maintained the notion of an 'invisible hand' by which the uncoordinated self-interest of individuals correlates with the interests and harmony or good of the whole society. This, as we saw, was central to Smith's writings on the harmonization of individuals' private interests with the progress of the whole society. The hand works because it is uncoordinated and unplanned, and there is no good resulting from any purposeful attempt to direct it for the public good. From the time Smith wrote such a notion has been central to liberalism. It has countered more interventionist ideas of the role and purpose of the state. It has militated against public planning and attempts at collective agency to co-ordinate the public interest on behalf of individuals. During the nineteenth and twentieth centuries it has fuelled countless concern with the issue of both the size and function of the state. Under invisible hand theory, the state represents what is *artificial*, standing over and against the 'nature-reserve' of uncoordinated initiatives of free spontaneous individuals. To compromise or infringe the individual's liberty is to interfere with nature. And because state action, except in relation to certain defensive measures that Smith set out, was seen as incompatible with liberty, rules were necessary which would limit both its power and scope.

Neoliberalism cannot be rendered compatible with this conception, for as we have seen, amongst those such as the *Ordoliberalen*, Human Capital theorists and Public Choice theorists, the state actively constructs the market. Far from existing within a protected and limited space, market relations now extend to cover all forms of voluntary behaviour amongst individuals. Rather than absenting itself from interfering in the private or market spheres of society, in the global economic era neoliberalism becomes a new authoritarian discourse of state management and control. Rather than being a form of political bureaucracy, which Weber (1921) saw as the supreme form of modernist rationality, neoliberalism constitutes a new and more advanced technology of control. It is both a substantive political doctrine of control and a self-driving technology of operations. It incorporates both more flexible and more devolved steering mechanisms than does bureaucracy. If, for Weber, bureaucracy constituted large-scale organization comprising a hierarchy of offices and lines of control, enabling efficiency, predictability, calculability and technical control, then neoliberalism, while incorporating these factors, goes beyond them to enable an extension of control in more devolved forms and in more flexible systems. This enables the function of control to be differentiated from the function of operations, or to use Osborne and Gaebler's (1992) metaphor, 'steering' from 'rowing'. It points to a more effective means of social engineering and control than classical bureaucracy, scientific management or the Fordist assembly line. Its overall rationale is to measure the costs of, and place a value on, all forms of human activity. It extends the market mechanism from the economic to the political to the social. Market exchanges now encapsulate all forms of voluntary behaviour amongst individuals.[5]

Thus, while subscribing to the doctrine of the *minimal* state, neoliberals have promoted the development of the *strong* state. While advocating privatization of resourcing and decentralization of provision of social services, neoliberal governments have built stronger state structures and introduced more robust modes of centralized control and regulation. These discourses are clearly evident in the educational policy agendas of the various nation-states that have embraced neoliberalism since the 1970s and 1980s. In the next three chapters, we present a critical account of neoliberal education policies in the context of a broader critique of neoliberalism's core assumptions and major claims. Building on this analysis, we then propose an alternative policy discourse for education based upon a reconceptualization of democracy for the new global era.

Notes

1 On this ground, it could be argued that Hayek and Friedman qualify as 'classical', and not 'neoliberals', for if 'neoliberalism' is defined, as we have suggested, as a positive form of state power, then Hayek and Friedman clearly are not included under such a definition. However, they would certainly be regarded as hugely influential precursors of neoliberalism.

2 There is an extensive literature on Agency Theory including Althaus (1997); Bendor (1988); Bergman and Lane (1990); Boston (1991, 1996), Boston et al. (1996); Braun (1993); Chan and Rosenbloom (1994); Deane (1989); Eisenhardt (1989); Heymann (1988); Jennings and Cameron (1987); Jensen and Meckling (1976); Kay (1992); Levinthal (1988); Moe (1984; 1990; 1991); Palmer (1993); Perrow (1986a; 1986b); Petersen (1993); Pratt and Zeckhauser (1985); Rees (1985a; 1985b); Scott and Gorringe (1989); Simon (1991); Thompson and Wright (1988); Treblicock (1995); Weingast (1984); Wistrich (1992).

3 For an introduction to Transaction Cost Economics see, Boston (1994), Boston et al. (1996), Bryson and Smith-Ring (1990), Dow (1987), Perrow (1986a; 1986b), Vining and Weimer (1990), Williamson (1975; 1983; 1985; 1991; 1992).

4 This section has been influenced by Lemke's (2001) excellent analysis, and by Burchell (1996).

5 This is the process which Ritzer (2000) describes as the 'McDonaldization of Society'.

9
Markets, Professionalism, Trust

Although in the last quarter of the twentieth century, neoliberalism constituted a dominant and effective discourse in OECD countries, any consideration of the micro-politics of education policy-making within different OECD countries reveals a contradictory and 'messy' picture as far as its specific applications are concerned. This chapter examines the effects of neoliberal restructuring on the nature and purposes of public education, with a particular focus on the reconstitution of citizenship and social relations within education by the discourses of marketization and managerialism.

Educational restructuring in England

As Ball (1990b; 1994) indicates in relation to the 'new right' in England, there were a number of ideological influences which competed to shape policies, including 'old reformist humanists', 'new progressives', 'neo-conservatives', 'conservative industrialists' and 'professionals' (Ball, 1990b: 7). Although Thatcherism involved 'a total reworking of the ideological terrain of educational politics' (ibid.: 8), the 'new right' constituted a blend of market liberals and neo-conservative factions. This resulted in complex effects and disagreements in practice within a broader unity. It opposed comprehensive and progressive educational initiatives, and it supported a broadly based restructuring programme which sought to re-establish traditional values and standards of 'excellence', impose discipline, authority and traditional norms of morality, and advocate rigid streaming, the use of formal exams, and corporal punishment. Ball (1990b: 41) thus represents Thatcherism as an 'amalgam', and as a 'loose aggregation', as 'a blending of tensions, a managing of nascent contradictions'.

What is significant in England, however, is the contestation over specific proposals between the various contending factions. While there was a unified front in relation to denigrating teachers, local educational authorities (LEAs) and comprehensives, not all groups advocated the same thing when it came to reconstruction and 'new right' policies were significantly amended in the process of legislation. Those more orientated towards Hayekian conceptions of the market supported a minimal state, opposed producer lobbies and maintained strong commitments to diversity in education, even opposing compulsory schooling and central control. They tended, like Sir Keith Joseph, Secretary of State for Education 1981–86, and his adviser Stuart Sexton, to support industry–school links, championing vocational schooling in its role of preparing young people for the workforce. They also tended to oppose, as Sir Keith did, state control of education. It was on these grounds that he opposed plans for a legislated national curriculum. Thus, the 1986 Education Act, for which he was responsible, still saw the role of planning and determining the curriculum as lying with the school, although it sought to bolster the power of management and governors over that of the teachers. As Ball (1990b: 170) argues, it was not until Kenneth Baker replaced Keith Joseph that the ground was cleared for the introduction of the National Curriculum in the Education Reform Act (ERA) of 1988. Baker, a more traditional conservative, more directly represented Prime Minister Thatcher's influence, and advanced the increasingly interventionist role that the state was assuming in the mid-1980s leading up to the ERA. Yet this more interventionist role was not something foreign to neoliberalism, but was in fact integral to it. Although Hayekian conceptions of the market represented a more classical liberal response and advocated a minimal state, neoliberals who came after Hayek, like James Buchanan or Oliver Williamson, or the German *Ordoliberalen*, advocated a positive (that is, directive) role for the state. In this sense, it is the Thatcherites, rather than the Hayekians, that constitute the true neoliberals. Neoliberalism thus supports a conservative 'strong state' position, which also supports an 'interventionist' or 'directive' state. In this sense, Stuart Hall's (1988b: ch. 8) characterization of Thatcherism as 'authoritarian populism' is indeed correct. As Hall (1988b: 152) expresses it in relation to Thatcherism, neoliberalism is in reality a 'highly contradictory strategy ... simultaneously, dismantling the welfare state, "anti-statist" in its ideological representation and highly state-centralist and *dirigiste* in many of its strategic operations'.

Educational restructuring in New Zealand

In New Zealand, the neoliberal revolution followed the election of the fourth Labour government in the 'snap' election of July 1984. At this time, the Treasury became the most powerful bureaucratic influence in state policy-making, pursuing an agenda based upon Human Capital Theory, Public Choice Theory and Transaction Cost Economics. By 1987 these doctrines were being applied to education policy. Hence the Treasury's brief to the government that year contained a graphic account of an education system that was relentlessly squeezed between fiscal and political pressures, such that the state, it was alleged, could no longer meet public expectations and political demands for further extension and improvement of educational provision.

Readers of this Treasury document were presented with the view that state intervention in education is neither equitable nor efficient. Without producing any evidence, the document asserts that such intervention for equity purposes would probably 'produce effects that reduce rather than further some kinds of equity' (New Zealand Treasury, 1987: 39). This assertion then becomes the major premise from which to advocate policies that would enable education to enter the marketplace and thus become more effective in delivering a service to consumers.

The major neoliberal policy response was contained in the New Zealand Department of Education's 1988 report of the Taskforce to Review Educational Administration (the Picot Report) and the White Paper, *Tomorrow's Schools*, that followed it. The Picot Report, named after the businessman who chaired the taskforce, contained proposals for an extensive restructuring of the New Zealand education system. The main thrust of the restructuring was to reduce the size of the central bureaucracy, to abolish regional education boards, and to convert each learning institution into a self-managing unit having its own elected Board of Trustees. Thus the new educational structure entailed a devolution of decision-making in a wide range of administrative areas, including resource allocation, staff appointments, support services and staff development. Boards of Trustees were given some discretion in these areas, but control was firmly invested in central state agencies, including the Ministry of Education, the Education Review Office and the Qualifications Authority. This control continues to be maintained through tightly circumscribed limits on local autonomy and contractual forms of accountability.

Similarities and differences

While there were many similarities between the New Zealand reforms and those that followed the Education Reform Act (1988) there were some major differences between England and New Zealand in terms of the way neoliberal policies were implemented. For a start, as Dale and Ozga (1993) point out, the background to the changes in New Zealand differed considerably from those in England and Wales. In New Zealand there were serious economic problems which were not experienced in England. As a consequence of these, New Zealand sought a new approach to managing the economy and reducing state expenditures through reforming public administration and reducing the size and scope of operations of the state. The reforms were presented from the start in terms of a necessary corrective to inherited deficiencies of the Keynesian mode of economic regulation in relation to welfare spending, the size of the state and the capture of key bureaucracies by producer interests. The state was seen as playing too great a role in relation to economic management, restricting the operations of the market, and creating unnecessary inefficiencies as a result of a 'top-heavy' and cumbersome bureaucracy. (See

Chapter 6 for an account of the political context for the sudden advent of neoliberalism in New Zealand.)

In England the 'crisis' was not simply concerned with administration but was identified as 'political' from the start and focused centrally on the ideological orientations of teachers, LEAs, and on developments within progressive and comprehensive education. Policy criticisms during the 1980s were preoccupied with standards which were seen as falling largely due to the progressive methods and left-wing political orientations of the teachers and LEAs, both of whom exercised too much autonomy, and therefore failed to be accountable to parents, employers and other interested groups. The ERA (1988) was thus much more encompassing than the New Zealand report of the Taskforce to Review Educational Administration (Picot Report). In addition to the issues of administration, it also dealt with matters such as the curriculum.

Behind these differences in approach there were also different sources of support for reform, as Dale and Ozga (1993) point out. Whereas in England, the criticisms of education contained both conservative and neoliberal elements, in New Zealand the sources of support were more consistently neoliberal. Whereas in England, the reforms thus marked a 'return to the past', in New Zealand they were orientated to the creation of a better future. Whereas in England, education was identified as the central issue from the outset, in New Zealand, the original impetus for reform was targeted as public administration. In New Zealand then, there was no 'discourse of derision' (Ball, 1990b) with respect to teachers or local schools as there was in England. As Brian Picot said, in launching the report of the Taskforce to Review Educational Administration (New Zealand Department of Education, 1988), the existing situation was one of 'good teachers/bad system' (Barry, 1996). In addition, the influence of traditional conservatives, supporting the causes of tradition, morality, standards, traditional subject disciplines, God, nation and family was not as significantly apparent in New Zealand. To the extent that neoliberal arguments did invoke political clothing in New Zealand they appended themselves to progressive left-wing concerns of enhancing equity in the areas of gender and race. But the central justifications were presented as a need to reform administration and make the system more efficient 'for the good of the country as a whole'. The state, it became clear, would direct proceedings to lessen bureaucracy by divesting traditional functions in preference for a devolutionary model which supported 'self-managing schools' which would be managed by local Boards of Trustees (BOTs) and would ultimately be funded on a per capita pupil basis (eventually labelled 'bulk-funding'). Finally, the conflicts and arguments proceeding legislation were of a different character to those evident in England, and ran along different axes: Labour Prime Minister David Lange, a staunch social democrat to the last, fell out with the architect of the reforms, Finance Minister Roger Douglas, and ultimately resigned from office as a result. There were occasional conflicts too over specific policies as well as between the various agencies of state (Treasury and State Services Commission) and between private sector interests such as the New Zealand Business Round Table (NZBRT) and the government over proposals for central control such as the New Zealand Qualifications Authority (NZQA).

Beyond these very different national contexts, and the much faster speed of reform in New Zealand (Dale and Ozga, 1993; Hood, 1991), both reform periods can be identified as distinctively neoliberal. Both constituted at the global level responses to the breakdown of the Keynesian welfare state, both advanced educational ideas that can be represented distinctively as 'new right', both were premised upon an increase in state control of education and social services, adapting them more directly to the requirements of the economy (see Figure 9.1). In this conception the state would 'steer' but not 'row', in the words of Osborne and Gaebler (1992). It would continue to control and direct from afar, but it would not regulate in the traditional 'bureaucratic' sense. Furthermore, what Stuart Hall (1988b: 163) says of Thatcherism, is equally true of New Zealand's Rogernomics (after Finance Minister, Roger Douglas):

> Thatcherism came into existence in contestation with the old Keynesian welfare state, with social democratic 'statism', which, in its view, had dominated the 1960s. Thatcherism's project was to transform the state in order to restructure society: to decentre, to displace, the whole post-war formation; to reverse the political culture which had formed the basis of the political settlement – the historic compromise between labour and capital – which had been in place from 1945 onwards.

This neoliberal transformation, however, has produced its own policy tensions, problems and contradictions. We shall examine some of these in the following sections of this chapter as we develop a critique of neoliberalism.

Markets and the state

The weaknesses of neoliberal approaches to public sector restructuring have become increasingly evident during the 1990s in OECD countries. The claim that private ownership is more efficient than public ownership is empirically less than self-evident and would need much more rigorous argumentation than has been provided to date. As Self (1989: 19) notes, for instance: 'Consumers do not only want the cheapest possible market goods, they also want safe drugs, wholesome foods, clean air and water, quiet and safe streets, unpolluted beaches, a beautiful countryside.' Further, says Self (1989: 19), deregulation often results in public hazards and other adverse effects (for example, water privatization in the UK upon health and river pollution; electricity provision in NZ upon public safety, environmental catastrophes such as oil spills, acid rain, atmospheric pollution, deforestation, noxious wastes and so on), all of which constitute increased reasons for public action. In other words, real individual wants and preferences value qualities such as good local services and amenities, the avoidance of urban congestion, all of which strengthen the case for effective public planning rather than the maximization of market preferences. In this, as Self (1989: 22) notes:

> The project of modeling government upon the market overlooks that government is there to control the market and needs an appropriate bureaucratic independence and integrity for this purpose. Its lack of any but a negative concept of 'public philosophy' blocks understanding of the broader role which governments today accept, and of the moral and intellectual resources essential to this task.

We have already noted in a previous chapter Keynes's discovery that the market has no inherent tendency to 'self-regulation'. Markets in fact generate inequality and encourage competition instead of co-operation as the central structuring norm of the community. In this sense, while markets are an important mechanism for the efficient performance and growth of the economic lives of individuals and communities, they must in their own right be regulated and controlled by the state.

If markets create inequality then unless regulated they cannot be sensitive to important issues like social need. On this basis consumer demand cannot be seen as equivalent to social need. Yet the notion of 'choice' entailed in neoliberal theory derives directly from a conception of consumer demand which is frequently confused with social need. Mistakenly believing that markets conform to a model of 'equality of opportunity', neoliberals overlook their inherent power inequalities. Consumer demand is skewed by people's ability to pay, and, because it is shaped by unequally distributed purchasing power, market forces are a poor indicator of social need. Products will not respond to needs of groups who cannot pay or which translate as weak demands due to differences in purchasing power. Markets breed inequality in relation to neglected/prosperous, high earners/low earners, wealth/poverty and success/failure. The extent to which this is so needs to be monitored on an ongoing basis through research by the state.

Markets and individual freedom

A series of related criticisms pertain to the issue of markets and rational choice. Of particular importance is that the consumer cannot be supposed to have perfect foresight or make rational decisions based on perfect knowledge or understanding of the situation. It is highly implausible, as Robert Lane (1993) points out, that all people can be represented as economic agents who can be relied on to make choices that are in all cases rational; that they are infinitely clear-headed about how to go about realizing their goals and obtaining their desires; that they are capable of foreseeing all of the consequences of their actions; that they can discover which is the best strategy to service their

	Classical liberal	Welfare liberal	Neoliberal
The state			
• Modes of regulation	'Negative' conception of state power; social contract; laissez-faire	Keynesian; state/market separation	'Positive' conception of state power; marketization of the state
• Core philosophical principles	Freedom of the individual and individual rights to 'life, liberty and property'	Egalitarian – aims to minimize differences between classes; 'new' rights to welfare and education	Enterprise economy, more support for the entrepreneurial spirit in private and public realms
• State and welfare	Encourage self-help. Leave assistance for individuals to local charities and voluntary societies	Supporting the causalities of social change through organized state welfare programmes	Limited support for the causalities of social change – targeted assistance; dismantling of welfare service provision
• State/individual/ group relations	Social contract based on theory of rights, or utility	Social contract based on theory of rights, or utility + interventionist	Aims to maximize diversity and choice between people
• Form of state power	Laissez-faire; negative conception of state power limited to defence, the enforcement of contract, and limited public works	Interventionist, provider of welfare services as well as universal, 'free' and compulsory education; plays a positive role in relation to economy and civil society	Strong state/reduced service and welfare expenditure; plays a 'positive' role in relation to economy and civil society; indirect rather than direct state direction control and surveillance of people's lives
• Conception of justice	Entitlement justice as in individual ethics (Kant) or Natural Law (Locke)	Distributive or 'end-state' justice (Rawls)	Entitlement justice according to market or legal criteria, that is, one deserves what one has gained by legal means (Nozick)
Human nature			
• Basic principles	Emphasizes individual capacities and natural rights	Emphasizes human needs and mutual obligations	Emphasizes individual desires and wants; an autonomous chooser
• Motives	Motives are largely self-interested (Hobbes) although capable of altruism, sympathy, and compassion (Locke, Smith)	Mixed between altruism, wants, self-love, compassion. People are co-operative and interdependent; sense of natural justice	Dominated by the economic motives, a self-interested chooser. People are competitive and self-interested
• Shaping forces	In terms of determining influences on people, emphasizes importance of nature over nurture	Emphasizes nurture and environmentalism in combination with nature. Sees people as only partially autonomous	Emphasizes nature and the genes. People are self-constructed, on basis of choices. Each individual is responsible for themselves
Education			
• Public or private good	Education is a private good. Parents have an obligation to educate their children (a private market)	Education is a public good. It aims to guide children in terms of social needs and individual talents (free and compulsory state	Education is publicly provided but privately distributed and accessed. Educators allow consumers to choose the

	Classical liberal	Welfare liberal	Neoliberal
• The purposes of education	Education has the potential to enhance persons in the full realization of all their abilities and competencies.	Education has the potential to enhance persons in the full realization of all their abilities and competencies.	Education will be used for the advancement of individuals who have paid for their skills
• The personal ends of education	Education produces the rational person and the ends of education are the development of mind and character and truth	Education has the potential to develop the moral, ethical, social, cultural and political awareness of all citizens; emphasizes needs, interests and growth	Education is a commodity which could be traded in the marketplace for money or status. The skills acquired in education will reflect the nature of the market
• The social ends of education	Education produces the rational person; and the independent citizen who can test the truth of things through reason	Education can assist the operation of the democratic process in society; a fundamental rite of citizenship	The state has no power to decide what kind of education is best for the individual, there will be freedom of choice in schooling
• Relations between the child and the society	Personal autonomy and reason as ends of education; child respected as independent person with rational critical faculties	Education can help promote the integration of society in terms of gender, race, class and creed	Education must be responsive to the needs of their clients in order to be competitive. Individuals will receive vouchers, which they can cash for a certain type of education
Knowledge			
• The purposes of knowledge	Worthwhile knowledge satisfies the development of character and mind	Worthwhile knowledge satisfies society's needs and individuals' interests and development	Worthwhile knowledge satisfies individuals' wants to compete; is a form of capital (that is, human capital)
• Power over knowledge and the curriculum	The worth of an education is judged by expert educationists, that is, teachers, principals and educational policy planners	The worth of an education is judged by expert educationists, that is, teachers, principals and educational policy planners	The worth of an education is judged by consumers, that is, parents and industry, in terms of the marketability of the knowledge
• The nature of knowledge	Education is broad and deep and emphasizes propositional knowledge and understanding which is not assessable in terms of outcome measures, but is dependent upon a particular context and the relationship with the teacher	Education is broad and deep and emphasizes propositional knowledge and understanding which is not assessable in terms of outcome measures, but is dependent upon a particular context and the relationship with the teacher	Education emphasizes performance knowledge and skills of use to employers, which are assessable in terms of measurable outcomes. Skills not dependent on a particular learning context, or a teacher to the same extent (that is, no provider capture)

Figure 9.1 *Classical liberal, welfare liberal and neoliberal policy perspectives on state, human nature, economy and educations*

chosen ends; or that each can experience the necessary feedback to keep their expectations in balance with the objective possibilities.

Individuals will clearly differ in their ability to act rationally in their own self-interest; some will be more successful than others. If this is so, then the critic of neoliberalism believes that there is no reason to structure society exclusively in the interests of those who can succeed. Indeed, as social democrats from John Stuart Mill to Keynes have argued, there is every reason not to do so because, in the main, human beings are not self-sufficient and fiercely independent but are connected to other people and the structures of social support in various relations of dependence and need (relations which will vary depending upon their age, gender, financial means, race or other factors at a specific time and place). If this is so, then the welfare liberals' demand for a state which is not exclusively geared to the self-interests of individuals, but is generally committed to an overall conception of the good in the interests of all individuals, is more likely to be acceptable to the vast majority of its citizens.

Neoliberals contend that all forms of state action, beyond the minimal functions of the defence of the realm and the protection of basic rights to life and property, are dangerous threats to liberty. For Hayek, as stated above, the proper functioning of markets is incompatible with state planning of any sort, and as such is both inefficient, and a threat to the freedom of the individual. It would be inefficient because real knowledge is locally generated in markets. Forms of central planning ignore this localistic character of knowledge and interfere with the market's self-regulating mechanism.

Socialist and social democratic analyses of the role of markets and state planning in socialist societies depart radically from Hayek's view that planning and markets are incompatible with each other. Studies by Dickinson (1933), Lange (1939), Dobb (1955), Brus (1972), Nuti (1981) and Nove (1983) have argued for the central importance (although not priority) of markets moderated by the state. Nove, in his book *The Economics of Feasible Socialism* (1983), argues against the case for generalized central planning as a desirable or workable alternative in western Europe. He recommends an active market economy moderated by a strong state as well as extensive state, social and co-operative property.

Hayek's arguments depend on a sharp dichotomy between markets and planning. For Hayek, mistakes and errors become 'entrenched' in the process of planning. Yet why they should become 'entrenched' rather than be 'correctable', is not clear. The issue is important, for the idea that administrative lethargy and proneness to error are endemic to all forms of planning, and are not 'correctable' through internally applied quality controls, is fundamental to the concept of 'capture' which has become an important theoretical term used in neoliberal policy reports throughout the western world. In addition, the extent to which Hayek's antipathy for planning is grounded in solid evidence or simply reflects his broader *anti*-communitarianism is problematic. Empirical studies of the history of planning in Britain, such as Wootton

(1945), argue that there is little sign of any road to serfdom, or significant erosion of the liberty of the individual, as a consequence of increases in state planning in the period between the two world wars (Tomlinson, 1990: 40).

For social democrats and welfare liberals, liberty is only one of the desirable attributes of social organization, and individual self-interest is not necessarily an appropriate basis for collective decisions (Wootton, 1945: 11; Tomlinson, 1990: 40). In exalting the liberty of the individual, neoliberals allow that the state can not have purposes and duties other than those arising from the purposes and interests of specific individuals or groups of individuals. If followed logically as a principle this would prevent the state undertaking projects for, or on behalf of, communities (for example, education, health and so on). It is not necessary to deny that there are many specific freedoms whose social value consists in allowing individuals to pursue their own ends, nor that the market is not the best means of allocation for many resources. The central issue is how far the liberty of the individual and the market can be extended before choices in certain areas need to be limited because of the undesirable consequences of unrestricted individual liberty on society generally. This might occur, for instance, in relation to allowing such things as unrestricted access to fishing reserves, or in relation to being prepared to tolerate enormous levels of poverty in the society.

It may be that under certain conditions a government that refuses to act with regard to the distribution of income and wealth may well be more coercive than a government that attempts redistribution. A more communitarian approach has attractions for all those who think of society as a community independent of individuals and who think of the well-being and liberty of individuals as in some way dependent upon the good or well-being of society. One argument for recognizing the importance of society independently of the individuals which constitute it relates to the fact that there are general interests, social benefits and public goods which cannot be identified with the interests of individuals. As a result, then, the protection and promotion of these interests must be the responsibility of the state. That is, in order to protect the liberties of all individuals, the state must act to restrain those forms of actions which would necessarily damage or curtail the liberties of any members of the community through either the intended or unintended actions of the labour market, the state, or any other person(s) or group(s) within society. The state should also act 'positively' to enhance the opportunities of all members of society. State action in relation to the environment (for example, clean air) or education has been advocated on this ground.

Negative and positive liberty

A further characteristic of the neoliberal concept of freedom as it pertains to the individual is that it is purely *negative* (relating to freedom *from* constraint) and it allows no notion of freedom *to* act. As we noted in Chapter 6, the concept of negative liberty relates only to the absence of coercion. As Isaiah Berlin (1969: 122) put it in his influential essay on the concept of freedom: 'Coercion implies the deliberate interference of other human beings within the area in which I could otherwise act. You lack political liberty or freedom only if you are prevented from attaining a goal by human beings. Mere incapacity to attain a goal is not lack of political freedom.' The central characteristics of negative liberty can thus be defined in terms of the protection of individuals' conduct and choices from external interferences and contraints. In short, *freedom is the absence of external coercion*, a position supported by all classical liberals. A government that acts to protect negative liberties (rights, contracts, property) is concerned with establishing and protecting the contractual relations and agreements in terms of which such choices can be made. It is not, however, concerned to provide for, or assist to realize, the positive capacities of individuals to achieve their objectives. In this sense, while such things as poverty, illiteracy, unemployment, or inadequate or non-existent health care, or education, may severely restrict what individuals are able to do, none of these are considered to diminish a person's 'freedom' or 'negative liberty'. It is a sufficient condition of being free that nothing stands in the way.

In Berlin's conceptual classification, 'negative' liberty is contrasted with 'positive' liberty in which freedom is represented as the product of men's active endeavours to realize a collective political, economic, social, or religious ideal in terms of altering the structures of the community environment in which people live. In this sense, while negative liberty offers *freedom from*, positive liberty offers *freedom to*. This distinction has been caricatured to suggest a demarcation between a *legitimate liberal state*, that simply acts to protect basic liberties, and an *illegitimate, or politically dangerous state*, that seeks to construct a substantive vision of the good society, seeing freedom as the public expression of a political will, and as exercised in the public, rather than the private, domain. Since Berlin's essay appeared, there have been a number of criticisms by writers such as MacCallum (1967), Taylor (1979), Gray (1980) and Skinner (1984), who have criticized either the use or the viability of the distinction as a conceptual contrast, especially when faced with concrete historical examples.

David MacCallum (1967) questioned whether such a conceptual distinction is viable at all. To be concerned with negative freedom *from* coercion is, he says, also to be concerned with positive freedom *from* coercion *to do* whatever one wants to do. In a more recent article, Luke Martell (1993) has also noted how the two forms of freedom are closely interrelated. If a person's negative rights are protected, but they still lack the opportunity to act, then freedom is *pointless*. As Martell (ibid.: 110) puts it:

> This makes the idea of liberty a nonsense because a person is just as unfree to pursue a path of action because of the lack of resources they have been left with as

a result of their position in the market as they are because the state has deliberately deprived them of a right to do so. One coercion may be more acceptable than another.

What Martell is saying is that negative liberty is achievable in a strictly inegalitarian society, which means that some have greater capacities to act freely than others do. The negative view also does not account for the fact that many of the obstacles to freedom may be *internal* rather than *external* to individuals' development, concerning such things as insufficient knowledge, skills, awareness, or resources to act freely in a meaningful and worthwhile sense, as T.H. Green argued in the late nineteenth century. Simply for the state to remove *external* obstacles does not necessarily assist someone *to act* freely. This sort of argument for a positive view of freedom would lead to state support for things like education, health care and welfare, and was in fact one of the important justifications for the welfare state in the late nineteenth and early twentieth centuries. Such a theory maintains that all people should have the resources and capacities to express and realize their freedom in their actions. This in turn entails a broadly egalitarian society, at least in the sense of offering equality of access, a minimum acceptable standard of living, as well as access to forms of cultural capital such as literacy and numeracy.

For classical liberals, the advocacy of negative over positive freedom constitutes the moral justification for *laissez-faire* and the restrictions on the role of the state. It is the positive role of the state that constituted the sources of totalitarianism.[1] This, in our view, is a weak argument, for to condemn the arbitrary imposition of a moral decision or goal by a political ruler, or government, while it certainly constitutes undemocratic conduct, is in no way incompatible with, and should not be confused with, a political authority promoting a substantive vision of the good life. Indeed, we will claim, in the next chapters, that it is *not* possible for a political authority *not* to promote, or act in accord with, such a substantive view or vision. Although our view is that the broad conceptual distinction between negative and positive liberty is useful in describing 'two such families of conceptions of political freedom', to use Charles Taylor's (1979: 175) expression, just because a state acts positively, which in the global era of the twenty-first century, *all must do*, does not mean that it promotes any propensity to totalitarianism. Indeed, we do not believe that there is any relationship at all between negative/positive state role, and propensity for democratic or non-democratic rule, and our position in this respect will become clearer in the final chapters of this study.

The de-professionalization of education

We argue that neoliberal governmental technologies comprise a new form of power which systematically undoes and reconstructs the practices of professionalism, and which alters the ways in which work is organized and managed under twenty-first century global capitalism.

This argument is most easily expressed in relation to political philosophy. The 'professions' constituted a mode of institutional organization characterized by a principle of *autonomy* which represented a form of power based on 'delegation' (that is, delegated authority) and underpinned by relations of trust. These relations characterized liberal governmentality. Under neoliberal (as opposed to liberal) governmentality, principal-agent, line-management chains of command, replace delegated power with forms of authoritative hierarchical relation, which erode, and seek to prohibit, an autonomous space from emerging. For teachers and academics this carries with it the effect of *de-professionalization*. This has involved increasing the specifications by management over workloads and curriculum content. Such hierarchically imposed specifications erode traditional conceptions of professional autonomy over work in relation to teaching, research and professional practice. In this sense, the neoliberal economic and management theories reviewed earlier, systematically deconstruct the space in terms of which professional autonomy is exercised. It is in this sense that they introduce into employment new forms of authoritarian relations.

Some writers on professionalism maintain the view that managerial or neoliberal forms of governmentality do not result in *de-professionalization*. Nixon et al (2001) speak of 'emergent' modes of professionalism, which entail new forms of professional identity, while writers like Halford and Leonard (1999) and Du Gay (1996) argue that professionals have constructed a new form of identity more suited to managerialism. As Halford and Leonard (1999: 120) put it, 'we cannot assume that this is in any way an automatic or linear process; or that individuals respond in ways which are consistent or coherent'. In this sense, they see managerial reforms as 'restructuring' the identity of professionals. Our argument is not to deny that new identities, comprising various forms and mixtures of resistance and compliance, will emerge, but simply to label whatever emerges as 'professional' is to trade on an elasticity in the concept that fails to acknowledge the differences between liberal and neoliberal regulation. What emerges may still be labelled 'professional', but amongst teachers and education workers generally, it involves 'de-professionalization' *in the sense* that autonomy and trust are replaced with new additional forms of accountability and control.

Traditional conceptions of professionalism involved an ascription of rights and powers over work in line with classical liberal notions of freedom of the individual and professional expertise. Market pressures increasingly encroach upon and redesign employees' traditional understandings of their rights, as both schools and higher education institutions adapt to market trends. The essence of contractual models involves a *specification* of tasks and duties, which is fundamentally at odds with the notion of delegated responsibility within liberal professionalism. Professionalism traditionally conveys the idea of an autonomous practice based upon the liberal conceptions of rights, freedom, and expertise. It conveys the idea of a power given to the subject, and of the subject's ability to make decisions in the workplace. It works on *trust*. Its ethical context is the 'public interest' or the 'public good'. No professional, whether doctor, lawyer or teacher, has traditionally wanted to have the terms of their practice and conduct dictated by anyone else but their peers, or determined by groups or structural levers that are outside their control. As a particular patterning of power, then, the organization of work in terms of professional authority is systematically at odds with neoliberal management, for neoliberals see the professions as self-interested groups who indulge in rent-seeking behaviour. In neoliberalism the patterning of power is established on contract, which in turn is premised upon a need for compliance, monitoring and accountability, organized in a management line and established through a purchase contract based upon measurable outputs.

Competition and marketization: the case of higher education

Closely related to de-professionalization is the concept of *competitive neutrality*. Increased competition represents improved quality within neoliberalism. One of the major objectives of the neoliberal reforms in education in OECD countries was to install market relations of competition as a way of increasing productivity, accountability and control. As Marginson (1997: 5) points out in relation to the marketization of higher education in Australia, for instance: 'Increased competition is meant to increase responsiveness, flexibility and rates of innovation ... increase diversity of what is produced and can be chosen ... enhance productive and allocative efficiency ... improve the quality and volume of production ... as well as strengthen accountability to students, employers, and government.' More indirect advantages are 'internationalization ... fiscal reduction ... and university–business links'. There is, he says 'an imagined line of causation from competition to consumer sovereignty to better efficiency and quality that is the virtuous ideal glowing at the core of micro-economic reform in higher education' (Marginson, 1997: 5).

In both higher and compulsory education, one key to the reform of provision has been to adapt the funding regime, which is seen as the central mechanism through which higher education institutions are linked with the market order. The reforms introduced are essentially a means of maximizing the competitive context in terms of which funding pressures would operate. In an environment of competitive neutrality, what it means in all forms of education is that 'user-pays' or 'per capita' funding schemes are made to serve as a mechanism for choice for students. This exerts a conservative pressure on course selection by students, as well as on course and programme development by schools and universities. Such schemes constitute a governmental technology for constituting students as self-reliant consumers and for disestablishing education as a 'right'. In addition, in both Britain and New Zealand, there has been a deregulation of control over the awarding of degrees and qualifications and over protected terms such as 'university', allowing a wide variety of higher education institutions to award qualifications and degrees. Overall, funding has been encouraged to 'follow the students'; that is, institutions get higher student fees and higher government funding, or lower fees and lower government funding. This has meant that schools and higher education institutions compete with each other for students, and that internal to educational institutions, departments and divisions will compete with each other for students as well. Although practices have been different in different countries, the logical neoliberal outcome is that education institutions can set their own fee levels, allowing each to compete with each other for students in relation to cost and service; and that in higher education institutions, research funding can become contestable as well.[2] What such a competitive ordering results in is a new type of quasi-market approach to education which conflicts with and interferes with traditional notions of professional autonomy.

Possible negative consequences of increasing the competition in education are that such policies result in a proliferation of the numbers of providers, as well as a proliferation of programmes among institutions. Forgetting that markets function imperfectly, competition is invariably seen in purely positive terms as a means of increasing efficiency and effectiveness. Within the higher education sector, however, there is any number of potential negative effects that policies of competitive neutrality can produce. Amongst the most important are that:

- they can contribute an in-built pressure which encourages unplanned expansion, resulting in educational providers that lack educational viability;
- they can result in needless and costly duplication of courses and programmes;
- they can result in the private sector siphoning off educational areas that are easily marketed;
- they distort the overall availability of provision, leading to the loss of programmes that cannot be sustained in market terms; and
- they lead to a 'dumbing down' of courses and qualifications, and result in a compromising of standards in order to compete for student-based income.

Marginson (1999) has observed that various organizational changes have accompanied these changes in Australian and New Zealand universities under the period of neoliberal restructuring. One of the consequences of marketization in higher education has been the increased emphasis on performance and accountability assessment, with the accompanying use of performance indicators and personal appraisal systems (Marginson and Considine, 2000). This has generated a concern with corporate loyalty and the use of discipline against employees who criticize their universities. The corporate model, moreover, has seriously eroded academic freedom and diminished the traditional role of academics as the intellectual critics of conventional wisdom. Universities in this model have become concerned with their market reputation and have become increasingly intolerant of adverse criticism of the institution by the staff. Such policies are the logical outcome of privatization: in the private sector employees are not permitted to criticize their employer in public. Under neoliberal corporatization many universities are employing advertising and public relations agencies to ensure that only positive statements appear about the university and its products.

Reconstituting professional work

In higher education, as in the workforce generally, what neoliberal reason involves is new, less visible forms of managing people. Notions such as *flexibility* are integral to neoliberal work and management relations. Flexible specialization requires malleable workers who continually train and retrain to meet the continuing changes of the economic process. As Richard Sennett (1998) explains in his insightful analysis of corporate capitalism, the promotion of flexibility is fundamental to the global economy in transforming the meaning of work.[3] What flexibility means is that work is being reorganized to adapt to the short term market trends and market volatility. 'Flexibility' redesigns skills and human capital as the personal responsiblility of the individual worker enabling the structures of both the economy and state maximum ability to accommodate change. Bourdieu (1998) refers to this process as 'flexploitation', where flexible specialization involves managerial strategies based on permanent uncertainty and insecurity in both employment and welfare provision. In Sennett's view this means the ethical basis of community is corroded and undermined. Thus, flexibility, while claiming to free people from the tyrannies of traditional work patterns, increases the numbers of temporary, low-paid and 'contract' employment opportunities throughout the workforce. Flexibility for Sennett embodies a mode of institutional adaptation whereby institutions are not charged with responsibilities for the welfare needs of their workers but, rather, the burdens of welfare, education and training are placed on the workers themselves at the lowest possible cost. Power in such a model is concentrated, focused and implemented while not appearing to be centralized. In Foucauldian terms, flexibility represents a micro-technology of power that sustains relations of governmentality.

Also occurring in conjunction with the neoliberal policies described above have been developments to make university courses and programmes more relevant to the world of work, as well as changes in the nature of knowledge. The rise of the professional doctorate (see Bourner et al., 2000) and criticisms of traditional academic programmes and courses are significant here (Becher et al., 1994; Clarke, 1998; DfEE, 1999; Harris, 1996; Pearson et al., 1991;

Pearson and Pike, 1989). As universities have adapted to the market order there has been growing concern about the limited impact of research on professional practice and a shifting emphasis towards evidence-based practice (Sackett et al., 1996).

In the compulsory education sector there has also been an intensification of managerialism with reference to the introduction of performance appraisal methods, performance-related pay, as well as temporary work contracts for teachers. This has resulted in a casualization of the workforce, the introduction of competitive 'student-centred' funding schemes, as well as the use of 'bidding' and 'target-setting', and the widespread use of 'league tables' as mechanisms to determine the distribution of resources. In addition, there has been a reorientation of the curriculum to 'tailor schooling more closely to the assumed demands of the economy' (Gewirtz, 2002a: 37).

In post-compulsory education, the concept of *lifelong learning* also represents an adaptation to neoliberal reason, and can be seen in Foucault's terms as a disciplinary technique aimed at shifting and effecting control. The concept emerged in the 1960s and 1970s in Europe and was promoted by organizations such as the *UNESCO*. Within the European Union it was promoted by groups such as the *OECD* and the *European Round Table* which sought to promote educational policies to develop a flexible and adaptable workforce. It is thus peculiarly adapted, as Bobbitt (2002) notes, to serve and promote the interests of the market state. In a post-welfare society, where the nation-state can no longer guarantee the security of its citizens, concepts such as 'lifelong learning' effectively constitute a privatization of educational responsibility. It constitutes a specifically adapted form of adult education where citizens are represented as consumers and are themselves responsible for their (re)training. As Colin Griffin (1999: 432) argues, governments in Europe used such educational strategies as a means of shifting the costs of learning and knowledge onto individual learners. As such, lifelong learning became linked to a policy package aimed at dismantling the welfare state. Although possible to redefine it in progressive democratic educational terms, as Thompson (2000: 134) suggests, adapted to neoliberal agendas, lifelong education 'represents a late capitalist solution to "investing in people" – in their human, cultural and social capital – as the key to future employment, economic growth, mobility and cohesion'.

The rebirth of managerialism

In that the neoliberal theories surveyed above aim to increase efficiency by engendering competition and improving accountability and monitoring, they introduce forms of managerialism that erode relations of trust and social capital in the social system as a whole. Although the neoliberal bodies of theory frequently linked economic and management theories (as in Agency

Theory or Transaction Cost Economics) such theories were also contiguous with and shaped by earlier forms of 'scientific management' theory, as developed in America in the early decades of the twentieth century. In 1911, Frederick Winslow Taylor published *The Principles of Scientific Management*, describing a system of management first used to make the northeastern railroads of the USA more efficient so that wages could be increased without increasing costs. Such a system involved breaking down the labour process into its component tasks, carrying out a 'time and motion' study of each task and planning more economical ways of reaching predetermined objectives. By the 1920s it was the dominant form of industrial management and had become the administrative counterpart of the Fordist mode of production. It also had a major influence on the administration of the public schools in the USA, which at that time were under attack for being wasteful of taxpayer's money and too much under the control of inefficient teachers. In his book *Education and the Cult of Efficiency*, the educational historian, Raymond Callahan (1962), describes how schools in the USA, in the period just after the First World War, became increasingly preoccupied with recording and reporting. Efficiency had not only to be done, but it had to be seen to be done. Efficiency was to be continually demonstrated through the incessant production of records and reports. Educational cost accounting became the order of the day. Teachers were required to keep records, accounting for every hour and every day of the week. Administrators were forever occupied in writing reports and policy statements. Needless to say, there was less and less time for teaching, and schools became places of tedium, ritualistic order and bland routine. Ironically, they became less and less efficient in an educational sense. By the late 1920s these attempts to reform American schools had produced a system that was weighed down by its own inertia and managerial oppression. The cult of efficiency had become a cult of managerialism which eventually proved to be totally unworkable in educational institutions. Liberation would come in the 1930s as the progressive educators, Dewey, Kilpatrick and others, succeeded in defeating managerialism and reconstructing American schooling on a basis of democratic educational values.

In its contemporary form, managerialism is preoccupied, if not obsessed, with the notion of 'quality'. Quality has become a powerful metaphor for new forms of managerial control. Thus, in the pursuit of quality, educational institutions must engage in 'objective setting', 'planning', 'reviewing', 'internal monitoring' and 'external reporting'. Policy formation and operational activities must be clearly separated. Governance, management and operations are all distinct functions assigned to different roles. The quality of education is reduced to key performance indicators, each of which can be measured and reported.

What this defines is an institutional culture in which ends are separated from means and where people are valued only for what they produce.

Neoliberalism involves the importation into education of instrumentalist values, grounded on such motives as the self-interest of the individual, and concepts such as 'provider capture', 'opportunism' and 'bounded rationality' or 'rent-seeking behaviour'. Neoliberal policy strategies are founded upon a conception of the person that is self-serving, competitive, and likely to be dishonest. It is such a conception that underpins proposals to separate policy formation and advice from policy implementation, or the separation of funder from provider. In this, while neoliberalism values efficiency, effectiveness and control, it devalues interpersonal trust. When used extensively to structure both the economy and the social, political and administrative structures of societies, it produces an institutional environment in which the norms of interpersonal trust become increasingly difficult to sustain, and which thereby serve, in the long term at least, to undermine the core values that enable both markets and democracy to work.

The culture of distrust

Although, on the surface, neoliberalism claims to institute procedures that control 'shirking', 'collusion' and 'opportunism', as Schick (1996: 25) points out, contractualism has some major limitations, which he identifies as:

- the high costs associated with administering the system to ensure compliance, for example. increased surveillance, monitoring, reporting, recording and so on;
- the weakening of collective interest and co-operative activity; and
- the erosion of public service values and their replacement with self-serving values.

Thus, Schick (1996: 25) concludes:

> The values of the Public Service include the trust that comes from serving others, the sense of obligation that overrides personal interest, the professional commitment to do one's best, the pride associated with working in an esteemed organization, and the stake one acquires from making a career in the Public Service.

Similarly, the New Zealand economist, Tim Hazeldine (1998: 216) criticizes the neoliberal practices of monitoring and quality assurance, noting that: 'Monitoring directly diverts resources from productive activities and, more insidiously, it fosters the sort of behaviour that it is supposed to prevent. People who are systematically not trusted will eventually become untrustworthy.' Trust is a relational concept. It is an attitude or disposition from which people will act towards each other in particular ways. These ways of acting and relating will presuppose principles such as fairness and respect and will entail virtues such as honesty (or veracity), friendliness and care. When conceived in this way, trust is inseparable from a way of life. It has to be sustained within a communal tradition, in which it is upheld by daily social interactions and practices. Otherwise, it gradually withers and disappears.

The implications of trust for both economics and democracy gained prominence in the early 1990s through such writers as Robert Putnam (1993) whose study provided empirical evidence for the importance of trust and co-operative behaviour in the emergence of economic prosperity in the northern regions of Italy. Putnam and his collaborators commenced their research in 1970 when Italy created new local governments for each of its regions, and over the next two decades they gathered data on the effectiveness of these governments in such fields as agriculture, housing and health services. Analysis of this empirical data has revealed a major contrast between southern Italy, with relatively weak social organizations, and the regions of the north in which people have a higher propensity to form organizations based not on kinship, but on what Putnam calls 'spontaneous sociability'. In these regions, civic community, good governance and economic prosperity have been facilitated by patterns of trust, co-operation and norms of reciprocity, all of which Putnam attributes to higher levels of what he calls 'social capital'. Social capital has three important components: trust, norms and networks. Norms and networks refer to embedded social values and ways of acting and communicating. Trust, which arguably is the most important of these factors, is a cumulative feature of any institution or social organization. The more there is, the more it will accumulate, or as Putnam (ibid.: 169) puts it – 'them as has, gets'. Thus: 'Most forms of social capital, such as trust, are what Albert Hirschman has called 'moral resources' – that is, resources whose supply increases rather than decreases through use and which become depleted if not used.' What this means is that trust breeds more trust and conversely distrust breeds more distrust, producing virtuous or vicious circles. The trustworthiness of an individual not only benefits the person, but every other person with whom he or she interacts. Conversely, once distrust becomes the norm it prevents people from acting in ways that would foster trust and there is no way of knowing whether distrust is justified. Norms of distrust, therefore, tend to be self-fulfilling (Gambetta, 1988: 234).

Secondly, trust is a basic ingredient of co-operation and this can lead to improved productivity and civic engagement. Putnam argues (1993: 170) that: 'In the civic regions of Italy, by contrast to Naples, social trust has long been a key ingredient in the ethos that has sustained economic dynamism and government performance.' The relationship between social trust and economic prosperity has been examined on a much larger scale by Francis Fukuyama in his 1995 book entitled *Trust: The Social Virtues and the Creation of Prosperity*. In a wide-ranging analysis of the relationship between culture and economic performance in North American, European and Asian societies, Fukuyama contrasts what he describes as low-trust societies (such as Chinese economic culture in Hong Kong and Singapore) with high-trust societies (such as Japan and Germany). His analysis shows that social trust is critical to economic prosperity. This is because most economic activity is carried out not by individuals pursuing their own interests but by groups or organizations requiring a high degree of social co-operation. The greater the level of trust within a society, the greater the propensity for co-operation. Moreover, just as social trust within a society can accumulate, it can also go into a vicious cycle of decline. It is a disturbing feature of American society that Fukuyama refers to as a 'crisis of trust'. He cites Putman's (1993) evidence of declining trust and sociability adding (Fukuyama, 1995: 310) that:

> Apart from opinion surveys, the decline of social trust is evident on both sides of the law, in both the rise of crime and civil litigation. Both reflect the decreasing trustworthiness of some Americans, and produce greater suspiciousness on the part of those who would normally be trusting and trustworthy themselves.

Writing within the tradition of civic republicanism, Philip Pettit (1997) documents the importance of civic trust for stable democracy and government. To say that the laws of a society must be embedded in networks of civil norms is to say that such laws must be supported by habits of civic virtue and good citizenship (ibid.: 245). These in turn require 'habits of civility' (Selznick, 1992: 389–90) which presuppose relations of trust and other norms such as tolerance. His point is that laws, if they are to be effective, must be embedded in norms, which include trust and tolerance as necessary conditions. Trust, then, is necessary to undergird the law, as well as engender obedience to the law, in order to satisfy the constraints associated with democratic contestability. Education, says Pettit, is a central institution in the production of such norms.

Trust and professional accountability

As Codd (1999) argues, neoliberalism exacerbates the erosion of trust. The restoration of trust presupposes a form of professional accountability in which the moral agency of the professional is fully acknowledged. This implies an internal form of accountability that differs significantly from the external form of accountability that belongs within the various discourses of neoliberalism. Figure 9.2 highlights the main differences between these two forms of accountability.

External (low-trust) accountability is based on line management. It is hierarchical and maintained by external controls and sanctions. It is largely an impersonal process that requires contractual compliance and a formal reporting and recording of information. In this form of accountability (represented by most current performance management and appraisal systems) the moral agency of the professional practitioner is greatly reduced. This occurs by invoking what Thompson (1985) refers to as (1) the ethic of neutrality, or (2) the ethic of structure. The ethic of neutrality is invoked when the practitioner assumes that responsibility for a decision or a policy rests with those who have greater authority. This fits the soldier whose role is 'not to reason why'. It is also consistent with a culture of managerialism. The ethic of structure is invoked when the practitioner assumes that moral responsibility is not possible because of existing political structures and power relationships. External accountability, therefore, does not depend upon moral agency. Obedience and conformity to organizational values are sufficient justification.

External	Internal
Low-trust	High-trust
Hierarchical (line) control	Delegated professional responsibility
Contractual compliance	Commitment, loyalty, sense of duty, expertise
Formal process of reporting and recording for line management	Accountable to multiple constituencies
Reduced moral agency • Ethic of neutrality • Ethic of structure	Enhanced moral agency • Deliberation • Discretion

Figure 9.2 *Two types of accountability*

Source: **Codd, 1999.**

Internal (high-trust) accountability is based on professional responsibility, with an underpinning conception of moral agency. It is maintained by internal motivations such as commitment, loyalty and sense of duty. It involves accountability to client beneficiaries and professional peers. In this form of accountability, the professional practitioner has the moral obligation to render an account to several different constituencies, which may have different, or even conflicting interests. This will involve judgement and sometimes the resolution of an ethical dilemma through a process of reflection or deliberation. This may be a collective process, shared with one's professional peers, but 'only the agent can have the responsibility for maintaining the standards of practice of the occupation' (Sockett, 1990: 229). In this form of accountability, the educational practitioner cannot avoid the exercise of professional discretion, where this may even require refusal to conform to managerial expectations or directives.

The contrast we are drawing between these two forms of accountability identifies specifically where the educational and public sector policies under neoliberal reason have had their most powerful effects in changing professional culture, and specifically the logic in terms of which management and administration are carried out. In addition, the ideological substance of these policies has carried some deep-seated and problematic ethical assumptions. Because these assumptions have become manifested in particular discourses and social practices they have had a real and pervasive effect in moving the professional culture of education – both schools and higher education institutions – towards externally imposed low-trust forms of accountability. In a recent paper on professional ethics, Andrew Brien argues that attempts to control ethical conduct directly through legislation or enforced codes are generally unsuccessful because they separate ethical action from the very virtues that comprise professional life. Thus, as Brien (1998: 394) states:

> These measures focus on what people do rather than the sort of person an agent is and so they fail to engender ethical norms. Such measures fail to take sufficient account of the fact that an important part of being a professional is being a certain sort of person who values certain things in certain ways.

Brien argues that cultivating a culture of trust can promote ethical conduct indirectly by providing an ideal of professionalism. He maintains (ibid.: 396) that 'on this view, trust is the essential and central element in the development of a professional culture and trustworthiness is the first virtue of professional life'.

In the 2002 BBC Reith Lectures, Onora O'Neill (2002) discusses the 'crisis of trust' in contemporary society. She argues cogently and persuasively that the contemporary (that is, neoliberal) culture of accountability distorts the proper aims of professional practice and fosters less, rather than more, trust between professionals and the public. In her view, the new modes of public accountability are primarily about control rather than professional integrity and this is seen, she suggests (ibid.: 52), when we ask '*to whom* the new audit culture makes professionals and institutions accountable, and *for what* it makes them accountable'. Although ostensibly the new culture aims to make them accountable *to the public* for the services they provide, O'Neill (2002: 53) observes that: 'the real requirements are for accountability *to regulators, to departments of government, to funders, to legal standards*. The new forms of accountability impose forms of *central control* – quite often indeed a *range of different and mutually inconsistent* forms of central control.' The question of how people can reverse the trends towards abandonment of trust in professional relationships, and resist forms of managerial control which aim to render all work visible through reporting systems and managerial procedures, calls for a number of suggestions. First, academics and teachers should strive to change their own individual practice, refusing where possible to enact neoliberal accountability rituals. Second, they should endeavour to promote democratic models of management based upon co-operation and collegial relationships.

We argue that neoliberal policies of accountability and managerial control, with an emphasis on role definition, planning and reporting, treat teachers and academics as workers rather than professionals and thereby diminish their commitment to the values and principles which ought to define the field of educational practice. The specification of objectives, performance reviews and other management techniques may encourage teachers to behave in ways that are antithetical to certain fundamental educational values such as altruism, intellectual independence and imagination. More generally, we argue that the restoration of a culture of trust and professional accountability within all educational institutions is a necessary prerequisite for the maintenance of a robust and prosperous democratic society. This will only be achieved, moreover, if the ideological force of neoliberalism (with its embedded values of possessive individualism and negative freedom) is resisted and replaced by a political commitment to values of community and democratic justice. It is this argument that we take further in the next chapter.

Notes

1   As even welfare rights were 'positive' rights, there was no doubt that Hayek (1944) was of the view that even a welfare state was the start of the 'slippery slope' leading down 'the road to serfdom'.
2   New Labour in Britain has regulated to protect higher education by imposing fee-level ceilings. Proposals to enable universities to set their own fee levels (the 'top-up' fees debate) reveal the tensions between neoliberalism and social democracy within the 'third way' political movement.
3   According to Sennett (1998: 46) the word 'flexible' entered the English language in the fifteenth century, and in relation to the characteristics of a tree in a wind, it referred to its capacity to 'yield and recover', 'the testing and restoration of its form'. Sennett (1998: 46) continues, 'Ideally, flexible human behaviour ought to have the same tensile strength: adaptable to changing circumstances, yet not broken by them … . The practices of flexibility, however, focus mainly on the forces of bending people'.

10

Discourses of Choice, Inequality and Social Diversity

At the dawn of the twenty-first century, neoliberalism presents an enormous threat to the provision of public education by democratic states. As a political force that continues to shape public policy both within nation-states and globally, neoliberals stand opposed to those who hold that education is a basic right of citizenship and that public schooling is a necessary institutional means for the advancement of social democracy. Throughout the 1990s, neoliberal governments in a number of OECD countries adopted policies that effectively reduced the state's responsibility for providing and maintaining a comprehensive and accessible public education system. Widespread acceptance for these policies was obtained in many instances by claims that they would reduce centralized bureaucratic structures for the governance and provision of education and give people more individual choice.

In spite of opposition from many educators concerned about questions of equity and social justice, the proposition that schools should compete for students in an educational marketplace and the related assertion that individuals (or their parents) should have greater freedom to choose the kind of education they will receive, have become the basis for widespread educational reform. It is precisely these claims, however, and their underlying neoliberal assumptions, that we shall challenge and critique in this chapter. We begin by considering briefly the rationale for school choice policies, particularly those contained within the educational reforms of the 1990s in both Britain and New Zealand. We then present the case against choice by drawing on the philosophical work of Ruth Jonathan. This is followed by a discussion of the contrasting ethical frameworks of neoliberal utilitarianism and Rawlsian 'social justice as fairness'. Our argument is that while Rawlsian liberalism provides a stronger ethical basis for educational policy than does neoliberalism, it does not sufficiently embrace a conception of democratic communitarianism. Thus, we argue in the next chapter for a form of 'thin' communitarianism that we derive from our reading of Foucault.

Choice in the 1990s

Choice policies throughout the western world have gained considerable popular support because they are perceived as removing bureaucratic constraints on personal freedom, thereby providing opportunities for people to make real choices in relation to their children's education. Thus, the promise of increased choice has been a powerful rhetorical element in the legitimation of neoliberal policies. In New Zealand, for instance, the Picot Report of 1988, which initiated the reform agenda, proclaims 'choice' as the first of its core values and states that this 'will involve providing a wider range of options both for consumers and for learning institutions' (New Zealand Department of Education, 1988: 4). The report begins by describing the 'the present administrative structure' as one which is 'over-centralized' and has 'too many decision points' such that 'almost everyone feels powerless to change things they see need changing' (ibid.: xi). Thus, the report (ibid.: 4) states that: 'Choice will involve providing a wider range of options both for consumers and for learning institutions ... . Only if people are free to choose, can a true co-operative partnership develop between the community and learning institutions.' *INDIVIDUALISM = WESTERN = NEOLIBERAL = CHOICE*

The Picot Report echoed the position advanced by the New Zealand Treasury in 1987 in its *Brief to the Incoming Government*. As the *Brief* (New Zealand Treasury, 1987: 41) states: 'Government intervention is liable to reduce freedom of choice and thereby curtail the sphere of responsibility of its citizens and weaken the self-steering ability inherent in society to reach optimal solutions through the mass of individual actions pursuing free choice without any formal consensus.' Such a statement is a clear expression of the neoliberal ideology that informs public choice theory. In its original formulation, it entailed a deeply individualistic approach to social policy. All state intervention, in this view, is essentially bad, and all social goods are reduced to private goods that can be achieved only by individuals exercising rational choice within a free market. 'Society' or the 'public' has no definable features and therefore no existence beyond the cumulative actions of individuals. Freedom to choose is no more than the absence of coercion or constraint by others. *How do we define "freedom"?*

Initially, the promotion of school choice in the New Zealand reforms was at odds with school zoning policies which had been introduced in the 1950s to promote equality of educational opportunity. Consequently, when the reforms commenced in 1989, a school zoning policy was retained, even though it could be seen to be anomalous within the overall neoliberal rationale of the reforms. When the more right wing National government assumed office in 1990, it moved to eliminate the anomaly and the 1991 Education Amendment Act abolished school zoning regulations thereby allowing schools to compete freely for students. The ideological rationale was once again that of maximizing parental choice. Many schools introduced their own admission criteria. Competition

COMPETITION = CHOICE = POLARIZATION AFFECTING THE POOR

between schools for both students and resources increased markedly and predictably some schools attracted more socially advantaged students.

There is now clear evidence of increased inequality amongst New Zealand schools (Gordon, 1994; Lauder and Hughes; 1999; Lauder et al., 1994; Wylie, 1994). This evidence has been assembled by two American researchers who visited New Zealand for five months in 1998 and carried out a comprehensive study of the New Zealand education reforms (Fiske and Ladd, 2000). Their analysis of enrolment and census data reveals increased ethnic and socio-economic polarization resulting directly from the school choice policies introduced in 1991.

In Britain, the Education Reform Act (1988) was informed by a strong discourse of choice. The major policies embraced by this Act were designed to increase competition between schools and encourage parental choice. In accordance with the 'free market' thrust of Thatcherism, and consistent with other moves towards privatization, schools were given the right to 'opt out' of local authority control. The rationale proclaimed that choice would generate competition which consequently would raise educational standards. Although the empirical evidence does not support such a theory (Halpin et al., 1991; Walford, 1992; Whitty et al., 1998) increasing numbers of schools continued to 'opt out' of local authority control (Bowe et al., 1992).

The number of directly funded (grant-maintained) self-managing schools further increased after the 1993 Education Act. This legislation resulted in the establishment of a new Funding Agency for Schools and 'streamlined' the procedures for 'opting out'. Greater diversity of schools was encouraged, together with more intense competition between schools. However, as Geoffrey Walford (1994: 142) points out:

> The major purpose of the 1993 Education Act, like the 1988 Education Reform Act before it, was not to build a more fair and generous education system, but to reconstruct a more differentiated and hierarchical system which will more closely aid social reproduction. The ideology of choice allows a partial masking of this process and, while choice may allow a few individuals to benefit, the majority have little to gain and much to lose.

Choice and the 'third way'

Under Tony Blair's New Labour, while choice initiatives still influence education policy, they have been adapted in accord with the policy agenda of the 'third way'. In Blair's (1998: 1) understanding:

> The Third Way ... draws vitality from uniting two great streams of left-of-centre thought – democratic socialism and liberalism – whose divorce this century did so much to weaken progressive politics across the West. Liberals asserted the primacy of individual liberty in the market economy; social democrats promoted social justice with the state as its main agent. There is no necessary conflict between the two.

In policy terms, Blair (ibid.: 18) sees the 'third way' as comprising four distinctive stances:

> Each taking progressive politics beyond the old dividing lines of left and right. On the economy, acceptance of fiscal disciplines together with investment in human capital, science and knowledge transfer. In civil society, a rights and responsibilities approach, strong on law and order but with social programmes to address the causes of crime. In public services, investment to ensure equality of opportunity, but also restructuring to provide more individually tailored services built around the needs of the modern consumer and to secure the public goods that markets, if left to themselves, could not provide. Foreign policy, robust on defence and committed to global justice.

In similar vein, Anthony Giddens (2000: 163) sees the 'third way' as 'concerned with restructuring social democratic doctrines to respond to the twin revolutions of globalization and the knowledge economy'. An important feature of third way politics, for Giddens, is that it recognizes the essential role that government and democratic institutions have in maintaining a prosperous market economy. Thus, an effective market economy requires a level of social cohesion that can only be sustained by a flourishing civil society. This involves a new relationship between the individual and the community founded upon two precepts: (1) no rights without responsibilities, and (2) no authority without democracy (Giddens, 1998: 64–8).

Notwithstanding these changes in broad underlying policy discourse, critics see the 'third way' as an amorphous amalgam of irreconcilable values, based upon an attempt to steer a middle way between a free market and a traditional welfare state (Callinicos, 2001). Whether the dual traditions are indeed compatible, or whether, as we argue, the new discourse is merely creating new tensions, centring on choice and social democracy, localism and central control, the 'third way' in our view is not a coherent alternative to neoliberalism. It appears, in both practice and theory, that the neoliberal emphasis on social competition and choice in 'third way' discourse remains paramount, and replaces traditional leftist concerns. We will support this with empirical research later, but potential tensions and contradictions are also occurring at the level of theory – not least within the concept of 'egalitarianism'. Giddens (2000: 85–6) argues, for instance, that 'egalitarianism at all costs' must be replaced by a 'dynamic life chances approach … placing the prime stress on equality of opportunity even if larger inequalities of outcomes are the result'. At the level of governance, New Labour has ushered in a 'new localism', where choice is realized through policy initiatives to establish 'specialist schools' which will operate as semi-autonomous management centres operationally freed from the regulatory structures of government control. Critics see this system as likely to take government policy backwards to a pre-comprehensive era, allowing for new tiers of selective schooling to emerge, reintroducing and further intensifying existing social class divisions. As the journalist Polly Toynbee (2002: 23) has noted in commenting on New Labour's education policy in the *Guardian*:

> Parents quickly decode the true meaning of 'difference', 'aptitude' and 'choice'. Give them any hint that one school is better than others, and they will queue to get in. The middle class navigates choice much better than the rest, and it is the rational and right thing to do – once one school is officially tagged as better, the other schools will get worse. Where middle-class children congregate, any 'chosen' school quickly becomes a self-fulfilling success.

→ CLASS MUST BE READ AS WHITE MIDDLE CLASS

The rationale for school choice

The fundamental rationale for choice ultimately traces its ancestry to the classical liberal conceptions of the rational autonomous individual who is presumed to be a person capable of deliberating upon alternatives and of deciding between different educational programmes according to individual needs, interests and desires. In the notion of choice is a conception of autonomy of the individual which presupposes that the choices made are the individual's own, that they are the independent result of freely made decisions, and that the outcomes have not been coerced, manipulated, or imposed by external institutions or by the logic of situation. Herein lies the problem of the conception of autonomous choice. POOR HAVE FEW "CHOICES" & FREEDOM

In the policy documents released in New Zealand after 1987 it is presumed that people are free to choose according to their ability to make rational decisions based on an evaluation of their preferences and interests in relation to variables concerned with the overall quality of education. In the Picot Report (New Zealand Department of Education, 1988: 4), for instance, it is said that:

> Choice will involve providing a wider range of options both for consumers and learning institutions … . Consumers need to be able to directly influence their learning institution by having a say in the running of it or by being able to turn to acceptable alternatives. Only if people are free to choose can a true cooperative partnership develop between the community and learning institutions.

Assumed in the notion of choice is the view that the quality of educational choices made by the consumer as consumer is superior to those offered to consumers by providers with expert knowledge. Consumers, it is held, know better than providers about which educational choice to make. Educators' knowledge in this model is considered as being of secondary importance. It is held that the choices of individual consumers are more rational and better both for the individual and for the community. Education is the glove that moves this 'invisible hand'.

Also implicit in the discourse of choice is subordination of state intervention to the operation of market mechanisms as a more effective way of promoting economic growth and a more efficient means of allocating and using scarce resources. The maximization of individual choice within a deregulated social environment is given priority over state-imposed responsibilities, duties and obligations. Property rights are given priority over social citizenship, or welfare rights, and economic efficiency is given priority over human needs in the allocation of resources. Choice is not only seen as a core value which will involve providing a wider range of options both for consumers and for learning institutions, but the creation of more choice is also represented as a way of ensuring greater efficiency and equity. The promotion of choice as a primary social objective which will guarantee both freedom of individuals and efficiency of social institutions reflect the dual claims entailed within choice theory: consumer sovereignty and market freedom.

Choice policies in Britain, New Zealand and throughout the western world reflect both elements of this double emphasis simultaneously. Educational proposals based on choice, such as voucher theories, can also be seen in terms of the freedom of individuals to seek to realize their own desires and preferences. Yet underpinning most choice proposals is a combination of rights claims concerning the freedom of individuals and utilitarian claims based on efficiency. As Kahne (1996: 94) says: 'This dual emphasis is possible because advocates endorse a particular kind of freedom – free markets. In perfectly competitive free market systems as individuals pursue their own conception of the good, they maximize aggregate utility. Choice proponents argue that their models simultaneously free individuals and improve educational services.'

Milton Friedman, (1955), and later with Rose Friedman (1980) developed such a dual perspective in his initial proposals for a school voucher scheme, arguing that providing parents with vouchers, which could be used to purchase educational services at either public or independent schools, would further both efficiency goals and rights-based objectives. On the one hand, such a scheme could enable parents to choose on the basis of quality which sort of school they preferred. On the other hand, choice will also improve the efficiency and effectiveness with which producers (educators, the state) will respond to consumers (parents, students) needs and desires. Schools that do respond to consumer demands will prosper, while those that do not will be forced to close. Hence choice initiatives in education for Friedman and Friedman in *Free to Choose* promote freedom as well as efficiency.

The American free market theorists, Chubb and Moe, in their book *Politics, Markets and America's Schools* (1990), place more emphasis on effectiveness than on freedom as an outcome of 'choice'. To a lesser extent than Friedman (1955), Friedman and Friedman (1980) and other earlier choice theorists (Coons and Sugarman 1978), who stress the importance of the free market in education, Chubb and Moe (1990) adopt the utilitarian argument for effectiveness and locate their theoretical perspective in relation to the 'effective schools research' (see Purkey and Smith, 1983, for a review). Hence, they claim that choice promotes higher student achievement outcomes, more desirable forms of school organization, fewer bureaucratic regulations, better school management and leadership structures, and higher quality overall in relation to a range of variables (clearer goals, greater teacher professionalism, wider range of academic programmes and so on).

School choice and inequality

What is neglected by advocates of choice, whether in terms of freedom or efficiency, is a consideration of the structural limits to choice imposed by the realities of the actual political and social context. Thus, less well off families have fewer options. Poor people must accept their neighbourhood schools regardless of the quality. Highly regarded wealthy schools are likely to be 'overchosen' with the practical outcome that the school will effectively 'choose' its customers rather than the other way round. General equity issues tend to be neglected such that an emphasis on choice will result in a corresponding increase in inequality and consequential social divisions between rich and poor schools and rich and poor communities. Hence there will be little incentive for schools in wealthy areas to admit children from disadvantaged sectors of the community, or from racial minorities.

The critics of choice, therefore, argue that choice proposals jeopardize the ability of public schooling to promote equal outcomes and equality of opportunity. In addition, those who run schools of choice will tend to structure admissions processes so as to avoid undesirable students, giving the schools rather than the consumers the ultimate 'choice'. Studies show that under choice schemes funds are directed to schools that represent predominantly middle-class (wealthy, white and well-behaved) students while less desired students are excluded from entry (Moore and Davenport, 1990).

Chubb and Moe's research has been criticized by a number of researchers (Glass and Matthews, 1991; Rosenberg, 1991; Tweedie, 1990) who question the adequacy of their methodology, the way they interpret their data, as well as the policy implications they derive from their analyses. With respect to their claim regarding the higher achievement of students in private (choice) schools compared with public schools, it is pointed out by the critics that they do not allow for the fact that parents currently choosing to pay for their children's education probably paid more emphasis to education than otherwise similar parents who use a neighbourhood school (Kahne, 1996: 99). All of these critics question the degree to which private schooling actually fosters significantly more effective schooling and some have pointed to the relatively minor nature of the differences put forward by Chubb and Moe as evidence (Kahne, 1996; Levin, 1989).

Chubb and Moe claim that systems of choice promote more flexible and superior organizational and administrative structures, and that 'public schooling is incompatible with effective schooling' (Chubb and Moe, 1990: 2). While choice policies are advocated by those who support private schooling, and even home schooling, governments in Britain, New Zealand, and other OECD and western countries have also promoted choice policies within the public system. In this context it is argued that increasing public school choice becomes a mechanism by which a quasi-market can be established, which it is assumed will improve educational services, foster innovation, attract and retain committed educators, and spur schools to be more responsive to consumers within limits laid down by the state. The empirical evidence, however, does not support these assumptions. The extent to which choice operates in private or in public schools is simply a matter of degree. Private schooling advocates want education to operate in the context of a free market, whereas public schooling advocates, if they are not simply militating against complete privatization, advocate limiting the extent to which market forces are allowed to operate in order to safeguard community interests (Levin, 1989).

The limits of choice

In the context of increased marketization choice operates within a collective (zero-sum) economic and social context. Although individual parents, who are presented with an opportunity *to choose* the school that their children will attend would be acting rationally by seizing that opportunity, the consequences, as Jonathan (1989; 1997) points out, if all other parents in similar social situations were to make similar choices, would be to severely reduce or eliminate the alternatives available to each individual.

Chester Finn (1990), educational adviser to the Reagan administration and one of the vanguard in the so-called 'excellence' movement in the USA, claims that parental choice is a direct form of accountability. People, in his words, 'will voluntarily exit from bad schools and head for good ones' (ibid:. 28). Such a comment undoubtedly has common-sense plausibility and after pointing out the unquestionable desirability of engaging parents more deeply in the education of their children, Finn (1990: 28) continues as follows: 'Educational choice ... by fostering competition among schools, will itself lead to diversity and individuality. In addition, choice can widen opportunities for disadvantaged and minority youngsters by giving them access to educational options not available in their immediate neighbourhoods.' The assumption here is that making choice available is exactly the same as enabling all people to choose. Given the choice between a 'good' school and a 'bad' school, any rational parent would always choose a 'good' school for their children. But so-called 'good' schools are only perceived as such when they can be distinguished from another group of schools that are perceived to be 'bad'. It is not possible, moreover, for all parents to be in comparable social positions from which to choose between 'good' and 'bad' schools.

Some will have available to them more financial and cultural resources than others will and their very choice of what they perceive to be a 'good' school becomes a self-fulfilling prophecy. Thus, the exercise of choice by some becomes a capacity to determine what is good, and therefore limits for others the opportunity to choose. In Jonathan's (1989: 333) argument, this follows from the nature of education as a 'positional' social good, because this is 'the sort of good whose worth to those who have it depends to some extent both on its general perceived value and on others having less of it'.[1]

Describing the effects of the 1988 Education Reform Act and other policies extending parental choice, Jonathan (ibid.: 323) argues that:

> It is probable that some schools will get better and others worse, with those parents who are most informed and articulate influencing and obtaining the 'best buy' for their children, thus giving a further twist to the spiral of cumulative advantage which results when the state is rolled back to enable 'free and fair' competition between individuals or groups who have quite different starting points in the social race.

The conclusion that this points to is that the promotion and enhancement of consumer opportunity and choice in education can be achieved only with a consequential cost in terms of social justice. In relation to this, Jonathan (1990: 16) maintains that:

> In the distribution of a 'positional' good such as education, measures to increase individual opportunity bring about a decrease in social justice and lead to a head-on clash between two commonly accepted duties of the state: to maximise individual freedom and to promote justice for the group as a whole – this clash being exacerbated in direct proportion to the resultant increase in social competition.

Thus, policies that promote educational choice, such as the removal of established geographical catchment areas for schools (zoning policies), have the effect not only of extending individual liberties but of ensuring that rational consumers will tend to use them to pursue their self-interest. When parents do this on behalf of their children, their actions have a prima facie moral justification. We expect parents to look after their children's interests. However, this overlooks other social realities relating to the scarcity of educational resources. Jonathan's argument, therefore, shows that policies which increase the discretionary power of educational consumers give priority to individual liberty over social justice. Thus, increasing parental choice of school inevitably also increases the level of social competition. As Jonathan (ibid.: 19) points out: 'Whereas, therefore, *individual parents* may acquire enhanced opportunities to benefit their children, it is also the case that *parents as a category of individuals* find the welfare of their children placed at increased risk in a climate of intensified competition.' In a later book-length study, Jonathan (1997) claims that market choice in education is an 'illusory freedom'. She provides a sustained philosophical critique of the 'new right' reforms in education under Thatcherism and a defence of public provision of education. Her

central thesis is that 'new right' policies, based as they are on neoliberal political and philosophical viewpoints, reinforce many of the central axioms of
classical liberalism especially those relating to the relations between the individual and society, the conception of freedom, the view of the self as a rational
maximizer, the separation of private and public spheres, and in their agnosti-
cism over the nature of the good.

As Jonathan maintains, one of the major points on which neoliberals depart
from classical liberals relates to the fact that most neoliberals in the twentieth
century do not advocate that education be provided by the market, as did their
classical counterparts, but only distributed and governed in accord with
market principles – that is, a quasi-market. So while we cannot treat the two
traditions as identical, what they share, says Jonathan, are certain ontological
and metaphysical assumptions. Especially pertinent in this regard is the view
that the neoliberal rationale for deregulated choice reflects a reassertion of
classical liberal faith in the effectiveness of markets and in the belief that only
individuals have the right to make choices. The major problems with liberalism (and more so neoliberalism) are its individualist orientation based on a
pre-social conception of the self, its contractarian commitments to a procedural framework of social justice, its representation of the social in terms of
an atomized reduction to private ends and its view of the state as a neutral
arbiter between differing individual standpoints. Because of its view of the
person as 'already formed', it neglects attention to the development or formation of preferences, of which education is a major practice, and of fundamental importance in relation to the issue of freedom, it mistakenly assumes
that the welfare of all will result from the promotion of the separate welfare
of each. As a consequence of this, says Jonathan, liberalism falters as a theoretical system. When subjected to critical scrutiny, the reality of the situation
is, in fact, precisely the opposite to the claims made. The state, far from reducing, is as large as ever, and the freedoms, far from increasing choice, are *illusory*. As she puts it (Jonathan, 1997: 27):

> The introduction of market forces into the evolution of the education system
> cannot be seen as a neutral procedure of 'rolling back the state' in order simply to
> devolve power to the people, with government seeking only to maximize individ-
> ual freedom. For by delegating to individuals decisions which, in aggregate, have
> substantial social, cultural and political effects, legislators are not lessening the
> extent to which they direct policy, but radically changing its direction: and the
> power of the state is not shrinking, but is rather being directed towards substantive
> change in the social order.

In a related way, Jonathan advances the argument that, as education is
society's most central social practice and one of society's primary sites for the
formation of preferences, it constitutes the 'limiting case of the free market'.
This is because education 'presupposes an arena of preference formation

which is exempt from the vagaries of the "hidden hand"'(ibid.: 5) on the grounds that the market is not, in itself, a self-sustaining order but requires a network of intermediary institutions to sustain it. Education is one of these for it provides forms of social capital that are essential to the effective operations of markets. As such, she claims (ibid.: 22), citing John Gray, it needs to be 'tended and nurtured by the state'.

From the perspective of either welfare state liberals or democratic communitarians like Dewey, unregulated choice proposals have several undesirable effects: they protect privilege; they deny all students equal access to education; they deny all students exposure to alternative perspectives; they limit the community's progress as a democratic community, and they undermine the basis of its integration, socially and politically. Such views seem supported by Moore and Davenport's (1990: 189) research on schools in America where they conclude that 'school choice schemes have become a new form of segregation ... based on race, income level and previous school experience'. Similarly, Michael Walzer (1983: 219) has stated that 'for most children, parental choice almost certainly means less diversity, more tension, and less opportunity for personal change, than they would find in schools to which they were politically assigned'.

Social selection and the 'third way'

In Britain, a recent report by Edwards and Tomlinson (2002) documents how New Labour has extended forms of social selection in education by expanding the numbers of specialist schools. These schools are permitted autonomy in the selection of their intake, making use of interview and aptitude tests. The establishment of specialist schools is a policy introduced in New Labour's first Education White Paper as a means of 'modernizing the comprehensive principle' (Edwards and Tomlinson, 2002: 32) by allowing comprehensive schools to develop and promote their own distinctive identities. Linked to the rejection of a 'one size fits all' model of governance, the policy sought to promote greater diversity in educational provision, resulting in rising numbers of 'specialist' comprehensives, 'advanced specialist schools', 'beacon schools', 'training schools' and 'city academies'. Of these, specialist schools have been the major mechanism for modernizing secondary education. From 200 in 1997, when New Labour came to power, the initial target of 500 was exceeded by the summer of 2000 (Edwards and Tomlinson, 2002: 34). As of December 2002, there are more than 700, comprising more that one-quarter of all state secondary schools. The new target is 2,000 by 2006. Defending comprehensive schooling as having resulted in huge advances in educational standards, Edwards and Tomlinson argue that the overall effect of parental choice through 'open enrolment' (that is, the abolition of geographical zoning policies) has been to increase social segregation. Amongst the other points they list are several that relate to the theme of 'covert social selection'. These are (ibid.: 11):

PSYCHOLOGICAL ASPECTS ARE ALSO KEY

- Some poor families have been enabled to avoid what they saw as poor schools, but the 'active choosers' tend to be middle class.
- The system introduced to police admissions has highlighted ways in which competing schools screen applicants to improve league table positions.
- It is average inner city schools that tend to lose children from higher socio-economic backgrounds to other comprehensives and local grammar schools.
- The most socially skewed intakes are in the most and least popular schools. Ethnic minority parents in particular are less likely to get their children into high-performing schools.
- All research confirms that a concentration of socially disadvantaged children in unpopular schools makes improved performance harder.

They then list a number of further points relating to the themes of 'diversity, standards and opportunity'. These are (ibid.: 11–12):

- So far the Specialist Schools Programme has increased differences between schools in intake and resources, without encouraging them to engage in conspicuous innovation in curriculum or pedagogy.
- Initial claims made for the superior performance of specialist schools have been questioned in the light of their prior funding and intake advantages.
- The temptation for specialist schools to use their entitlement to select 10 per cent of their intake on aptitude will increase as more such schools compete for pupils in their local market.
- It is not clear that the government has found a way of developing types of school that are 'simply' different without being unequal in esteem, resources, and the chances available to their pupils.

Thus, parental choice has resulted in intensified resource differences between schools, and the promotion of new types of schooling is resulting in new inequalities. Consumer choice has increased segregation and 'open' enrolment schemes have increased the opportunities for escaping unsuccessful schools. In this context, choice becomes a fiction when viewed in the context of class competition. As Edwards and Tomlinson (ibid.: 28) state:

> But enrolment is not open when schools are over-subscribed. The 'quasi-market' created in urban areas marked a deliberate shift from secondary schools as local (community) institutions to schools as competing providers, proximity to a child's home being least relevant for those parents inclined to seek the 'best buy' and able to meet the travel costs.

The evidence so far, say Edwards and Tomlinson (ibid.: 28) is that: 'Choice has increased differences between schools in relation to intake and resources, but has done more to encourage them to play safe than to engage in conspicuous innovation in curriculum or pedagogy.'

Because of its wide popular support, the ideology of choice presents a major challenge to educational administrators committed to equality of access and opportunity. Education policies that promote choice at the cost of equity and social justice cannot be reversed until the political opportunities for such a change exist within the macrosocial context. Only by experiencing and monitoring the real social effects of these policies will people gradually work collectively to change them through the same democratic processes that have put them in place.

For democratic communitarians like Dewey, the very essence of a community is that it is self-determining and egalitarian. While they support the liberal emphasis on creating a society that supports autonomy, they are cautious about recognizing an irreducible plurality of individual values and conceptions of the good as entailed in choice schemes. As individual identity depends upon collective support, a development of identity to the exclusion of an emphasis on the interests of the community will be dysfunctional to it. Thus, the unbridled pursuit of individual choice can be detrimental to social cohesion and community well-being.

Discourses of diversity and devolution

Choice policies throughout the western world have been linked to attempts to create markets or quasi-markets and have traded upon *discourses of diversity* and *devolution*, echoing concerns for 'localism' in contrast to what Tony Blair calls the 'one size fits all' model of public service provision. In this sense, choice policies have been associated with the dismantling of centralized educational bureaucracies, and with the attempt to create devolved systems of education. These have been associated with institutional autonomy and a variety of forms of school-based management, the enhancement of parent power, an increased emphasis on community involvement, more efficient management, more transparent accountability, as well as deregulation, devolution, dezoning and greater school autonomy, all of which assist schools in responding to market forces (Whitty et al., 1998).

Under the 'third way', choice policies have continued to be promoted as part of a complex diversity agenda. This agenda not only promotes quasi-markets and competition, but also is linked to new models of governance and a shift in the role of the state. As Tony Blair stated at the Labour Party Conference held at Bournemouth in 2002: 'Just as mass production has departed from industry, so the monolithic provision of services has to depart from the public sector. Out goes the big state. In comes the enabling state' (cited in Wintour, 2002: 13). This idea of an 'enabling state' as the vehicle by which devolution and diversity are managed is central to 'third way' policy initiatives on education and health policies of New Labour in Britain. In education, it has involved the expansion and development of specialist schools as part of the 'post-comprehensive era'. This has resulted in new legislation to encourage successful specialist schools to operate autonomously, to expand and to encourage school takeovers. Choice policies which enable parents to secure the school of their preference are being encouraged along with privatization initiatives to extend private sector involvement in public services through a proliferation of public–private partnerships (PPPs), private finance initiatives (PFIs) and public interest companies (PICs). As such, the enabling state constitutes a model of semi-autonomous public services supposedly free of Whitehall control. Both schools and hospitals are being granted autonomy where they can establish new directions to travel. Controls are being released on local Councils, and voluntary organizations are being allowed to run public services. New Labour think tanks, such as the New Economics Foundation, the New Local Government Network and the Institute of Public Policy Research represent this agenda as moving beyond old distinctions between the state and the market. The idea is that services funded by the state need not be run by the state. Such a model thus entails an increased role for the private sector, with increased choice and greater diversity of provision.

The discourse of diversity under the 'third way' is also rationalized in terms of social democratic arguments, which serve to cloak or mask the disequalizing impacts of these neoliberal policies. In this, diversity is represented as a progressive value, as part of the celebration of difference, and of the acceptance of the 'politics of recognition'. Diversity under the 'third way' is championed as both 'community building' and 'anti-bureaucracy'. David Walker (2002: 13) cites Giddens (2002) who represents localism as the 'freedom to do things differently'. It is more flexible. Centralization excludes people from democratic processes. Localism is seen as more 'innovative' and fosters 'participation' and 'democratic citizenship'. This discourse is both a celebration of the local and a depreciation of the centre. The centre is said to be bureaucratic, overloaded and inefficient. A faith in localism is a faith in 'local people'; things are better organized locally. Matthew Taylor (cited in Walker, 2002: 12), of the New Labour think tank, the Institute of Public Policy Research, states that only locally can 'meaningful debate about public health priorities and needs take place'. Part of the argument here is that the public services are better managed under local control, they are more accountable, and that the 'knowledge management capacities of the centre are finite' (ibid.: 12).

In addition to these arguments, the discourse of 'third way' diversity is fed by political arguments from both the left and right. From the right, there has traditionally been suspicion of centralized power and a celebration of the local as 'democratic', and even, 'natural' (ibid.: 12–14). From the left, political writers like R.H. Tawney and G.D.H. Cole championed localism as a democratic discourse, in that citizens at the local, community level could *participate* more effectively as citizens, which led to more effective *self-government*, which in turn led to *self-realization* and *self-development*. What is important here, is that neoliberal arguments for choice are now masked or cloaked by arguments for diversity from a variety of quarters.

The necessity of state control

Whether this 'third way' model really does manage to reconcile neoliberal and social democratic agendas is highly doubtful. Neoliberal choice schemes implement quasi-markets which are inherently and cumulatively inegalitarian. Local communities are constituted by groups and institutions that are unequal in power and influence. The issues of 'equality', 'professional standards', 'expertise' and 'justice' require *uniformity* in provision and enforcement. The rights of citizenship depend upon an *authority* in terms of which they can be uniformly applied. This is especially relevant over different geographical areas. In addition, as Walker (2002: 25) argues 'at the heart of the argument for devolution is a wish to see more difference ... . But "difference" will eat into fairness'.

The discourse of localism also operates in relation to governance. According to Rhodes (2000), the new governance narrative, which is espoused by New Labour, is based on (1) networking, (2) partnerships, (3) autonomy of providers, (4) interdependence between organizations and (5) trust. The state's role is to facilitate and co-ordinate without treading on the autonomy of foundation hospitals, schools or higher education institutions. In reality the state underemphasizes its control for although it may not actively be delivering services, it can still be seen to be effecting control, and at least some studies claim that this control, rather than being less, is simply taking a different form (Cloke et al, 2000: 130; Rhodes, 1997a; 1997b; 2000). In addition, in that the power of the state is being reorganized rather than reduced in its relationship to local groups, the organization of governance in networks and partnerships is producing new obstacles as far as traditional democratic forms of accountability are concerned. A governance model which delegates power to local agencies is producing problems relating to representation, accountability, openness to criticism, as well as to the democratic rights of consumers or users. Furthermore, the ability of local agencies to work together, or coordinate service provision, is offset by the differences in power and influence between them; by the adherence to traditional norms of exclusivity and non-cooperation; by the inequalities between the different partners or actors providing services in the state, voluntary and private spheres; and by the fragmentation of services across different sectors (Dickson et al., 2002).

Thus, whether new models of governance based on networks and partnerships can constitute a solution to traditional forms of state bureaucracy or markets, or overcome the limitations inherent in them, is unlikely. Research by Rhodes (2000), Cochrane (2000) Cloke et al. (2000), Glendinning et al. (2002) and others casts doubt on whether patterns of state control have significantly altered, and whether ad hoc adjustments and interference are not constantly required to overcome inequities, unfairness and inequalities that arise when localistic solutions to policy operate. As Karl Polanyi (1957; 1969) observed with reference to the rise of the welfare state in the late nineteenth and early twentieth centuries, the growth of central state involvement in economic and social policy arose not because of any predetermined political plan or conspiracy, but on an ad hoc basis because of the sheer complexity of government. This complexity is likely to increase at pace given the inherently individualist and self-serving nature of neoliberal reason which operates as a Trojan horse within the 'third way' diversity discourse. In the end, what is likely is that the resources and manpower invested in 'steering' becomes as great if not greater than in 'rowing' until it is not clear what the differences between them are.

Paradoxically, the dual aims of localism and state 'steering' will likely result in a greater and greater role for the state as it attempts to level out the bumps and potholes in the playing field, provide reasonable mechanisms of representation and accountability, and ensure some measure of rights and fair treatment for the unsuspecting and often unenlightened public whose education and welfare is at stake. This seems to be what is indeed happening in 'third way' policy delivery. In Britain, Railtrack, which was privatized under Thatcher, has recently returned to public ownership due to the sheer operational chaos that private ownership produced. More recently, British Energy has had to be 'bailed out' financially by the state. The government had to underwrite its risks due to the sensitive place it occupies in the economy, which, of course, was one of the reasons for nationalizing it in the first place. Under private ownership it has become obvious that neither managerial efficiency nor public safety are guaranteed. The history of the past few years in Britain is littered with examples of the failings of privately run prisons, schools and hospitals. It is a situation, as Roy Hattersley (2002: 18) has quipped, of 'taxpayers servicing the debt, and shareholders receiving the dividends'.

Contrary directions in the 'third way'

Sharon Gewirtz (2002a, 2002b) has highlighted the tension between neoliberal and social democratic elements of 'third way' policy in relation to New Labour's education agenda in England since 2000. She claims that implicit within the 'third way' are two notions of educational success, which are in tension with each other. On the one hand, neoliberal policies continue to promote commitments to marketization, privatization and competition. These have involved such things as (1) continued policies which fund schools on a 'per capita' basis, thus promoting competition; (2) intensifying managerialism based on such policies as 'target-setting', 'performance monitoring', 'performance pay' and the use of competitive techniques (such as 'bidding') for the distribution of resources; (3) an expansion of privatization through the PFI; and (4) an 'intrumentalization' of the curriculum, relating it more directly to the world of work.

On the other hand, says Gewirtz (2002a: 37) New Labour has introduced a variety of 'humanistic' more social-democratic-type policies which mark a 'significant departure from the reforms of the Conservatives'. These have involved such things as (1) a commitment to increased investment as a proportion of GDP; (2) additional funds for disadvantaged children; (3) a commitment to narrowing educational inequalities through wider policies of economic and social regeneration; (4) encouraging collaboration and cooperation between schools; (5) encouraging policies focused on widening participation in educational attendance and decision-making; (6) encouraging policies that value and support teachers through professional development; and (7) supporting the broadening of the curriculum. In examining both types of 'success' policies, Gewirtz (2002a: 39) concludes that: 'Whilst, from a social justice perspective, the humanistic strands are clearly to be welcomed … the intensification of the managerial business-friendly element is in danger of undermining the possibility of the more humanistic strands being realised.' Furthermore she argues that managerialism has a corrosive effect on school life and ensures risks to quality, sustainability, democratic accountability, and equality (ibid.: 39).[2]

If the 'third way' attempt to marry social democracy and neoliberalism in terms of governance produces tensions between the two divergent theoretical systems that make it up, the rise of the discourse of the 'third way' does suggest a more positive message in that it speaks to a more *active* state than was entailed under traditional laissez-faire models. Indeed, even if the state under the 'third way' seeks to change the form of its operation, from traditional bureaucracy to governance through networks, the model still speaks to the idea of a *strong* state. The idea of an enabling state is indeed compatible with a conception of the state that sets up the rules of the game, that passes legislation to enforce minimum conditions of acceptable treatment for all of the various groups in society (children, the aged, women, ethnic minorities and so on) and that seeks to ensure adequate protection and rights for all through the framing and introduction of legislation. The notion of 'enabling', like that of 'steering', does not of itself speak to the size of the state and, conceivably, a state that 'steers' might be just as big as a state that 'rows'. At the same time, so long as the state can assure the important platforms of universal entitlement, equality of opportunity and equality before the law, then the attempt to actively co-opt the citizenry in running their own lives can only be seen as positive and a major back-down from the discourse of a reduced state which became the catchword of neoliberal reason during the Thatcher years. If the state is to be brought back as the major defender of citizenship rights, educational policies will need to be informed by a renewed ethic of social justice. It is this theme that we address in the next chapter.

Notes

1   The notion of education as a 'positional good' is a notion she takes from Hollis (1982) which characterizes the fact that education has a 'special complexity' as a good as in that its exchange value for individuals depends on its relative position within the hierarchical and competitive structure of the society. This results in large measure from its scarcity value owing to the fact that the advantage that accrues from being educated derives from the fact that not all people have the same advantage. In Hollis's (1982: 237) words, educational attainments are like 'numbered lithographs' having additional worth to those who gain them precisely because not everybody gains them.

2   Some independent confirmation of the view that the privatization initiatives of New Labour did not show the results intended was provided in January 2003, when the Audit Commission, the independent watchdog on government spending in England, delivered a political bombshell in a report comparing 17 of the first 25 schools to be built in terms of the Private Finance Initiative with 12 schools constructed with traditional public finance. Its conclusion was that schools designed and financed by the private sector are no cheaper, or better, than those built and run by councils.

11
Democracy, Citizenship and the 'Thin' Community

The debate over choice policies identifies a philosophical dilemma that lies at the heart of education and social policy. Fundamentally, it is a dilemma in which two conflicting ethical frameworks are called upon to justify different elements of the same overall set of reform policies. The philosophical and ethical theory that underlies marketization and provides a rationale for 'choice' policies can be recognized as entailing two specific forms of liberalism. Traditional social contract versions of liberalism rationalized choice in relation to the belief in the rational capacity of the self-interested individual. Classical economic versions rationalized it in terms of the belief in laissez-faire as the guiding principle for the state. In this chapter, we argue against both of these forms of liberalism in favour of a notion of social justice that is based upon a 'thin' communitarianism. We claim that, if social democracy is to survive, policies pertaining to educational choice and diversity must be subordinate to a prior commitment by the state to the continuation, strengthening and expansion of a universal public education system.

Conflicting ethical frameworks: utilitarianism and social justice

In the nineteenth century, utilitarianism became the major rationale for choice. While this version of liberalism was at one level more collectivist, in terms of the ends which justified action, it was still embedded in the rational calculations of individuals. In terms of this theory, as promulgated by writers like Jeremy Bentham and John Stuart Mill, a moral decision is justified if it produces the 'greatest happiness for the greatest number' of people. Such happiness is calculated in terms of the consequences for society as a whole, rather than the consequences for any particular individuals or groups within the society. Thus, in the distribution of a good such as education, utilitarianism would seek to maximize the average distribution even if the disparities were wider as a result. Efficiency, according to utilitarian ethic, means that as many people as possible get more of what they want even if some end up getting less. This may be achieved by increasing both opportunities for choice and competition among individuals.

Education, in neoliberal utilitarian terms, is considered to be a *preferred good*, that is something we expect some to want and others not to want. Although it is referred to as a 'good' it is typically defined as representing the sum total of individuals' preferences. It is something we choose or earn and because it involves the acquisition of marketable skills, it does not differ essentially from other exchangeable commodities. Such preferred goods do not produce positive externalities or benefits to others apart from those who receive them.

The distributive principle within a utilitarian framework is that of utility, which means that a preferred good such as education is distributed so as to gain optimal average benefits for all, even if the least advantaged become worse off. This entails an ethical position that differs in a number of essential ways from the *social justice ethic* that traditionally informed educational policy-making under the welfare state. The major differences between these two ethical frameworks are summarized in Figure 11.1.

	Neoliberal Utilitarianism	Social Justice as fairness
Primary social objective	Choice	Equity
What is distributed?	Education as a preferred good (exchangeable commodity)	Education as a primary social good
Distributive principle	Utility (optimal average benefits for all – even if disparities are wider)	Fairness (inequalities are justified only if they benefit those who are disadvantaged)
Main criterion for resource allocation	Efficiency (invest to maximize aggregate gains)	Need (invest to improve opportunities for least advantaged)
Major educational outcome	Increased educational productivity	Fairer distribution of educational benefits
Major social effect	Disproportionate acquisition of resources by most advantaged (profit by some)	Redistribution of benefits by limiting choice (welfare for all)

Figure 11.1 *Ethical frameworks for educational policy*

217

'Social justice as fairness' refers to an ethical framework in which equity is given priority over choice as the primary social objective. As we saw in Chapter 7, Green and Hobhouse both advanced such a conception in the late nineteenth and early twentieth centuries. One twentieth-century philosopher who theorizes a conception of social justice as an alternative to choice theory is John Rawls. In its simplest form, equity is taken to mean 'redress', that is, giving more to the less advantaged. In the social justice theory advanced by Rawls, however, equity is given a more subtle and extended definition. Essentially, for Rawls (1971: 302), equity is embodied in two principles of social justice. The first principle is that: 'Each person is to have an equal right to the most extensive total system of equal basic liberties compatible with a similar system of liberty for all.' The second principle, which he calls 'the difference principle' is: 'Social and economic inequalities are to be arranged so that they are both to the greatest benefit of the least advantaged and attached to offices and positions open to all under conditions of fair equality of opportunity.' In addition, Rawls (ibid.: 303) posits a 'General Conception': 'All social primary goods – liberty and opportunity, income and wealth, and the bases of self respect – are to be distributed equally unless distribution of any or all of these goods is to the advantage of the least favoured.'

Thus Rawls's conception of 'justice as fairness' is to allow each individual to advance 'in a fair way'. Rawls argues that these principles have a rational basis and thus constitute an Archimedean point for judging the basic social structures of a society. His theory of justice is an attempt to identify the deep structures which shape our common-sense judgements about what is right and proper. Rather than the utilitarian view which seeks to maximize aggregate happiness, Rawls provides a modern contract theory extending the traditional theory of social contract as set down by Locke, Rousseau and Kant, and which he summarizes in shorthand form with the phrase 'justice as fairness'.

The rationale for implementing justice as fairness is relatively straightforward. Rawls posits a modern 'thought-experiment' which involves ascertaining the principles by which rational people would distribute resources in society uninfluenced by knowledge of their own social situation, their own wealth, or their future life plans or prospects. He imagines (ibid.: 136) such people making such decisions behind this 'veil of ignorance' about their own position or prospects in such a society in order to ensure fairness by removing 'the effects of specific contingencies which put men at odds and tempt them to exploit social and natural circumstances to their own advantage'. Rawls conceptualizes such people in the position of erecting a new social contract and charges them as rational beings with establishing the social arrangements according to principles which reason dictates and which, in turn, will enable basic political and economic policies to be derived in the interests of the least well off, as well as upholding the basic rights and duties of its members.

The application of these principles to education would mean that resources were to be allocated 'so as to improve the long-term expectation of the least favoured' (ibid.: 101) rather than simply evening out existing inequalities or improving the economic efficiency of the system. Because education is necessary to the very formation of people's wants, it constitutes what Rawls calls a *primary good* (ibid.: 62). Primary social goods are things that all reasonable people would want because without them they cannot even choose the kind of life they would want. For example, reasonable people would want to be able to participate in decisions that affect their welfare, and to be able to develop skills and acquire knowledge necessary for participation in the political economic institutions of society. Education, in these terms, becomes defined as a basic human right and functions as a necessary prior condition for liberty. It is not something we can simply choose to have from a position of not having it. Education is not something we simply acquire: it changes who we are.

Rawls argues that a just society is one in which primary goods are distributed fairly, according to people's needs. This implies that (ibid.: 107): 'Resources for education are not to be allotted solely or necessarily mainly according to their return as estimated in productive trained abilities, but also according to their worth in enriching the personal and social life of citizens, including here the less favoured.' Within this view, educational policies are justified by the extent to which they produce a fairer distribution on education benefits, rather than in terms of economic efficiency or improved consumer choice. Social justice obliges the state to invest in education, not to maximize the gains for all, nor to allow some to profit at the expense of others, but rather to safeguard conditions of welfare for all and where necessary to limit the choice of some in order to redistribute the benefits more fairly.

For Rawls (ibid.: 3), then, 'justice is the first principle of social institutions, as truth is of systems of thought'. As such it offers an alternative to utilitarianism, libertarianism and meritocratic theories. As Kahne (1996: 21) puts it:

> He faults utilitarians for violating individual rights when they attempt to maximize aggregate utility, libertarians for permitting distribution of positions and rewards to be influenced 'by ... factors [both native abilities and social and economic status] so arbitrary from a moral point of view' ... and those who support meritocratic systems because he feels the distribution of natural assets is every bit as arbitrary as that of social assets. 'Equality of opportunity', he writes, 'means an equal chance to leave the less fortunate behind in the personal quest for influence and social position'.

In relation to education, Rawls's commitment to the disadvantaged under the difference principle would not necessarily mean that the relatively more successful or 'gifted' students would be neglected at the expense of the worst off. Yet, the educational emphasis on meritocracy would be modified, and although incentives could still be linked to performance, they would be structured so as to benefit the worst off first.

According to Kahne (1996: 22–4), Rawls's (1971: 100–1) proposals are similar in many respects to those of James Coleman (1968) who wanted to shape policy within liberal agendas to compensate those – to use Rawls's words – 'born into less favourable social positions'. Yet unlike Coleman, Rawls wants to compensate 'those with fewer native talents' as well:

> In order to treat all persons equally, to provide genuine equality of opportunity, society must give more attention to those with fewer native talents and to those born into less favourable social positions. The idea is to redress the bias of contingencies in the direction of equality. In pursuit of this principle greater resources might be spent on the education of the less rather than the more intelligent.

This view contrasts strongly with the neoliberal position in which the state invests in education to improve the overall productive capacity of its citizens. The aim of neoliberal policy is to achieve a maximum return on investment. Where this involves an unequal distribution of resources, it is based upon the ability of people to profit from those resources and it is assumed that the resulting increased productivity eventually will provide benefits for all. However, this 'trickle-down' theory of economic and social justice, which is commonly used in defence of neoliberal policies, does not bear closer ethical scrutiny. As Ronald Dworkin (1985: 209) points out:

> Children denied adequate nutrition or any effective chance of higher education will suffer permanent loss even if the economy follows the most optimistic path of recovery. Some of those who are denied jobs and welfare now, particularly the elderly, will in any case not live long enough to share in that recovery however general it turns out to be.

Dworkin (ibid.: 209) argues that neoliberal utilitarianism, which 'attempts to justify irreversible losses to a minority in order to achieve gains for the large majority' is contrary to the principle that people must be treated with equal concern. Thus, the utilitarian ethic, which gives priority to the maximization of people's opportunity to have what they happen to want, denies the principle of equity that is central to social justice as fairness.

Rawls and his communitarian critics

Rawls's version of socially democratic liberalism is one alternative to the neoliberal organization of schooling according to 'choice' and has appeal to all those who think of society as a community independent of the specific individuals within it, or who think of the well-being and liberty of individuals as in some way mutually related to the well-being and good of society. As such, Rawls reinstates social contract theory as an alternative to utilitarianism as the basis for a new welfare state. Whether Rawls's principles of justice are defendable as rational principles which necessarily constitute an Archimedean point for moral and political philosophy is highly contentious (see Lukes, 1977). Irrespective of their rational basis, however, they could be *politically* argued for, and on this ground Rawls's principle of justice could be seen as a useful philosophical guideline for a revised welfare state. It may be possible too, to link Rawls's arguments with more communitarian viewpoints which justify a 'positive' dimension to state policy in the interests of equity and justice. For many twentieth-century communitarians such as Michael Sandel (1982) or Michael Walzer (1981; 1983; 1990), however, Rawls's conception is too individualist, embodying a classical liberal conception of the self and society. For Rawls, in *A Theory of Justice* (1971: 143), the rational individual is exclusively concerned with finding the solution, that is, those principles of justice, that most clearly advance his own interests. He is the classical *homo economicus*:

> A rational person is thought to have a coherent set of preferences between the options open to him. He ranks these options according to how well they further his purposes; he follows the plan which will satisfy more of his desires rather than less, and which have a greater chance of being successfully executed.

In addition, says Sandel (1982), a certain range of conceptions of the good will be unable to flourish in Rawlsian society because the individualist and asocial metaphysical foundations of liberal principles generate an inability to acknowledge or even perceive the types of goals that communities inevitably must strive for and the social objectives they must fulfil.[1] Rawls's individual is essentially the self-interested autonomous chooser of classical liberalism and in this context his principles of justice constitute 'limiting' ethical boundaries within which market exchanges can take place.

In his later work, *Political Liberalism* (1996), Rawls presents a further defence of 'justice as fairness', where he seeks to justify and revise his position in the light of criticism.[2] Although he reasserts the basic elements of the approach, he makes several noteworthy amendments, qualifications, or 'clarifications'. Early on, he addresses two issues. First, he rejects a metaphysical conception of the person as a 'self-interested chooser', claiming (Rawls, 1996: 19) that his approach posits individuals who are only 'free and equal':

> The basic idea is that in virtue of their two moral powers (a capacity for a sense of justice and for a conception of the good) and the powers of reason (of judgement, thought, and inference connected with these powers), persons are free. Their having these powers to the requisite minimum degree to be fully cooperating members of society makes persons equal.

Secondly, he qualifies (ibid.: 24) the contractual device of the original position as a 'device of representation' which 'must be regarded as both hypothetical and nonhistorical': 'It describes the parties, each of whom is responsible for the essential interests of a free and equal citizen, as fairly situated and as reaching an agreement subject to conditions that appropriately limit what they can put forward as good reasons.'

Notwithstanding these changes to his position, Rawls still seeks to maintain that 'political liberalism' is neutral over different ways of life and ends, and agnostic between diverse cultural viewpoints. For this purpose he distinguishes 'political liberalism' from what he terms 'comprehensive doctrines', which he claims assert a particular moral, religious or philosophical truth. For Rawls a doctrine is fully comprehensive if it claims to organize all relevant values into a systematic whole. Hence, while a 'political' discourse is limited and impartial with respect to different versions of the good, a 'comprehensive' discourse represents a whole world view – something like a *Weltanschauung* – of which Hegelianism, Marxism, religious doctrines or certain formulations of liberalism (such as those of Kant or Mill) are examples. Central to the distinction is the rejection of monism and the defence of pluralism. As he states in his essay 'Priority of the right and ideas of the good' (Rawls, 1988: 201) 'justice as fairness does indeed abandon the idea of political community if by that ideal is meant a political society united in one (partially or fully) comprehensive religious, philosophical or moral doctrine'.

Rawls's argument here entails positing a qualitative distinction between two types of discourse. Politically, he traces the origins of his argument to the distinction between the 'liberties of the moderns' from the 'liberties of the ancients'. While Rawls's argument may be useful in order for him to differentiate his own pluralistic conception as against the monistic and autocratic societies that Benjamin Constant (the originator of the distinction) had in mind, it certainly cannot be applied to pluralistic conceptions of communitarianism, or for that matter to Habermas, for neither assert a 'comprehensive philosophical, moral or religious doctrine' of the 'monistic' sort Rawls says he objects to.

The distinction between a 'political' doctrine and a 'comprehensive' doctrine opens up significant problems for Rawls. They are problems which strike at the heart of his claim that liberalism constitutes a neutral discourse. As Callan (1997: 13) maintains, 'the distinction between political and comprehensive liberalism is far more porous than its devotees suppose, and Rawls's political liberalism in particular is really a disguised instance of comprehensive liberalism'. Reich (2002) maintains a similar argument, making the point that to acknowledge that education must play an essential role in constructing autonomous citizens and producing the necessary political virtues (as Rawls does at times in both *A Theory of Justice* and *Political Liberalism*) 'makes political liberalism much more comprehensive than Rawls wants to admit' (ibid.: 51). Essentially, Rawls argues that liberalism is neutral (not comprehensive) because it adheres only in the public sphere, while cultural and religious diversity is allowed to flourish in the private sphere. Hence, while political liberalism is the official public discourse, citizens are free in their private lives to live non-autonomously. Yet, as Reich (ibid.: 50) argues, utilizing an expression from Amy Gutmann, the values of the public realm 'spill over' into the private. As he comments (ibid.: 49):

> By containing autonomy within the political domain, Rawls's theory of justice remains a political conception rather than a comprehensive conception. In our nonpublic identities, autonomy and the political virtues are not binding. Ultimately, Rawls's distinction ... fails, for autonomy ... is less a capacity that we switch on or off at will than a sort of character that colors our lives as a whole.[3]

Reich's point here is that as political liberalism must structure all public sphere activities and processes, including education, the identities of all the diverse cultural groups in the polis will be affected through such socialising practices, thus undermining citizens private right to structure their lives freely in terms of the comprehensive discourses of their choice.[4]

In a related sense, another general objection to Rawls's 'political/comprehensive' distinction, is that it maintains that political liberalism is *neutral* in relation to different ways of life, whereas comprehensive doctrines assert particular values. While Rawls recognizes that liberalism cannot be completely neutral to all actions or ways of life, including those that are intolerant or operate outside the law, it can be neutral to all *reasonable* comprehensive doctrines.[5] As he puts it (Rawls, 1996: 375) in response to Habermas, 'The central idea is that political liberalism moves within the category of the political and leaves philosophy as it is. It leaves untouched all kinds of doctrines – religious, metaphysical, and moral – with their long traditions of development and interpretation'. Education serves as a good example, and shows also why Rawls's argument fails. Whereas education structured in terms of a comprehensive doctrine would need to inculcate whatever distinctive doctrine it adhered to, education in accord with political liberalism would be neutral with respect to the broad diversity of views in society. But, as has now been pointed out by many critics,[6] the argument of liberal neutrality is seriously flawed, for the liberal state privileges certain ways of life over others, as the example of education shows only too clearly. As Reich (2002: 38) argues:

> The demands and effects of liberal citizenship are decidedly non-neutral, favoring some cultural groups over others. Liberalism consciously and purposefully urges upon citizens a certain kind of character that outlines at least minimally the kind of person we are to be, which in turn affects the way cultural groups are able to form the character of their adherents. To use a familiar phrase, liberalism is about soulcraft as well as statecraft.

William Kymlicka (1995: ch. 5) makes a similar argument when he claims that states cannot be neutral with respect to such educational issues as *language policy* or *national holidays*. In addition to these matters, one can add educational issues such as the content or pedagogy of the educational curriculum, or non-educational issues such as marriage laws, taxation policies or public health issues. As Reich (2002: 39) maintains:

education reveals the way that liberal neutrality is impossible in two powerful ways: (1) *in practice*, the historical operation of schools in liberal states demonstrates the clear privileging of some cultural groups over others, both in aim and in effect; and (2) *in theory*, the presuppositions that liberal theorists make about citizenship point to the imperative for a sort of civic education whose aims are decidedly non-neutral for cultural groups. The blinkered vision of contemporary liberal theorists when considering education has led many to ignore the actual practice of educational institutions and, worse, to ignore or underestimate the theoretical demands that liberalism places on a certain kind of civic education.

The concern with neutrality indicates that Rawls's 'political/comprehensive' distinction serves a broader epistemological function beyond a mere concern with the issue of pluralism and monism. Indeed, to distinguish liberal from comprehensive discourses in terms of 'neutrality/partiality' is to go well beyond a concern with 'pluralism/monism'. Rawls tends to assume that 'comprehensive' doctrines are inevitably 'monistic', yet, as Callan (1997: 19) observes, comprehensive doctrines are 'variable in the degree to which they can be reconciled with pluralism'. In that the 'political/comprehensive' binary denotes broader relations than a concern with the issues of pluralism and monism, it invokes resonances with other dualisms that appear within liberalism. Indeed, as Spragens (1981: 45) notes, the liberal mind-set creates philosophical and political dualisms of its own divided along lines such as 'us vs. them', 'reliable concrete knowledge vs. ideology', 'empiricistic vs. non-empiricistic theories', 'practice vs. theory', 'individual vs. community' or 'open/closed'. Our view is that Rawls's 'political/comprehensive' binary dualism is of this order. As Spragens (ibid.: 45) continues:

> We might characterize this dominant [liberal] paradigm as *epistemological manicheanism*. In its relation to the human understanding the world was divided into two. On the one side lay the kingdom of light, the land of the intelligible. In it, all was transparent and comprehensive with certitude. On the other side lay the kingdom of darkness, the land of the unintelligible. In it all was inpenetrable to the best efforts of the human mind.

With the reformulations and clarifications of his position in *Political Liberalism*, Rawls also faced other difficulties. The modifications or qualifications, put forward to answer his critics, cause unresolvable downstream tensions in terms of his commitment to any philosophically consistent form of liberalism. Rawls may claim to be redefining the contours of 'political liberalism' which, in a way, he is trying to do, yet the difficulties remain. On the one hand, he collapses any meaningful distinction between liberalism and comunitarianism. This appears with his redefinition of the human subject as essentially social in nature. It appears again with his argument that his theory of justice is 'political/not metaphysical'. It also appears when Rawls accepts that political liberalism and classical republicanism are not in opposition (Rawls,

1996: 205). Further, it seems (ibid.: 206) that 'civic humanism' as a form of Aristotelianism is only problematic because it places too great a stress on 'participation' as the basis of citizenship. As to the acceptance of a view of the individual as 'social', Rawls's clarification at one level may appear to resolve the issue at stake, yet leaves remaining problems associated with liberalism's methodological and epistemological individualism, and its inability to theorize 'collective properties', or any meaningful conception of 'community'.[7]

In responding to Habermas, Rawls (1996: 424, 432) accepts that all theories of justice posit substantive ends or goals, and argues that procedural and substantive ends cannot be separated.[8] His claim that liberalism is a *substantive* doctrine is directly problematic in this regard, for classical liberals have traditionally maintained that liberalism maintains *no* substantive conception of the good. This indeed was the basis for the claims to liberal neutrality. This was Constant's (1988) view, who argued that the liberal state must be 'neutral' over conceptions of the good life, recognizing only individuals' values and preferences. This was also the position taken by Isaiah Berlin (1969) in his famous essay on liberty. The identification of a good is impossible, in Berlin's view, as individuals manifest such diversity of opinion over the nature of the good. Because of this irreducible pluralism over values and preferences, and consequent incompatibility over versions of the good, individual freedom is all that remains. It is only as a consequence of this axiom that the state can be represented as the *enemy*, rather than the *precondition*, of freedom.

Notwithstanding such traditional liberal arguments, in accepting justice as fairness as a substantive doctrine, Rawls has come to accept that liberalism itself *implies* a substantive conception of the good. While we may well wonder how he squares this view with his arguments about liberal neutrality, communitarians and others will welcome the change in his views. The argument by liberals that within its policy prescriptions liberalism does not invoke a particular preferred shape to society, or that it does not advocate the establishment of a social good over and above what individuals desire, cannot rule out substantive commitments about what society should be like. As Luke Martell (1992: 156) states, for instance:

> It all sounds very nice until you realize that what it does, in effect, is to let in just another particular substantive vision of society as consisting of the sum total of individuals' preferences over which individuals have no overall control. In this sense, liberalism is in fact a highly substantive doctrine – one which posits a competitive individualist society immune to overall democratic direction.

In recognizing liberalism as a substantive doctrine, there are various other consequences, however. If justice as fairness is committed to substantive values and ends, then it is asserting a conception of the good – not of *primary* goods, but of *the* good. Yet, to open liberalism to an objective theory of 'the good', in this way, is to open the door to a theory of collective properties, and of community.

Yet, Rawls wants to defend a form of liberal pluralism that does not involve accepting a general objective conception of well-being for all, as for liberals, individual morality is seen as a private question, each person pursuing their own good in their own way. This is to say that, consistent with the liberal tradition, Rawls continues to assert the priority of the right over the good. Yet this makes a conception of community as a collective property essentially a fiction as all we have in an ontological sense is an aggregate of individuals.[9]

It is on this point that William Galston maintained that neutralist liberals like Rawls, Dworkin and Ackerman could not avoid reference to a substantive theory of the good.[10] Without being explicit, says Galston (1991: 92) they 'covertly rely on the same triadic theory of good which assumes the worth of human existence'. In a similar vein, Chantal Mouffe (1993: 31) maintains that Rawls compounds his difficulties, in seeking to adapt his theory in response to criticism, for 'it is only within a specific community, defining itself by the good that it postulates, that an individual with his rights can exist'. Rawls could, she says, accommodate this once he distinguished between a moral and a political good. If a political good could constitute an overarching structure of association, institutions and rules, then the diverse moral ends of individuals could be accommodated. Yet, although Rawls belatedly made such a distinction,[11] his liberal assumptions are poorly equipped to conceptualize the political and collective dimensions of life. As Mouffe (ibid.: 33) puts it, '[e]very consistent individualism must negate the political, since it requires that the individual remains *terminus a quo* and *terminus ad quem*'. Hence she concludes that trying rationally to found a welfare state project, offering reasonable equality, no matter how progressive, based upon a liberal conception of the subject, must run aground. If the individual is a social and historical being, which we as Foucauldians maintain, then the right cannot precede the good. In this respect, as Galston (1982: 506, cited in Mouffe, 1993: 47) notes, as Rawls adapts his position, he creates further difficulties:

> He still maintains the priority of the right but his new emphasis on the conception of the moral person undermines such a priority, since if justice is desirable because it aims at our good as moral persons, then justice as fairness rests on a specific conception of the good, from which the 'constraints' of right and justice are ultimately derived.

Rawls's problems here stem, fundamentally, from the deep attachments between liberalism and atomistic individualism. Individualism can be broken down into three different types: ontological, epistemological and political individualism. Ontological individualism holds that only individuals are real, and that the individual is 'prior' to society and is the sovereign legislator of the moral law.[12] Epistemological individualism is the doctrine that the individual human mind constitutes a reliable foundation for knowledge,[13] and political individualism holds that social policies and state actions are to be judged good or bad only in so far as they serve the desires and purposes of individual members of society. In an extreme sense, the political individualist adopts the view, as Margaret Thatcher did, for instance, that 'society does not exist – all there are, are individuals'. Although Rawls would clearly claim not to accept Margaret Thatcher's extreme formulation, the difficulties he faces, given the deep ontological and epistemological attachments between liberalism and individualism, relate to (1) how a theory of collective properties can emerge, and (2) how the relations between the individual and the society can be adequately theorized and reconciled. His attempted reformulations in *Political Liberalism* are in our view far from convincing in these respects.

The consequences of these problems become apparent again when Rawls seeks to respond to another of Habermas's (1995) criticisms, a criticism which Habermas sees as crucial. Habermas claims to see an unresolvable antagonism between *public and private autonomy*, or between *ancient and modern liberties*, which he claims, in the history of modern thought liberals have failed to understand. Whereas liberals have accepted a conception of private autonomy as theorized in the liberty of the moderns, and which exists as a *natural* condition, *prior to society*, the republican tradition derives autonomy from the principle of popular sovereignty, as expressed in *democratic law*, as a *condition of society*. In Habermas's view, Rawls shares the liberal assumption that there exist individual rights prior to the democratic process, which results in a model of a just society where 'liberal rights ... constrain democratic self-legislation' (Habermas, 1995: 128–9). Charles Lamore (1999: 617) summarizes Habermas's position:

> [Habermas's] view is that citizens must be able to see all their political principles, even those establishing individual rights, as rooted in their autonomous political will. Such a self-understanding is blocked by a conception that gives rights, as he believes Rawls's theory does, a status prior to the democratic process.

Rawls's (1996: 433) response is to claim that these public and private conceptions of freedom as embedded in ancient and modern conceptions are not mutually inconsistent but 'co-original' or 'co-equal'. While these complex philosophical arguments cannot be treated fully here, this response exposes the serious tensions Rawls faces between trying to ward off criticisms and endeavouring to protect the distinctiveness and integrity of his position *as liberal*. It is difficult to see, to borrow Sandel's phrase, how liberty can be *both* 'prior to its ends', *and* 'derivative' from them. But such are the dilemmas and problems that Rawls creates when trying to defend political liberalism from his critics. To put the matter bluntly, Rawls's reformulation is a good example, to use Spragen's (1981: 5) words, of the 'incapacity of liberalism's deepest assumptions – ontological, epistemological and anthropological – to sustain its finest aspirations and ideals'. It is because of the problems that afflict Rawls's liberal approach *at its very core* that we now seek to resolve the problems of liberty and choice from a communitarian perspective.

Communitarianism as the basis of social democracy

A more throughgoing democratic communitarianism of the sort advanced earlier in the century by John Dewey (1916; 1935; 1963) or, more recently, by Michael Sandel (1982), Charles Taylor (1985; 1994), Michael Walzer (1983; 1990) or Alasdair MacIntyre (1981; 1988; 1991) can be distinguished from liberal conceptions of education and society on a number of important dimensions. The most important of these are: (1) a critique of individualism, including individual rights and a recognition of the 'common good' including the shared values and practices of a community; (2) a positive conception of the role of the state, and (3) a recognition of the social nature of the self. It is our view that communitarianism, if suitably modified, offers a more viable philosophical basis for social democracy in the twenty-first century than does Rawlsian 'political liberalism'. Our argument focuses on each of these three aspects.

(1) The common good

Communitarians place greater emphasis on the 'common good', that is, on collective goods including the shared values and practices of a community. While collective goods are institutional and include such things as buildings used for sports and intangible goods such as education, community values also include the shared norms and beliefs that constitute a society's cultural belief systems. Communitarians are committed to the value of strong communities and argue that the bonds among people weaken as the population becomes more diverse. As this happens, the number of shared values and goals in society lessens and there is a corresponding increase in the emphasis on individual rights and goals. In addition, communitarians argue that individual values are derived from community values and not from human nature. Hence the weakness of the liberal position.

Communitarians would argue that Rawls's deontological conception essentially constitutes a rights-based morality which decentralizes any notion of the 'common good' and does not allow for a conception of public goods over and above the sum of individual private desires and preferences. As Seung-Hwan Lee (1992: 241) puts it:

> A rights-based morality does not give central place to the common good and a shared life. Rather it emphasizes the notion of what each member of the community is entitled to claim from other members. The moral bonds of the community are founded on mutual respect, demonstrated by recognizing the rights of each individual, rights such as those of freedom, property and well-being.

Communitarians argue that as the common good is not simply the sum of individual rights-based actions, it cannot be reduced to them. Hence a conception based on rights will not ensure many community ends (housing for the elderly, clean water, and so on). This differs fundamentally from rights and utilitarian conceptions. In contrasting his communitarian conception of the good with Bentham's, Philip Selznick (1992: 537) states:

> The alternative [to Bentham's view] is to think of the common good as more profoundly systemic, not reducible to individual interests or attributes, yet testable by its contribution to personal well-being. The common good is served, for example, by institutions that provide collective goods, such as education or public safety. The strength or weakness of these institutions is a communal attribute, not an individual one.

For communitarians, liberal individualism is incoherent because people's identities are not reducible to individual preferences and beliefs, and also because ethics, as Alasdair MacIntyre (1988) has said, cannot be represented in individualist terms. Rather, ethical decisions can only be understood in the context of a community.

(2) A positive role for the state

A state which is limited in terms of a negative conception of its role will serve neither community ends, nor the 'common good'. To ensure the conditions for social justice and harmony a state must act positively in relation to issues such as education and health in order to provide and maintain the conditions necessary for individual rights and freedoms to be effective. The essential argument for a positive role for the state was put forward by social democratic liberals at the end of the nineteenth century. To the 'negative' rights of 'life, liberty and estate' they added new 'positive' rights to knowledge, education, health and minimum sustenance of life's basic resources. Such a conception of the state's role has been traditionally supported by social democrats. As the current British Home Secretary, David Blunkett (2002) writes, for instance:

> I prefer a positive view of freedom, drawing on another tradition of political thinking that goes back to the ancient Greek polis. According to this tradition, we only become fully free when we share, as active citizens, in the government of the affairs of the community. Our identity as members of a collective political community is a positive thing. Democracy is not just an association of individuals determined to protect the private sphere, but a realm of active freedom in which citizens come together to shape the world around them. We contribute and we become entitled.

In Hobhouse's view, one's entitlement to rewards and gain must be balanced by one's obligations to society. What liberal conceptions of democracy obscured, said Hobhouse, was the interdependence between individuals and the social structure or, in other words, the social and moral obligation of the society (acting through the vehicle of the state) to assist in arranging the social futures of each rising generation. As he argued in his classic study, *Liberalism* (1911: 189–90), in his justification for redistributive policies of progressive taxation, the state has an obligation to legislate reasonable conditions of equality on the basis that while a society should provide the conditions for enterprise, all individuals are correspondingly indebted to society for the conditions and structures provided, and on this basis, individuals should contribute in direct proportion to the luck or good fortune they experience.

(3) The social nature of the self

What is common to all democratic forms of communitarianism is their rejection of the liberal conception of a pre-social (that is, natural) self. In contrast, they maintain that the nature of the self is social and depends to a large extent on the community. As Charles Taylor (1985: 190–1) puts it:

> What has been argued in the different theories of the social nature (of human beings) is not just that they cannot physically survive alone, but much more that they only develop their characteristically human capacities in society. The claim is that living in a society is a necessary condition of the development of rationality, in some sense of this property, or of becoming a moral agent in the full sense of the term, or of becoming a fully responsible autonomous being.

Or, as expressed by Michael Sandel (1982: 11): 'We are conditioned beings "all the way down". There is no point of exception, no transcendental subject capable of standing outside society or outside experience. We are at every moment what we have become, a concatenation of desires and inclinations with nothing left over to inhabit a noumenal realm.'

Rawls's view, like that of Locke, and like Kant, posits a conception of the self which is 'atomistic', says Taylor (1985: 292, 309):

> We can describe as atomist views of the human good for which it is conceivable for man to attain it alone … . The basic error of atomism in all of its forms is that it fails to take account of the degree to which the free individual with his own goals and aspirations is himself only possible within a certain kind of civilization; that it took a long development of certain institutions and practices, of the rule of law, of rules of equal respect, of habits of common deliberation, of common association, of cultural self-development, and so on, to produce the modern individual, and without these the very sense of oneself as an individual in the modern meaning of the term would atrophy.

Communitarians claim that liberals overemphasize the autonomy of individuals, as in Kantian ethics, for instance: that they perpetuate a myth of the pre-social individual; that they adhere to an arrogant universalism, as in the social contract tradition; and that they neglect the central role of community in providing necessary structures of learning, of language and of opportunity. In this, communitarians claim that the philosophical anthropology of liberalism is an incoherent one in that it underemphasizes the *interdependence* of people. In addition, it fails to account satisfactorily for social, or ethical experiences, because evaluation and judgement are treated *asociologically*, as mere subjective preferences. As Glendon (1991: 109) puts it:

> Neglect of the social dimension of personhood has made it extremely difficult for us to develop an adequate conceptual apparatus for taking into account the sorts of groups within which human character, competence, and capacity for citizenship are formed. In a society where the seedbeds of civic virtue – families, neighbourhoods, religious associations, and other communities – can no longer be taken for granted, this is no trifling matter.

Dewey (1927: 158) also criticized the liberal conception of 'the self':

> At the basis of the scheme lies what Lippman has well called the idea of the 'omnicompetent' individual: competent to frame policies, to judge their results, competent to know in all situations demanding political action what is for his own good ... . (It) held that ideas and knowledge were functions of a mind or conciousness which originated in individuals by means of isolated contact with objects. But, in fact, knowledge is a function of association and communication, it depends upon tradition, upon tools and methods socially transmitted, developed and sanctioned.

Forms of communitarianism

Amongst communitarians there are 'strong' programmes and 'weak' programmes in relation to the extent to which individuals are seen as constrained by traditional roles or community norms. Joseph Kahne (1996) has distinguished one group of traditional conservative communitarians, represented by Plato and Aristotle, and another group of democratic communitarians, represented by Dewey. In order to characterize the type of communitarianism advanced by Plato in *The Republic*, Kahne (1996: 32) cites Dewey's (1916: 88) own description, from *Democracy and Education*:

> No one could better express than [Plato] the fact that a society is stably organized when each individual is doing that for which he has aptitude by nature in such a way as to be useful to others (or to contribute to the whole to which he belongs); and that it is the business of education to discover these aptitudes and progressively to train them for social use.

Plato's is a traditional conservative communitarianism which sees individuals as directly subservient to community-defined roles and positions, which, in turn are conceptualized as hierarchical, narrow and unchanging. Liberal criticisms of this view tend to represent it as authoritarian on the basis that it erodes individual liberty, autonomy and rights.[14] For Dewey, on the other hand, the form of communitarianism is both weaker, in that there is an attempt to balance both individual rights and goals with community ends and values; and more dynamic, in that he is especially interested in the mechanisms by which communities change. In addition, weaker forms of communitarianism may recognize structures (related to knowledge or biology) which transcend particular communities both historically and cross-culturally, and still claim that many important dimensions of individual welfare and development (including learning, psychological health, and so on) depend in important respects on the nature of the community. Contemporary writers who may be held to fit within this broad category include Joseph Raz (1986; 1994) Martha Nussbaum (1990; 1994a; 1994b; 1992; 1996; 1997; 2000a; 2000b) and Amartya Sen (1979; 1985; 1988; 1992; 1993; 1999; 2002).

In the sense that Dewey sought to combine communitarian elements with certain liberal and democratic elements, there is a similarity with Green and Hobhouse, the 'welfare state liberals' of the late nineteenth century, who sought to preserve the liberal emphasis on rights, and a 'positive' role for the state, while acknowledging the central importance of 'collective goods' over and above individual preferences and desires, thus rejecting the classical liberal conception of a pre-social autonomous self. In this sense, it is the rejection of the philosophical anthropology underpinning liberalism, together with the implications this has for theorizing the relations between individual and society, that makes a shift in philosophical discourse all important. If the self is socially and historically constituted, then the development of our identities depends upon state action and community support. Freedom, too, rather than being a natural inborn capacity, will depend on politically structured opportunities. This also entails a role for education, and the state, in that the state must protect freedom and ensure safety and support for the development of identities. In that rights are important, they are not conceptualized as natural or pre-social, but rather as politically distributed, and understood, in combination with *duties*, within the context of a historically changing democratic community.

Dewey's democratic conception of community is valuable, also, in that it retains fundamental liberal insights, whilst not justifying them according to liberal arguments. While recognizing that the capacity for choice and autonomy depends upon community background, and that there are many valuable ways of life, it acknowledges and recognizes the importance of freedom or liberty. In this sense, it clearly rejects the conservative communitarians' stress on unity or consensus, tradition and authority. Rather, as in Miller's (2000: ch. 6) notion of 'communitarians of the left', community can be seen as promoting equality and as actively determining cultural patterns, rather than merely accepting or endorsing authority and tradition, as is the case, says Miller, with 'conservative communitarians' or 'communitarians of the right'. In that it is democratic, community in this sense accords each person an equality of status, and a moral equality as citizen before the law.

Towards a 'thin' communitarianism

Compared with traditional conservative versions of communitarianism, such a conception constitutes a 'thin' communitarianism of the sort that is evident in

Foucault's work (Olssen, 2002b). In his analysis of the Greeks and Greco-Romans, for instance, Foucault reinstates a form of communitarianism which, ultimately, is necessitated by the social *conditions* of selfhood and which underlies his conceptions of self-creation and ethics. Such a communitarianism is 'thin' in the sense that, contra Spinoza, Hegel, Herder, Rousseau and Marx, it has no common bond or goal which is characterized by integration or consensus. In this sense, the 'thin' community does not eclipse liberty or the rights of individuals in preference for belonging, social cohesion, or co-operation. The model of community is, as William Corlett (1993) describes it, 'without unity'. This is to say, the model is not a *totalizing* one, which presupposes unity between individual and collective. Rather, it is a *detotalizing* one, where society comprises a minimal structure of norms, rules, understandings, practices and agreements necessary to permit individual agency and social difference to take effect and function. There are, of course, substantive commitments directed to certain preferred ways of life, dictated by the decisions already taken in history, embedded in traditions, customs, modes of thinking, values and institutions that already exist in the present when individuals arrive on the scene. These commitments dictate a comprehensive way of life within limits, but do not seek to 'integrate' or 'unify' the social structure, and are quite compatible with diversity and difference *internal to such a way of life*. Conceptions such as 'autonomy' or 'democratic citizenship' fit within such a model.

In this sense, the 'thin' community still posits an irreducible conception of the good. In ontological terms, such a conception displays affinities to the conception of 'the good' espoused by Nussbaum (1990, 1992, 2000a, 2000b). Nussbaum's conception incorporates "an account of the most important functions of the human being, in terms of which human life is defined" (1992: 214). It recognizes that all individuals and all cultures have certain developmental and lifestyle needs. Such a conception, she says, is 'vague, and this is deliberately so ... for it admits of much multiple specification in accordance with varied local and personal conceptions. The idea is that it is better to be vaguely right than precisely wrong' (ibid.: 215). Such a conception is not metaphysical in that it does not claim to derive from a source exterior to human beings in history. Rather, it is as 'universal as possible' and aims at 'mapping out the general shape of the human form of life, those features that constitute life as human wherever it is' (ibid.: 216). Nussbaum calls this her 'thick vague theory of the good' (ibid.: 214). Hence, her list of factors constitutes a formal list, allowing for difference or variation within each category. Amongst the factors are: (1) mortality: all human beings face death; (2) various invariant features of the human body, such as 'nutritional, and other related requirements' regarding hunger, thirst, the need for food and drink and shelter; (3) cognitive: 'all human beings have sense perception ... the ability to think'; (4) early development; (5) practical reason; (6) sexual desire; (7) affiliation with other human beings; and (8) relatedness to other species and to nature (ibid.: 216–19).

Nussbaum classifies such a conception, following the influential writings of W.V.O. Quine, Donald Davidson, Hilary Putnam and Nelson Goodman, as an 'internalist essentialism' (ibid.: 208) which is 'an historically grounded empirical essentialism' (ibid.: 208). Within its broad end, and subject to the limits necessary for its realization and continuance, it permits and recognises a multitude of identities and projects and ways of life.[15]

This sort of 'capabilities' approach has not only been advanced by Nussbaum but by Sen (1979; 1985; 1992; 1993; 1999; 2002). For Sen (1999: 295), the development of capabilities is part of the expansion of freedom. Criticizing Human Capital Theory for narrowly considering human beings as part of the productive economic process, Sen (1999: 295) maintains that:

> The acknowledgement of the role of human qualities in promoting and sustaining economic growth – momentous as it is – tells us nothing about why economic growth is sought in the first place. If, instead, the focus is, ultimately, on the expansion of human freedom to live the kind of lives that people have reason to value, then the role of economic growth in expanding these opportunities has to be integrated into that more foundational understanding of the process of development as the expansion of human capability to lead more worthwhile and more free lives.

The form of 'thin' communitarianism we are advocating is broadly compatible with such an approach. Foucault's emphasis on 'self-creation' can be held to *presuppose* a range of capabilities *as necessary*. Such an approach, as Nussbaum argues, enables both international comparisons, and concentrates on the actual conditions which provide for the functional needs of individuals and groups. Such an approach also provides for education, for a politics based on the capabilities approach presupposes that a society provides necessary public education by which capabilities can be developed. Under such an approach it is the business of education to provide for the production of such capabilities. Taking Foucault's emphasis on 'self-creation' as fundamental, we can say that a number of things are clearly required. These include: (1) basic material and institutional supporting structures and resources, (2) training and knowledge, (3) non-humiliation, respect and dignity, (4) a protected space where autonomy can be practised, (5) structures that permit dialogue and communication. Unlike Nussbaum, we have replaced Rawls with Foucault as the major influence on justice and ethics. Foucault's is a non-liberal conception, yet one which protects traditional liberal ideals as regards 'liberty' and 'autonomy' in the context of the development of the virtues necessary for a global community.[16] By stressing 'capabilities' such an approach is not advocating a utilitarian ethics, nor a traditional rights-based approach, nor a teleology of functioning in the Aristotelian sense, nor even a Kantian approach, but simply focuses on the political virtues and collective arrangements wherein survival can be assured and individual development and self-creation can take place.

In addition, a Foucauldian-inspired 'thin' community has other characteristics. Importantly, it is established and reproduced by voluntary acts of free and equal citizens. In addition, to speak of 'community', is to speak of an all-encompassing arena, *without fixed borders*. In this sense, it is not to be understood as a 'bounded' territory or region, but rather it moves across borders, and links politically to forms of republicanism and cosmopolitanism (as we shall see in the final chapter). Also important, such a community is not incompatible with universalism. 'Thin' communitarianism thus overcomes the relativism whereby ethical reasoning must be *internal* to a particular community tradition.[17] Further, common values and practices are only required to the extent they are necessary for democratic continuity and survival. Finally, it comprises antecedent values, norms and institutions that recognize the priority of the social to the individual.

In terms of its social ontology such a conception is therefore more coherent than modern natural law liberalism. Given that human beings can only make meaningful choices for their lives against a background context of alternatives constituted in a community, it will be argued further that Foucault's stress on self-creation and liberty as the basis of ethics would require a strong state that could protect these conditions. Individual autonomy to choose presupposes, in this sense, the existence of structures that are institutionally embodied. As a consequence, 'thin' communitarians stress balancing the rights and freedoms of individuals to pursue their own interests with an equal interest in the rights and interests of the community. Such a conception is 'thin' in that the plurality of ends, goals and values are either institutionally permitted or, in that they conflict, democratically negotiated. In this conception, the reciprocal or inter-related links between individual and collective are kept clearly in balance.

Community, liberty and justice

Such a view also effects a conception of freedom as encompassing both positive duties and negative rights. In this, liberty and autonomy are seen as constituted by society in terms of meaningful civic functioning. Only in society is freedom realizable and determinate. As in the classical view, it is held that liberty cannot operate in the absence of law. Contrary to the idea of a 'natural liberty', as is expressed in the social contract tradition, liberty is conceived as socially and historically constituted, for it is only through the civil law of society that liberty becomes definite and bounded. In his *Commentaries on the Laws of England*, the eighteenth-century legal and political philosopher, William Blackstone depicted liberty in such a way, seeing 'civil liberty' as consisting in 'protecting the rights of individuals by the united force of society' (cited in Heyman, 1992: 85). Civil liberty must be supplemented by 'political liberty', which is more collective, and can be defined as the power of a community to govern itself, and for its citizens to participate in self-government. Such a conception is both positive and negative: the positive freedom of a community is its power to make and enforce laws for the public good; the negative conception entails that it is free to the extent that it is not interfered with. As Heyman (1992: 87–8) points out, in such a classical conception, both senses of freedom are governed by the laws of the constitution which both confers and limits governmental power. Political liberty, thus, enables individuals to achieve goals through collective action, for example, the protection of rights, as requiring in Blackstone's sense, 'the unified force of society'. For these purposes, the economy would be regulated as necessary to increase the civil liberty of individuals to pursue their own good (see Blackstone, 1979).

Crucially, in this 'quasi-Foucauldian' approach, unlike for Rawls or Habermas, there is no Kantian tribunal of transcultural reason that could ground moral decisions or justify policy outcomes. There are, however, pragmatic factors, like the importance of peaceful coexistence for survival or stability, that can justify policy outcomes. It can be agreed too, as Nussbaum (2000b: 124) has stated, that the core capabilities and basic needs of humans can be the object of an 'overlapping consensus' 'among people who otherwise have very different comprehensive conceptions of the good'. This essentially reinstates a theory of human need as fundamental. But for such a shared interest in 'necessity', the outcomes of democratic deliberations would simply bare the character of what Rawls would call a modus vivendi, or 'treaty'. It is 'necessity' that makes deliberation important. And it is 'necessity' that dictates that there will be some common 'overlapping' values. What results is a new 'settlement' or 'pact' or 'agreement' which enables life to be lived in the presence of fundamental disagreements over values, practices and ways of life.

There is also present within Foucault's approach a general conception of *democratic justice* that could underpin such a model of community in a normative sense.[18] In his discussions about 'domination', and the 'equalization of power relations', Foucault (1991a) is advancing a political principle that speaks to both liberty and equality. In terms of equality, equalizing power would mean fighting for marginalized and oppressed groups. In relation to liberty, it presupposes the irreducible moral status of each person and would oppose governmental policies that conflicted with or inhibited self-creation. As Mitchell Dean (1999b: 184) puts it, the law is important in Foucault's political conception according to whether 'it allows rather than inhibits the self-directed use and development of capacities'. This echoes Foucault's view that liberty requires a certain political structure, given that liberty itself involves the exercise of power. Under certain situations, the power relations in terms of which liberty is realized make its expression impossible. In this situation, there results a *state of domination*, says Foucault (1991a: 12), in which power relations become fixed 'in such a way that they are perpetually asymmetrical [in which case] the margin of liberty is extremely limited'. Foucault gives the example of the traditional conjugal relation in the eighteenth and nineteenth centuries:

236

We cannot say that there was only male power; the woman herself could do a lot of things: be unfaithful to him, extract money from him, refuse him sexually. She was, however, subject to a state of domination, in the measure where all that was finally no more than a certain number of tricks which never brought about a reversal of the situation.

Such states of domination entailed relations of power that:

> instead of being variable and allowing different partners a strategy which alters them, find themselves firmly set and congealed. When an individual or social group manages to block a field of relations of power ... to prevent all reversibility of movement ... we are facing what can be called a state of domination. (Ibid.: 3)

In his criticism of Habermas, Foucault (ibid.: 18) proceeds to state a conception whereby power relations can be 'equalized' in order: 'To give oneself the rules of law, the techniques of management, and also the ethics, the ethos, the practices of self, which would allow these games of power to be played with a minimum of domination.' As against totalizing approaches, such as Marxism, Hegelianism and liberalism, the normative emphasis of Foucault's position is that all power relations must be characterized by *openness* (that is, not be 'set' or 'congealed'). As a consequence, such principles give a normative basis to a conception of democratic justice, while recognizing that justice may require different things at different times and places. Such a conception is universal, in Rorty's (1998: 52) sense, in terms of 'reach', but not in terms of 'validity'. This is to say, unlike Rawls and Habermas, it does not seek to encourage deliberation in order to arrive at a supposed 'rational consensus', but simply to achieve a 'settlement'. Such a conception, based upon power relations that must remain dialogically open, and, through *resistance*, is normatively skewed towards power equalization, is also *context-sensitive* to the specific contingencies of historical circumstance.

'Thin' communitarianism can also reconcile the two discourses of justice, centring around *distribution* and *recognition* that have divided academic debate over recent decades.[19] While it recognizes a conception of democratic justice, and the universality of a rights culture as fundamental, this does not mean that the *recognition of distinct identities and differences*, as argued for by multiculturalists are not important. In Nancy Frazer's (1997: 12) view, the importance of a critical theory of recognition is that it embraces a broader conception of cultural and political domination, rather than mere economic inequality, as the core of an argument for justice. For Frazer, justice today requires a concern with both redistribution *and* recognition, that is, with a cultural politics of difference and a social politics of equality. Recognition politics must be grounded, however, in a theory of human rights. This gives rise to a number of interrelated conceptions of justice: first, socioeconomic justice, which requires equality of resources, of the sort that Rawls (1971; 1996) and Dworkin (1981; 1985) have argued for; secondly, justice requires that people

237

have equal 'capabilities to function', of the sort that Sen (1985) and Nussbaum (1990; 1992; 1994b) have argued for; and, thirdly, justice requires a politics of recognition, of the sort that Charles Taylor (1994) and Iris Marion Young (1990; 1995; 1997) have argued for. But the concern for distribution and recognition pulls in opposite directions, says Frazer (1997: 16), constituting a 'redistribution–recognition dilemma':

> Recognition claims often take the form of calling attention to, if not performatively creating, the putative specificity of some group and then of affirming its value. Thus they tend to promote group differentiation. Redistribution claims, in contrast, often call for abolishing economic arrangements that underpin group specificity … . Thus, they tend to promote group dedifferentiation.

'Thin communitarianism' aims to cut across the redistribution–recognition divide to render it amenable to resolution. It aims to affirm both redistribution and recognition in democratically approved ways. Thus 'thin communitarianism' is a 'discourse of diversity' *within limits*. If a rights culture is fundamental, then multicultural diversity cannot be permitted to the extent that it undermines the degree of cohesion and consensus necessary for groups to live and work together, or for a 'reflexive equilibrium' to develop.[20] While not all cultural identities can be valorised on this basis, radical democrats must protect social and economic equality, the recognition of difference, and the protection of security for all.[21] This means, as Frazer (1997: 186) says 'cultural differences can be freely elaborated and democratically mediated only on the basis of social equality'. There can be 'no recognition without redistribution' (ibid.: 187).

In line with our Foucauldian approach, the principles of consensus and diversity will be brought to bear differently in different societies and at different points in time. Foucault himself recognized that consensus was not unimportant to societies, at least in relation to basic agreements. In spite of his wish to accord a greater respect to diversity, he accepted that the consensus model could operate in politics as a *critical principle*, but not as a *regulatory principle*. He made this point in 1983 (Foucault, 1984c: 379) in response to a a panel of interviewers:

> I would say, rather, that it is perhaps a critical idea to maintain at all times: to ask oneself what proportion of nonconsensuality is implied in such a power relation, and whether that degree of nonconsensuality is necessary or not, and then one may question every power relation to that extent. The farthest I would go is to say that perhaps one must not be for consensuality, but one must be against nonconsensuality.

Communitarianism and educational choice policies

In relation to education, democratic communitarians hold that the extent to which systems of choice operate must be balanced by the needs of the community through control by the state. Too much 'choice' tends to undermine community integration and promotes sectarian decisions in terms of class (wealth), race and creed. Not only do 'choice' policies promote private interests at the expense of community interests but also they insulate community subgroups from communicating with those who hold alternative perspectives. Hence on this basis democratic communitarians would argue against the interest group politics of choice advocates like Milton Friedman or Chubb and Moe. Rather, they support public schooling as a means for promoting shared goals for their children and more generally their community. In this context, they emphasize the need for public debate, inclusive community forums, and a more expansive relationship between the school and the community. Michael Walzer (1983), for instance, places emphasis on these issues and argues that some children need protecting by the state from their parents, as some parents may not always choose what is in the interests of their children. On this basis, choice plans, if pushed very far, undermine the process of democratic deliberation by permitting the wealthy to ignore the less well off members of the community, thereby inadequately representing the diverse populations which make it up.

In Dewey's communitarian view, the two central traits of a democratic community are (1) the existence of shared interests amongst members of groups in common and (2) interaction with other groups (Dewey, 1916: 100). Joseph Kahne (1996: 105) cites two questions from Dewey (1916: 100) which are:

1 How numerous and varied are the interests which are consciously shared?
2 How full and free is the interplay with other forms of association?

In relation to Dewey's questions, Kahne (1996: 106) asks two further questions concerning their implications for education policy:

1 Will school choice proposals constrain or promote interaction among students of varied communities?
2 Will school choice proposals increase or decrease the number of interests students consciously share?

From Dewey's point of view, choice proposals would be seen to *constrain* interaction among different groups and *decrease* the number of interests students consciously share. Hence the development of private interests exacerbates conflict and undermines the democratic functioning of the community. As Dewey (1916: 99) puts it:

> The isolation and exclusiveness of a gang or clique brings its anti-social spirit into relief. But this same spirit is found wherever one group has interests 'of its own' which shut it out from full interaction with other groups, so that its prevailing purpose is the protection of what it has got, instead of reorganization and progress through wider relationships. It marks nations in their isolation from one another, families which seclude their domestic concerns as if they had no connection with larger life; schools when separated from the interests of home and community; the division of rich and poor; learned and unlearned.

Similarly, Dewey (ibid.: 96–7) argues that families cannot be seen as isolated from the community:

> (The family enters) intimately into relationships with business groups, with the schools, with all the agencies of culture, as well as with other similar groups, so that it plays a due part in the political organization and in return receives support from it. In short, there are many interests consciously communicated and shared; and there are varied and free points of contact with other modes of association.

The arguments for public schooling restated

In relation to education, the neoliberals' argument is for extending private schooling which ignores the 'social benefits' that publicly provided education brings. These benefits are related to issues such as citizenship, tolerance, literacy and the democratic functioning of a community. As the 'social benefits' of education, they cannot be reduced to individual self-interest, or rendered intelligible within a market perspective. Similarly, the view that standards can be raised through comparison and competition and that increasing systematic appraisal and accountability will lead to increased efficiency and hence productivity is highly questionable.

The provision of public education is based on a number of historically important rights and claims. The 'positive' rights associated with social democratic liberalism entailed that a universal and free education was the indispensable prerequisite to the freedom of the individual (Levinson, 1999). Such education was to be compulsory because children needed to be protected against the individual self-interest of their parents. Such rights underpinned the goals of a democratic society to ensure its reproduction through a common set of skills and values. Public education thus served the community by addressing social needs. Schools provided students with a common set of values and knowledge, thus creating the basis for citizenship and the democratic functioning of society. Schooling also contributed to scientific and cultural progress and played an important role in economic and social growth, ensuring the conditions for full employment.

The public benefits of education cannot simply be seen as the sum of individual private benefits. Norms such as political or civic tolerance, literacy, or the values required for democratic functioning adhere to the quality of a community and are not reducible to the psychological characteristics of individuals. In short, essential to producing the public benefits of schooling, all children must experience certain common benefits which are not safeguarded by a privatized education without the regulation and monitoring of the state. In a private system some parents will not be able to obtain schooling for their children at all; others might seek schooling that reinforces sectarian religious, political, ethnic or cultural ends. As a consequence, certain social benefits are not safeguarded and important issues to do with the regulation and control over such things as the 'quality of teacher training' or 'the nature of the curriculum' are not protected. Universal and compulsory education established common uniform features in order to guarantee skills such as literacy and numeracy as the universal common basis necessary for active citizenship and democratic participation.

Even Milton Friedman (1962: ch. 6) considers education as a public good in the sense that it contributes to goods that are public, specifically as Harry Brighouse (2000: 41) puts it, to the 'stability of the civic polity'.[22] In Brighouse's (ibid.: 41–2) words:

> Social stability is valuable to everyone: it provides a framework within which different people can plan and pursue diverse ends with confidence and security. It exhibits jointness in supply and consumption, nonrivalness and nonexcludability, and compulsoriness. If some significant level of education for almost the whole population is essential for civic stability in a modern society, then a system of almost universal compulsory education is needed to provide this public good.

In addition to this public good function, Brighouse (2000: 45) also considers education important in that it contributes to *social justice*, a point we take up further in the next chapter.

By the intrinsic nature of their social organization, private schools, argues Levin (1989), are also likely to neglect areas concerned with specific aspects of schooling, such as the curriculum, which are necessary to public benefits such as tolerance or citizenship. This is so, he argues, because private schooling is less likely to introduce students to, and encourage in them, a tolerance of diverse cultures and values. In a related sense, reflecting the specific social attributes on which they are based, they are likely to undermine the level of social and cultural integration, thus exacerbating differences in relation to class, race and religion within the community.

In that private schooling cannot provide for important social benefits, a suitably public-provided education can account for individual 'choice' through the provision of a greater variety of options and offerings within the public system. To this extent a publicly provided education can adapt itself flexibly to individual preferences thus reconciling the twin goals of (1) preserving the 'public goods' of education and (2) protecting individual rights (which have historically given to parents the ability to decide exactly how and where their children will be educated, and to withdraw them from the state system if they so wished). For the welfare liberal, the ideals of public education depend on a conception of schooling as a shared experience rather than based on 'choice'. Hence, while a public system can produce private benefits (such as individual qualifications and skills), a private system cannot provide for the social benefits which are necessary to the functioning of a democratic society and which education under the welfare state has historically provided. In fact, extensive privatization is likely to undermine the public basis of a democratic, literate society itself. For the communitarian, as our identities are socially constituted, they depend upon state action and community support. The state must support development and provide opportunities if autonomy is to be assured, and education is the major vehicle by which this can be done.

In the final chapter, we return to the theme of globalization and argue that the 'education nation-state', with strong institutions of democratic citizenship, offers the only positive way forward in a world that is increasingly threatened by global conflict, terror and catastrophe.

Notes

1 This type of failing also lies behind Sen's (1985) criticism that Rawls is too concerned to equalize the distribution of basic *primary goods*, seen as *commodities*, rather than a broader understanding of *capabilities to function*, for to be concerned with the latter would entail a theory of collective processes and societal structures, which Rawls, given his residual attachment to liberal individualism, is unable to address.

2 This work constitutes a major revised formulation. In it, Rawls also draws insights from a series of articles where he sought to expand and defend the justice as fairness conception. See Rawls (1975; 1980; 1985; 1987; 1988).

3 See also Will Kymlicka (1995: 132, n. 9) for a similar point.

4 Seemingly, the only way Rawls can maintain such an argument is by adherence to a conception of the subject which is 'prior to its ends', that is, which is 'non social', 'pre-formed', where autonomy is a natural attribute.

5 In his later work, Rawls seeks to qualify the sense in which political liberalism is neutral. See *Political Liberalism* (Rawls, 1996: 192). It can also be noted that the sense in which the neutrality thesis applies to liberals like Rawls, Dworkin and Ackerman is quite different. See Mouffe (1993: 136).

6 See for instance Kymlicka (1995), Young (1990), Selznick (1992), Callan (1997) and Reich (2002).

7 Why, if identity is now social, does he not appreciate the importance of education and other institutions that shape character? The fact that Rawls makes so few references to education in both *A Theory of Justice* and *Political Liberalism* reinforces that his *real* adherence is to a classical liberal conception of the subject. (There are only a handful of brief references to education in both works together. The major comment appears in *Political Liberalism* on pp. 199–200).

8 Rawls's response to Habermas originally appeared in the *Journal of Philosophy*, 92 (March 1995) immediately following Habermas's (1995) 'Reconciliation through the public use of reason: remarks on John Rawls's Political Liberalism'. Rawls's response is included as Lecture IX in the 1996 edition of *Political Liberalism*.

9 Rawls's insistence on the priority of the right over the good creates con-

tradictions with the other concessions he makes. See Habermas (1995), Lamore (1999) and Mouffe (1993).

10 See Dworkin (1978); Ackerman (1989).

11 See Rawls (1985: 224) where he announces his theory is political not moral.

12 This is Kant's transcendental position in maintaining that all individuals inhabit both noumenal and phenomenal worlds.

13 Both Descartes and Locke warrant a reliable foundation for knowledge of 'clear and distinct ideas', or 'sense impressions', to be taken as 'self-evident' truths. Although Descartes saw the *Cogito*, and Locke *experience*, as the starting point, in both cases direct simple ideas constituted the atomic components of reliable knowledge in thoroughly individualistic terms.

14 Miller (2000: 103–4) identifies Roger Scruton (1980) as an example of a contemporary 'conservative communitarian' of the political right, in that a characteristic of conservative communitarians is that they support the inclusive community as a source of social unity.

15 Nussbaum (1990; 1992) represents her approach as a 'soft' version of Aristotelian essentialism, which is, she says (1992: 205) an 'essentialism of a kind', which gives an '(historically embedded and historically sensitive) account of the central human functions' (1992: 243, fn. 6). Her faithfulness to Aristotle's thought has been questioned however (see Arneson, 2000, Mulgan, 2000). In her defence against these charges, Nussbaum makes it clear that her relation to Aristotle is 'inspirational' and works at the level of a commitment to basic postulates rather than in terms of a detailed commitment to the detail of Aristotle's positions on particular topics. Foucault's approach incorporates a Nietzschean emphasis on 'self-creation' and rejects the Aristotelian stress on essentialist teleology concerning the subject. The two approaches are otherwise quite compatible in terms of the relations between the individual and the social, and of the individual as a social being.

16 Although 'liberty' and 'autonomy' are central to such a community, they are politically provided for rather than being the essential attributes of persons or their rational faculties. The notion of autonomy is also heavily qualified in the Foucauldian sense, for given the degree of interdependence between persons and community, and the sense in which reason is conditioned, autonomy is precisely what individuals do not have. While a certain level of self-reliance is attainable, it can only be achieved through education and knowledge, and even then it will always be partial and limited, for individuals are far more dependent upon, and conditioned by, the structures of social support than the liberal conception acknowledges. It is in this sense, that the liberal conception of 'autonomy' has been integrally tied to 'non-' or 'pre-social' conceptions of the rational self that were integral to the discourse of classical liberalism. Failure to recognize these historical constraints and conditions in terms of which the liberal

notion of the autonomy of reason developed has led to inappropriate recent attempts to recast autonomy in a social constructionist light (for example, Reich, 2002). In a Foucauldian sense, the conditions for liberty must be politically provided for. There is no sovereign, or founding, or universal form of subject, for the individual is an effect of power. (see Foucault, 1982a, 1994a)

17 This was one of the criticisms of early forms of communitarianism. See Onora O'Neill (2000: 445)

18 Although Foucault never really was interested in normative political philosophy, we are extending his approach in this direction, because we consider it a weakness of the Foucauldian approach. In this sense our model of a republican 'thin' communitarianism can only really be said to be 'inspired' by Foucault in the same sense as Nussbaum is 'inspired' by Aristotle (see note 15 above). We would claim that our approach is broadly consistent with Foucault's thought in terms of ontological and epistemological commitments.

19 In terms of 'distribution', writers like Rawls (1971; 1996), Sen (1985; 1988; 1992; 1999) or Dworkin (1981; 1985). In relation to 'recognition', writers like Charles Taylor (1994) or Iris Marion Young (1986; 1990; 1995; 1997). For an account, see Frazer (1997).

20 This concept belongs to Rawls (1971; 1996), and refers to a public process of reflection in which policies are assessed for consistency and coherence, at various levels of generality, and with practice, in what Rawls seemed to suggest is an historical process of successive approximations to a consensual agreement over fundamental values.

21 The identities of groups such as terrorists, or neo-nazis would not in our conception warrant 'recognition'. Recognition is subordinate to the requirements of democracy which will be discussed further in Chapter 11.

22 Brighouse (2000: 41) cites Garrett Cullitty (1995: 3–4)who defines the concept of 'public good' as comprising the following characteristics: (1) '*Jointness of supply*: if a public good is available to one member of the group for which it is public, then it is available to every other member at no cost to any member', (2) '*Non-excludability* (or *non-exclusiveness*): if anyone else is enjoying it, no-one else can be prevented from doing so without excessive cost to would-be excluders', (3) '*Jointness in consumption*: one person's consumption of the good does not diminish the amount available for consumption by anyone else', (4) '*Compulsoriness*: if anyone receives the good, no-one else can avoid doing so without excessive cost', (5) '*Equality*: if anyone receives the good, everyone receives the same amount', (6) '*Indivisibility*: there can be more than one consumer of the good and each consumes total output'. Brighouse (ibid.: 41)comments that 'the most usual features included are the first four'.

12
Globalization, Democracy and Education

In the first part of this chapter we complete our critique of neoliberalism by emphasizing its abject failure to offer viable policy responses to the emerging economic, social and political crises of global capitalism. This political philosophy, having delivered obvious policy disasters within nation-states, bears the prospect of even greater catastrophes as it expands at the global level. It is therefore imperative, we contend, to seek an alternative way forward before it is too late. Such an alternative course must initially be forged, in our view, at the level of the nation-state. Thus our argument presents a case for the construction of a non-bureaucratic welfare state which has radical democratization as its central *raison d'être*. Essential to the creation and maintenance of this robust form of participatory democracy, we argue, is a strong democratic system of public education that has education for citizenship as its primary aim.

It is somewhat paradoxical in our view that globalization and education comprise the dual mantras of 'third way' politics, which claims to be an alternative both to the neoliberalism of the 1980s and 1990s and to the 'old style' socialism of the Keynesian welfare state. According to Anthony Giddens (1998), arguably the most influential theorist of 'third way' politics, it rejects both the market fundamentalism of neoliberalism and the state domination of Keynesian welfarism. It emphasizes the renewal of civil society, inclusiveness and social responsibility, but also embraces individualism, economic freedom and globalization. The British Prime Minister, Tony Blair, asserted in March 2001 that 'the ideas associated with the third way are still the wave of the future for progressive politics' (Blair, 2001: 3). Furthermore, in Blair's view, 'Politics in all countries today is about how to combine dynamic markets with strong communities' (ibid.: 9). However, critics of the 'third way' (Callinicos, 2001; Hall, 1998; Hobsbawm, 1998) regard it as merely a 'softer' version of neoliberalism. Indeed, Callinicos (2001: 123) who is trenchant in his criticism, states that: 'Far from renewing social democracy, the Third Way amounts to an attempt to mobilize the political capital of the reformist left in support of a project that abandons substantial reforms altogether and instead embraces neoliberalism.'

Similarly, Jane Kelsey (2002) criticizes the 'third way' rhetoric of the post-

1999 Labour-led New Zealand government, suggesting that such rhetoric enables governments of the centre-left 'to rationalize their role in consolidating neoliberalism' (Kelsey, 2002: 54). The 'third way', she argues, 'is less a political theory than a programme of political management'. It remains committed to the neoliberal agenda of globalization, albeit globalization with a social face. She would agree with Callinicos (2001: 120) that: 'What is needed is a break with the very logic of capital, and its replacement by a different one – one that, at the minimum, gives priority to human needs and subjects the allocation of resources to democratic control'. While it continues to follow the logic of global capital, the 'third way', contrary to its rhetoric of social democracy, offers a neoliberal road to greater economic injustice on a global scale.

The failure of neoliberalism

Neoliberalism is not only hostile to the welfare state, it is also hostile to social democracy. This is not surprising, given that the welfare state is the product of social democracy. It is the institutional embodiment of the struggle for citizenship rights: that is, rights to health, education and employment opportunities, within a social environment of collective responsibility. In contrast, neoliberalism emphasizes individual rights to property ownership, legal protection and market freedom, within a social environment of enterprise and competition. Such an environment is not conducive to democratic economic development because, as MacEwan (1999: 5) argues: 'Neoliberalism prevents the implementation of programmes that would allow people to exercise political control over their economic affairs, involve people in solving their own economic problems, and serve the material needs of the great majority.'

The fact that state controls have been shunned throughout the western world over the last quarter of a century has seen a huge escalation of inequality in the distribution of incomes and wealth. MacEwan (ibid.: 68) cites the United Nations *Human Development Report* (UNDP, 1992: 34):

> Between 1960 and 1989, the countries with the richest 20% of the world population increased their share of the global GNP from 70.2% to 82.7%. The countries with the poorest 20% of the world population saw their share fall from 2.3% to 1.4%. The consequences for income distribution have been dramatic. In 1960, the top 20% received 30 times more than the bottom 20%, but by 1989 they were receiving 60 times more … . Even these figures conceal the true scale of injustice since they are based on comparisons of average per capita incomes of rich and poor *countries*. In reality, of course, there are wide disparities within each country between rich and poor *people*.

Castells (1996: 219–20) and Esping-Andersen (1993) also note a growing world trend in income inequality. In addition, as MacEwan (1999: 68–9) points out, growing income inequality reflects the fact that income has been growing more rapidly in rich countries than poor countries. Whether one's basis of comparison is pre-war or post-war, or somewhat later, the conclusion is that there has been a relative deterioration in the countries of the South compared to countries of the North. Although the 1970s provided some minor exceptions to the trend, by the late 1980s 'the devastation wrought by the debt crisis and the "structural adjustment programmes" it engendered was dramatic' (ibid.: 69). Within America, as Hertz (2002: 57–8) points out, '97 per cent of the increase in income has gone to the top 20 per cent of families over the past twenty years'.

Charles Beitz (1979) maintained a quarter of a century ago that even though interdependence produced absolute gains for most countries in a global polity, evidence still suggested that it widened the income gap between rich and poor countries. From what we can now see about globalization, this is even more so, and Beitz's (1979: 146) message is still apt:

> Because states have differing factor endowments and varying access to technology, even 'free' trade can lead to increasing international distributive inequalities (and, on some views, to absolute as well as relative declines in the well-being of the poorest classes) in the absence of continuing transfers to those least advantaged by international trade.

The problem for nation-states intent on reducing inequalities within their borders is that redistributive policies tend to result in less private appropriation and, consequently, less capital accumulation, less economic growth and less taxation. Hence, governments with fewer scarce resources to reallocate will need to increase taxation levels which, in a global economy, produces a vicious cycle of social unrest, capital flight and economic contraction. As Kapstein (1999: 116) points out:

> The appropriate policy answer, then, is to find the point where sufficient redistribution has occurred to prevent domestic turmoil, but where taxation remains low enough to encourage investment. Where that point may be found, of course, will differ across societies. The problem is that, in a global economy with mobile capital, states may be unable to engage in the very redistributive measures that are needed to promote political stability and, in turn, economic growth.

Neoliberals are bereft of any adequate policy solutions to this enormous political problem facing all modern capitalist states. They argue that the logic of globalization dictates a greater role for markets uninterrupted by government regulatory controls. To embark on direct initiatives to improve wages or prevent poverty would require government intervention (for example, progressive taxation) which would scare off private investors, who would therefore take capital out of the country and scare off foreign investment. Hence, the logic of the global system results in TINA: 'there is no alternative'.

Our view is that there are alternatives to neoliberalism which have more theoretical coherence than the poorly formulated 'third way' options. Although neoliberalism has constituted conventional economic dogma for the last 40 years, we argue that it cannot be defended solely on economic growth grounds, and more importantly, as we shall see, that it cannot be defended on political or educational grounds.

Although the economic arguments against neoliberalism are not as important as the political arguments against it, there are plenty of economists in recent times who remain steadfastly opposed (Armstrong et al., 1984; Bronk, 1998; Gerschenkron, 1962; Hutton, 2002; MacEwan, 1999; Self, 2000; Sen, 1999). On economic grounds, the claim that international growth and stability can be achieved without government constraint or regulation, based as it is in a naive confidence in the self-regulating capacity of markets, is empirically less than self-evident. This claim essentially involves the argument that free trade is a basic operating principle and that economic growth is fastest when the movement of goods, services and capital is unimpeded by government regulations. Invoking arguments drawn originally from David Ricardo concerning the theory of 'comparative advantage'[1] the free traders' argument is based upon the economic sub-arguments that investment depends on the level of savings, savings rise and fall with the level of income, free trade leads to higher income, which leads to higher savings, higher investment and higher economic growth. Hence, the free movement of goods and capital is optimal because it increases the prospects for direct foreign investment, and therefore increases the availability of foreign funds. But the argument that economic growth is possible when regulation is minimized is deeply flawed. Although neoliberalism allows for the free movement of goods, services and capital, there has not been an equal respect for the free movement of labour across national boundaries. More to the point however, there is compelling evidence that the massive initial growth of the rich G-7 countries[2] has been a result, not of free trade, but of extensive regulation. This view is consistent with Eric Hobsbawm's (1968: 31) argument in relation to British industry. He claims that it 'could grow up, by and large, in a protected home market until strong enough to demand free entry into other people's markets, that is: "Free Trade"' (ibid.: 31). MacEwan (1999: 37) also notes that tariff protection played a large role in the emergence of US industry, claiming that 'only after the Second World War, when US industry's dominant position in the world economy was secure, did a steady and lasting reduction of tariffs take place'.

Even today, there has been a tendency by the richest countries to selectively protect industries at particular times. Those that have achieved major developmental growth since the Second World War have also had stronger more regulative control over foreign commerce, with regard to both trade and investment. One of the most notable cases here is the Japanese who in the post-Second World War period have consistently rejected free trade and extensive foreign investment in favour of state-assisted promotion of its national businesses.

Armstrong et al. (1984) and MacEwan (1999) document how Japan has protected its industries since the 1950s, starting with the auto industry, applying
quotas and very high tariffs in the 1950s and 1960s, almost prohibiting foreign
investment, placing regulatory controls on Japanese businesses that imported
foreign technology (requiring them to substitute the imported components with
Japanese copies within a certain time frame). Similarly the Japanese computer
industry has been protected in more recent times.

South Korea, too, has adopted similar protectionist policies to Japan protecting its domestic markets since the 1960s, favouring Korean-owned firms and
using state industries and agencies to assist with national production goals, using
'credit policies' and 'price controls' to protect industrial development (Amsden,
1989; Hart-Landsberg, 1993). Countries like South Korea and Taiwan have
avoided foreign direct investment and writers like Peter Evans (1979; 1987)
claim that the relationship between foreign direct investment and economic
growth suggest a negative correlation. Other noted economists (Helpman and
Krugman, 1985; Krugman, 1986; Stewart, 1986) have also argued that a free
trade argument cannot be supported on purely economic grounds.

The neoliberal globalization thesis also ignores the persistence and likely
increasing importance of the nation-state and the crucial role of governments
in influencing the structure and dynamics of the new international economy
(Carnoy et al., 1993). On this point, we would agree with Stephen Cohen
(1990) that the international economy is not truly global in the way that it has
sometimes been represented. Not only are markets far from fully integrated,
but capital flows are restricted by banking and currency regulations, the
mobility of labour is undermined by immigration controls and multinationals
must still base their operations in their 'home' countries. In this sense market
openness is far from reciprocal. Although America and Europe have become
relatively open markets for trade and foreign direct investment, many
economies, including the Japanese, Korean, Taiwanese, Indian and Russian
(Castells, 1996: 98–9) have maintained a high degree of protection.

Rebirth of the welfare state

We would argue in fact that state regulation today is crucial for the global
economy, and for democracy in the world. Because education and skills are
crucial for the global economy, and for the mass labour force, it is imperative
that states support educational development. When the institutions of civil
society are weak so civic stability and authority are undermined. Even accepting a new level of economic interdependence between nations, and a shift
from post-industrialism to the informational society, unless we are to lapse
into a form of technological determinism, we must still see the capacity of
individual nation-states, both individually and in blocks, to resist the pressures
of international capital and the agencies of neoliberal control. A number of

things make education pivotal here. If nations are going to compete in the global marketplace, then:

- the generation and production of added value will be crucial;
- to add value will require the generation and production of knowledge and skills; and
- the nation-state will progressively need to offset the destabilizing effects of capital in order to guarantee these resources.

In this context, the welfare state becomes a decisive productive force because (1) it contributes to added value, economically, (2) it insures the social conditions of existence, and (3) it enhances cultural capacity. In this sense, the state cannot be seen as merely a redistributive agency, or as unproductive. Although, as Castells (1999: 54) notes, when states become players in the global economy, they have, as always, the potential for national agency on the basis of the defence of the specific national interests they represent. The function of the state is to construct a new welfare polity that stabilizes and insures the social conditions of existence for the citizenry. We describe this as a *non-bureaucratic welfare state*.

The difference between this conception of a welfare state and traditional Keynesian conceptions is important here. There is no reason why a revised welfare state should be statist or overly centralized. Proponents of forms of 'associational socialism' (Cohen and Rogers, 1995; Hirst, 1995) or of decentralized democratic social democracy (Bobbio, 1987) have called for radical, democratic alternatives based on citizenship, parliamentary democracy, the rule of law, the strengthening of the institutions of civil society and liberal democracy, as well as decentralization. This model of radical democratic community has much to teach welfare liberals who have traditionally supported the institutions of liberal democracy. Essentially, the future for a revived welfare state lies in its commitment to democratization through new limited forms of decentralization, citizenship and participation. Such commitments can also, under certain circumstances, imply the extension of democracy from the polity to the economy and to civil society. This model of welfare democracy supports the strengthening of the institutions of civil society, from student and citizen involvement in schools and public services, to consumer representatives on the boards of large business enterprises, to new radical, pluralist, decentralized and participatory forms of democracy.

This constitutes a different response to the crisis of the state from that of neoliberalism. Rather than rejecting ideas of the common good and of collectivism, this response to statism is not to abandon the state altogether and replace it with radical forms of decentralization, or to abandon public goods in favour of privatization and markets, but rather to bring both markets and state institutions under greater democratic control. This might conceivably mean then any or all of the following:

1 Decentralize state powers into civil society but maintain ultimate state regulation and control. The state's function becomes an 'ethical' function of ensuring democratic justice, including the equitable distribution of resources and capabilities, as well as the existence and maintenance of democratic processes.

2 Strengthen controls and checks of central government over employers and all corporate actors in terms of the functions named in point (1) above. Reciprocally, strengthen the controls and checks of the associations of civil society over government. As all that can make the state legitimate is its democratic mandate, to frustrate or disregard due democratic procedure or contestation is to call its own legitimacy into question.

3 Promote a more active role for citizenry. Although this would emphasize participation to a greater extent than post-Schumpeterian realist conceptions, it would not put a requirement of classical forms of participation of citizens within voluntary associations. Rather, participation would be increased partly through more direct reliable communications with the citizenry over issues of concern. New forms of communications technology offer possibilities for better communications and dialogue between leaders, institutions, the state and the citizenry.

Controls on government can be extended through legal and constitutional safeguards, through extending the separation and devolution of state powers, through promoting a vibrant civil society, increasing the number and strength of counteracting centres of power to the state, and promoting a strong role for independent associations. None of these undermines or erodes the state's role of ensuring the 'equalization of power', including the equitable distribution of resources and capabilities within society. Activities of specific individuals or groups of individuals will be restrained only to the extent they conflict with the rights of other individuals or with certain democratically negotiated public goods.

In Britain, Paul Hirst (1995; 2000a) is one recent author who has advocated a theory of associational democracy utilizing a Durkheimian emphasis on democracy as a two-way communication between governors and governed, centring on the state and corporativist occupational groups in the polity. As the basis of making democracy more effective in an increasingly fragmented society, Hirst advocates an associative democracy model which involves devolving many state functions to society while retaining public funding and central control. Such a conception contributes to a model of a revised welfare state.

In Hirst's account, 'associative self-governance' would establish democratic legitimacy for organizations, reduce the need for external governance and make possible radical administrative decentralization. Rather than privatization, Hirst advocates devolved service provision to self-governing voluntary associations which are governed by constitutional democratic rules of the society. Organizations would receive public funds proportionate to membership for providing public services. Options of voice and exit could still apply. Efficiency measures such as limited use of 'user-pays' to steer public policy could still be used without accepting limitations on the size of the public sector, or ideological commitments to increased privatization. While such proposals would make radical decentralization possible, effectively removing many tasks from central government, and while market technologies could be used as 'tools' *if effective and fair*, overall participation would not be dependent on ability to pay.[3] In this sense, says Hirst (2000a: 29–30), associational self-government would extend representative democracy rather than replace it, and 'national democracy would be … strengthened and made viable by a democratized civil society'. This would not only turn state organizations from top-down state-administered bureaucracies into democratically self-governing associations, thus separating service provision from supervision, but such associations would check the power of other corporate entities, including the state. In Hirst's view, such a model of associative democracy is neither statist nor laissez-faire. It confronts fragmentation via democratization.

The model of a decentralized welfare society advanced here is compatible with the notion of community, which has been advocated as the basis of a revived welfare state since the 1970s (Joppke, 1987; Le Grand, 1982). The model is compatible, too, with Peters and Marshall's notion of an empowerment community which they argue is consistent with a genuine state of participatory democracy (Peters and Marshall, 1988a; 1988b; 1988c; 1988d; 1988e; 1990). Such a notion of community embodies the strengthening of the institutions of civil society and an increase in the opportunities for democratic participation. There is nothing inherently wrong with arguments for devolution of authority to schools or other community agencies. Such a devolution must be accompanied, however, by participatory structures that are genuinely democratic. This would entail moves towards a more responsive, community-based, service delivery welfare state which might involve power sharing, devolved decision-making, as well as forms of community-based public ownership of business enterprises (along the lines in New Zealand of the Trustee Savings Banks, prior to the 1990s, for example).[4] Such a conception is consistent with those that advocate a conceptual shift from the notion of a 'welfare state' to that of a 'welfare society' in which family, voluntary societies, local bodies, trade unions and employers play a greater role (Davey and Dwyer, 1984). It is a welfare state which is sensitive to institutional abuses of power, which is committed to the twin goals of full employment and equality of opportunity as well as to universal welfare entitlements and Keynesian demand management. It is a welfare state which constitutes a viable alternative to the bureaucratic welfare state. In Joppke's (1987: 250) words, 'it pursues the egalitarian project of a non-bureaucratic decentralized and self-reliant welfare society'. Consistent with Peters and Marshall's 'empowerment community', it is based on the values which encourage and promote co-operative rather than competitive behaviour and which make for a sense of cohesion and community. As Peters and Marshall (1990: 81) put it:

> This is tantamount to arguing simply that a welfare state ought to be concerned with developing a sense of *communal* rather than *self* interest, that values of the private and the individual ought not to be privileged or aggrandized over those of the public and the community; and that collective provision based on communal interest is potentially more egalitarian, socially responsible and democratic than similar services provided by the free market.

This is a far cry from the neoliberal's conception. It rejects the notion of the market as a superior mechanism for allocating resources in society or as the instrument of a self-regulating or spontaneously ordered social system. It supports the notion that the real purposes of central planning are the creation of a genuinely free society, and that collective powers of the state are used only to protect individual rights and to enable individuals to pursue their own goals in their own way. Moreover, this conception of the state supports the idea that such a welfare society is committed to the principle of equality, although it acknowledges that the concept of equality, and its relationship to liberty, needs careful theorizing. Gregor McLennan (1993: 109) notes that the concept can be recast in more precise terms which include a focus on *access, needs fulfilment, social justice, and self-realization*. In addition, the term sometimes conflates concerns such as equality of opportunity with universal provision and with equality of outcomes.

In this sense, such a conception is not so decentralized that it abandons an 'umpiring' role for the state. One of the state's central roles is ensuring democratic justice to inhabitants within its territorial borders. As equality is a central dimension of such a conception, state control over regulatory and distributional matters is of vital importance. One reason why the state needs to be strong relates to the inherently disequalizing tendencies in devolved patterns of governance where overall control is not retained by a strong centre. As Walker (2002: 17) maintains, the state alone is competent to regulate markets and the movements of capital in spite of globalization. The fact is, he says, referring to the European Union, that 'the national government retains the capacity to inspect, regulate and where necessary curtail financial markets … . To put it in pseudo-quantitative terms: market size times taxable capacity equals veto power over most species of capital' (ibid.). What in turn legitimates the state's authority is its own subjection to the democratic principles that empower it to act.

Revising the globalization thesis

In seeing an important role for the state, we are not disputing that what is called the 'globalization thesis' does refer to a process with certain ascertainable effects.

What we are rejecting is the neoliberal version of this thesis. Thus we accept the realities of globalization and we can agree with Castells (1996: 97) that the global economy has shown some marked patterns of integration, including:

- the increasing interpenetration of markets, which received further impetus after the Uruguay Round of the General Agreement on Tariffs and Trade (GATT);
- the birth of the World Trade Organization (WTO);
- the slow but steady progress in European integration/unification;
- the signing of the North American Free Trade Agreement (NAFTA);
- the intensification of economic exchanges in Asia;
- the gradual incorporation of Eastern Europe and Russia into the global economy;
- the quasi-legal integration of capital markets; and
- the growing role played by trade and foreign investment in economic growth everywhere.

Castells notes (1996: 97) that the global economy is internally diversified into three major regions:

- North America, including Canada and Mexico (after NAFTA);
- the European Union; and
- the Asia-Pacific region, centred on Japan.

Regionalization corrupts, or at least substantially modifies, the version of globalization theory advocated by neoliberals in that it constitutes a context for the emergence of new regulatory controls within particular regions. Naomi Klein tells the story of the emergence of 'fortress continents' which she says is the model being employed by NAFTA and the European Union. After 9/11, in Klein's view (2003: 23) this model has taken on a new urgency:

> A fortress continent is a block of nations that join forces to extract favourable trade terms from other countries, while patrolling their shared external borders to keep people from those countries out. But if a continent is serious about being a fortress it also has to invite one or two poor countries within its walls, because someone has to do the dirty work and heavy lifting. It is a model being pioneered in Europe, where the European Union is currently expanding to include 10 poor eastern bloc countries, at the same time as it uses increasingly aggressive security methods to deny entry to immigrants from even poorer countries, like Iraq and Nigeria.

Regionalization makes the relationship of the nation-state to globalization more complex. Regional blocks with an assortment of institutions, associations and accords create a new constraint on the nation-state, and both erode and confirm its sovereignty in important respects. The relation of Britain to the European Union, for instance, in accepting European conventions and accords, and even in accepting the euro as currency, surrenders certain aspects of sovereignty, and means that sovereignty of the state is no longer, in all matters, coincident with the national borders of its territory. But, of course, the acceptance of such 'constraints' and 'conditions' also enables new possibilities in conformity with national development, in the context of existing regional and global economic and political exigencies.

It is important, however, not to misrepresent what globalization *means* in this sense. In that Held and McGrew (2000) distinguish between the 'hyperglobalizers' who see globalization as ubiquitous, and the 'sceptics' who regard it as little more than a myth (Shipman, 2002), we have difficulty with both these views. Nevertheless, in that 'sceptics' emphasize the uneven patterns of integration of countries to the world economy, and deny that 'globalization' is a novel development, emphasizing the origins of 'transnational flows' prior to 1914, we are largely in agreement. Globalization cannot be seen as a qualitatively new development, but rather as the intensification of a process that is age-old.[5] We would only point out that this does not mean that globalization is not effecting new changes. With the 'globalizers' and 'hyperglobalizers' we can agree that states have a diminished capacity to protect their borders against private international decision-making, but we would argue, only in some arenas, and only on some issues. This is as much because certain issues (environmental issues, trade issues, health issues) have become global issues of concern, as it is that states have been divested of control. Where states traditionally had control, we consider they still have it; where states were weak in the face of international pressure, or from a particular country or block of countries, they continue to be so. Sometimes, too, as Pheng Cheah (1998: 31) points out, global institutions 'can become an alibi for economic transnationalism, which is often US economic nationalism in global guise'.

If, at the level of governance, globalization is complex and fragmented, at the cultural level we can also agree that globalization is having a marked effect. We can agree with Pheng Cheah (ibid.: 32) that an 'alternative spatialization of politics' is under way. We can also agree with Arjun Appadurai (1993) that contemporay 'global culture flows' create conflict between existing global forms and the separateness of the nation-state. Appadurai's (1993: 418) thesis of growing interconnectedness through travel, technology and communications, where global institutional forms are 'both instances and incubators of a postnational global culture' is we think largely correct. However, in our view, Appadurai's thesis needs qualifying. Just as national and global governance can coexist, we would maintain that global culture can *coalesce* with national identity, and compromises national consciousness only in certain respects, not all of which can be seen as negative; for example, in relation to norms of democratic justice, which we think warranted and important. Furthermore we see no contradiction, or pressures toward mutual exclusivity between the global and national domains in relation to culture.

Our view is not one of 'globalization *or* the nation-state', but of 'globalization *and* the nation-state'. By this we mean that while globalization is effecting major changes, the role of the state is changing, but this does not mean that it is diminishing. It still has a highly significant role in relation to work, welfare, education and defence. It is still the superior agency, hierarchically relating to all other constituents in a definite territory with clear boundaries. While it is affected to a greater extent in the twenty-first century by international pressures and greater interdependence this is not a qualitatively new form of development. What has emerged, as Hirst (2000b: 178) argues, is a 'division of labour between local, national and supra-national levels and between public and private government'. As Hirst (ibid.: 185) argues, 'we still have a world of states. The change is that we now have many other agencies too'. Although sovereignty is a changing relation, and is frequently sold on one issue to be retained or strengthened on another, over most governance capacities states still retain sovereignty, or they control the conditions in terms of which it is transferred. In this sense Hirst argues that while sovereignty is not total, it never was, for state power has never existed *independent* of an international context. As governance becomes more complex and multi-levelled, so too, sovereignty alters both its scope and domain. Sovereignty is not then, Hirst (ibid.: 183) says, a 'zero-sum game': the existence of global agencies and regional blocks does not substantially weaken the nation-state.

Having said this, we can still agree that globalization is a significant phenomenon. Key governmental functions are undergoing relocation and the forms of governance are changing from state to global, to inter-state, to non-governmental and to private market mechanisms. As a process then, we can make more sense of globalization by defining it in terms of two interrelated phenomena: (1) as a high degree of global *interconnectedness*, as a consequence of changes in science and technology; and (2) as a discursive system, pursued at the policy level by powerful states and international capital. This enables us to distinguish two senses of globalization which we will call 'Globalization I' and 'Globalization II'. The essential features of Globalization I are:

- increased speed and volume of private trans-border transactions, especially related to capital and communications systems;
- new developments in technology which have assisted mobility of cross-border flows (electronic clearing systems, the Internet); and
- the increasing possibility of transport (cheaper air fares, and so on).

The essential features of Globalization II are:

- the replacement of the Bretton Woods agreement with neoliberal orthodoxy (open borders, floating exchange rates, abolition of capital controls, and so on);
- deregulation and liberalization of government policy and establishment of highly integrated private transnational systems of alliances;

- privatization and marketization: the establishment of central banks (for example, the European Central Bank) which reside inside countries but adopt a market-independent monetary policy and which are largely autonomous from political interference.[6] Also, the growth of private international authorities, including consultants, advisers and arbitration specialists; and
- the increased size and power of transnational corporations (Hertz, 2002).

These two forms of globalization, while related, can be seen as conceptually distinct. Globalization I leads to growing *interconnectedness* between countries. As McGrew (2000: 3–4) states:

> Globalization has been variously concerned with action at a distance (whereby the actions of social agents in one locale can come to have significant consequences for 'distant others'); time–space compression (referring to the way in which instantaneous electronic communication erodes the constraints of distance and time on social organisation and interaction); accelerating interdependence (understood as the intensification of enmeshment among national economies and societies).

Not all of these developments necessarily 'undermine' the state, however. New technologies, although they may undermine the nation-state in a cultural sense, may not unduly affect it in a political sense, or may even enhance it. Instant forms of recording and transcription enable the documenting of abuses in new important senses. Hence, what technology can do is provide new possibilities in relation to democracy. As Castells (1997: 300) notes:

> What the power of technology does is to extraordinarily amplify the trends rooted in social structure and institutions: oppressive societies may be more so with the new surveillance tools, while democratic participatory societies may enhance their openness and representativeness by further distributing political power with the power of technology ... thus the direct impact of new information technologies on power and the state is an empirical matter, on which the record is mixed.

The point of distinguishing two types of globalization is that neoliberalism structures the character of globalizing processes that have already taken place. Neoliberalism drives Globalization II. Competition, for instance, is increased as a consequence of being associated with neoliberal endorsement of free trade, open economies and marketization. In this sense, Globalization II requires a great deal of state power to sustain it. The creation of markets has been engineered by particular policies. As Hirst (2000b: 179) notes, it was public policy, not market pressures, which led to deregulation of capital markets and removal of exchange controls in the late 1970s and early 1980s. As he states: 'What is supposed to be an inevitable market-driven global process is actually substantially a product of public policy ... . It was influential economic policy elites and state officials in advanced states that shaped the deregulatory free-market vision of world trade' (ibid.).

States are not, however, surrendering their sovereign capacities. Rather, they are implementing control mechanisms to adapt to the changing architecture of global power. Regulatory controls operate to offset or negate competitive effects. One means of doing this, as Wiener (2001) points out, is by *harmonizing* governance and legal arrangements, with the transnational. In this process states are disciplining transnational systems as much as the other way around.[7] Another mechanism of state adaptability is through *privatization of responsibility*. Thus, criminal responsibility over use of financial resources, which has become an issue linked with terrorism post 9/11, has been devolved to (or imposed on) private sector banks, just as the governance issues connected with intellectual property rights has placed liability on Internet service providers, and tends to stress 'self-enforcement'. What results, says Wiener, is a form of neoliberal multi-level governance which acts through domestic law, where state borders are losing practical relevance. This is not a response to the technological imperatives, but to deliberate state policies. Whereas Bretton Woods insulated national economies from shock, and provided for greater control, under neoliberalism interdependence alters this protection system. One of the major effects means that states act in concert, seeking to harmonize policies and laws to ensure the effectiveness of measures taken at the national level.

Kanishka Jayasuriya (2001) maintains that globalization has also ushered in a new form of economic constitutionalism which has changed the role of the nation-state with respect to its legal institutions and the rule of law. This is to say, there has been a changing *architecture* of power, both globally and within the state, which is serving to *transform* the processes of governance and the nature of sovereignty. Crucial in this transformation is the shift from political constitutionalism to 'a kind of economic constitutionalism' (Jayasuriya, 2001: 443). As Jayasuriya (2001: 452) continues: 'Economic constitutionalism refers to the attempt to treat the market as a constitutional order with its own rules, procedures and institutions that operate to protect the market order from political interference'. Although states will continue to be important, it will not be possible, as Jaysuriya (ibid.: 448) states, to put 'the sovereignty genie back in the conventional state bottle'. Many decisions of importance – economic, environmental, human rights, health – will be global in nature. Issues such as climate change, AIDS, international debt, the dominance of the G-7 countries, the depletion of natural resources, poverty, nuclear proliferation, defining the rules of world trade, policing world financial markets and evolving common standards for all sorts of activities (for example, nuclear power), will increasingly become argued about and resolved in the global arena. In this sense many aspects of sovereignty will be increasingly global. Autonomous regional and global agencies will replace the state in relation to specific areas of control.

Cosmopolitan democracy

In the context of this more fragmented state and global order, writers such as McGrew (2000) and Jayasuriya (2001) question the applicability of liberal democratic models of democracy. These models were developed in the context of an autonomous state system that has largely ignored the impact of globalization. The established territorial patterns of liberal democracy appear increasingly to be unable to deal with the complex issues and problems which transcend states' borders. In this sense, as McGrew (2000: 404–5) states, the scale of human social organization no longer *corresponds with* the nation-state. If this is so, then the nation-state can no longer be seen as the repository of democratic life, and new forms of global democracy must be entertained.

Jayasuriya (2001) advocates a republican cosmopolitan order. Republicanism is a conception of political order and government based on classical models of the Greek and Greco-Roman polis. Although the republican assumption of a uniform public sphere needs adjusting, the idea of democracy working in and through a global civil society is not unfeasible, given the proliferation of new technologies of communication. As Jayasuriya demonstrates, such an analysis is useful as a starting point when seeking to understand how democracy can be modified to operate effectively at the global level. Essentially what is being suggested is the creation of alternative authority structures to the nation-state where groups and social movements can represent effective citizen mobilization within the global arena, policing governance through the establishment of public democratic organizations. In Jayasuriya's (ibid.: 455) words, it 'seeks to build not a managerial civil society, but a political civil society composed of publicly accountable associations and regulatory entities'. Although Jayasuriya relates the argument to Habermas, such a conception is equally compatible with the Foucauldian notion of the public sphere, based on deliberative processes, that we have outlined. Similar to Jayasuriya, and Habermas, it fits too within a 'neo-republican' conception of the political order as 'freedom from domination' which is one of the central elements of republican thought.

The notion that republican principles of political organization can include nation-state, regional, and global levels has a long history in political thought. Immanuel Kant (1932) developed such a conception in his *Perpetual Peace*, first published in 1795, which was an extension and development of his 1784 essay 'Idea toward a universal history in a cosmopolitan respect'. According to Kant, the ideal of republican government is extendable to the international arena, and represents the Enlightenment ideal of 'perpetual peace' through a free federation of states. Kant proposed a federation of republican states on the basis that peace might be achieved between states under a system of international law. Kant himself acknowledges debts for the conception to early modern thinkers like Hugo Grotius and Samuel Pufendorf but his more immediate sources of inspiration are Rousseau and Charles-Irénée Castel (Wood, 1998: 60). As Allen Wood (1998: 62) states:

> Kant's philosophical project ... is truly cosmopolitan in intent, not limited by any geographic or cultural borders. Its articles are meant not merely as precepts of a *ius gentium*, applying to the relations between sovereign states, but beyond this also as principles of a *ius cosmopoliticum*, which regards *all* peoples of the earth as a 'single universal community' or 'universal state of humankind' founded on a 'universal right of humanity'.[8]

For Kant, then, the solution to the relations between states resided in the development of republican states and their organization into a peaceful federation of states operating under the rule of the cosmopolitan law. Such a conception has clearly provided a model for those like Daniele Archibugi (1998) or David Held (1995) in their models of cosmopolitan democracy. Held argues that contemporary forms of globalization are undermining existing patterns of liberal democracy, centred as they are on the nation-state. Held (ibid.: 279–80) claims that because there is no global *demos*, there is no locus for decisions beyond or between states. Conventional democratic theory applies to life *within*, but not *between*, states. In Held's view democracy is threatened by being confined to the national level. According to Held (ibid.: 237) national democracies require safeguarding 'by elaborating and reinforcing democracy from the "outside" through a network of regional and international agencies and assemblies that cut across spatially limited locales'. Through such interlinking global networks individual nation-states are rendered accountable in relation to transnational democratic norms. Such proposals do not involve a conception of world government but rather a common framework of interlocking and overlapping institutions and agencies.

While the cosmopolitan ideal expresses some important insights, the approach needs serious modification. In Kant's original formulation, it expresses the overly abstract faith that international relations and global governance can be run according to deontological principles of universal reason. Not only does it fail to relate issues of global justice to the lives and communities of actual contexts, but also it potentially ignores the realities concerning the global power of transnational capital, and the 'uneven' development that is the inevitable consequence of global markets. As Bellamy and Castiglione (1998: 154) point out, it champions a 'free-standing' conception of human rights based on 'individualism, universality and generality'. Additionally, there is inadequate understanding of how democracy works in and through communities and agencies at the global or national levels.

This is not to say that cosmopolitan conceptions should be entirely discarded. Bellamy and Castiglione (ibid.: 162) maintain that 'it would be mistaken to regard the cosmopolitan and the communitarian arguments as totally at odds with each other ... . Rather, they offer contrasting but to some degree compatible accounts of how we should think about individuality, rights and their relationship to the societies that embody them'. They maintain (ibid.: 162) that 'cosmopolitan morality only makes sense to the extent that it is embedded within a communitarian framework', a position they dub as 'cosmopolitan communitarianism'.

In a recent reformulation of their position, Held and McGrew (2002: 99) argue that cosmopolitan social democracy represents a middle ground between the extremes of neoliberal globalization and statist or Marxist anti-globalization. They argue (ibid.: 131) for a new politics of globalization in which:

> Accordingly, the project of cosmopolitan social democracy can be conceived as a basis for uniting around the promotion of the impartial administration of law at the international level; greater transparency, accountability and democracy in global governance; a deeper commitment to social justice in the pursuit of a more equitable distribution of the world's resources and human security; the protection and reinvention of community at diverse levels (from the local to the global); and the regulation of the global economy through the public management of global financial and trade flows, the provision of global public goods, and the engagement of leading stakeholders in corporate governance.

Community, as we envisage it, is 'without borders'. While this means they are characterized by differences of custom, tradition and practice, communities are also characterized by certain commonalities in structure and belief, networked throughout and across them. Such commonalities, already identified in relation to writers like Sen and Nussbaum, are expressed by Jana Thompson (1998: 191) as constituting universal cosmopolitan principles regarding peace and security, the self-determination of communities, the freedom of individuals and individual well-being. In this sense, as we conceptualize community, the limits to a particular community are not the limits of justice and democracy. This is to say that communities without borders permit 'bridgeheads' that enable transnational democracy based on certain shared ends and values. Our conception also recognizes an idea of 'multiple overlapping' communities in that individuals can identify with many different communities – ethnic, religious, political and social – at the same time. In a global world, identity becomes more complex, and the processes of identity attachment cannot be confined to a single territorial state. At the same time, our conception recognizes that individuals derive their identities from socially embedded communities that they do not themselves choose.

Just as all communities have some common interests, and in this sense belong to a 'community of communities', so there is a common good for humanity expressing the core of these values and species necessities. In the contemporary era the necessary objectivism of the good becomes more evident. Such a conception of the good can harbour general principles of right, just as communitarianism can harbour certain cosmopolitan principles.

261

Democracy, survival and international relations

These models of cosmopolitan and radical global democracy are in direct opposition to the standard model of international relations as an anarchic system of states each pursuing their own interest. This standard view of international relations accords with the Westphalian model of free independent states, organized and run on the basis of autonomy and non-interference. Such a conception is essentially Hobbesian. That is, it represents an extrapolation from Hobbes's views about individuals in the state of nature to ethical scepticism concerning relations between states in the international arena.[9] For Hobbes, there were no *effective* moral principles in the state of nature.[10] The fact that one individual cannot trust another individual to abide by a moral rule or norm, makes it pointless acting in such a way oneself – which is why life in the state of nature is 'solitary, nasty, brutish and short'. In the international system of states, ethical scepticism means that there are no moral restrictions on a state's interpretation of its own interests. Hence, as moral rules would be inappropriate, the system is seen as 'anarchic'. Each state should pursue its own interests, as Beitz (1979: 51–2) puts it, 'in the absence of reliable expectations of reciprocal compliance', that is, given there is no possibility of a community of states acting in accord with a moral rule or principle at all. Since the Peace of Westphalia, which ended the Thirty Years War in 1648, the anarchic conception of independent states has been seen as the ruling view.[11]

Kant rejected such a conception, as did Grotius and Pufendorf before him. Rather than support an anarchic conception of international relations based on individual state interests, they supported an ethical view of the role of the state acting in accord with an objective moral rule.[12] Initial plausibility of a such a view can be seen in the existence of human rights accords, international charters and initiatives towards international peace, which would seem to suggest that some conception of international morality does exist and does influence states in their actions towards each other. Before the Peace of Westphalia, Grotius had defined international relations as a moral community of states.[13] Pufendorf also developed a conception of the 'morality of states', interpreting international relations from within a natural law tradition.[14]

Globalization, terrorism and weapons of mass destruction (WMD) make such a model, based on an 'ethical' conception of the global order, more of a necessity than a plausible option in the twenty-first century. A number of factors reinforce this. The rise of international terrorism and WMD alters the 'equation', for it makes individual and collective survival an important ethical concern. The possibilities with respect to issues like climate change, SARS and AIDS add further to such concerns. All these possibilities, together with the democratization of knowledge, and of access to nuclear knowledge and technology, makes the challenges facing humanity potentially formidable. In this situation, survival constitutes a new imperative to justify a global law of morality amongst nations. Acting according to principles becomes compelling if by so doing acts of terrorism are *minimized*, and the possibilities for survival are *enhanced*. Similarly, the possibility of AOT or of violence increases the need for a discourse of safety and security. We may not agree with Hobbes on very much, but the priority of *security* over *freedom*, was indeed a profound insight. Globalization and terrorism raise the issue of 'survival' both for individuals and nations. It is in my interest to treat you fairly and impartially on the basis of respect if it reduces the chances for terrorism and enhances those of survival. It is in the interests of my country to act similarly.

Such a thesis would argue that given these new realities of AOT and WMD, the *self-interest* of states, like the *self-interest* of individuals, is a poor basis for action and ethics. Indeed, actions calculated in terms of short-term interests may not be realized as in the long-term interests of either. The interests of survival are normative in that they impose requirements of action in the interests of all. The self-interests of humanity cannot be calculated on the basis of the interests of each, however, but must involve a collective consideration. This necessitates a conception of democracy, as Beitz (1979: 58) puts it, which expresses a 'moral point of view':

> The moral point of view requires us to regard the world from the perspective of one person among many rather than from that of a particular self with particular interests, and to choose courses of action, policies, rules, and institutions on grounds that would be acceptable to any agent who was impartial among the competing interests involved ... . From the moral point of view ... one views one's interests as one set of interests among many and weighs the entire range of interests according to some impartial scheme.

Democracy must in this light be seen as a *comprehensive discourse* of (1) *safety and security*, (2) *freedom and autonomy*, (3) *inclusion*, (4) *fairness and justice*, and (5) *equality of resources and capabilities*. *Safety and security* express themselves in children's telephone 'help-lines', women's refuges, or human rights accords for the treatment of ordinary citizens, or prisoners, or so on. *Inclusion* warrants that no one is excluded from democratic entitlement, and constitutes the basis on which safety and security can be assured. *Freedom* incorporates freedom *from* domination and freedom *for* the development of capabilities. *Justice and fairness* promises treatment in a public arena according to publicly stated criteria embodied in constitutional laws and rules. *Equality* of resources and capabilities ensures opportunities and conditions for the development for all. In that treating people fairly and reasonably on the basis of respect minimizes terrorism and increases the chances for survival, democratic justice based on an equalization of power and non-domination becomes an objective good. It is in the interests of both the individual and the collectivity. In an age of terrorism, where a global *Leviathan* is clearly undesirable, *a comprehensive discourse of democracy becomes the best answer to the Hobbesian problem of order.*

Such a conception requires institutions committed to conflict resolution, ongoing debate and communication, as well as the mutual survival of different traditions. Such a democratic conception is not utilitarian, but presupposes rights and entitlements which are universally given to all. Rights in this conception are not natural, but are given by the state as the collective expression of the will of the people. Such rights are necessary to self-creation and constitute recognition that a space of autonomy is necessary to self-development of both individuals and groups. The events of 9/11 may hopefully reintroduce a concern for rights, and other themes within liberal constitutionalism, as fundamental to the emancipatory and progressive concerns of thin communitarianism as we have advocated it. Such a conception of democracy also underpins multicultural rights by recognizing different group aspirations yet underpinning them with a rights culture. Unlike liberal conceptions of democracy, it is not insensitive to diversity and does not seek cultural homogeneity through the uniform application of a single standard or rule.

Democracy, multiculturalism and justice

In that democracy must respect multiculturalism, so multiculturalism must respect democracy. Democratic norms must necessarily cross-cut multicultural groups to protect three conditions: (1) that the basic rights of all citizens individually and as groups (freedom of speech, thought, assembly, expression, lifestyle choice and so on) are safeguarded, (2) that no person or group is manipulated into accepting values represented by public institutions and (3) that public officials and institutions are democratically accountable in principle and practice.

Democracy in this sense must constitute a new universal.[15] In this sense, it is more basic as a set of procedural norms and rules than are the rights of any minority to do what they like. We must move away from any conception of multiculturalism whereby cultural minorities can be completely unresponsive to outside cultures, or where prohibitions against group members leaving the culture can be enforced. No minority and no culture, can guarantee their own survival forever, as openness to the world outside is a necessary principle of democracy. This openness is indeed a core principle of cosmopolitanism, which must infuse citizenship education post 9/11. The point here is that a democratic rights culture must underpin any conception of multiculturalism, so defined.

By making a 'rights culture' universally applicable, in this sense, limits are placed upon the 'discourse of diversity' that multiculturalism entails. This does not mean that the recognition of distinct identities and differences, as argued for by multiculturalists, are not important. Liberalism has clearly failed to sufficiently acknowledge such insights from 'the politics of recognition', tending to represent justice as the *imposition of a single standard or rule* to all of the diverse groups within the social structure. Yet, while we can accept that multiculturalists have contributed something important in arguing for the recognition of distinct cultural identities, based on ethnicity, race, religion, gender or class, as Kymlicka (1999) has argued, such arguments cannot be used to legitimate 'internal restrictions' (for example, prohibiting group exit) which violate or contradict democratic principles, or interfere with the rights of others, individuals or groups. By the same token, multicultural advocacy may result in 'external protections' to counter group disadvantage or marginalization. Such claims may themselves vary from one historical period to another, and should thus be deliberated and enacted through the democratic process itself.

Although multiculturalism advances a 'discourse of diversity', it is different from, and largely unrelated to, the 'discourse of diversity and devolution' advanced by neoliberalism. In relation to neoliberalism, diversity is sponsored by the market mechanism, which results in compounding and cumulative inequalities. With multiculturalism, diversity may also be dysfunctional to the extent that it undermines the degree of societal cohesion necessary for different groups to work and live together. The extent to which multicultural diversity reinforces norms of intolerance and conflict also takes on a new and altered significance post 9/11. Clearly the balance of contending forces between the common interests of society, and the subgroupings within it, and the overall extent to which diversity is recognized and permitted, is itself a question of democratic deliberation and adjudication, which may alter in different places and times.[16]

It can also be argued that such a view of democracy is not only compatible with, but strongly coerces a conception of *global distributive justice*. If anything threatens survival, and increases the prospects for terrorism, it is the cumulative and compounding inequalities driven by neoliberal reason. Both Charles Beitz (1979) and Onora O'Neill (1988; 2000) have inquired into applying principles of distributive justice to the international arena. In Beitz's (1979: 144, 149–50) view:

> International economic cooperation creates a new basis for international morality. If social cooperation is the foundation of distributive justice, then one might think that international economic interdependence lends support to a principle of global distributive justice … . In an interdependent world, confining principles of social justice to democratic societies has the effect of taxing poor nations so that others may benefit from living in 'just' regimes.

Central to Beitz's (ibid.: 151) argument is the notion that national boundaries should not be seen as having 'fundamental moral significance' for '[s]ince boundaries are not coextensive with the scope of social cooperation, they do not mark the limits of social obligations'.

Although Beitz seeks to apply Rawls's 'justice as fairness' conception, O'Neill acknowledges that liberalism's abstract principles are incompatible with the specificity required to apply to the international community. The very abstractness necessary to be relevant transnationally, she states, makes it irrelevant to the ideals of a concrete *Sittlichkeit*. Because deontological solutions are universalist they ignore context. This is the problem with Rawls. He subordinates *Sittlichkeit* (ethical life in community) to *Moralität* (abstract individualist principles).[17] Hence, his deontological principles cannot be linked to the 'discourse and experience of particular communities' (O'Neill, 1988: 718). In prioritizing distribution over recognition, he is unable to achieve policy flexibility. Although Rawls in his later 'political/not metaphysical' writing sought to correct the problem, he paid a heavy price for trying to accommodate his critics.[18] Our 'thin communitarianism' answers this criticism, because it is structured along republican/global lines. It can retain an internationalist focus, can be related to specific communities, and is concerned with survival. It is not as abstract as Rawls, for *Moralität* operates in and through *Sittlichkeit*. It also avoids the problems of utilitarianism, in that it attributes 'rights'; it can explain why majorities should not tyrannize minorities; and it can explain why some groups, and some countries, should not be sacrificed to benefit others.

In addition to this, the principles of non-domination and power equalization, or dispersal, do not determine outcomes in specific instances. They present a guide but they do not dictate the solution. In this sense, they can be sensitive to both 'distribution' and 'recognition'. What fills the void is *deliberation*. If principles do not determine outcomes but *underdetermine* them, then deliberation in an open contestable environment becomes crucial. Thus, it is through deliberation that the outcome is achieved, and sometimes constructed (Miller, 2000: ch. 1). The final resolution will be in accord with moral norms prevailing in the communities involved, and represents a 'reasonable' settlement.[19] It will also be consistent with global principles of justice, however.

This is where the deontological liberals like Rawls's need amendment. They remain tied to universalizing theory unrelated to context. As O'Neill (1988: 720) says 'the move from abstract principles to a determinate situation is part and parcel of all ethical reasoning, indeed of all practical reasoning'. Deontological liberals have little to say about the processes of history or differences of situation or demands for recognition. They seek merely to 'apply principles', prefer abstract accounts and apply a single standard to all situations.

Similarly with Habermas's discourse ethics. As with Habermas the resolution of conflict occurs according to norms inherent in language and communication in the public sphere, there is, as with Rawls, a naive overlooking of strategic relations of power. Foucault agrees with Habermas that the misuse of power is the central problem of our era. But whereas Habermas seeks resolution through universals and context-independent standards of the ideal speech situation, in a way similar to Rawls,[20] Foucault concentrates his attention upon the historically contingent context-dependent inequalities in power that seek strategic redress. In this he posits a series of strategies and tactics of resistance as power acts against power. Thus we disagree with Habermas's Kantian argument that there is a universal transhistorical foundation for determining truth claims or policy claims (Habermas, 1987b: 294). Our view is that Habermas's theory of communicative action is idealist in the sense that it introduces the reality of a non-contextualized, transhistorical reason, which introduces a fatal problem into his work. Because Foucault's position posits power as always present in terms of which all communication works, dialogic communication is always, inevitably, a conversation shaped by relations of power incorporating the expression of interests. For Foucault, democratic norms have historical validity to the extent they are historically valued. While it makes little sense to ask if these norms are 'universally true', the value of democratic deliberation and communication is constituted in a settlement anchored in norms of the historical present. Whereas for Habermas, power distorts communication in relation to an ideal form, for Foucault power is contingent and can be either enabling or constraining depending on circumstances. Thus, Foucault's work is anchored by contextualism in the norms of the present. While he rejects metaphysical universals as anchoring democracy, he seeks recourse to norms of power, resistance and criticism. In this sense, it is historically conditioned situations that form the basis for analysis, not metaphysical universals.

Foucault's approach also supports a more republican conception of political organization. Republicanism is committed to a substantive conception of society and to the good. Freedom is seen as non-domination, which links to equality, community, civic virtue and an emphasis on constitutionalism and checking the power of government. Such a conception of freedom developed in a republican tradition from the time of the Roman Empire, and was further developed after the English Civil War by writers like James Harrington. In the eighteenth century, republican thought became popular in England, France and America.[21] Such a view rejects the liberal conception of negative freedom as non-interference. By focusing on freedom of some over others, freedom is seen as immunity from arbitrary control. Focusing on freedom as non-domination also means that it is not necessary to see freedom exclusively linked to civic participation.[22] Pettit (1997: 38) also maintains that it is different from 'interference' because one can be enslaved without interference. For Pettit (ibid.: 35) interference does not necessarily mean loss of liberty, if it is not arbitrary, but accepted by legitimate authority. As for William Blackstone, for James Harrington, in *Oceana*, says Pettit (ibid.: 39) 'liberty ... is the liberty *by* the laws'. Freedom depends *on the law*, and hence, *on the constitution*.[23] As Pettit (ibid.: 173) says: 'We find constitutionalism in place whenever there are legally established ways of constraining the will of the powerful, even if the constraints are not recorded in a formal constitution.' Non-domination also entails the principle that powers should be dispersed, or 'equalized' as we have been saying. For Montesquieu (1900), and republicans that followed him, it was this principle of dispersion, or equalization, that entailed the separation of powers. Such a principle becomes a core political principle which can

267

support policies of bi-cameral arrangements for two houses of parliament, decentralization of power in federal systems, binding governments to international covenants or conventions, or permitting semi-autonomous institutions or associations within the polis (Majone, 1996; Pettit, 1997: 178–9).

Such a principle can also function economically to support policies of redistribution and 'equalization'; not according to Rawls's formula, but according to a formula that is context appropriate. Non-domination also supports two educationally important processes: *deliberation* and *contestation* which are important for how principles are put into practice in determinate historical settings. Contestation underpins and qualifies consent in such a schema, and becomes an open democratic entitlement. The concept of deliberation, as Miller (2000: 9) puts it, 'starts from the premise that political preferences will conflict and that the purpose of democratic institutions must be to resolve this conflict'. Deliberation presupposes a different conception of democracy from traditional 'realist' liberal models which refer to a narrow system of representative government and a means of changing governments through a system of elections.[24] The deliberative model also implies a different regulative ideal. In this sense, it is part of a variety of mechanisms aiming to *deepen* democracy, and presupposes a different conception of human nature. Whereas the liberal model gives weight to each person's preferences as a rational decision-maker, each with 'pre-formed' beliefs and opinions, the deliberative conception of democracy requires seeing outcomes as being fashioned, and seeing beliefs and values as being moulded, in the process of discussion (ibid.: 9).

Deepening democracy through education

Democracy, as John Dewey (1916: 87) pointed out, is more than a form of government; it is 'primarily a mode of associated living, of conjoint communicated experience'. Dewey (ibid.: 87) held that democracy is characterized by a 'widening of the area of shared concerns and the liberation of a greater diversity of personal capacities'. But democracy has to be seen as more than merely participating in society. While practices which extend discussion and consultation are necessary to the democratic process, they are not sufficient for the achievement of democratic outcomes unless they arise out of an overriding concern for justice and are accompanied by a prior commitment to basic moral principles such as fairness, freedom and respect for persons. Discussion and consultation, as democratic practices, will lead to justifiable decisions only if there exists a prior commitment to these fundamental principles under which various claims and interests can be appraised and compared.

If there is no commitment to substantive principles, democracy may be reduced to mere 'rule by the majority' and as the philosophers Benn and Peters (1959: 354) argued many years ago, to treat democracy as 'rule by the majority' is to ignore its moral significance. It is an essential requirement of democracy, they argue, that: 'every claim should be given a hearing. If it fails in this, the majority principle becomes a mere assertion of the power of numbers, and fifty-one in a hundred possess no intrinsic moral authority over the other forty-nine' (ibid.). Only when we have a community educated into a deeper understanding of democratic principles will it be possible to involve that community in a discussion which might become purposeful and effective in bringing about worthwhile social change. Thus, education for democratic citizenship is education that places high value on the qualities of open-mindedness, tolerance of diversity, fairness, rational understanding, respect for truth, and critical judgement. This conception of democratic education is fully elaborated in the work of Amy Gutmann (1987: 14) who, following in the footsteps of John Dewey, has developed a democratic theory of education that: 'focuses on what might be called "conscious social reproduction" – the ways in which citizens are or should be empowered to influence the education that in turn shapes the political values, attitudes, and modes of behaviour of future citizens'. When it is understood in this way, education for democratic citizenship entails much more than merely another curriculum reform and it certainly requires more than a framework of learning outcomes. What it requires, above all else, is a teaching profession whose members embody within their own practices the values and dispositions of democratic citizenship, and who have the capability to create democratic learning environments within their schools and classrooms.

In 1937, Dewey delivered an address to American school administrators in which he argued that democratic principles were essential to the very nature and purpose of educational institutions. He expressed this view at a time when political democracy, in Europe and elsewhere, was being threatened by the forces of fascism. The vulnerability of democratic institutions (for example, parliament, elections, political parties) when confronted with these opposing forces convinced Dewey that democracy could survive only if it pervaded all areas of social life. Thus, he argued (Dewey, 1987:225) that:

> unless democratic habits of thought and action are part of the fiber of a people, political democracy is insecure. It can not stand in isolation. It must be buttressed by the presence of democratic methods in all social relationships. The relations that exist in educational institutions are second only in importance in this respect to those which exist in industry and business, perhaps not even to them.

For Dewey, education is a social process and the social relationships that are embodied within educational institutions will be those that shape the ends of the educative process. Because the aim of education is to free individuals from barriers that would prevent them co-operating and supporting each other as members of inclusive communities, it is necessary for the institutions of learning to also be inclusive democratic communities. It is through education, Dewey argues, that democracy gives rise to community. Thus, democracy, in

Dewey's (ibid.: 220) terms, requires an expression of faith in the capacity of all human beings, such that 'each individual has something to contribute, whose value can be assessed only as it enters into the final pooled intelligence constituted by the contributions of all'. The basic democratic freedom, Dewey (ibid.: 220) argues, 'is not the right of each individual to do as he pleases' but 'freedom of mind and of whatever degree of freedom of action and experience is necessary to produce freedom of intelligence'. It is important to note that by 'intelligence' Dewey does not mean 'IQ' or 'cleverness' – he means reflective thought. It is through this notion that he links democracy with education. A democratic community is one in which people are educated to engage in reflective thought and to contribute to collective action. Such a community fosters what Brown and Lauder (2001: 218–19) call 'collective intelligence', a form of capacity-building which they define as 'empowerment through the *development and pooling of intelligence* to attain common goals or resolve common problems'.

This conception of democracy has important implications for educational policy, particularly as it relates to the education and professionalism of teachers. According to Dewey (1987: 222), it is the role of the school, no less than the family, 'to influence directly the formation and growth of attitudes and dispositions, emotional, intellectual and moral'. It follows, therefore, that teachers will be able to impart democratic values better in an environment which embodies such values in its practices.

An educational environment in which deliberative democracy could be nurtured would need to be based upon a reconstruction of teacher professionalism. This point is cogently made in relation to the British context by Carr and Hartnett (1996: 195), who argue that:

> From the perspective of a democratic society, the professionalism of teachers is based on a recognition of their right to make autonomous judgements about how, in particular institutional and classroom contexts, to develop their students' capacity for democratic deliberation, critical judgement and rational understanding. Without this kind of professional autonomy teachers have no protection against external coercion and pressure, and they quickly become neutral operatives implementing the 'directives' of their political masters and mistresses.

In contrast to this democratic ideal, neoliberalism fosters a culture of individualism, competitiveness and mistrust. The emphasis on managerialism and performativity within educational institutions has undermined the professionalism of teachers and produced a major barrier to the formation of inclusive democratic communities. Neoliberalism has reconstructed teachers as managed professionals who can operate efficiently and effectively within global educational markets. For the managed professional, who is little more than a skilled technician, performativity replaces the critical reflection and professional judgement of the autonomous professional. The managed professional has specified competencies, is extrinsically motivated within a contractual relationship, and produces what the performance indicators can measure (Codd, 1998; Robertson, 1998).

Deliberation

Deliberative democracy, according to Miller (2000: 9), entails a different regulative ideal from that which prevails under neoliberalism:

> The deliberative ideal also starts from the premise that political preferences will conflict and that the purpose of democratic institutions must be to resolve this conflict. But it envisages this occurring through an open and uncoerced discussion of the issue at stake with the aim of arriving at an agreed judgement. The process of reaching a decision will also be a process whereby initial preferences are transformed to take account of the views of others.

In Miller's (2000: 17) view, the cooperative strategies entailed in deliberation override self-interest.[25] He concludes that there is 'good reason to expect the deliberative process to transform initial policy preferences (which may be based on private interest, sectional interest, prejudice, and so on) into ethical judgements on the matter in hand' (ibid.: 18). Thus, deliberation is 'the process whereby individual preferences are transformed into ethically-based judgements about matters of common concern' (ibid.: 22).

In a deliberative democracy, openness of debate is an insurance against knowingly strategic action, or collusion in agenda-setting or making decisions. Thus, a deliberative democratic community is ideally one where the participants not only contribute freely, but also where they are prepared to change their views in the light of evidence and cogent argument. It is a community in which 'the decisions reached reflect not simply the prior interests or prior opinions of the participants, but the judgements they make after reflecting on the arguments made on each side, and the principles or procedures that should be used to resolve disagreements' (ibid.: 142). In deliberation, an understanding of the need for exceptions, the recognition of differences, or the need for modifications can be brought to light and assessed.

The aim of deliberation is not to reach an *epistemic consensus* but to reach a final decision that represents 'a fair balance between the different views expressed in the course of the discussion, and to the extent that it does, even those who would prefer some other outcome can recognise the decision as legitimate' (ibid.: 4).

Clearly then, deliberative democracy presupposes an educated citizenry who have some sense of collective identity and shared values. Although accepted values of democratic justice will be important in the shaping of outcomes, pragmatic factors such as the effects on the peace and stability of the community will also be important.

Contestation

Contestation is central to deliberation and to freedom in republican conceptions of democracy. As Philip Pettit (1997: 180) observes, public decisions can be held to be legitimate 'so far as they are capable of withstanding individual contestation ... under procedures that are acceptable to all concerned'. The right to contest thus replaces arbitrariness in decision-making. In Pettit's (ibid.: 185) words 'to require public decision-making to be contestable is to insist that decision-making satisfy a democratic profile'. Hence, the decision-making model is premised on contestation before consent. A government will be democratic to the extent that people can contest whatever it decides. To stop contestation is to undermine its legitimacy.

Essentially, here, is the idea of democracy as self-rule. Foucault's notion of 'speaking the truth to power' captures this idea of contestability as well. For Foucault (2001d: 11) such a right is embodied in the classical Greek notion of *parrhesia*, which means 'frankness in speaking the truth'.[26] But someone is said to use *parrhesia* 'only if there is a risk or danger for him in telling the truth ... the *parrhesiastes* is someone who takes a risk' (ibid.: 16). In addition:

> The function of *parrhesia* ... has the function of criticism ... . *Parrhesia* is a form of criticism, either towards another or towards oneself, but always in a situation where the speaker or confessor is in a position of inferiority with respect to the interlocutor. The *parrhesiastes* is always less powerful than the one with whom he speaks.

Finally, 'in *parrhesia*, telling the truth is regarded as a duty (ibid.)'. Foucault (ibid.: 19–20) draws these elements together thus:

> *Parrhesia* is a kind of verbal activity where the speaker has a specific relation to truth through frankness, a certain relationship to his own life through danger, a certain type of relationship to himself or other people through criticism ... and a specific relation to moral law through freedom and duty. More precisely, *parrhesia* is verbal activity in which a speaker expresses his personal relationship to truth, and risks his life because he recognizes truth telling as a duty to improve or help other people (as well as himself). In *parrhesia*, the speaker uses his freedom and chooses frankness instead of persuasion, truth instead of falsehood or silence, the risk of death instead of life and security, criticism instead of flattery, and moral duty instead of self-interest and moral apathy. That, then, quite generally, is the positive meaning of the word *parrhesia* in most of the Greek texts ... from the Fifth Century B.C. to the Fifth Century A.D.

Contestability, then, is a precondition for democracy in the republican ideal. The right to contest decisions presupposes that decision-making is conducted in such a way that a basis for contestation exists, and that there are channels, mediums and forums by which views can be expressed and conflicts resolved. Such a principle supports a 'debate-based' society whereby communities can move towards agreed outcomes, whereby settlements can be reached and preferences formed. As such, to emphasize contestation is to accept conflict and abandon the quest for an unobtainable ideal of consensus. Politics in this sense is agonistic in that it is conceived as the non-antagonistic resolution of the political. As a consensus without exclusion is not possible, it warns against the possibility of a final harmonious form of democracy. As Chantal Mouffe (2000: 128) writes: 'Agonism forces us to nurture democratic contestation, to accept responsibility for our actions, and to foster the institutions in which political action, with all its limitations, can be pursued. Only under these conditions is pluralist democracy possible.'

Contestation also functions at the global level of international politics. In this respect Rob Walker's (1988; 1991; 1994; 1995) emphasis on the role of critical social movements as the basis of a theory of radical democracy 'beyond borders' is worthy of consideration. In this, as McGrew (2000: 413) summarizes it, such movements constitute 'a "bottom up" theory of the democratization of world order'. As a theory of progressive politics, this form of radical democracy operates through 'grassroots' social movements, such as women's movements, environmental or peace movements, or political movements, which express resistance to international as well as national institutions and authorities. Such a view of global justice constitutes a check on nation-states at a number of levels. It puts nation-states under an obligation to respect human rights in line with critical debate and policies formulated at the regional or global levels. In addition, it puts nation-states under obligations not to exploit or oppress individuals, or other communities. Finally, it creates the conditions whereby all nations' actions are monitored, and accountable at supra-national levels, and where they have the chance to achieve their own regime of justice internally, in conformity with global principles.[27]

The rise of the education state: educating the democratic capabilities

Education is pivotal in the formation of a deliberative contestatory democracy. Such a conception of society depends upon the creation of a normative culture which can make constitutional and legal codes operative. Pettit (1997: 245) cites Philip Selznick (1992: 389–90) who talks about the need for 'habits of civility'. The purpose of education is to help construct a socially established normative culture that provides security and builds the *capabilities* for democracy. These might include techniques of debate and legal eristic, of meeting procedure and political activism. In addition, norms of trust and civility are necessary to underpin law, and to satisfy the constraints associated with contestability and deliberation. Trust in democratic principles must cut across a wide range of groups – gender, ethnic, prisoners, war widows, gays, those with special needs. Common democratic principles must cut across group differences, and practices based on tolerance and trust are commonly required by all groups. As Pettit (1997: 248–9) says:

> It is extremely doubtful that governments would have been forced to take account of environmental considerations, even in the inadequate measure to which they currently do so, if people were not generally responsive to a norm requiring concern for the common good: a norm requiring efforts on behalf of that good even when free-riding looks like the rational self-interested response ... . If the law is to be kept on track ... then there has to be a form of civility available that will drive not just a politics of difference but a politics of common concern.

Pettit (1997: 249) notes with respect to the politics of difference:

> that, while it requires partial forms of civility in order to be effective, it also requires a disposition on the part of people, even people of quite different perspectives, to display a civility that relates to the society as a whole. Let people cease to countenance society-wide norms in their enthusiasm for more local affiliations, and the republic will degenerate into a battlefield of rival interest groups.

Pettit's point is that state action is fundamental in the nurturing of trust and other 'habits of civility'. From our point of view these are democratic capabilities which education is fundamental in producing. Such capabilities involve not only norms of tolerance and civility, but the skills of deliberation in all its complex forms. Education lies between what Pettit (1997: 255) calls the 'stark choice between the invisible hand and the iron hand: between the strategy of marketing and a strategy of management'. Education is the 'third estate' between the free market and the autocratic hand of regulation and management. Such collective norms become central to personal identity, to personal aims and ambitions, and to dreams, which are only possible within a community. Such communitarian *civicness* attests to the irrepressibly social nature of selfhood. Without cultural models and normative values – of care, of solidarity, of compromise, of negotiation, of tolerance, of legal debate and eristic – there can be no global society or polity. Trust and civility become part of the 'conditions of liberty' as Gellner (1994) states. Yet, what enables trust and civility is prior reliance on the rules and laws. That is, the prior existence of a comprehensive discourse of democracy.

Although such a conception requires a theory of community, we have described this as a 'thin' community, a 'community without unity', without fixed borders, which can incorporate the essential features of liberal constitutionalism. It thus avoids the problems of conservative communitarianisms. The practical import of such a conception is indeed well captured by Self (2000: 233–4):

> Communitarianism offers a strong answer to the atomistic liberalism of neoliberal thought, but as a doctrine it tends to expect too much from autonomous movements within society and to pay too little attention to the importance of the polit-

ical framework, both for restraining excesses of communitarian zeal and for pro-moting its positive benefits. Democratic governments should bend over backwards to devolve functions and initiatives downwards into society, but they still need to organize some redistribution of resources to assist poorer communities, some basic standards of public services and a framework of common rights and duties for all citizens.

Education for democracy, as Dewey argued nearly a century ago, requires democracy in education. Only when we have teachers educated into a deeper understanding of democratic principles will it be possible to involve the wider community in a discussion which could lead to democratic educational reform. This means that there must be a reciprocal relationship between dem-ocratic change in education and democratic change in society. Thus, in the words of Carr and Hartnett (1996: 189):

> a key task for a democratic theory of education is to articulate a conception of edu-cation which recognises that without a democratic development of society a more democratic system of education cannot be promoted, and that without a more democratic system of education the democratic development of society is unlikely to occur.

Education is seen to be a key force in this reconstruction of democratic citi-zenship. It is, in Giddens's words, 'the main public investment that can foster both economic efficiency and civic cohesion' (Giddens, 2000: 73). Education, Giddens argues, 'needs to be redefined to focus on capabilities that individu-als will be able to develop through life' (ibid.: 74). Education can give stabil-ity to civil society by inculcating norms of trust and responsibility, and without such norms markets cannot prosper and democracy cannot survive.

It is against this background that the New Labour government in Britain set up an advisory group in 1997 under the chairmanship of Bernard Crick, to provide a statement of aims and a broad framework for citizenship education in schools. After a decade of educational reform in that country, this was an admission that something was seriously missing from the National Curriculum. The final report of the Advisory Group on Citizenship, entitled *Education for Citizenship and the Teaching of Democracy in Schools* (known as the Crick Report) was released in September 1998 and has been subse-quently adopted as policy by the British government.

This means that there is to be a statutory requirement on schools to ensure that education for citizenship is part of the entitlement of all pupils. The Crick Report emphasizes that citizenship education is education for citizenship, it is not just knowledge about citizenship and civic society. It has three interrelated elements, each of which is to be included in the curriculum. These are social and moral responsibility, community involvement and political literacy. The purpose of citizenship education in schools, according to the Crick Report, is:

to make secure and to increase the knowledge, skills and values relevant to the nature and practices of participative democracy; also to enhance the awareness of rights and duties, and the sense of responsibilities needed for the development of pupils into active citizens; and in so doing to establish the value to individuals, schools and society of involvement in the local and wider community. (Advisory Group on Citizenship, 1998: 40)

As an educational aim, this statement points in quite a different direction from the competitive individualism of Margaret Thatcher's enterprise culture. The emphasis throughout this report is on 'active citizenship' which includes 'the learning of the skills, values, attitudes, understanding and knowledge needed for both community involvement and preparation for involvement as citizens of our parliamentary democracy and the wider political world' (ibid.: 23). Emphasis should also be given, according to this report, to whole-school issues including school ethos, organization and daily practices.

Rather than detailing specific programmes of study, the Crick Report proposes a broad framework for citizenship education, including specific learning outcomes for each of the key stages in the National Curriculum. It is suggested that: 'schools should make every effort to engage pupils in discussion and consultation about all aspects of school life on which pupils might reasonably be expected to have a view, and wherever possible to give pupils responsibility and experience in helping to run parts of the school' (Advisory Group on Citizenship, 1998: 55). The aim, clearly, is to induct young people into democratic practices and procedures. However, this view of democracy, which takes it to be a set of practices, is limited, for it provides no account of the underlying principles of which such practices are merely the outward manifestation.

Although many of its proposals are sound, part of the problem of the Crick Report is that democracy is still conceptualized in a too narrow, overly Eurocentric, even nationalistic, sense, starting with the struggles in the seventeenth century and proceeding 'onwards and upwards' to universal enfranchisement. We have advocated a broader, multi-level conception of democracy spanning national, regional and global levels, and including a diverse range of capabilities. Democracy is embedded in the values of mutual equal respect and survival, and includes norms and practices of reciprocity, of deliberation, of contestation, of dialogue, and of fair treatment by due process. In this, as the American Walter Parker (2001: 9) observes, it is concerned not only with *learning about* democracy, but with *involvement in* democracy. The approach to education cannot be exclusively *curricular*, but must incorporate as well, the *extracurricular* focus on both *direct* and *indirect* learning through participation in the governance of the school, in school-community forums, and in inter-school forums for broader educational relations. In America, one group favouring extracurricular approaches include those like Noddings (1992) and Kerr (1997) who advocate an ethics of care; another group includes those interested in promoting the required skills for deliberative democracy, such as Power et al. (1989) and Sadker and Sadker (1994); while writers like Michael Apple (1975; 2001) favour active, real-world, participation. Education for democracy, if it is to be effective, will involve a transformation of the culture of public schooling. In the words of Beane and Apple (1999: 26) it involves:

> enhancing participation at the grass roots and in the school, empowering individuals and groups who had heretofore been largely silenced, creating new ways of linking the real world and real social problems with the school so that the school is integrally connected to the experiences of people in their daily lives.

While the Crick Report aims to teach democracy, and aims to foster the skills of sharing and deliberation, it does not involve students in democracy in any meaningful participatory or multicultural sense.

What is crucial in the world post 9/11 is that it is a global world, a world which urges us to recognize those people and cultures that occupy the world in addition to us, as those others who are inhabiting the cities, libraries and schools we think of as ours, a world which is increasingly cosmopolitan, if not in the sense we travel more or at all, but certainly in the sense that what happens in one part of the globe, now affects us all. Multicultural citizenship is now a matter of vital concern.

In the preceding chapters, we have argued for a reconceptualization of liberal politics for the global era – an era in which the realities of economic globalization and the dangers of international terrorism must be reconciled with national and local concerns for security, social justice, political democracy, environmental sustainability and human rights. By tracing the recent history of liberalism, we have shown that classical liberal thought is Janus-like in its political manifestations, pointing in contrary directions and giving rise both to Keynesian welfarism and to 'new right', neoliberalism. But globalization, we argue, brings a new set of demands to the liberal tradition.

While rejecting the neoliberal globalization thesis, we support a revised version in which there is both a continuing role for the democratic nation-state and a legitimate need for autonomous forms of regional and global governance. As a possible basis for such governance, we support the idea that a republican democratic polity could be constructed at a supra-national level. Consistent with our Foucauldian 'thin' communitarian position, we support Held and McGrew's (2002) notion of global 'cosmopolitan social democracy', and we see the rise of the education state as fundamental to the emergence of this new world order.

Notes

1 The theory of 'comparative advantage' played an important role in economics, for it provided an intellectual rationale for free trade economics. It essentially responds to the criticism that under free trade conditions, if

one country produces everything more efficiently than others do, then neoliberal theories of free trade run into trouble. The problem, it is claimed, disappears if each country specializes in the production of those goods where it has a 'comparative advantage'. Ricardo initially developed his case for free trade using the example of trade between Britain and Portugal, in which British cloth was exchanged for Portuguese wines (Ricardo, 1966 [1817]: ch. 7). The error of this argument was that cloth for wine was not a result of free trade but was made possible by the 1703 Methuen Treaty in which Portuguese wines were given preference in British markets over French wines, as a means by which to open the Portuguese markets to British cloth (MacEwan, 1999: 37–8).

2 Group of Seven: France, Germany, Japan, the UK, the US, Canada and Italy.

3 Although Hirst does not advocate monetarist policies, on specific issues, such as transport congestion in large cities, a 'congestion tax' has been introduced in London in order to reduce traffic. Such policies can be adopted without the need to reduce the public sector, or to adopt such charges on essential services, such as health and education.

4 These were publicly owned and operated by community boards until the 1990s when they were sold as part of a privatization initiative.

5 Globalization can be seen as spreading or developing with technological changes, effected no doubt initially by the invention of such instruments as the alphabet, and the printing press. Twentieth-century developments in transport and electronic communications have obviously had a major impact in intensifying globalization.

6 The European Central Bank acts independently, has its own 'legal' personality, is not responsive to any immediate local community, and is protected under Article 106 (2) of the EC Treaty.

7 In this process, the contours and size of a new welfare state is being negotiated globally, as an 'excessive' welfare state will lead to capital flight, tax competition and uncompetitiveness.

8 Cited from Kant's original German edition of *Perpetual Peace* (1795).

9 Many writers, like Charles Beitz, have based their critique of this model of international relations and ethics on the inappropriateness of this analogy (see Beitz, 1979: 64).

10 As Charles Beitz (1979: 146) notes, Hobbes (1968) did maintain that there were natural principles and he proposes 19 laws of nature (see Hobbes, 1968: ch. 15). The difficulty in international relations, as in the state of nature, as Hobbes held it to be, was in the difficulty in being sure that others would act on them.

11 Stephen Krasner (1993) maintains that this Westphalian system was not in fact inherent in the treaties signed in 1648.

12 For contemporary work in this tradition, see the English school of Martin

Wright (1992) and Hedley Bull (1977).

13 Grotius's was a 'pre-liberal' conception and, notably, he argued against the principle of 'non-interference', arguing that it is sometimes justifiable (see Beitz, 1979: 71). It was Wolff and Vattel who later argued for an absolute principle of non-interference, arguing that unlimited respect for another state's autonomy upheld stability. Wolff's view marked the application of 'pure' classical liberal principles ('autonomy', 'non-interference' and so on) to international relations. Although Wolff argued that no state had a right to interfere in another state's sovereign affairs, the entire 'community of states' had such a right (see Beitz, 1979: 75).

14 Although he argued against Hobbes, as Beitz (1979: 60) notes, he produces similar conclusions about the weakness of moral rules in international relations.

15 Once again, in Rorty's (1998: 52) sense, we mean universal in terms of *reach*, not in terms of *validity*.

16 Sharon Gewirtz (2003) suggests that official government support towards state funding of 'faith-based' schools in England has altered post 9/11, suggesting that forms of religious separatism over education are being seen as socially dysfunctional for the production of democratic values, such as tolerance.

17 *Sittlichkeit* pertains to 'ethical life'. We have added the phrase 'in community' because Hegel, in the *Philosophy of Right* (para. 144), identifies ethical life with the 'objective ethical order'. It is through this conception of ethical life that Hegel asserts the primacy of the social over the individual.

18 See Charles Lamore (1999). Onora O'Neill (2000: 445) refers to his 'nearly communitarian writing' with specific reference to Rawls (1985).

19 The reference to the word 'reasonable' is Rawls's of course. The concept is apt for a settlement will invariably be a mix of factors, reflecting principles of justice, the potential effects of a policy on the stability of the community, and its acceptance by the majority of those affected. In this sense any particular policy settlement reflects a mix of pragmatic, moral and political factors.

20 Richard Rorty (1998: 53) argues there is a great deal of similarity.

21 Amongst some of the republican writers on these continents are Machiavelli, Montesquieu, Rousseau, de Tocqueville, Harrington, Price, Wollstonecraft, Madison, Hamilton, Jay and Paine. See Pocock (1975), Skinner (1978), Pettit (1997) and Honohan (2002).

22 Participation needs more extensive theorization within political theory than it has had to date. It must be seen also as a continuum of action, varying in terms of extent and kind. Our view would be that nearly all people participate to some degree in an active sense of joining voluntary civic groups and associations. It need not be seen as the only good in rela-

tion to citizenship, however. We would agree with Iain McLean (1986: 143), however, that traditional arguments between realist liberals who support a narrow conception of representative democracy based on elections, and more classical versions of democracy based on participation in the public sphere often represent little more than a 'dialogue of the deaf'. While we believe that democracy needs 'deepening' and that participation in the public life is an important component of citizenship, we simply do not accept realist arguments against such a position, as should be now obvious.

23 This is a difference between republicanism and liberalism. For liberalism, freedom is a natural condition and exists outside of society. Although not a liberal in the modern sense, Robert Filmer encapsulates the liberal notion when he notes that perfect liberty would require the absence of laws. As Filmer (1991: 268) states, 'for it is no law except it restrain liberty'. For Hobbes (1968: 264) also, liberty resides 'in the silence of the laws'. Harrington (1992: 20) attacks this viewpoint in his *Oceana*. (see Pettit, 1997: 38)

24 Such a model can be seen associated with Joseph Schumpeter's (1976) *Capitalism, Socialism and Democracy*, especially pp. 250–83 ('Two concepts of democracy').

25 Miller (2000: 17) gives the example of a game strategy where individual self-interest dictates that each group member keeps money and invests it on their own, but when pursued co-operatively as a collective, when the money is pooled, far greater wealth is produced. His major focus is in critiquing neoliberal theories of democracy, especially, Arrow's general possibility theorem that denies the possibility of amalgamating voter preferences to reach a collective social decision. Essentially, Arrow maintained that no collective rule could be rational. All decision rules are arbitrary which means all outcomes reflect strategic manipulation. The interesting point here is the thesis that collective endeavour produces higher and better outcomes for the individuals and the group, than individual endeavour. This maxim could also be applied to learning theory.

26 Foucault (2001d: 11) explains that '*Parrhesia* is ordinarily translated into English by "free speech" (in French by *franc-parler*, and in German by *Freimüthigkeit*). *Parrhesiazomai* or *parrhesiazesthai* is to use *parrhesia*, and the *parrhesiastes* is the one who uses *parrhesia*, i.e., the one who speaks the truth'.

27 A good example of a grassroots movement is the continued existence of the Global Justice Movement, which has shown signs of growing in numbers and strength. As George Monbiot (2003) notes, in 2002 40,000 members gathered at the World Social Forum in Porto Alegre, Brazil, and in 2003 more than 100,000 from 150 countries attended. Another meeting, in 2003, held in Florence, titled 'Another Europe is Possible',

organized by the European Social Forum, attracted some 40,000 intellectuals, students, social activists, radical economists and concerned individuals, expressing solidarity with those who had attended similar meetings and protests in Genoa, Prague, Seattle and London over the proceeding three years. The meeting expressed 'anti-globalization' protests against agencies like the IMF, World Bank (WB), WTO and NAFTA. At Florence in 2002, says John Vidal (2002) they advocated open borders, a universal right to work and to have a home, the regulation of MNCs, a Tobin tax on financial markets, no GM foods or pollution, no privatization of public services, the public ownership of the media, and an end to racism. In addition 'there was almost complete consensus on three issues: that "neoliberalism" – the free market ideas espoused by the IMF and G7 – is a violent political and economic doctrine; that trade with poor countries should be fair; and that one vote every four years given to political parties run by self-serving elites is no way to run modern, complex democracies in a globalized economy' (Vidal, 2002: 18).

Bibliography

Ackerman, B. (1989) *Social Justice and the Liberal State*. New Haven: Yale University Press.

Addison, P. (1975) *The Road to 1945*. London: Cape.

Advisory Group on Citizenship (1998) *Education for Citizenship and the Teaching of Democracy in Schools*. (Crick Report) London: Qualifications and Curriculum Authority.

Althaus, C. (1997) 'The application of agency theory to public sector management', in G. Davis, B. Sullivan and A. Yeatman (eds), *The New Contractualism*. Melbourne: Macmillan Education, pp. 137–53.

Althusser, L. (1969) *For Marx* (trans. Ben Brewster). London: Penguin Books.

Althusser, L. (1970) *Reading Capital*. London: New Left Books.

Althusser, L. (1971) 'Ideology and ideological state apparatuses', in L. Althusser, *Lenin and Philosophy and Other Essays*. London: New Left Books.

Amsden, A.H. (1989) *Asia's Next Giant: South Korea and Late Industrialization*. New York: Oxford University Press.

Andrew, E. (1988) *Shylock's Rights: A Grammar of Lockean Claims*. Toronto: Toronto University Press.

Anyon, J. (1991) 'The retreat of Marxism and socialist feminism: postmodern and poststructural theories in education', *Curriculum Inquiry*, 24 (2): 115–33.

Appadurai, A. (1993) 'Patriotism and its futures', *Public Culture*, 5 (3): 418–28.

Apple, M.W. (1975) 'The hidden curriculum and the nature of conflict', in W. Pinar (ed.), *Curriculum Theorizing: The Reconceptualists*. Berkeley: McCutchan, pp. 95–119.

Apple, M.W. (1982a) *Education and Power*. London: Routledge and Kegan Paul.

Apple, M.W. (ed.) (1982b) *Cultural and Economic Reproduction in Education*. London: Routledge and Kegan Paul.

Apple, M.W (1986) 'National reports and the construction of inequality', *British Journal of Sociology of Education*, 7: (2): 171–90.

Apple, M.W. (1996) *Cultural Politics and Education*. New York: Teachers College Press; Buckingham: Open University Press.

Apple, M.W. (1999) *Power, Meaning and Identity*. New York: Peter Lang.

Apple, M.W. (2000) *Official Knowledge*, 2nd edn. New York: Routledge.

Apple, M.W. (2001) *Educating the 'Right' Way: Markets, Standards, God, and Inequality*. New York: Routledge.

Apple, M.W. and Beane, J.A. (eds.) (1999) *Democratic Schools: Lessons from the*

Chalk Face. Buckingham: Open University Press.

Archibugi, D. (1998) 'Principles of cosmopolitan democracy', in D. Archibugi, D. Held and M. Köhler (eds), *Re-Imagining Political Community*. Cambridge: Polity Press/Blackwell, pp. 198–228.

Armstrong, P., Glynn, A. and Harrison, J. (1984) *Capitalism since World War II: The Making and the Breakup of the Great Boom*. London: Fontana.

Arneson, R.J. (2000) 'Perfectionism and politics', *Ethics*, 111 (1): 37–63.

Aronowitz, S. and Giroux, H. (1991) *Postmodern Education: Politics, Culture and Social Criticism*. Minneapolis, MN: University of Minnesota Press.

Ashcraft, R. (1987) *Locke's Two Treatises of Government*. London: Unwin Hyman.

Ball, S.J. (ed.) (1990a) *Foucault and Education: Disciplines and Knowledge*. London: Routledge.

Ball, S.J. (1990b) *Politics and Policy Making in Education: Explorations in Policy Sociology*. London: Routledge.

Ball, S.J. (1993) 'What is policy?: texts, trajectories and toolboxes', *Discourse*, 13 (2): 10–17.

Ball, S.J. (1994) *Education Reform: A Critical and Post-Structuralist Approach*. Buckingham: Open University Press.

Barker, E. (1928). *Political thought in England: 1848–1914*, 2nd edn. London: Thornton Butterworth.

Barrett, M. (1988) *The Politics of Truth*. Cambridge: Polity Press.

Barry, A., Osborne, T. and Rose, N. (1996) *Foucault and Political Reason: Liberalism, Neo-Liberalism and Rationalities of Government*. Chicago: University of Chicago Press.

Barry, A. (1996) *Someone Else's Country: The Story of the New Right Revolution in New Zealand*. (Video, edited by Shane Loader, narrated by Ian Johnstone). Wellington: Community Media Trust in association with Vanguard Films.

Barry, N.P. (1983) 'Review article: the new liberalism', *British Journal of Political Science*, 13: 93–123.

Barry, N.P. (1986) *On Classical Liberalism and Libertarianism*. London: Macmillan.

Barry, N.P. (1987) *The New Right*. London: Croom Helm.

Barthes, R. (1977) 'The death of the author', in R. Barthes, *Image–Music–Text*. Glasgow: Fontana/Collins.

Beane, J.A. and Apple, M.W. (1999) 'The case for democratic schools', in M.W. Apple and J.A. Beane (eds), *Democratic Schools: Lessons from the Chalk Face*. Buckingham: Open University Press, pp. 1–29.

Becher, T., Henkel, M. and Kogan, M. (1994) *Graduate Education in Britain*. London: Jessica Kingsley.

Beck, U. (1992) *Risk Society: Towards a New Modernity*. London: Sage.

Becker, G. (1964) *Human Capital: A Theoretical and Empirical Analysis with Special Reference to Education*, republished 1975. New York: Columbia University Press.

Becker, G. (1976) *The Economic Approach to Human Behaviour*. Chicago: University of Chicago Press.

Beitz, C. (1979) *Political Theory and International Relations*. Princeton, NJ: Princeton University Press.

Bellamy, R. and Castiglione, D. (1998) 'Between cosmopolis and community: three models of rights and democracy within the European Union', in D. Archibugi, D.

Held and M. Köhler (eds), *Re-Imagining Political Community*. Cambridge: Polity Press/Blackwell, pp. 152–78.

Belsey, C. (1980) *Critical Practice*. London: Methuen.

Bendor, J. (1988) 'Review article: formal models of bureaucracy', *British Journal of Political Science*, 18 (3): 353–95.

Benn, S.I. and Peters, R.S. (1959) *Social Principles and the Democratic State*. London: Allen and Unwin.

Bentham, J. (1950) *A Theory of Legislation*. London: Routledge and Kegan Paul.

Bergman, M. and Lane, J. (1990) 'Public policy in a principal–agent framework', *Journal of Theoretical Politics*, 2: 339–52.

Berlin, I. (1964) 'Hobbes, Locke and Professor Macpherson', *Political Quarterly*, 35, 444–68.

Berlin, I. (1969) *Four Essays on Liberty*. Oxford: Oxford University Press.

Blackstone, W. (1979) *Commentaries on the Laws of England*. Chicago: University of Chicago Press. (A facsimile of the first edition of 1765–69).

Blair, T. (1998) *The Third Way: New Politics for the New Century*. London: Fabian Society.

Blair, T. (2001) 'Third Way, phase two', *Socialist Renewal*, New Series, No. 4: 3–9.

Blair, T. (2003) 'The Left should not weep if Saddam is toppled', *Guardian*, 10 February, p. 18.

Blaug, M. (1970) *An Introduction to the Economics of Education*. London: Penguin.

Blunkett, D. (2002) 'Civic rights', in 'Big brother: the secret state and the assault on privacy, part two', *Guardian*, 14 September, pp. 22–3.

Bobbio, N. (1987) *The Future of Democracy*. Cambridge: Polity Press.

Bobbitt, P. (2002) *The Shield of Archilles*. London: Allen Lane.

Bordo, S. (1990) 'Feminism, postmodernism, and gender-scepticism', in L. Nicholson (ed.), *Feminism/Postmodernism*. New York: Routledge, pp. 133–56.

Bosanquet, N. (1983) *After the New Right*. London: Heinemann.

Boston, J. (1991) 'The theoretical underpinnings of public sector restructuring in New Zealand', in J. Boston, J. Martin, J. Pallot and P. Walsh (eds), *Reshaping the State: New Zealand's Bureaucratic Revolution*. Auckland: Oxford University Press, pp. 1–26.

Boston, J. (1994) 'Purchasing policy advice: the limits to contracting out', *Governance*, 6 (1): 1–30.

Boston, J. (1996) 'Origins and destinations: New Zealand's model of public management and the international transfer of ideas', in G. Davis, and P. Weller (eds), *New Ideas, Better Government*. Sydney: Allen and Unwin.

Boston, J., Martin, J., Pallot, J. and Walsh, P. (1996) *Public Management: The New Zealand Model*. New York: Oxford University Press.

Bourdieu, P. (1977a). *Outline of a Theory of Practice*. Cambridge: Cambridge University Press.

Bourdieu, P. (1977b) 'The economics of linguistic exchanges', *Social Science Information*, 16 (6): 645–68.

Bourdieu, P. (1998) 'Job Insecurity is Everywhere Now', in P. Bourdieu (ed.) *Acts of Resistance*. Bristol: Polity Press, pp. 81–7.

Bourner, T. , Bowden, R. and Lang, S. (2000) 'The adoption of professional doctorates in English universities: Why here? Why now?' Presentation for the Professional Doctorates 3rd Biennial International Conference, Doctoral Education and Professional Practice: 'The next generation'. University of New England, Armidale, NSW, Australia, 10–12 September.

Bowe, R., Ball, S. and Gold, A. (1992) *Reforming Education and Changing Schools*. London: Routledge.

Bowles, S. and Gintis, H. (1986) *Democracy and Capitalism: Property, Community, and the Contradictions of Modern Social Thought*. New York: Basic Books.

Braun, D. (1993). 'Who governs intermediary agencies? Principal–agents relations in research policy making', *Journal of Public Policy*, 13 (2): 135–62.

Brien, A. (1998) 'Professional ethics and the culture of trust', *Journal of Business Ethics*, 17 (4): 391–409.

Brighouse, H. (2000) *School Choice and Social Justice*. Oxford: Oxford University Press.

Bronk, R. (1998) *Progress and the Invisible Hand: The Philosophy and Economics of Human Advance*. London: Little, Brown.

Brown, P. and Lauder, H. (2001) *Capitalism and Social Progress: The Future of Society in a Global Economy*. Basingstoke: Palgrave.

Brus, W. (1972) *The Market in a Socialist Economy*. London: Routledge and Kegan Paul.

Bryson, J. and Smith-Ring, P. (1990) 'A transaction-based approach to policy intervention', *Policy Studies*, 23: 205–29.

Buchanan, J. (1960) *Fiscal Theory and Political Economy*. Chapel Hill, NC: University of North Carolina Press.

Buchanan, J. (1969) *Cost and Choice*. Chicago: Markham.

Buchanan, J. (1975). *The Limits of Liberty: Between Anarchy and Leviathan*. Chicago: University of Chicago Press.

Buchanan, J. (1978) 'From private preferences to public philosophy: the development of public choice', in J. Buchanan (ed.), *The Economics of Politics*. London: Institute of Economic Affairs, reading 18.

Buchanan, J. and Tullock, G. (1962) *The Calculus of Consent: Logical Foundations of Constitutional Democracy*. Ann Arbor, MI: University of Michigan Press.

Bull, H. (1977) *The Anarchical Society*. New York: Columbia University Press.

Burbules, N.C. and Torres, C.A. (2000) 'Globalization and education: an introduction', in N.C. Burbules and C.A. Torres (eds), *Globalization and Education: Critical Perspectives*. London: Routledge.

Burchell, G. (1991) 'Peculiar interests: civil society and governing "the system of natural liberty"', in G. Burchell, C. Gordon and P. Miller (eds), *The Foucault Effect: Studies in Governmentality*. Chicago: University of Chicago Press.

Burchell, G. (1996) 'Liberal government and techniques of the self', in A. Barry, T. Osborne and N. Rose (eds), *Foucault and Political Reason*. Chicago: University of Chicago Press, pp. 19–36.

Cable, V. (1999) *Globalization and Global Governance*. London: Royal Institute of International Affairs.

Callahan, R.E. (1962) *Education and the Cult of Efficiency*. Chicago: University of Chicago Press.

Callan, E. (1997) *Creating Citizens: Political Education and Liberal Democracy*. Oxford: Clarendon Press.

Callinicos, A. (1989) *Against Postmodernism: A Marxist Critique*. Cambridge: Polity Press.

Callinicos, A. (2001) *Against the Third Way: An Anti-Capitalist Critique*. Cambridge: Polity Press.

Capella, J.-R. (2000) 'Globalization, a fading citizenship', in N.C. Burbules and C.A. Torres (eds), *Globalization and Education: Critical Perspectives*. London: Routledge.

Carmichael, D.J.C. (1983) 'C.B. Macpherson's "Hobbes": a critique', *Canadian Journal of Political Science*, 16 (1): 61–80.

Carnoy, M. and Levin, H. (1976) *The Limits of Educational Reform*. New York: Longman.

Carnoy, M. and Levin, H. (1985) *Schooling and Work in the Democratic State*. Stanford, CA: Stanford University Press.

Carnoy, M., Castells, M., Cohen, S.S. and Cardoso, F.H. (1993) *The New Global Economy in the Information Age*. University Park, PA: Pennsylvania State University Press.

Carr, W. and Hartnett, A. (1996) *Education and the Struggle for Democracy*. Buckingham: Open University Press.

Castells, M. (1996) *The Rise of the Network Society: The Information Age: Economy, Society and Culture (Vol. 1)*. Oxford: Blackwell.

Castells, M. (1997) *The Power of Identity: The Information Age: Economy, Society and Culture (Vol. 2)*. Oxford: Blackwell.

Castells, M. (1999) 'Flows, networks and identities: a critical theory of the information society', in M. Castells, F. Ramon and P. Freire et al., *Critical Education in the New Education Age*. Lanham: Rowman and Littlefield.

Chan, S. and Rosenbloom, D. (1994) 'Legal control of public administration: a principal–agent perspective', *International Review of Administrative Sciences*, 60: 559–74.

Cheah, P. (1998) 'Introduction, part II: the cosmopolitical – today', in Pheng Cheah and Bruce Robbins (eds), *Cosmopolitics: Thinking and Feeling Beyond the Nation*, Cultural Politics vol. 14. Minneapolis, MN: University of Minnesota Press.

Cherryholmes, C. (1988) *Power and Criticism: Poststructural Investigations in Education*. New York: Teachers College Press.

Chia, Tai Tee (1989) *Has the Value of the Degree Fallen? Cross Sectional versus Time-series Evidence*, Centre for Economic Policy Research, Discussion Paper No. 201. Canberra: Australian National University.

Chomsky, N. (1999) *Profit Over People: Neoliberalism and Global Order*. New York: Seven Stories Press.

Chouliaraki, L. and Fairclough, N. (1999) *Discourse in Late Modernity: Rethinking Critical Discourse Analysis*. Edinburgh: Edinburgh University Press.

Chubb, J. and Moe, T. (1990) *Politics Markets and America's Schools*. Washington, DC: Brookings Institute.

Clarke, C. (1998) 'Resurrecting research to raise standards'. *ESRC Updates ESRC Corporate News*, http://www.esrc.ac.uk.

Clarke, J. and Newman, J. (1997) *The Managerial State*. London: Sage.

Clarke, S. (1988) *Keynesianism Monetarism and the Crisis of the State*. Cheltenham: Edward Elgar.

Cloke, P., Milbourne, P. and Widdowfield, R. (2000) 'Partnership and policy networks in rural local governance: homelessness in Taunton', *Public Administration*, 78 (1): 111–13.

Cochrane, A. (2000) 'New labour, new urban policy', *Social Policy Review*, 12: 184–204.

Codd, J. (1988) 'The construction and deconstruction of educational policy documents', *Journal of Education Policy*, 3 (3): 235–47.

Codd, J. (1990a) 'Educational policy and the crisis of the New Zealand state', in S. Middleton, J. Codd and A. Jones (eds), *Education Policy Today: Critical Perspectives*. Wellington: Allen and Unwin.

Codd, J. (1990b) 'Policy documents and the official discourse of the state', in J. Codd, R. Harker and R. Nash (eds), *Political Issues in New Zealand Education*. Palmerston North: Dunmore Press.

Codd, J. (1994) 'Educational markets and the meaning of choice', paper presented at the Annual Conference of the New Zealand Association for Research in Education, Christchurch, New Zealand, 2–4 December.

Codd, J. (1998) 'Professional accountability and the education of teachers', *Delta*, 50 (2): 149–62.

Codd, J.A. (1999) Educational reform, accountability and the culture of distrust, *New Zealand Journal of Educational Studies*, 34 (1), pp. 45–53.

Cohen, J. and Rogers, J. (1995) *Associations and Democracy*, ed. Erik Olin Wright, London: Verso.

Cohen, S. (1990) *The Indian Army: Its Contribution to the Development of a Nation*. Delhi: Oxford University Press.

Coleman, J.S. (1968) 'The concept of equality of educational opportunity', *Harvard Educational Review*, 38 (1): 7–36.

Collini, S. (1979) *Liberalism and Sociology: L.T.Hobhouse and the Political Argument in England 1880–1914*. Cambridge: Cambridge University Press.

Connelly, W. (1993) 'Democracy and contingency', in J. Carens (ed.), *Democracy and Possessive Individualism: The Intellectual Legacy of C.B. Macpherson*. New York: State University of New York Press.

Constant, B. (1988) *Political Writings*, trans. and ed. Biancamaria Fontana. Cambridge: Cambridge University Press.

Coons, J. and Sugarman, S. (1978) *Education by Choice: The Case for Family Control*. Berkeley, CA: University of California Press.

Corlett, W. (1993) *Community without Unity: A Politics of Derridean Extravagance*. Durham, NC, and London: Duke University Press.

Cox, R.W. (1980) 'Social forces, states and world orders', *Millennium: Journal of International Studies*, 10 (2): 126–55.

Cox, R.W. (1996) *Approaches to World Order*. Cambridge: Cambridge University Press.

Cranston, M. (1978) 'Keynes: his political ideas and their influence', in A.P. Thirwall (ed.), *Keynes and Laissez-Faire*. London: Macmillan.

Cullitty, G. (1995) 'Moral free riding', *Philosophy and Public Affairs*, 24 (1): 3–34.

Dahl, R. (1999) 'Can international organisations be democratic?: a skeptic's view', in I. Shapiro and C. Hacker-Cordon (eds), *Democracy's Edges*. Cambridge: Cambridge University Press.

Dale, R. (1986a) *Industry Vocationalism and Employers' Needs*. Milton Keynes: Open

University Press.

Dale, R. (1986b) *Introducing Education Policy: Principles and Perspectives*, E333 Module 1. Milton Keynes: Open University Press.

Dale, R. (1989) *The State and Education Policy*. Milton Keynes: Open University Press.

Dale, R. (1999) 'Specifying globalization effects on national policy: a focus on the mechanisms', *Journal of Education Policy*, 14 (1), 1–17.

Dale, R. (2000) 'Globalization: a new world for comparative education', in J. Schriewer (ed.), *Discourse Formation in Comparative Education*. Frankfurt am Main: Peter Lang, pp. 87–110.

Dale, R. and Ozga, J. (1993) 'Two hemispheres – both "new right"? 1980s education reform in New Zealand and England and Wales', in B. Lingard, J. Knight, and P. Porter (eds), *Schooling Reform in Hard Times*. London: Falmer Press, pp. 63–87.

Davey, J. and Dwyer, M. (1984) *Meeting Needs in the Community: A Discussion Paper on School Service*. Wellington: New Zealand Planning Council.

Davidson, A (1986) 'Archaeology, genealogy, ethics', in D. Cousins Hoy (ed.), *Foucault: A Critical Reader*. Oxford: Blackwell.

Davidson, A. (1997) *Foucault and his Interlocutors*. Chicago and London: University of Chicago Press.

Dean, M. (1999a) *Governmentality: Power and Rule in Modern Society*. London: Sage.

Dean, M. (1999b) 'Normalising democracy: Foucault and Habermas on democracy, liberalism and law', in S. Ashenden and D. Owen (eds), *Foucault Contra Habermas*. London: Sage, (pp. 166–94).

Deane, R.S. (1989) 'Reforming the public sector', in S. Walker (ed.), *Rogernomics: Reshaping New Zealand's Economy*. Auckland: GP Books.

Deleuze, G. (1999) *Foucault*. Minneapolis, MN: University of Minnesota Press.

Denison, E.F. (1962) *The Sources of Economic Growth in the United States and the Alternatives Before Us*. New York: Committee for Economic Development.

Department of Education and Employment (DfEE) (1999) 'Baroness Blackstone welcomes boost to university teaching standards', DfEE press release 287/99, 23rd June.

Derrida, J. (1976) *Of Grammatology*. Baltimore, MD: Johns Hopkins University Press.

Derrida, J. (1978) *Writing and Difference*. Chicago: University of Chicago Press.

Derrida, J. (1981) *Positions*. Chicago: University of Chicago Press.

Dewey, J. (1916) *Democracy and Education*. New York: Macmillan.

Dewey, J. (1927) *The Public and its Problems*, rep. 1954. Athens, OH: Swallow Press.

Dewey, J. (1932) *Ethics*. New York: Henry, Holt and Co.

Dewey, J. (1935) *Liberalism and Social Action*. New York: Capricorn.

Dewey, J. (1963) *Experience and Education*. New York: Collier.

Dewey, J. (1974). *The Child and the Curriculum, the School and Society*. London: University of Chicago Press.

Dewey, J. (1981) 'My pedagogic creed', reprinted in J. McDermott, *The Philosophy of John Dewey*. Chicago: University of Chicago Press.

Dewey, J. (1987) 'Democracy and educational administration', in J.A. Boydson (ed.), *John Dewey: The Later Works, 1925–1953*. Carbondale and Edwardsville, IL: Southern Illinois University Press.

Dickey, L. (1986) 'Historicising the "Adam Smith problem": conceptual, historiographical and textual issues', *Journal of Modern History*, 58: 579–609.

Dickinson, H. (1933) 'Price formation in a socialist community', *Economic Journal*, 43 (170): 237–50.

Dickson, M., Gerwirtz, S., Halpin, D., Power, S. and Whitty, G. (2002) 'Beyond markets and hierarchies? Networks, partnerships and the Experience of Education Action Zones', paper presented to King's College Market Forces Seminar, King's College, University of London, 29 October 2002.

Dobb, M. (1955) *On Economic Theory and Socialism*. London: Routledge and Kegan Paul.

Dow, G. (1987) 'The function of authority in transaction-cost economics', *Journal of Economic Behaviour and Organization*, 8: 13–38.

Downs, A. (1957) *An Economic Theory of Democracy*. New York: Harper and Row.

Dreyfus, H. and Rabinow, P. (1982) *Michel Foucault: Beyond Structuralism and Hermeneutics* (with an afterword by Michel Foucault). Chicago: University of Chicago Press.

Du Gay, P. (1996) *Consumption and Identity at Work*. London: Sage.

Dunn, J. (1968) 'Justice and the interpretation of Locke's political theory', *Political Studies*, 161: 68–87.

Dunn, J. (1969) *The Political Theory of John Locke*. Cambridge: Cambridge University Press.

Dworkin, R. (1978) 'Liberalism', in S. Hampshire, (ed.), *Public and Private Morality*. Cambridge: Cambridge University Press.

Dworkin, R. (1981) 'What is equality? Part 2: equality of resources', *Philosophy and Public Affairs*, 10 (4): 283–345.

Dworkin, R. (1985) *A Matter of Principle*. Cambridge: Harvard University Press.

Easton, B. (1980) *Social Policy and the Welfare State in New Zealand*. Auckland: Allen and Unwin.

Edwards, T. and Tomlinson, S. (2002) *Selection Isn't Working: Diversity, Standards and Inequality in Secondary Education*. A Catalyst Working Paper. London: Catalyst Forum.

Eisenhardt, K.M. (1989) 'Agency theory: an assessment and review', *Academy of Management Review*, 14 (1): 57–74.

Ellesworth, E. (1989) 'Why doesn't this feel empowering?: working through the repressive myths of critical pedagogy', *Harvard Educational Review*, 59 (3): 297–324.

Esping-Andersen, G. (ed.) (1993) *Changing Classes*. London: Sage.

Esping-Andersen, G. (ed.) (1996) *Welfare States in Transition: National Adaptations in Global Economies*. London: Sage, in association with the United Nations Institute for Social Development.

Evans, P. (1979) *Dependent Development: The Alliance of Multinational, State and Local Capital in Brazil*. Princeton, NJ: Princeton University Press.

Evans, P. (1987) 'Class, state and dependence in East Asia: lessons for Latin America', *Boston Sunday Globe*, 27 August.

Ewart, B. and Boston, J. (1993) 'The separation of policy advice from operations: the case of defence restructuring in New Zealand', *Australian Journal of Public Administration*, 52 (2): 223–40.

Fairclough, N. (1989) *Language and Power*. London: Longman.

Fairclough, N. (1992) *Discourse and Social Change.* Cambridge: Polity Press.

Fairclough, N. (1995) *Critical Discourse Analysis: The Critical Study of Language.* London: Longman.

Fane, G. (1975). 'Education and the managerial efficiency of farmers', *Review of Economics and Statistics*, 57 (4): 452–61.

Fay, B. (1975) *Social Theory and Political Practice.* London: Allen and Unwin.

Fay, B. (1987) *Critical Social Science: Liberation and its Limits.* Cambridge: Polity Press.

Ferguson, A. (1996) *An Essay on the History of Civil Society*, Ed. Fania Oz–Salzberger. New York: Cambridge University Press.

Filmer, R. (1991) *Patriarcha and Other Writings*, ed. J.P. Sommerville. Cambridge: Cambridge University Press.

Finn, C. (1990) 'Why we need choice', in W.L. Boyd and H.J. Walberg (eds), *Choice in Education: Potential and Problems.* Berkeley, CA: McCutchan.

Fiske, E.B. and Ladd, H.F. (2000) *When Schools Compete: A Cautionary Tale.* Washington, DC: Brookings Institute.

Fitzsimmons P. and Peters, M. (1994) 'Human capital theory and the industry training strategy in New Zealand', *Journal of Education Policy*, 9 (3): 245–66.

Flew, A. (1975) 'J.S. Mill: socialist or libertarian?', in M. Ivens (ed.), *Prophets of Freedom and Enterprise.* London: Kogan Page, for 'Aims for Industry'.

Forbes, D. (1976) 'Sceptical Whiggism, commerce and liberty', in T. Wilson and A.S. Skinner (eds), *Essays on Adam Smith.* Oxford: Clarendon Press, pp. 179–201.

Foucault, M. (1970) *The Order of Things: An Archaeology of the Human Sciences.* New York: Vintage Books.

Foucault, M. (1972) *The Archaeology of Knowledge*, trans. A.M. Sheridan Smith. London: Routledge.

Foucault, M. (1977a) *Discipline and Punish: The Birth of the Prison*, trans. A. Sheridan. New York: Pantheon.

Foucault, M. (1977b) 'A preface to transgression', in Donald Bouchard (ed.), *Language, Counter-Memory, Practice*, trans. Donald Bouchard and Sherry Simon. Ithaca, NY: Cornell University Press, pp. 29–52.

Foucault, M. (1977c) 'Nietzsche, genealogy, history', in Donald Bouchard (ed.), *Language, Counter-Memory, Practice*, trans. D. Bouchard and S. Simon. Ithaca, NY: Cornell University Press, pp. 139–64.

Foucault, M. (1978a) 'Politics and the study of discourse', *Ideology and Consciousness*, 3: 7–26, first published in *Esprit*, 1968.

Foucault, M. (1978b) *The History of Sexuality Vol. 1: An Introduction*, trans. R. Hurley. New York: Pantheon.

Foucault, M. (1979) *Discipline and Punish: The Birth of the Prison.* New York: Pantheon.

Foucault, M. (1980a) 'Truth and power', in C. Gordon (ed.), *Power/Knowledge: Selected Interviews and Other Writings 1972–1977.* Brighton: Harvester Press, pp. 109–33.

Foucault, M. (1980b) 'The confession of the flesh', in C. Gordon (ed.), *Power/Knowledge: Selected Interviews and Other Writings 1972–1977.* Brighton: Harvester Press, pp. 194–228.

Foucault, M. (1981) 'The order of discourse' trans. I. McLeod, in R. Young (ed.), *Untying the Text*. London: Routledge.

Foucault, M. (1982a) 'The subject and power', an afterword, in H.L Dreyfus and P. Rabinow, *Michel Foucault: Beyond Structuralism and Hermeneutics*. Brighton: Harvester Press.

Foucault, M. (1982b) 'Michel Foucault: Vorlesungen zur Analyse der Machtmechanismen 1978', partially complete transcription of a lecture given at the Collège de France in 1978, translation in German by A. Pribersky in *Der Staub und die Wolke*, Bremen: Impuls, pp. 1–44.

Foucault, M. (1984a) 'What is enlightenment?', trans. C. Porter, in P. Rabinow (ed.), *The Foucault Reader*. New York: Pantheon, pp. 31–50.

Foucault, M. (1984b) 'Politics and ethics: an interview', trans. C. Porter, in P. Rabinow (ed.), *The Foucault Reader*, New York: Pantheon, pp. 373–80.

Foucault, M. (1984c) 'Preface to the history of sexuality, volume two', in Paul Rabinow (ed.), *The Foucault Reader: An Introduction to Foucault's Thought*. London: Penguin Books, pp. 333–9.

Foucault, M. (1984d) 'La Phobie d'Etat', partial transcription of lecture at Collège de France delivered on 31 January 1979. *Libération*, 30 June/1 July, p. 21.

Foucault, M. (1988a) 'Practicing criticism', trans. A. Sheridan, in L.D. Kritzman (ed.), *Politics, Philosophy, Culture: Interviews and Other Writings, 1977–1984*. New York: Routledge, pp. 152–8.

Foucault, M. (1988b) 'Power and Sex', in L.D. Kritzman (ed.), *Politics, Philosophy, Culture: Interviews and Other Writings, 1977–1984*. (pp. 110–24) New York: Routledge.

Foucault, M. (1988c) 'Politics and reason', in L.D. Kritzman (ed.), *Politics, Philosophy, Culture: Interviews and Other Writings, 1977–1984*. New York: Routledge, pp. 57–85).

Foucault, M (1991a) 'The ethic of care of the self as the practice of freedom: an interview', trans. J.D. Gauthier, in J. Bernauer and D. Rasmussen (eds), *The Final Foucault*. Cambridge, MA: MIT Press.

Foucault, M. (1991b) 'Governmentality', in G. Burchell, C. Gordon and P. Miller (eds), *The Foucault Effect: Studies in Governmentality*. Chicago: University of Chicago Press, pp. 87–104.

Foucault, M. (1992) 'La Population', (transcription of lecture of 25 January 1978 rendered by S. Olivesi, in 'Memoire de DEA de philosophie sous la direction de Monsieur P. Macherey', Université de Paris I, Année 1991–92, in Foucault Archive (A 271).

Foucault, M. (1993) 'About the beginning of the hermeneutic of the self', transcription of two lectures in Dartmouth on 17 and 24 November 1980, ed. M. Blasius, *Political Theory*, 21 (2): 198–227.

Foucault, M. (1994a) 'Two lectures', in M. Kelly (ed.) *Critique and Power: Recasting the Foucault/Habermas Debate*. Cambridge, MA: MIT Press.

Foucault, M. (1994b) *Dits et Écrits: 1954–1988*, (eds) D. Defert and F. Ewald with J. Lagrange, 4 vols. Paris: Éditions Gallimard.

Foucault, M. (1994c) 'La philosophie analytique de la politique', in D. Defert and F. Ewald with J. Lagrange (eds), *Dits et Écrits: 1954–1988*, 4 vols. Paris: Éditions Gallimard, vol. 3 , no. 232, pp. 534–551.

Foucault, M (1994d) 'Linguistique et sciences sociales', in D. Defert and F. Ewald with J. Lagrange (eds), *Dits et Écrits: 1954–1988*, 4 vols. Paris: Éditions Gallimard, vol. 1, no. 70, pp. 821–42.

Foucault, M. (1997a) 'Security, territory and population', in P. Rabinow, (ed.), *Michel Foucault: Ethics, Subjectivity and Truth*. London: Penguin, pp. 67–71.

Foucault, M. (1997b) 'The birth of bio-politics', in P. Rabinow (ed.), *Michel Foucault: Ethics, Subjectivity and Truth*. London: Penguin, pp. 73–9.

Foucault, M. (2001a) '"Omnes et Singulatim"': toward a critique of political reason', in J.D. Faubion (ed.), *Michel Foucault: Power, The Essential Works 3*. London: Penguin, pp. 298–325.

Foucault, M. (2001b) 'The risks of security', in J.D. Faubion (ed.), *Michel Foucault: Power, The Essential Works 3*. London: Penguin, pp. 365–81.

Foucault, M. (2001c) 'Confronting governments: human rights', in J.D. Faubion (ed.), *Michel Foucault: Power, The Essential Works 3*. London: Penguin, pp. 474–5.

Foucault, M. (2001d) *Fearless Speech*, ed. J. Pearson. Los Angeles, CA: Semiotext(e).

Frazer, N. (1997) *Justice Interruptus: Critical Reflections on the 'Postsocialist' Condition*. New York and London: Routledge.

Friedman, M. (1952) *Essays in Positive Economics*. Chicago: University of Chicago Press.

Friedman, M. (1953) 'The methodology of positive economics', in M. Friedman, *Essays in Positive Economics*. Chicago: University of Chicago Press.

Friedman, M. (1955) 'The role of government in education', in R.A. Solo (ed.), *Economics and Public Interest*. New Brunswick, NJ: Rutgers University Press.

Friedman, M. (1962) *Capitalism and Freedom*. Chicago: Chicago University Press.

Friedman, M. (1967) 'Value judgements in economics', in S. Hood (ed.), *Human Values and Economic Policy*. New York: New York University Press.

Friedman, M. (1970) *The Counter-Revolution in Monetary Theory*. London: Institute of Economic Affairs.

Friedman, M. and Friedman, R. (1980) *Free to Choose*. London: Penguin.

Frye, N. (1957) *Anatomy of Criticism*. Princeton, NJ: Princeton University Press.

Fukuyama, F. (1995) *Trust: The Social Virtues and the Creation of Prosperity*. London: Penguin.

Gale, T (2001) 'Critical policy sociology: historiography, archaeology and genealogy as methods of policy analysis', *Journal of Education Policy*, 16 (5): 379–93.

Galston, W.A. (1982) 'Moral personality and liberal theory: John Rawls' "Dewey Lectures"', *Political Theory*, 10 (4):492–519.

Galston, W.A. (1991) *Liberal Purposes: Goods Virtues and Diversity in the Liberal State*. Cambridge: Cambridge University Press.

Gambetta, D. (1988) 'Can we trust trust?', in D. Gambetta (ed.), *Trust: Making and Breaking Co-operative Relations*. Oxford: Blackwell, pp. 213–37.

Gamble, A. (1986) 'The political economy of freedom', in R. Levitas (ed.), *The Ideology of the New Right*. Cambridge: Polity Press.

Gellner, E. (1994) *Conditions of Liberty: Civil Society and Its Rivals*. London: Hamish Hamilton.

Geras, N. (1987) 'Post-Marxism?', *New Left Review* 1(63), May–June: 40–82.

Gerschenkron, A. (1962) *Economic Backwardness in Historical Perspective*.

Cambridge, MA: Harvard University Press.

Geuss, R. (1981) *The Idea of a Critical Theory*. Cambridge: University of Cambridge Press.

Gewirtz, S. (2002a) 'Can managerial means be harnessed to social democratic ends? critical reflections on new labour's "third way" policies for schooling in England', *Prospero: A Journal for New Thinking in Philosophy for Education*, 8 (3): 36–47.

Gewirtz, S. (2002b) *The Managerial School: Post-Welfarism and Social Justice in Education*. London: Routledge.

Gewirtz, S. (2003) 'Faith-based schooling and the invisible effects of September 11th: The view from England', Centre for Public Policy Research, Department of Education and Professional Studies, King's College London. Provided in personal communication.

Giddens, A. (1982) *Profiles and Critiques in Social Theory*. London: Macmillan.

Giddens, A. (1985) *The Nation-State and Violence*. Cambridge: Polity Press.

Giddens, A. (1987) *Social Theory and Modern Sociology*. Cambridge: Polity Press.

Giddens, A. (1998) *The Third Way: The Renewal of Social Democracy*. Cambridge: Polity Press.

Giddens, A. (1999) *Runaway World: How Globalization is Shaping Our Lives*. London: Profile Books.

Giddens, A. (2000) *The Third Way and its Critics*. Cambridge: Polity Press.

Giddens, A. (2002) Address to Annual Conference of Chartered Institute of Finance and Accountancy, 13 June, London.

Glass, G. and Matthews, D. (1991) 'Are data enough?', *Educational Researcher*, 20 (3): 24–7.

Glendinning, C., Powell, M. and Rummery, K. (2002) *Partnerships, New Labour and the Governance of Welfare*. Bristol: Policy Press.

Glendon, M.-A. (1991) *Rights Talk: The Impoverishment of Political Discourse*. New York: Free Press.

Gordon, C. (1991). 'Government rationality: an introduction', in G. Burchell, C. Gordon and P. Miller (eds), *The Foucault Effect*. Hemel Hempstead: Harvester Wheatsheaf, pp. 1–51.

Gordon, C. (2001) 'Introduction', in J.D. Faubion (ed.), *Michel Foucault: Power, The Essential Works 3*. London: Penguin.

Gordon, I., Lewis, J. and Young, K. (1977) 'Perspectives on policy analysis', *Public Administration Bulletin*, 25 (1): 26–35.

Gordon, L. (1994) 'Is school choice a sustainable policy for New Zealand?: A review of recent research findings and a look to the future', New Zealand Annual Review of Education. Te Arotake a Tau o te Ao o te Matauranga i Aotearoa, ed. Hugo Manson, 4: 9–24.

Gottdiener, M. (1995) *Postmodern Semiotics: Material Culture and the Forms of Postmodern Life*. Oxford: Blackwell.

Gould, S.J. (1981) *The Mismeasure of Man*. New York: W.W. Norton.

Gramsci, A. (1971) *Selections from the Prison Notebooks (SPN)*, eds and trans. Q. Hoare and G. Nowell Smith. London: Lawrence and Wishart.

Gray, J. (1980) 'On negative and positive liberty', *Political Studies*, 28: 507–26.

Gray, J. (1984) *Hayek on Liberty*. Oxford: Blackwell.

Gray, J. (1986) *Liberalism*. Buckingham: Open University Press.

Gray, J. (1998) *False Dawn: The Delusions of Global Capitalism*. London: Granta Books.

Green, T.H. (1888) *Works of Thomas Hill Green*, vol. 3, ed. R.L. Nettleship. London: Longmans, Green.

Green, T.H. (1890) *Works of Thomas Hill Green*, vol. 2, 2nd edn, ed. R.L. Nettleship. London: Longmans, Green.

Greer, P. (1992) 'The Next Steps Initiative: the transformation of Britain's civil service', *Political Quarterly*, 63: 222–7.

Griffin, C. (1999) 'Lifelong learning and welfare reform', *International Journal of Lifelong Education*, 18 (6): 431–52.

Grosz, E. (1989) *Sexual Subversions*. Sydney: Allen and Unwin.

Gutmann, A. (1987) *Democratic Education*. Princeton, NJ: Princeton University Press.

Gutmann, A. (1992) 'Communitarian critics of liberalism', in S. Avineri and A. de Shalit (eds), *Communitarianism and Individualism*. Oxford: Oxford University Press.

Haakonssen, K. (1981) *The Science of a Legislator: The Natural Jurisprudence of David Hume and Adam Smith*. Cambridge: Cambridge University Press.

Habermas, J. (1971a) *Knowledge and Human Interests*, trans. J. Shapiro. Boston, MA: Beacon Press.

Habermas, J. (1971b) *Toward a Rational Society*. Boston, MA: Beacon Press.

Habermas, J. (1975) *Legitimation Crisis*, trans. T. McCarthy. Boston, MA: Beacon Press.

Habermas, J. (1979) *Communication and the Evolution of Society*. Boston, MA: Beacon Press.

Habermas, J. (1984) *The Theory of Communicative Action, Vol. 1*, trans. T. McCarthy. Boston, MA: Beacon Press.

Habermas, J. (1987a) *The Philosophical Discourse of Modernity*, trans. F. Lawrence. Cambridge, MA: MIT Press.

Habermas, J. (1987b) *Theory of Communicative Action, Vol. 2. System and Lifeworld: A Critique of Functionalist Reason*, trans. T. McCarthy. Boston, MA: Beacon Press.

Habermas, J. (1994a) 'Some questions concerning the theory of power: Foucault again', in M. Kelly (ed.), *Critique and Power: Recasting the Foucault/Habermas Debate*. Cambridge, MA: MIT Press.

Habermas, J. (1994b) *Between Facts and Norms: Towards a Discourse Theory of Law and Democracy*. London: Polity Press.

Habermas, J. (1995) 'Reconciliation through the public use of reason: remarks on John Rawls's Political Liberalism', *Journal of Philosophy*, 92 (3): 109–31.

Halford, S. and Leonard, P. (1999) 'New identities? Professionalism, managerialism and the construction of self', in M. Exworthy and S. Halford (eds), *Professionals and the New Managerialism in the Public Sector*. Buckingham: Open University Press.

Hall, P. (1989) *The Political Effect of Economic Ideas: Keynesianism Across Nations*. Princeton, NJ: Princeton University Press.

Hall, S. (1986) 'Variants of liberalism', in J. Donald and S. Hall (eds), *Politics and Ideology*. Philadelphia, PA, and Buckingham: Open University Press, pp. 34–69.

Hall, S. (1988a). 'Brave new world', *Marxism Today*, October, 24–9.

Hall, S (1988b) *The Hard Road to Renewal: Thatcherism and the Crisis of the Left*. London and New York: Verso, in association with *Marxism Today*.

Hall, S. (1998) 'The great moving nowhere show', *Marxism Today: Special Issue*, November–December: 9–14.

Halpin, D., Power, S. and Fitz, J. (1991) 'Grant-maintained schools: making a difference without being really different', *British Journal of Educational Studies*, 39 (4): 409–24.

Hardt, M. and Negri, A. (2001) *Empire*. Cambridge, MA: London, Harvard University Press.

Harrington, J. (1992) *The Commonwealth of Oceana and A System of Politics*, (ed.) J.G.A. Pocock, Cambridge: Cambridge University Press.

Harris, M. (1996) *Report of the HEFCE, CVCP, SCOP Review of Postgraduate Education*. Bristol: HEFCE.

Hart, H.L.A. (1955) 'Are there any natural rights?', *Philosophical Review*, 64 (2): 175–91.

Hart-Landsberg, M. (1993) *The Rush to Development: Economic Change and Political Struggle in South Korea*. New York: Monthly Review Press.

Hartwell, R.M. (1995) *A History of the Mont Pelerin Society*. Indianapolis, IN: Liberty Fund.

Hattersley, R. (1987) *Choose Freedom: The Future for Democratic Socialism*. London: Penguin.

Hattersley, R. (2002) 'The silly season', *Guardian*, 30 August, p. 18.

Hayek, F. (ed.) (1935) *Collectivist Economic Planning*. London: Routledge and Kegan Paul.

Hayek, F.A. (1944). *The Road to Serfdom*. London: Routledge and Kegan Paul.

Hayek, F.A. (1945) 'The use of knowledge in society', *American Economic Review*, 35 (4): 519–30.

Hayek, F.A. (1949) 'Individualism: true and false', in F.A. Hayek, *Individualism and Economic Order*. London: Routledge and Kegan Paul.

Hayek, F.A. (1952a) *The Sensory Order*. London: Routledge and Kegan Paul.

Hayek, F.A.(1952b) *The Counter-Revolution in Science: Studies in the Abuse of Reason*. Glencoe, IL: Free Press.

Hayek, F.A. (1960) *The Constitution of Liberty*. London: Routledge and Kegan Paul.

Hayek, F.A. (1967) *Studies in Philosophy, Politics and Economics*. London: Routledge and Kegan Paul.

Hayek, F.A. (1973) *Law, Legislation and Liberty. Volume 1*. London: Routledge and Kegan Paul.

Hayek, F.A.(1976) *Law, Legislation and Liberty. Volume 2: The Mirage of Social Justice*. London: Routledge and Kegan Paul.

Hayek, F.A. (1978) *New Studies in Philosophy, Politics, Economics and the History of Ideas*. Chicago: University of Chicago Press.

Hayek, F.A. (1979) *Law, Legislation and Liberty. Volume 3: The Political Order of a Free Society*. London: Routledge and Kegan Paul.

Hazeldine, T. (1998) *Taking New Zealand Seriously*. Auckland: HarperCollins.

Heald, D. (1983) *Public Expenditure: Its Defence and Reform*. Oxford: Martin

Robertson.

Hede, A. (1991) 'The Next Steps Initiative for civil service reform in Britain: the emergence of managerialism in Whitehall?', *Canberra Bulletin of Public Administration*, 65: 32–40.

Hegel, G.W.F. (1942) *The Philosophy of Right*, trans. T.M. Knox. Oxford: Clarendon Press.

Held, D. (1991) 'Democracy, the nation-state and the global system', *Economy and Society*, 20 (2): 138–72.

Held, D. (1995) *Democracy and the Global Order: From Modern State to Cosmopolitan Governance*. Cambridge: Cambridge University Press.

Held, D. (1996) *Models of Democracy*, 2nd edn. Cambridge: Polity Press.

Held, D. and McGrew, A. (eds) (2000) *The Global Transformations Reader: An Introduction to the Globalization Debate*. Cambridge: Polity Press.

Held, D. and McGrew, A. (2002) *Globalization/Anti-Globalization*. Cambridge: Polity Press.

Held, D., McGrew, A., Goldblatt, D. and Perraton, J. (1999) *Global Transformations: Politics, Economics, Culture*. Cambridge: Polity Press.

Helpman, E. and Krugman, P. (1985) *Market Structure and Foreign Trade*. Cambridge, MA: MIT Press.

Henry, M. (1993). 'What is policy? A response to Stephen Ball', *Discourse*, 14 (1): 102–5.

Hertz, N. (2002) *The Silent Takeover: Global Capitalism and the Death of Democracy*. London: Arrow Books.

Herz, J.H. (1976) *The Nation State and the Crisis of World Politics*. New York: McKay.

Heyman, S. (1992) 'Positive and negative liberty', *Chicago-Kent Law Review*, 68 (1): 81–98.

Heymann, D. (1988) 'Input Controls and the Public Sector: What Does Economic Theory Offer?', paper prepared for the Fiscal Affairs Department, International Monetary Fund, Washington, DC.

Hill, C. (1963) 'Review article: possessive individualism', *Past and Present*, (24), April: 86–9.

Hill, C. (1975) *The World Turned Upside Down*. London: Penguin.

Hill, M. (1993) *The Welfare State in Britain*. Cheltenham: Edward Elgar.

Himmelfarb, G. (1984) *The Idea of Poverty: England in the Early Industrial Age*. New York: Faber, pp. 42–144.

Hindess, B. (1990) 'Liberty and equality', in B. Hindess (ed.), *Reactions to the Right*. London: Routledge, pp. 7–31.

Hirsch, E.D. (1967) *Validity in Interpretation*. New Haven: Yale University Press.

Hirschman, A.O. (1977) *The Passions and the Interests: Political Arguments for Capitalism Before its Triumph*, Princeton, NJ: Princeton University Press.

Hirst, P. (1990) 'Democracy: socialism's best answer to the right', in B. Hindess, (ed.), *Reactions to the Right*. London: Routledge, pp. 148–76.

Hirst, P. (1995) 'Can secondary associations enhance democratic governance?', in J. Cohen and J. Rogers (eds), *Associations and Democracy: The Real Utopia's Project*, Vol. 1, series ed. E.O. Wright. London: Verso, pp. 101–13.

Hirst, P. (2000a) 'Democracy and governance', in J. Pierre (ed.), *Debating Governance*. Oxford: Oxford University Press, pp. 13–35.

Hirst, P. (2000b) 'Globalization, the nation state and political theory', in N. O'Sullivan (ed.), *Political Theory in Transition*. London and New York: Routledge, pp. 172–89.

Hirst, P. and Thompson, G. (1996) *Globalization in Question*. Cambridge: Polity Press.

Hobbes, T. (1968) *Leviathan*, ed. C.B. Macpherson. London: Penguin (Pelican edition).

Hobhouse, L.T. (1911) *Liberalism*. London: Williams and Norgate.

Hobsbawm, E.J. (1968) *Industry and Empire*. London: Penguin.

Hobsbawm, E.J. (1998) 'The big picture: the death of neoliberalism', *Marxism Today: Special Issue*, November–December: 4–8.

Hollis, M. (1982) 'Education as a positional good', *Journal of the Philosophy of Education*, 16 (2): 235–44.

Honohan, I. (2002) *Civic Republicanism*, London and New York: Routledge.

Hont, I. and Ignatieff, M. (1983) *Wealth and Virtue: The Shaping of Political Economy in the Scottish Enlightenment*. Cambridge: Cambridge University Press.

Hood, C. (1991) 'A public management for all seasons?', *Public Administration*, 69, Spring: 3–19.

Hospers, J. (1971) *Libertarianism: A Political Philosophy for Tomorrow*. Los Angeles: Nash.

Hoy, D.C. (1986) *Foucault: A Critical Reader*. Oxford: Blackwell.

Hume, D. (1898) *Essays, Moral, Political and Literary*, eds T.H. Green and T.H. Grose. Harlow: Longman.

Hume, D. (1978) *A Treatise of Human Nature*, ed. L.A. Selby-Bigge, 2nd edn, revised by P.H. Nidditch. Oxford: Clarendon Press.

Hundert, E.J. (1977) 'Market society and meaning in Locke's political philosophy', *Journal of the History of Philosophy*, 15: 33–44.

Hutcheon, L. (1989) *The Politics of Postmodernism*. London: Routledge.

Hutton, W. (1996) *The State We're In*. London: Vintage.

Hutton, W. (2002) *The World We're In*. London: Little Brown.

Jaggar, A.M. (1983) *Feminist Politics and Human Nature*. Hemel Hempstead: Rowman and Allanheld/Harvester Press.

James, B. and Saville-Smith, K. (1989) *Gender, Culture and Power*. Auckland: Oxford University Press.

Jarvis, P. (ed.) (2001) *The Age of Learning: Education and the Knowledge Society*. London: Kogan Page.

Jayasuriya, K. (2001) 'Globalization, sovereignty, and the rule of law: from political to economic constitutionalism?', *Constellations*, 8 (4): 442–59.

Jennings, S. and Cameron, R. (1987) 'State owned enterprise reform in New Zealand', in A. Bollard and R. Buckle (eds), *Economic Liberalisation in New Zealand*. Auckland: Allen and Unwin.

Jensen, M. and Meckling, W. (1976) 'Theory of the firm: managerial behaviour, agency costs and ownership structure', *Journal of Financial Economics*, 3: 305–60.

Jesson, B. (1989a) *Fragments of Labour: The Story Behind the Labour Government*. Auckland: Penguin.

Jesson, B. (1989b) 'The libertarian Right in New Zealand: the demise of social democracy and the rise of a new orthodoxy', paper presented for the Stout Research Seminar, 'The New Right: an analysis', 3–4 March.

Jessop, B. (1982) *The Capitalist State: Marxist Theories and Methods*. Oxford: Blackwell.

Jonathan, R. (1989) 'Choice and control in education: parental rights and social justice', *British Journal of Educational Studies*, 37 (4): 321–38.

Jonathan, R. (1990) 'State education service or prisoner's dilemma: the "hidden hand" as source of educational policy', *British Journal of Educational Studies*, 38 (2): 116–32.

Jonathan, R. (1997) 'Illusory freedoms: liberalism, education and the market', *Journal of the Philosophy of Education*, 31 (1), special issue: 1–220.

Joppke, C. (1987) 'The crisis of the welfare state, collective consumption and the rise of new social actors', *Berkeley Journal of Sociology*, 32: 237–60.

Kahne, J. (1996) *Reframing Educational Policy: Democracy, Community and the Individual*. New York: Teachers College Press, Columbia University.

Kant, I. (1932) *Perpetual Peace*, preface by N.M. Butler, Los Angeles, CA.: US Library Association.

Kapstein, E.B. (1999) *Sharing the Wealth: Workers and the World Economy*. New York: W.W. Norton.

Kay, N. (1992) 'Markets, false hierachies and the evolution of the modern corporation', *Journal of Economic Behaviour and Organisation*, 17: 315–34.

Keane, J. (1993) 'Stretching the limits of the democratic imagination', in J. Carens (ed.), *Democracy and Possessive Individualism: The Intellectual Legacy of C.B. Macpherson*. New York: State University of New York Press.

Keat, R. (1991) 'Introduction: Starship Britain or universal enterprise', in R. Keat and N. Abercrombie (eds), *Enterprise Culture*. London: Routledge.

Kedgley, C.W. and Wittkopf, E.R. (1989) *World Politics*. London: Macmillan.

Kelsey, J. (2002) *At the Crossroads: Three Essays*. Wellington: Bridget Williams Books.

Kemp Smith, N. (1966) *The Philosophy of David Hume*. London: Macmillan.

Kenway, J. (1990) Education and the Right's discursive politics: private versus state schooling', in S.J. Ball (ed.), *Foucault and Education: Disciplines and Knowledge*. London: Routledge.

Kerr, D. (1997) 'Towards a democratic rhetoric of schooling', in J.I. Goddard and T.J. McMannon (eds), *The Public Purpose of Education and Schooling*. San Franscisco: Jossey-Bass, pp. 73–83.

Keynes, J.M. (1931a) 'The end of laissez-faire', in J.M. Keynes, *Essays in Persuasion*. London: Macmillan, pp. 312–22.

Keynes, J.M. (1931b) 'Am I a liberal?', in J.M. Keynes, *Essays in Persuasion*. London: Macmillan, pp. 323–38.

Keynes, J.M. (1931c) 'The pure theory of money: a reply to Dr Hayek', *Economica*, 2 (34): 387–97.

Keynes, J.M. (1974) (New edn.) *The General Theory of Employment, Interest and Money*. London: Macmillan.

Kincheloe, J. (1991) 'Educational historiographical meta-analysis: rethinking methodology in the 1990s', *Qualitative Studies in Education*, 4 (3): 231–45.

King, D. (1987) *The New Right – Politics, Markets and Citizenship*, London: Macmillan.

Klein, N. (2000) *No Logo*. London: Flamingo.

Klein, N. (2003) 'Fortress continents', *Guardian*, 16 January, p. 23.

Krasner, S. (1993) 'Westphalia and all that', in J. Goldstein and R.O. Keohane (eds), *Ideas and Foreign Policy: Beliefs, Institutions and Political Change*. Ithaca, NY: Cornell University Press.

Krugman, P. (ed.) (1986) *Strategic Trade Policy and the New International Economics*. Cambridge, MA: MIT Press.

Kymlicka, W. (1989) *Liberalism, Community and Culture*. Oxford: Clarendon Press.

Kymlicka, W. (1995) *Multicultural Citizenship*. Oxford: Clarendon Press.

Kymlicka, W. (1999) 'Liberal complacencies', in S.M. Okin (ed.), *Is Multiculturalism Bad for Women?* Princeton, NJ: Princeton University Press.

Lacan, J. (1977) *Ecrits*. London: Tavistock.

Laclau, E. and Mouffe, C. (1985) *Hegemony and Socialist Strategy: Towards a Radical Democratic Politics*, trans. W. Moore and P. Commack. London: Verso.

Lamore, C. (1999) 'The moral basis of political liberalism', *Journal of Philosophy*, 96 (12): 599–625.

Lane, R. (1993) *The Market Experience*. Cambridge: Cambridge University Press.

Lange, O. (1939) *On the Economic Theory of Socialism*, ed. B. Lippincott. Minneapolis, MN: University of Minnesota Press.

Laslett, P. (1964) 'Market society and political theory', *Historical Journal*, 7 (1): 150–4.

Lather, P. (1991) *Getting Smart: Feminist Research and Pedagogy within the Postmodern*. New York: Routledge.

Lauder, H. and Hughes, D. (1999) *Trading in Futures: Why Markets in Education Don't Work*. Buckingham: Open University Press.

Lauder, H., Hughes, D., Waslander, S., Thrupp, M., McGlynn, J., Newton, S. and Dupuis, A. (1994) *The Creation of Market Competition for Education in New Zealand*, Smithfield Project, Phase One, First Report to The Ministry of Education. Wellington: Ministry of Education.

Lave, J. and Wenger, E. (1991) *Situated Learning: Legitimate Peripheral Participation*. Cambridge: Cambridge University Press.

Le Grand, J. (1982) *The Strategy of Equality*. London: Allen and Unwin.

Lee, S.-H (1992) 'Was there a concept of rights in confucian virtue-based morality', *Journal of Chinese Philosophy*, 19: 241–50.

Lehmann, W.C. (1960) *John Millar of Glasgow*. Cambridge: Cambridge University Press.

Lemke, T. (2001 '"The birth of bio-politics": Michel Foucault's lecture at the Collège de France on neo-liberal governmentality', *Economy and Society*, 30 (2): 190–207.

Letwin, W. (1972) 'The economic foundation of Hobbes' politics', in M. Cranston and R. Peters (eds), *Hobbes and Rousseau*. New York: Anchor, pp. 143–64.

Lévi-Strauss, C. (1969) *The Elementary Structures of Kinship*, trans. J. Harle Bell, J. Richard von Sturmer and R. Needham. London: Eyre and Spottiswoode.

Levin, H. (1989) 'Education as a public and private good', in N.E. Devins (ed.), *Public Values, Private Schools*. London and New York: Falmer Press, pp. 215–32.

Levinson, M. (1999) *The Demands of Liberal Education*. New York: Oxford University Press.

Levinthal, D. (1988) 'A survey of agency models of organisation', *Journal of Economic Behaviour and Organisation*, 9: 153–85.

Levitas, R. (ed.) (1986) *The Ideology of the New Right*. Cambridge: Polity Press.

Lindgren, J.R. (1973) *The Social Philosophy of Adam Smith*. The Hague: Martinus Nijhoff.

Lindsay, G. (1997) 'Threats to freedom then and now: the Mont Pelerin society after 50 years', *Policy*, Autumn: 18–20.

Linklater, A. (1996) 'Citizenship and sovereignty in the post-Westphalian state', European *Journal of International Relations*, 2 (1): 77–103.

Locke, J. (1958) *Essays on the Law of Nature*, ed. W. von Leyden. Oxford: Clarendon Press.

Locke, J. (1959) *An Essay Concerning Human Understanding*, 2 vols. New York: Dover.

Locke, J. (1960) *Two Treatises of Government*, ed. Peter Laslett. Cambridge: Cambridge University Press.

Locke, J. (1979) *Treatise on Civil Government and A Letter Concerning Toleration*, ed. C.L. Sherman. New York: Irvington.

Luke, A. (1995) 'Text and discourse in education: an introduction to critical discourse analysis', in M.W. Apple (ed.), *Review of Research in Education*, 21. Washington: American Educational Research Association, pp. 3–48.

Lukes, S. (1977) *Essays in Social Theory*. New York: Columbia University Press.

Lyas, C. (1973) 'Personal qualities and the intentional fallacy', in G. Vesey (ed.), *Philosophy and the Arts*, London: Macmillan, pp. 194–210.

MacCallum, G.G. (1967) 'Negative and positive liberty', *Philosophical Review*, 76: 312–34.

McCann, P. (ed.) (1977) *Popular Education and Socialisation in the Nineteenth Century*. London: Methuen.

McCarthy, T. (1994) 'The critique of impure reason: Foucault and the Frankfurt school', in M. Kelly (ed.), *Critique and Power: Recasting the Foucault/Habermas Debate*. Cambridge, MA: MIT Press.

McCloskey, R.G. (1951) *American Conservatism in the Age of Enterprise*. New York: Harper and Row.

MacCormick, N. (1999) *Questioning Sovereignty*. Oxford: Clarendon Press.

McCulloch, G. (1991) 'Serpent in the garden: conservative protest, the "new right" and New Zealand educational history', *History of Education Review*, 20 (1): 73–89.

Macdonell, D. (1986) *Theories of Discourse*. Oxford: Blackwell.

MacEwan, A. (1999) *Neo-Liberalism or Democracy? Economic Strategy, Markets, and Alternatives for the 21st Century*. London: Zed Books.

McGrew, A. (2000) 'Democracy beyond borders?', in David Held and Anthony McGrew (eds), *The Global Transformations Reader: An Introduction to the Globalization Debate*. Cambridge: Polity Press, pp. 405–19.

McGrew, A. and Lewis, P.G. et al. (1992) *Global Politics: Globalization and the Nation-State*. Cambridge: Polity Press.

McGrew, T. (1992) 'Conceptualising global politics', in A. McGrew and P.G. Lewis et

300

al., (eds), *Global Politics: Globalization and the Nation State*. Cambridge: Polity Press.

McGuire, M. and Ball, S. (1994) 'Researching politics and the politics of research: recent qualitative studies in the UK', *Qualitative Studies in Education*, 7 (3): 269–85.

MacIntyre, A. (1981) *After Virtue*. London: Duckworth.

MacIntyre, A. (1984) *Is Patriotism a Virtue?*, Lawrence, KS: Department of Philosophy, University of Kansas.

MacIntyre, A. (1988) *Whose Justice? Which Rationality?* London: Duckworth.

MacIntyre, A. (1991) 'I'm not a communitarian, but … ', *The Reponsive Community*, 1 (3): 91–2.

McKean, R. (1974) 'Property rights within government, and devices to increase governmental efficiency', in E.G. Furubotn and S. Pejovich (eds), *The Economics of Property Rights*. MA: Ballinger.

McLean, I. (1986) 'Mechanisms for democracy', in D. Held and C. Pollitt (eds), *New Forms of Democracy*. London: Sage/The Open University.

McLennan, G. (1993) 'The concept, history, situation and prospects of social democracy: a modest overview', *Sites*, 26, Autumn: 103–14.

Maclure, S. (1970) *One Hundred Years of London Education: 1870–1970*. London: Penguin.

McPherson, A. and Raab, C. (1988) *Governing Education*. Edinburgh: Edinburgh University Press.

Macpherson, C.B. (1962).*The Political Theory of Possessive Individualism: Hobbes to Locke*. Oxford: Oxford University Press.

Macpherson, C.B. (1970) 'Progress in the Locke industry', *Canadian Journal of Political Science*, 3 (2): 324–5.

Macpherson, C.B. (1973) *Democratic Theory: Essays in Retrieval*. Oxford: Oxford University Press.

Macpherson, C.B. (1977) *The Life and Times of Liberal Democracy*. Oxford: Oxford University Press.

Macpherson, C.B. (1980) 'Editor's introduction', in J. Locke, *Second Treatise of Government*, ed. C.B. Macpherson. Indianapolis, IN: Hackett.

Machado, R. (1992) 'Archaeology and epistemology', in T.J .Armstrong trans., *Michel Foucault: Philosopher*. New York: Harvester Wheatsheaf, pp. 3–19.

Majone, G. (1996) 'Regulatory legitimacy', in G. Majone (ed.), *Regulating Europe*. London: Routledge.

Mander, J. and Goldsmith, E. (eds) (1996) *The Case Against the Global Economy*. San Francisco: Sierra Club Books.

Mandville, B. (1970) *The Fable of the Bees*, ed. and Introduction P. Harth. London: Penguin.

Mansbridge, J. (1993) 'Macpherson's neglect of the political', in J. Carens (ed.), *Democracy and Possessive Individualism: The Intellectual Legacy of C.B. Macpherson*. New York: State University of New York Press.

Marginson, S. (1992) *The Free Market: A Study of Hayek, Friedman and Buchanan and the Effects on the Public Good*. Kensington, NSW: Public Sector Research Centre, University of New South Wales.

Marginson, S. (1993) *Education and Public Policy in Australia*. Melbourne: Cambridge University Press.

Marginson, S. (1997) 'Competition and contestability in Australian higher education, 1987–1997', *Australian Universities Review*, 40 (1): 5–14.

Marginson, S. (1999) 'Harvards of the antipodes? Nation-building universities in a global environment', *Access: Critical Perspectives on Cultural and Policy Studies in Education*, 18 (2): 1–20.

Marginson, S. and Considine, M. (2000) *The Enterprise University: Governance, Strategy, Reinvention*. Melbourne: Cambridge University Press.

Margolis, J. (1993) *The Flux of History and the Flux of Science*. Berkeley, CA: University of California Press.

Marshall, C. (1997) 'Dismantling and reconstructing policy analysis', in C. Marshall (ed.), *Feminist Critical Policy Analysis I: A Perspective from Primary and Secondary Schooling*. London: Falmer Press.

Marshall, J. (1989) 'Michel Foucault and education', *Australian Journal of Education*, 33 (2): 99–113.

Marshall, J. (1990) 'Foucault and educational research', in S.J. Ball (ed.), *Foucault and Education: Disciplines and Knowledge*. London: Routledge, pp. 11–28.

Marshall, J. (1995) 'Skills, information and quality for the autonomous chooser', in M. Olssen and K.M. Matthews (eds), *Education, Democracy and Reform*. Auckland: New Zealand Association for Research in Education/Research Unit for Maori Education, pp. 44–58.

Martell, L. (1992) 'New ideas of socialism', *Economy and Society*, 21 (2): 152–72.

Martell, L. (1993) 'Rescuing the middle ground: neo-liberalism and associational socialism', *Economy and Society*, 22 (1): 100–13.

Matheson, A. (1997) 'The impact of contracts on public management', in G. Davis, B. Sullivan and A. Yeatman (eds.), *The New Contractualism?* Melbourne: Macmillan, pp. 164–79.

Meek, R. (1963) *The Economics of Physiocracy*, Cambridge, MA: Harvard University Press.

Middleton, S. (1990) 'Women, equality, and equity in liberal educational policies 1945–1988', in S. Middleton, J. Codd and A. Jones (eds), *New Zealand Education Policy Today*. Wellington: Allen and Unwin, pp. 68–93.

Mill, J.S. (1859) *On Liberty*, ed. C.V. Shield. Indianapolis, IN: Bobbs Merrill Library of Liberts Arts (1956 edition).

Mill, J.S. (1924) (New edn.) *Autobiography*. London: Oxford University Press.

Mill, J.S. (1965) 'Chapters on socialism', in V.W. Bladen, J.M. Robson and J. Mercel eds, *Collected Works*. Toronto: University of Toronto Press.

Mill, J.S. (1965) (New edn.) 'Principles of political economy', vol. 2 of *Collected Works*, ed. J.M. Robson. Toronto: Toronto University Press.

Mill, J.S. (1975) *The Subjection of Women*. Oxford: Oxford University Press.

Millar, J. (1990) *Observations Concerning the Distinction of Ranks*. Bristol: Thoemmes.

Miller, D. (1980) 'Hume and possessive individualism', *History of Political Thought*, 1 (2): 261–78.

Miller, D. (2000) *Citizenship and National Identity*. Cambridge: Polity Press.

Miller, D. and Estrin, S. (1986) 'Market socialism: a policy for socialists', in I. Forbes (ed.), *Market Socialism: Whose Choice?* Fabian Tract 516. London: Fabian Society.

Minogue, K.R. (1963) 'The political theory of possessive individualism', *History*, 48: 219–20.

Mises, L. von (1949) *Human Action*. New Haven, CT: Yale University Press.

Mises, L. von (1951) *Socialism*. London: Cape.

Mises, L. von (1958) *Theory and History*. London: Cape.

Mishra, R. (1999) *Globalization and the Welfare State*. Cheltenham: Edward Elgar.

Moe, T. (1984) 'The new economics of organisations', *American Journal of Political Science*, 28: 739–75.

Moe, T. (1990) 'Political institutions: the neglected side of the story', *Journal of Law, Economics and Organization*, 6: 213–53.

Moe, T. (1991) 'Politics and the theory of organization', *Journal of Law, Economics and Organization*, 7: 106–29.

Monbiot, G. (2001) *The Captive State*. London: Pan Books.

Monbiot, G. (2003) 'Stronger than ever', *Guardian*, 28 January, p. 19.

Montesquieu, Charles de Secondat., Baron de (1900) *The Spirit of Laws*, trans. T. Nugent. New York: Colonial Press.

Moore, D. and Davenport, S. (1990) 'Choice: the new improved sorting machine', in W.L. Boyd and H.J. Walberg (eds), *Choice in Education: Potential and Problems*. Berkeley, CA: McCutchan.

Mouffe, C. (1993) *The Return of the Political*. London: Verso.

Mouffe, C. (2000) 'For an agonistic model of democracy', in N. O'Sullivan (ed.), *Political Theory in Transition*. London and New York: Routledge, pp. 113–30.

Mulgan, R. (2000) 'Was Aristotle an "Aristotelian social democrat"', *Ethics*, 111 (1): 79–101.

Muller, J.Z. (1993) *Adam Smith in his Times and Ours: Designing the Decent Society*. New York: Free Press.

Nelson, R.R. and Phelps, E.S. (1966) 'Investment in humans, technological diffusion and economic growth', *American Economic Review*, 56 (1/2): 69–75.

New Zealand Department of Education (Taskforce to Review Educational Administration) (1988) *Administering for Excellence: Effective Administration in Education* (Picot Report). Wellington: Government Printer.

New Zealand Treasury (1984). *Economic Management: Brief to the Incoming Government*. Wellington: New Zealand Treasury.

New Zealand Treasury (1987) *Government Management: Brief to the Incoming Government, Vol. II: Education Issues*. Wellington: New Zealand Treasury.

Nicholls, D. (1962) 'Positive liberty', 1880–1914', *American Political Science Review*, 56 (1): 114–28.

Nietzsche, F. (1969) *On the Genealogy of Morals*, trans. W. Kaufmann. New York: Random House.

Nixon, J., Marks, A., Rowland, S. and Walker, M. (2001) 'Towards a new academic professionalism: a manifesto of hope', *British Journal of the Sociology of Education*, 22 (2): 227–44.

Noddings, N. (1992) *The Challenge to Care in Schools*. New York: Teachers College Press.

Nove, A. (1983) *The Economics of Feasible Socialism*. London: Allen and Unwin.

Nozick, R. (1974) *Anarchy, State and Utopia*. Oxford: Blackwell.

Nussbaum, M. (1986) *The Fragility of Goodness: Luck and Ethics in Greek Tragedy and Philosophy*. Cambridge: University of Cambridge Press.

Nussbaum, M. (1990) 'Aristotelian social democracy', in R.B. Douglas, G. Mara and H. Richardson (eds), *Liberalism and the Good*. New York: Routledge.

Nussbaum, M. (1992) 'Human functioning and social justice: in defense of Aristotelian essentialism', *Political Theory*, 20 (2): 202–46.

Nussbaum, M. (1994a) *The Therapy of Desire*. Princeton, NJ: Princeton University Press.

Nussbaum, M. (1994b) 'Human capabilities, female human beings', in M.C. Nussbaum and J. Glover (eds), *Women, Culture, Development: A Study of Human Capabilities*. Oxford: Clarendon Press, pp. 61–104.

Nussbaum, M. (1996) *For Love of Country*. Boston, MA: Beacon Press.

Nussbaum, M. (1997) *A Classical Defence of Reform in Liberal Education*. Cambridge, MA: Harvard University Press.

Nussbaum, M. (2000a) *Women and Human Development: The Capabilities Approach*. Cambridge: Cambridge University Press.

Nussbaum, M. (2000b) 'Aristotle, politics, and human capabilities: a response to Antony, Arneson, Charlesworth, and Mulgan', *Ethics*, 111 (1): 102–40.

Nuti, D. (1981) 'Socialism on earth', *Cambridge Journal of Economics*, 5: 391–403.

O'Connor, J. (1973) *The Fiscal Crisis of the State*. New York: St Martin's Press.

O'Connor, J. (1984) *Accumulation Crisis*. Oxford: Blackwell.

O'Neill, A-M. (1996) 'Privatising Public Policy: Privileging Market Man and Individualising Equality Through Choice within Education in Aotearoa/New Zealand'. *Discourse* 1996 17 (3): 403–16.

O'Neill, O. (1986) *Faces of Hunger: An Essay on Poverty, Development and Justice*. London: Allen and Unwin.

O'Neill, O. (1988) 'Ethical reasoning and ideological pluralism', *Ethics*, 98 (4): 705–22.

O'Neill, O. (2000) 'Transnational justice', in D. Held and A. McGrew (eds), *The Global Transformations Reader: An Introduction to the Globalization Debate*. Cambridge: Polity Press, pp. 442–52.

O'Neill, O. (2002) *A Question of Trust*, BBC Reith Lecture 2002, Cambridge: Cambridge University Press.

Offe, C. (1984) *Contradictions of the Welfare State*. London: Hutchinson.

Ogden, C.K. and Richards, I.A. (1923) *The Meaning of Meaning*. London: Routledge and Kegan Paul.

Ohmae, K. (1990) *The Borderless World*. London: Collins.

Ohmae, K. (1996) *The End of the Nation State: The Rise of Regional Economies*. London: HarperColllins.

Olssen, M. (1995) 'Wittgenstein and Foucault: the limits and possibilities of constructivism', *Access: Critical Perspectives on Education Policy*, 13 (2): 71–8.

Olssen, M. (1996a) 'Michel Foucault's historical materialism', in M. Peters, W. Hope, J. Marshall and S. Webster (eds), *Critical Theory, Poststructuralism and the Social Context*. Palmerston North: Dunmore Press, pp. 82–105.

Olssen, M. (1996b) 'In defence of the welfare state and publicly provided education: a New Zealand perspective', *Journal of Education Policy*, 11 (3): 337–62.

Olssen, M. (1998) 'Education policy, the cold war and the "liberal-communitarian" debate', *Journal of Education Policy*, 13 (1): 63–89.

Olssen, M. (1999) *Michel Foucault: Materialism and Education*. Wesport: Bergin and Garvey.

Olssen, M. (2000) 'Ethical liberalism, education and the "New Right"', *Journal of Education Policy*, 15 (5): 481–508.

Olssen, M. (2002a) 'The neo-liberal appropriation of tertiary education policy: accountability, research and academic freedom', 'State of the Art' monograph no. 8. Wellington: New Zealand Association for Research in Education.

Olssen, M. (2002b) 'Michel Foucault as "thin" communitarian: difference, community, democracy', *Cultural Studies–Critical Methodologies*, 2 (4): 483–513.

Olssen, M. (2003) 'Structuralism, poststructuralism, neo-liberalism: assessing Foucault's legacy', *Journal of Education*, 18 (2): 189–202.

Olssen, M. and Morris-Matthews, K. (1997) (eds), *Education Policy in New Zealand: the 1990s and Beyond*. Palmerston North: Dunmore Press.

Organization for Economic Co-operation and Development (OECD) (1987) 'Structural adjustment and economic performance' monograph. Paris: Organization for Economic Co-operation and Development.

Organization for Economic Co-operation and Development (OECD) (1993) *Economic Surveys 1992–1993: New Zealand*. Paris: Organization of Economic Co-operation and Development.

Osborne, D. and Gaebler, T. (1992) *Reinventing Government: How the Entrepreneurial Spirit is Transforming the Public Sector, from Schoolhouse to Statehouse, City Hall to the Pentagon*. Reading, MA: Addison-Wesley.

Osborne, T. (1993) 'On liberalism, neo-liberalism and the "liberal profession" of medicine', *Economy and Society*, 22 (3): 345–56.

Ozga, J. (2000) *Policy Research in Educational Settings: Contested Terrain*. Buckingham: Open University Press.

Palmer, K. (1993) *Local Government Law in New Zealand*, 2nd edn. Sydney: Law Books.

Parker, W.C. (2001) 'Educating democratic citizens: a broad view', *Theory into Practice*, 40 (1): 6–13.

Payne, G., Dingwall, R., Payne, J. and Carter, M. (1981) *Sociology and Social Research*. London: Routledge and Kegan Paul.

Pearson, R. and Pike, G. (1989) *The Graduate Labour Market in the 1990s*. IMS Report No. 167. Brighton: Institute of Manpower Studies.

Pearson, R., Seccombe, I., Pike, G., Holly, S. and Conner, H. (1991). *Doctoral Social Scientists and the Labour Market*. IMS Report No. 217. Brighton: Institute for Manpower Studies.

Perrow, C. (1986a) 'Economic theories of organisation', *Theory and Society*, 15 (6): 11–45.

Perrow, C. (1986b) *Complex Organisations: A Critical Essay*. New York: Random House.

Peters, M. (1992) 'Starship education: enterprise culture in New Zealand', *Access:*

Critical Perspectives on Education Policy, 11 (1): 1–12.

Peters, M. and Marshall, J. (1988a) 'Social policy and the move to "Community"', in *The Report of the (NZ) Royal Commission on Social Policy, III*, Part 1. Wellington: Government Printer, pp. 655–76.

Peters, M. and Marshall, J. (1988b). 'Social policy and the move to "Community": practical implications for service delivery', in *The Report of the Royal Commission on Social Policy, III*, Part 1. Wellington: Government Printer, pp. 677–702.

Peters, M. and Marshall, J. (1988c) 'Te Reo o Te Tai Tokerau: community evaluation, empowerment and opportunities for oral Maori language reproduction', in *The Report of the Royal Commission on Social Policy, III*, Part 1. Wellington: Government Printer, pp. 703–43.

Peters, M. and Marshall, J. (1988d) 'Empowerment and the ideal learning community: theory and practice in Tai Tokerau', in C. Wylie (ed.), *Proceedings of the First Research into Educational Policy Conference*, 17–19 August. Wellington: NZCER.

Peters, M. and Marshall, J. (1988e) 'The politics of "choice" and "community"', *Access: Critical Perspectives on Cultural and Policy Studies in Education*, 7: 84–109.

Peters, M. and Marshall, J. (1990) 'Education, the new right, and the crisis of the welfare state in New Zealand', *Discourse*, 11 (1): 77–90.

Pettit, P. (1997) *Republicanism: A Theory of Freedom and Government*. Oxford: Oxford University Press.

Petersen, J. (1993) 'The economics of organisation: the principal–agent relationship', *Acta Sociologica*, 36: 277–93.

Pilger, J. (2002) *The New Rulers of the World*. London: Verso.

Plant, R. (1985) *Equality, Markets and the State*. London: Fabian Society.

Plant, R. (1988) *Citizenship Rights and Socialism*. London: Fabian Society.

Pocock, J.G.A. (1975) *The Machiavellian Moment: Florentine Political Theory and the Atlantic Republican Tradition*. Princeton, NJ: Princeton University Press.

Polanyi, K. (1957) *The Great Transformation*. Boston, MA: Beacon Press.

Polanyi, K. (1969) 'The Birth of the Liberal Creed', in K.J. Rea and J.T. McLeod (eds), *Business and Government in Canada*. Toronto: Methuen, pp. 7–20.

Pope, A. (1805) *An Essay on Man*. (New edn.) Boston, MA: Manning and Loring.

Porter, M.E. (1990) *The Competitive Economy of Nations*. London: Macmillan.

Poster, M. (1984) *Foucault, Marxism and History: Mode of Production vs Mode of Information*. Cambridge: Polity Press.

Power, F.C., Higgins, A. and Kholberg, L. (1989) *Lawrence Kholberg's Approach to Moral Education*. New York: Columbia University Press.

Pratt, J. and Zeckhauser, R. (eds) (1985) *Principals and Agents: The Structure of Business*. Boston, MA: Harvard University Press.

Prunty, J. (1984) *A Critical Reformulation of Educational Policy Analysis*. Geelong: Deakin University Press.

Prunty, J. (1985) 'Signposts for a critical educational policy analysis', *Australian Journal of Education*, 29 (2): 133–40.

Purkey, S. and Smith, M. (1983) 'Effective schools: a review', *Elementary School Journal*, 83 (4): 427–52.

Putnam, R. (1993) *Making Democracy Work: Civic Traditions in Modern Italy*. Princeton, NJ: Princeton University Press.

Rajchman, J. (1985) *Michel Foucault: The Freedom of Philosophy*. New York: Columbia University Press.

Rand, A. (1961) *For the New Intellectual*. New York: Signet.

Rand, A. (1964) *The Virtue of Selfishness*. New York: Signet.

Raphael, D.D. (1977) *Hobbes: Morals and Politics*. London: Allen and Unwin.

Rawls, J. (1971) *A Theory of Justice*. Cambridge: Harvard University Press.

Rawls, J. (1975) 'Fairness to goodness', *Philosophical Review*, 84: 536–54.

Rawls, J. (1980) 'Kantian constructivism in moral theory', *Journal of Philosophy*, 77 (9): 515–72.

Rawls, J. (1985) 'Justice as fairness: political not metaphysical', *Philosophy and Public Affairs*, 14 (3): 223–51.

Rawls, J. (1987) The idea of an overlapping consensus', *Oxford Journal of Legal Studies*, 7 (1): 1–25.

Rawls, J. (1988) 'The priority of the right and ideas of the good', *Philosophy and Public Affairs*, 17 (4): 251–76.

Rawls, J. (1996) *Political Liberalism*. New York: Columbia University Press.

Raz, J. (1986) *The Morality of Freedom*. Oxford: Clarendon Press.

Raz, J. (1994) *Ethics in the Public Domain*. Oxford: Clarendon Press.

Reeder, D. (ed.) (1977) *Urban Education in 19th Century London*. London: Taylor and Francis.

Rees, J.C. (1966) 'A re-reading of Mill on liberty', in P. Radcliff (ed.), *Limits of Liberty: Studies of Mill's On Liberty*. Belmont, CA: Wadsworth, pp. 87–107.

Rees, R. (1985a) 'The theory of principal and agent: part 1', *Bulletin of Economic Research*, 37 (1): 1–26.

Rees, R. (1985b) 'The theory of principal and agent: part 2', *Bulletin of Economic Research*, 37 (2): 75–95.

Rees-Mogg, W. (1974) *The Reigning Illusion*. London: Hamish Hamilton.

Rehg, W. and Bohman, J. (2001) *Pluralism and the Pragmatic Turn: The Transformation of Critical Theory*. Cambridge, MA: MIT Press.

Reich, R. (1991) *The Work of Nations: A Blueprint for the Future*. New York: Vintage Books.

Reich, Rob (2002) *Bridging Liberalism and Multiculturalism in American Education*. Chicago and London: University of Chicago Press.

Rhodes, R.W. (1997a) *Understanding Governance: Policy Networks, Governance, Reflexivity and Accountability*. Buckingham: Open University Press.

Rhodes, R.W. (1997b) 'From marketization to diplomacy: it's the mix that matters', *Public Policy and Administration*, 12 (2): 31–50.

Rhodes, R.W. (2000) 'Governance and public administration', in J. Pierre (ed.), *Debating Governance*. Oxford: Oxford University Press, pp. 54–90.

Ricardo, D. (1966) *The Works and Correspondence of David Ricardo, Vol. 1, On the Principles of Political Economy and Taxation*. Cambridge: Cambridge University Press.

Riesman, D. (1990) *The Political Economy of James Buchanan*. College Station, TX: Texas A&M University Press.

Ritchie, D.G. (1895) *Natural Rights*. London: Swan Sonnenschein.

Ritzer, G. (2000) *The McDonaldization of Society*, Thousand Oaks, CA: Pine Forge

Press.

Robertson, J. (1983) 'Scottish political economy beyond the civic tradition: government and economic development in the "Wealth of Nations"', *History of Political Economy*, 4, Winter: 579–609.

Robertson, S. (1998) 'Quality, contractualism and control: orchestrating the sectoral settlement in teachers' work in New Zealand', *New Zealand Journal of Educational Studies*, 33 (1), 2–33.

Roper, B. (1991) 'From the welfare state to the free market: explaining the transition', *New Zealand Sociology*, 6: (1): 38–63.

Roper, R. (1997) 'New Zealand's postwar economic history', in C. Rudd and B. Roper (eds), *The Political Economy of New Zealand*, Auckland: Oxford University Press, pp. 3–21.

Rorty, R. (1998) 'Justice as a larger loyalty', in Pheng Cheah and Bruce Robbins (eds), *Cosmopolitics: Thinking and Feeling Beyond the Nation*. Minneapolis, MN: University of Minnesota Press, pp. 45–58.

Rose, N. (1979) *The Pschological Complex: Pyschology, Politics and Society in England, 1869–1939*. London: Routledge and Kegan Paul.

Rose, N. (1993). 'Government, authority and expertise in advanced liberalism', *Economy and Society*, 22 (3): 283–99.

Rose, N. (1996) 'Governing "advanced" liberal democracies', in A. Barry, T. Osborne and N. Rose (eds), Foucault and Political Reason. Chicago: University of Chicago Press, pp. 37–64.

Rosenau, J.N. (1980) *The Study of Global Interdependence*. London: Frances Pinter.

Rosenberg, B. (1991) 'Not a case for market control', *Educational Leadership*, 48 (4): 307–16.

Rosenberg, N. (1963) 'Mandeville and laissez-faire', *Journal of the History of Ideas*, 24, April–June: 183–96.

Rosenberg, W. (1977) 'Full employment: the fulcrum of the welfare state', in A.D. Trlin (ed.), *Social Welfare and New Zealand Society*. Wellington: Methuen.

Rothbard, M. (1978) *For a New Liberty: The Libertarian Manifesto*, 2nd edn. London and New York: Collier-Macmillan.

Rubenstein, D. (1969) *School Attendance in London 1870–1904*. Hull: University of Hull Press.

Rugman, A.M. (2001) *The End of Globalization: Why Global Strategy is a Myth and How to Profit for the Realities of Regional Markets*. New York: AMACOM.

Rupert, R. (2000) *Ideologies of Globalization: Contending Visions of a New World Order*, London: Routledge.

Ryan, A. (1965) 'Locke and the dictatorship of the bourgeoisie', *Political Studies*, 13: 219–30.

Ryan, A. (1988) 'Hobbes and individualism', in G.A.J. Rogers and A. Ryan (eds), *Perspectives on Thomas Hobbes*. Oxford: Clarendon Press.

Sackett, D.L., Rosenberg, W.M.C., Muir Gray, J.A., Brian Haynes, R. and Scott Richardson, W. (1996) 'Evidence-based medicine: what is it and what it isn't', *British Medical Journal*, 312: 71–2.

Sadker, M.P. and Sadker, D.M. (1994) *Failing at Fairness: How America's Schools Cheat Girls*. New York: Scribner.

Said, E. (1978) *Orientalism*. London: Routledge and Kegan Paul.

Said, E. (1983) *The World, the Text and the Critic*. Cambridge, MA: Harvard University Press.

Sandel, M. (1982) *Liberalism and the Limits of Justice*. Cambridge: Cambridge University Press.

Saussure, F. de (1974) *Course in General Linguistics*. London: Fontana/Collins (originally published in French, 1916).

Saville, J. (1977) 'The welfare state: an historical approach', in M. Fitzgerald, P. Halmos, J. Muncie and D. Zeldin (eds), *Welfare in Action*. London and Henley: Routledge and Kegan Paul/Open University Press, pp. 4–9.

Sawicki, J. (1991) *Disciplining Foucault: Feminism, Power and the Body*. New York: Routledge.

Scheurich, J. (1994) 'Policy archaeology: a new policy studies methodology', *Journal of Education Policy*, 9 (4): 297–316.

Schick, A. (1996) *The Spirit of Reform: Managing the New Zealand State Sector in a Time of Change*, a report prepared for the New Zealand State Services Commission and the Treasury. Wellington: State Services Commission.

Schultz, T. (1960a) 'Investment in man: an economist's view', *Social Science Review*, 33 (2): 109–17.

Schultz, T. (1960b) 'Capital formation by education', *Journal of Political Economy*, 68 (6): 571–83.

Schultz, T. (1961) 'Investment in human capital', *American Economic Review*, 51 (1): 1–17.

Schultz, T. (1975) 'The value of the ability to deal with disequilibrium', *Journal of Economic Literature*, 13 (3): 827–46.

Schumpeter, J. (1976) *Capitalism, Socialism and Democracy*. London: Routledge.

Scott, G. (1997) 'The new institutional economics and the shaping of the state in New Zealand', in G. Davis, B. Sullivan and A. Yeatman (eds), *The New Contractualism*. Melbourne: Macmillan Education, pp. 154–63.

Scott, G. and Gorringe, P. (1989) 'Reform of the core public sector: New Zealand experience', *Australian Journal of Public Administration*, 48 (1): 81–92.

Scruton, R. (1980) The Meaning of Conservatism. London: Penguin.

Self, P. (1989) 'What's wrong with government?: The problem of public choice', *Political Quarterly*, 6: 317–44.

Self, P. (2000) *Rolling Back the Market: Economic Dogma and Political Choice*. London: Macmillan.

Sellars, W. (1997) *Empiricism and the Philosophy of Mind*. Cambridge, MA: Harvard University Press.

Selleck, R.J.W. (1968) *The New Education: The English Background 1870–1914*. Melbourne: Pitman and Sons.

Selznick, P. (1992) *The Moral Commonwealth: Social Theory and the Promise of Community*. Berkeley, CA: University of California Press.

Sen, A. (1979) 'Utilitarianism and welfarism', *Journal of Philosophy*, 76: 463–89.

Sen, A. (1985) *Commodities and Capabilities*. Amsterdam: North-Holland.

Sen, A. (1988) *On Ethics and Economics*. Oxford: Blackwell.

Sen, A. (1992) *Inequality Reexamined*. Oxford: Clarendon Press.

Sen, A. (1993) 'Capability and well-being', in M. Nussbaum and A. Sen (eds), *The Quality of Life*, Oxford: Clarendon, pp. 30–53.

Sen, A. (1999) *Development as Freedom*. Oxford: Oxford University Press.

Sen, A. (2002) *Rationality and Freedom*. Cambridge, MA: Belknap Press..

Sennett, R. (1998) *The Corrosion of Character*. New York: W.W. Norton.

Shapiro, I. (1986). *The Evolution of Rights in Liberal Theory*. Cambridge: Cambridge University Press.

Shipman, A. (2002) *The Globalisation Myth*. Cambridge: Icon.

Shonfield, A. (1965) *Modern Capitalism: The Changing Balance of Public and Private Power*. London: Oxford University Press.

Simkins, T. (2000) 'Education reform and managerialism: comparing the experience of schools and colleges', *Journal of Education Policy* 15 (3): 317–32.

Simon, H. (1991) 'Organizations and markets', *Journal of Economic Perspectives* 5 (2): 25–44.

Simonson, H.P. (1971) *Strategies in Criticism*. New York: Holt, Rinehart and Winston.

Skidelsky, R. (1978) 'The American response to Keynes', in A.P. Thirwall (ed.), *Keynes and Laissez-Faire*. London: Macmillan.

Skinner, Q. (1978) *The Foundations of Modern Political Thought*, 2 vols. Cambridge: Cambridge University Press.

Skinner, Q. (1984) 'The idea of negative liberty: philosophical and historical perspectives', in R. Rorty, J.B. Schneewind and Q. Skinner (eds), *Philosophy in History – Essays on the Historiography of Philosophy*. Cambridge: Cambridge University Press, pp. 193–221.

Smith, A. (1976a) *The Theory of Moral Sentiments*, eds D.D. Raphael and L. Macfie. Oxford: Clarendon Press. (Originally published 1759, revised edn. 1790.)

Smith, A. (1976b) *An Inquiry into the Nature and Causes of the Wealth of Nations*, eds R.H. Campell and A.S. Skinner. Oxford: Clarendon Press. (Originally published 1776.)

Sockett, H. (1990) 'Accountability, trust, and ethical codes of practice', in J.I. Goodlad, R. Soder and K.A. Sirotnik (eds), *The Moral Dimensions of Teaching*. San Franscisco: Jossey-Bass.

Sommerville, J.P. (1992) *Thomas Hobbes: Political Ideas in Historical Context*. London: Macmillan.

Soros, G. (2002) *George Soros on Globalization*. New York: Public Affairs.

Soroos, M.S. (1986) *Beyond Sovereignty*. Columbia, SC: University of South Carolina Press.

Spragens, T.A. (1981) *The Irony of Liberal Reason*. Chicago and London: University of Chicago Press.

Sreenivasan, G. (1995) *The Limits of Lockean Rights to Property*. Oxford: Oxford University Press.

Stewart, M. (1986) *Keynes and After*, 3rd edn. London: Penguin.

Stiglitz, J. (2002) *Globalization and Its Discontents*. London: Penguin.

Strange, S. (1995) 'Political economy and international relations', in K. Booth and S. Smith (eds), *International Relations Theory Today*. Cambridge: Polity Press.

Strike, K. (1989) *Liberal Justice and the Marxist Critique of Education*. New York: Routledge.

Sturt, M. (1970) *The Education of the People.* London: Routledge and Kegan Paul.

Sutch, W. (1966) *The Quest for Security in New Zealand.* London: Oxford University Press.

Taylor, C. (1979) 'What is wrong with negative liberty', in A. Ryan (ed.), *The Idea of Freedom.* Oxford: Oxford University Press., pp. 175–93.

Taylor, C. (1985) *Philosophy and the Human Sciences: Philosophical Papers 2.* Cambridge: Cambridge University Press.

Taylor, C. (1989) 'Foucault on freedom and truth', in D.C. Hoy (ed.), *Foucault: A Critical Reader.* Oxford: Blackwell.

Taylor, C. (1994) 'The politics of recognition', in A. Gutmann (ed.), *Multiculturalism and the Politics of Recognition.* Princeton, NJ: Princeton University Press, pp. 25–73.

Taylor, F. (1911) *The Principles of Scientific Management.* New York: Harper.

Taylor, M. (2002) 'Labour's core problem', *Financial Times,* 16 April.

Taylor, S. (1997) 'Critical policy analysis: exploring contexts, texts and consequences, *Discourse,* 18 (1): 23–35.

Teichgraeber, R.F. (1986) *'Free Trade' and Moral Philosophy: Rethinking the Sources of Adam Smith's 'Wealth of Nations'.* Durham, NC: Duke University Press.

Thomas, K. (1965) 'The social origins of Hobbes' political thought', in K. Brown (ed.), *Hobbes' Studies.* Cambridge, MA: Harvard University Press, pp. 185–236.

Thompson, D.F. (1985) 'The possibility of administrative ethics', *Public Administration Review,* 45, September–October: 555–61.

Thompson, G. (1990) *The Political Economy of the New Right.* London: Pinter.

Thompson, J. (1998) 'Community identity and world citizenship', in D. Archibugi, D. Held and M. Köhler (eds), *Re-Imagining Political Community.* Cambridge: Polity Press/Blackwell, pp.179–97.

Thompson, J. (2000) 'Life politics and popular learning', in J. Field and M. Leicester (eds), *Lifelong Learning.* London: Routledge Falmer, pp. 134–46.

Thompson, J.B. (1982) 'Universal pragmatics', in J.B. Thompson and D. Held (eds), *Habermas: Critical Debates.* London: Macmillan, pp. 116–33.

Thompson, J.B. (1984) *Studies in the Theory of Ideology.* Cambridge: Polity Press.

Thompson, S. and Wright, M. (eds) (1988) *Internal Organisation, Efficiency and Profit.* Oxford: Philip Allan.

Tomlinson, J. (1988) *Can Government Manage the Economy?* Fabian Tract 524. London: Fabian Society.

Tomlinson, J. (1990) 'Market socialism: a basis for socialist renewal', in B. Hindess (ed.), *Reactions to the Right.* London: Croom Helm, pp. 32–49.

Tomlinson, J. (1991) 'Why wasn't there a "Keynesian revolution" in economic policy everywhere?', *Economy and Society,* 20 (1): 103–19.

Tomlinson, J. (1999) *Globalization and Culture.* Cambridge: Polity Press.

Tomlinson, S. (2001) *Education in a Post-Welfare Society.* Buckingham: Open University Press.

Tooley, J. (1996) *Education Without the State.* London: Institute of Economic Affairs.

Torres, C. (1989) 'The capitalist state and public policy formation: framework for a political sociology of educational policy making', *British Journal of Sociology of Education,* 10 (1): 81–102.

311

Townshend, J. (2000) *C.B. Macpherson and the Problem of Liberal Democracy*. Edinburgh: Edinburgh University Press.

Toynbee, P. (2002) 'Lessons in class warfare', *Guardian*, 6 December, p. 23.

Treblicock, M. (1995) 'Can government be reinvented?', in J. Boston (ed.), *The State Under Contract*. Wellington: Bridget Williams Books.

Trlin, A.D. (1977) *Social Welfare and New Zealand Society*. Wellington: Methuen.

Trombadori, D. (1991) *Remarks on Marx: Conversations with Duccio Tombadori*, trans. R.J. Goldstein and J. Cascaito. New York: Semiotext(e).

Trosa, S. (1994) *Next Steps: Moving On*. London: HMSO.

Troyna, B. (1994a) 'Reforms, research and being reflexive about being reflective', in D. Halpin and B. Troyna (eds), *Researching Education Policy: Ethical and Methodological Issues*. London: Falmer Press, pp. 1–14.

Troyna, B. (1994b) 'Critical social research and education policy', *British Journal of Education Studies*, 42 (1): 70–84.

Tuck, R. (1989) *Hobbes*. Oxford: Oxford University Press.

Tully, A. (1980) *Discourse on Property: John Locke and his Adversaries*. Cambridge: Cambridge University Press.

Tully, A. (1988) *Meaning and Context: Quentin Skinner and his Critics*. Oxford: Polity Press.

Tully, A. (1993) 'The possessive individualism thesis: a reconsideration in the light of recent scholarship', in J. Carens (ed.), *Democracy and Possessive Individualism: The Intellectual Legacy of C.B. Macpherson*. New York: State University of New York Press.

Tweedie, J. (1990) 'Should market forces control educational decision-making?', *American Political Science Review*, 84 (2): 549–54.

United Nations Human Development Programme (UNDP) (1992) *Human Development Report*. New York and Oxford: Oxford University Press.

Vico, G. (1968) *The New Science of Giambattista Vico*, trans. T.G. Bergin and M.H. Fisch. Ithaca, NY: Cornell University Press.

Vidal, J. (2002) 'Florence builds a bridge to a brand new social paradise', *Guardian*, 11 November, p. 18.

Viner, J. (1958) 'Adam Smith and laissez-faire', in J. Viner (ed.), *The Long View and the Short: Studies in Economic Theory and Policy*. Glencoe, IL.: Free Press.

Viner, J. (1963) '"Possessive individualism" as original sin', *Canadian Journal of Economics and Political Science*, 29 (4): 548–59.

Vining, A. and Weimer, D. (1990) 'Supply and government production failure: a framework based on contestability', *Journal of Public Policy*, 10: 1–22.

Voltaire, F. (2000) *Treatise on Tolerance*, trans. B. Masters, ed. S. Harvey, Cambridge: Cambridge University Press.

Waldron, J. (1987) *'Nonsense on Stilts': Bentham, Burke and Marx on the Rights of Man*. London and New York: Methuen.

Waldron, J. (1988) *The Right to Private Property*. Oxford: Clarendon Press.

Walford, G. (1992) 'Educational choice and equity in Great Britain', in P.W. Cookson (ed.), *The Choice Controversy: Current Debates and Research*. Newbury Park, CA: Corwin Press.

Walford, G. (1994) *Choice and Equity in Education*. London: Cassell.

Walker, D. (2002) *In Praise of Centralism: A Critique of the New Localism.* London: Catalyst Forum.

Walker, R.B.J. (1988) *One World, Many Worlds: Struggles for a Just World Peace.* Boulder: Lynne Rienner.

Walker, R.B.J. (1991) 'On the spatio-temporal alternatives of democratic practice', *Alternatives*, 16 (2): 243–62.

Walker, R.B.J. (1994) *Inside/Outside.* Cambridge: Cambridge University Press.

Walker, R.B.J. (1995) 'International relations and the concept of the political', in K. Booth and S. Smith (eds), *International Relations Theory Today.* Cambridge: Polity Press, pp. 306–27.

Wallerstein, I. (1974) *The Modern World System.* New York: Academic Press.

Walzer, M. (1981) 'Philosophy and democracy', *Political Theory*, 9 (3): 379–99.

Walzer, M. (1983) *Spheres of Justice.* New York: Basic Books.

Walzer, M. (1990) 'The communitarian critique of liberalism', *Political Theory*, 18 (1): 6–23.

Weber, M. (1921) *Economy and Society*, Totowa, NJ: Bedminster.

Weingast, B. (1984) 'The congressional-bureaucratic system: a principal agent perspective', *Public Choice*, 4: 147–91.

Werhane, P.H. (1991) *Adam Smith and his Legacy for Modern Capitalism.* New York and Oxford: Oxford University Press.

West, E.G. (1994) *Education and the State*, 3rd edn, revised and extended. Indianapolis, IN: Liberty Press.

Whitty, G., Power, S. and Halpin, D. (1998) *Devolution and Choice in Education: The School, the State and the Market.* Buckingham: Open University Press.

Wiener, J. (2001) 'Globalization and disciplinary neoliberal governance', *Constellations*, 8 (4): 462–79.

Wilkes, C. (1989) 'The art of the state: the Jessop thesis and the case of Labour monetarism in New Zealand', in New Zealand Public Service Association (eds), *Private Power or Public Interest?.* Palmerston North: Dunmore Press.

Williams, R. (1983) *Towards 2000.* London: Chatto and Windus.

Williamson, O.E. (1975) *Markets and Hierarchies.* New York: Free Press.

Williamson, O.E. (1983) 'Organisational innovation: the transaction-cost approach', in J. Ronen (ed.), *Entrepreneurship.* Lexington, MA: Heath Lexington, pp. 101–34.

Williamson, O.E. (1985) *The Economic Institutions of Capitalism: Firms, Markets, Relational Contracting.* New York: Free Press.

Williamson, O.E. (1991) 'Comparative economic organization: the analysis of discrete structural alternatives', *Administrative Science Quarterly*, 36: 269–96.

Williamson, O.E. (1992) 'Markets, hierarchies and the modern corporation: an unfolding perspective', *Journal of Economic Behaviour and Organisation*, 17: 335–52.

Williamson, O.E. (1994) 'Institutions and economic organization: the governance perspective', paper prepared for the World Bank's Annual Conference on Development Economics, 28–29 April, Washington, DC.

Wimsatt, W. and Beardsley, M. (1954) 'The intentional fallacy', in W.K. Wimsatt (ed.), *The Verbal Icon.* London: Methuen, pp. 3–18.

Winch, D. (1978) *Adam Smith's Politics: An Essay in Historiographic Revision.* Cambridge: Cambridge University Press.

Wintour, P. (2002) 'Parties consign welfare state to history', *Guardian*, 12 October, p. 13.

Wistrich, E. (1992) 'Restructuring government New Zealand style', *Public Administration*, 70 (1): 119–35.

Wittgenstein, L. (1953) *Philosophical Investigations*, trans. G.E.M. Anscombe. Oxford: Blackwell.

Wolfe, A. (1977) *The Limits of Legitimacy: Political Contradictions of Late Capitalism*. New York: Free Press.

Wood, A. (1998) 'Kant's project for perpetual peace', in P. Cheah and B. Robbins (eds), *Cosmopolitics: Thinking and Feeling Beyond the Nation*, Cultural Politics, vol. 14. Minneapolis, MN: University of Minnesota Press.

Wood, E. (1978) 'C. B. Macpherson: liberalism, and the task of socialist political theory', in R. Miliband and J. Saville (eds), *The Socialist Register*. London: Merlin Press.

Wood, E. (1981) 'Liberal democracy and capitalist hegemony: a reply to Leo Panitch on the task of socialist political theory', in R. Miliband and J. Saville (eds), *The Socialist Register*. London: Merlin Press.

Wood, E. (1986) *The Retreat from Class*. London: Verso Press.

Wood, N. (1980) 'Thomas Hobbes and the crisis of the English aristocracy', *History of Political Thought*, 1 (3): 437–52.

Wood, N. (1984) *John Locke and Agrarian Capitalism*. Los Angeles: University of California Press.

Wootton, B. (1945) *Freedom Under Planning*. London: Allen and Unwin.

Wozniak, G. (1984) 'The adoption of interrelated innovations: a human capital approach', *Review of Economics and Statistics*, 66 (1): 70–9.

Wright, M. (1992) *International Theory: The Three Traditions*. New York: Holmes and Meier.

Wylie, C. (1994) *Self-Managing Schools in New Zealand: The Fifth Year*. Wellington: New Zealand Council for Educational Research.

Young, I.M. (1986) 'The ideal of community and the politics of difference', *Social Theory and Practice*, 12 (1): 1–26.

Young, I.M. (1990) *Justice and the Politics of Difference*. Princeton, NJ: Princeton University Press.

Young, I.M. (1995) 'Together in difference: transforming the logic of group political conflict', in W. Kymlicka (ed.), *The Rights of Minority Cultures*. Oxford: Oxford University Press, pp. 155–78.

Young, I.M. (1997) 'Polity and group difference: a critique of the ideal of universal citizenship', in R.E. Goodin and P. Pettit (eds), *Contemporary Political Philosophy*. Oxford: Blackwell, pp. 256–72.

Young, M. (1961) *The Rise of Meritocracy*. London: Penguin.

Index